INVISIBLE ON EVEREST

INNOVATION AND THE GEAR MAKERS

BY

MIKE C. PARSONS AND MARY B. ROSE

northern liberties press

Philadelphia, Paris,
Kuala Lumpur, London

Published in association with Cheyne Books.

northern liberties press, *An Imprint of Old City Publishing*

Northern Liberties Press
628 North 2nd Street
Philadelphia, PA 19123, USA

Published by:
Old City Publishing, Inc.

Visit our web site at: oldcitypublishing.com

Published in association with Cheyne Books. Dek Palmer Mountaineering Series Editor.

0-9704143-5-8 (Hardcover)

Library of Congress Cataloging-in-Publication Data

Parsons, Mike, 1942-
  Invisible on Everest : innovations and the gear makers / by Mike Parsons and Mary B. Rose.
      p. cm.
  ISBN 0-9704143-5-8
  1. Mountaineering--Equipment and supplies--History. 2. Mountaineering--History. I. Rose, Mary B. II. Title.
  GV200.15 .P37 2003
  688.7'682'2--dc21
                                    2003006028

Printed at : Thomson Press (I) Ltd., Web : www.thomsonpress.com

TABLE OF CONTENTS

Corporate sponsors of *Invisible On Everest*:

GRIVEL

KARRIMOR

THE NORTH FACE

TRANGIA AB

To the next generation of innovators:
We hope this book will provide a little inspiration and a positive take off platform regardless of whether your innovation is a style of outdoor/mountain movement or a product to help achieve it. Knowing your sustained determination we wish you a touch of luck and good timing.

FOREWORD

BY

DOUG SCOTT

Mike Parsons and Mary Rose have put together a fascinating history of equipment used in wild places from Derbyshire crags to Himalaya Peaks, as well as the great Polar ice caps.

Parsons has been manufacturing equipment since 1960 and has supplied numerous expeditions with clothing and rucksacks, including many expeditions I participated in since 1967. To complement his intimate knowledge of the subject he consulted widely and incorporated the wisdom of many climbing friends. This book was, however, a genuine partnership between Mike Parsons' business and sporting knowledge and Mary Rose's skills as a business historian. In 1974, after five years research I produced **Big Wall Climbing**, in which I addressed the origins and development of technical climbing equipment. I know first hand how difficult it is to accurately research the subject, but how interesting it is to see the overall picture and to put the record straight. It is worth checking out the Norfolk jackets used on the early attempts on Everest. You will discover here that the Everest explorers actually had the advantage of clothing concepts, used on Polar journeys, to keep out the wind and to stave off frost bite so may not have been quite so exposed as popular myth has it.

Innovations made by our climbing compatriots on the continent have never previously been told in the English language, and probably not in any other language either, which gear freaks should find interesting.

There is more to this book than just equipment. Parsons and Rose have brought to light the characters involved and from an unusual angle. Armchair mountaineers and committed climbers will find this book of enormous interest.

Doug Scott CBE
March 2003

ACKNOWLEDGEMENTS

This book has combined interviews, e-mails and archival and library research and could not have been written without the help, advice, support and more than anything enthusiasm from countless people. When David Tonks suggested contacting Mike Parsons for an interview, little did he realise this would lead to a joint book, but we are very glad that he put us in touch. The outdoor trade has a justified reputation for friendliness, and experience over the last two and a half years, has confirmed this on so many occasions. Insights into the period after 1960 have come from interviews and e-mail exchanges. with Gill Aldersley, Marion Barnes, (Berghaus) Paul Bibby, (Peter Storm) Keith Black, (Regatta) John Brailsford, Dave Brook, Rab Carrington, (Rab) John Cleare, Diana Condell (Imperial War Museum) Hazel and Pat Constance, Gordon Davison, (Berghaus) Alan Day, (Blacks) Derryck Draper, Mick Farnworth, (Karrimor) Jon Gale, (Berghaus) Peter Gildersleve, (Capricorn Fulton Harris) Ian Gundle, (Field and trek) Tony Howard, (Troll) Hermann Huber, (Salewa) Pete Hutchinson, (ME) Bill O'Connor, Tony Lack,(Pindisports) Bob Lawford, Ken Ledward, (KLETS) Peter Lockey, (Berghaus) Jen Longbottom, (Karrimor) Peter Lumley, (Outdoor Trade and Industry) Vin Machin, Stéphane Pennequin, Bill Ruthven (Mount Everest Foundation), Mark Vallance, (Wild Country) Shane Whinser (Royal Geographic Society),Bill Wilkins (Ultimate Equipment) and Tony Woods (Craghoppers/Regatta now Berghaus). Since Mike Parsons, as past owner of Karrimor, was co-author of the book, Mary Rose conducted all the research Chapter 8 and was careful to ensure that neither Mike nor his prime competitors – Peter Lockey and Gordon Davison of Berghaus – knew in advance what the other had told her. This led to sustained e-mail exchanges and Peter and Gordon must have wondered at times just how many more queries could possibly come down the line. We cannot thank them enough for their help and also for lending us a collection of Berghaus and LD Mountain Centre catalogues. Pete Hutchinson has also helped with technical information on down and we are particularly grateful to him for arranging for the loan of transparencies in the possession of Mountain Equipment. Alan Day has been most generous with time, knowledge, advice and enthusiasm and lent us his collection of Blacks' catalogues and correspondence. These give a wonderful record of outdoor clothing and equipment from the 1930s onwards. Tony Lack could not have been more helpful and lent us his collection of Pindisport catalogues, photographs, scrapbooks and trade periodicals. Both Alan and Tony were always available at the end of the telephone to talk through some aspect of the trade and generally catch up with the project's progress. Hazel and Pat Constance have an unrivalled knowledge of camping, tents and stoves which they shared with us generously, along with their hospitality. Again they remained in touch as the research progressed. Ken Ledward has provided regular help, sharing his knowledge and especially his enthusiasm for outdoor education , clothing and equipment - whether at the Royal on a Friday evening or at his home in the Newlands valley. Peter Lumley likewise has stayed in touch and as well as interest and enthusiasm, lent us correspondence and periodicals from his collection. Without the sustained help and enthusiasm from Hermann Huber, it would not have been possible to penetrate the origins and history of climbing equipment in the German speaking world. He lent us the wonderful catalogue of Heinrich Schwaiger, which gave such an intriguing insight into early German retailing and lent us several out of print books. Stéphane Pennequin gave so freely of his information and pictures about Pierre Allain and the origins of nut development, regardless of his own book aspirations. John Brailsford provided us with personal insights into the processes of the metalworking industry and much other information on the origins of equipment. Bill O'Connor was very supportive finding and then lending us important books from his collection and picture library, which filled crucial gaps. Roger Mear provided critical analytical support for the polar chapter. Some of the research was carried out in libraries and would have been very much more difficult without the services of the British Library and the Public Record Office. Without the keepers of various special collections we would have made little progress and so are mentioning these by name. The Fell and Rock Club of the English Lake District house their library at Lancaster University and it has been invaluable. We are especially grateful to the librarian Peter Osborne for allowing us to use the collection as a source of illustrations, and to Gill Aldersley for the story of the Sid Cross interview. Margaret Ecclestone, the Alpine Club Librarian, has been enthusiastic about this project since it began in 2000 and every visit to Charlotte Road has been a pleasure. She has especially helped in the research into women's clothing and, without her advice on the use of the AC Tract collection, chapter 4 would have looked very different. Andrew Tatham ensured that every visit to the Royal Geographical Society archives, to consult the Everest Files, was as fruitful and valuable as possible. He has remained interested in the progress of the research, even after his departure from Kensington Gore. Bob Headland, at the Scott Polar Research Institute, ensured that our intensive one week visit to use his archives was as constructive as possible and saved us much time by ensuring the files we selected really did relate to clothing and equipment. We are also grateful to Richard Golland the keeper of printed books at the Imperial War Museum for his help and advice. For an illustrated book, the advice of photo-librarians is invaluable and both Sue Lawford of the AC and Lucy Martin of SPRI have helped us enormously. I should also like to thank Pauline Hubner of the Royal Geographical Society.

We have worked to a very tight deadline and we could not have completed the book without research assistance. Ann Prior of Lancaster University carried out a survey of a number of outdoor periodicals in the Fell and Rock Collection with exceptional interest and enthusiasm. Pam Mansfield has a marvellous eye for detail and we thank her for patiently helping us with our proof reading. However, without the sustained help of Mary's partner Tony Breakell, this book could not have been completed. He carried out extensive research with her in the British Library, the PRO and at SPRI and created a comprehensive database of all research materials, without which we would have been lost (as would many of our materials!). He also undertook the massive task of compiling the index. His knowledge, enthusiasm and legendary common sense has made the work so much easier. We are eternally grateful to both our partners, Tony and Marian who deserve thanks for living with a project that has engulfed us and eaten our time and energy and for their enthusiasm for it.

We were keen to ensure that we had feedback as we wrote and many people have read part, or all, of the manuscript as it evolved. The footnotes reveal that we continued to receive comments and e-mail right up to final submission of the manuscript. Thanks are due to Ken Ledward, Peter Lockey, Tony Lack, Derryck Draper, Alan Day, Andrew Tatham, John Innerdale, Roger Mear, Hermann Huber, John Brailsford, Bill O'Connor, Roger Mear, Marian Parsons, Margaret Ecclestone and Katrina Honeyman for their comments and insights. We also gained feedback from conference papers given at the Association of Business Historians Conference (University of Portsmouth), the European Business History Association Conference (Norwegian School of Management, Oslo) and the Management Theory and Practice Conference (Lancaster University) in 2001 and the Costume Society Conference (Manchester Metropolitan University) in 2002.

Time has been vital for writing this book and Mary Rose is grateful to Lancaster University for study leave from August 2001-March 2002 which helped tremendously. In addition, a grant from Lancaster University Management School provided assistance for research expenses. Transcribing interview tapes is a tedious process and thanks are especially due to Helen Towers and Carol Clark for struggling with tapes made at trade shows, in pubs and in cars and with the laughter which punctuated one interview and threatened to deafen Helen. Finally we should thank Dek Palmer, Ian Mellanby and Guy Griffiths for their enthusiasm for publishing our book and the help they have given us.

It is certain that in a work of this kind which has no precursors, we will make some errors and omissions. If you have knowledge or personal experiences which you think how relevant we would be most pleased to hear from you; please contact us via e-mail

Mike Parsons e-mail address: mike@KIMM.com

Mary Rose e-mail address: m.rose@lancaster.ac.uk

Or alternatively through our website www.invisibleoneverest.com

Mike Parsons and **Mary Rose**
November 2002.

CHAPTER 1
Introduction
How this book came to be written

Mike C. Parsons

Noel Odell seemed to already tower above me even before he raised his arm, sweeping it across an imaginary skyline and explaining how he saw Mallory and Irvine disappear into the clouds in 1924. The only other listener was HRH Prince Philip. The occasion was a London reception organised by Chris Bonington for his suppliers, of which I was one. I had pulled out the stops before for Bonington, supplying a mass of custom-made gear for Annapurna South Face expedition 1970. Here we were again in 1975, for the Everest South West face expedition. When we, as suppliers put ourselves out, Bonington reciprocated wonderfully well with unusual experiences. In 1970 it was a visit to 10 Downing Street and an informal meeting with Harold Wilson. On this occasion it was a cocktail reception in the City of London with HRH Prince Philip. Steadily the number of people in the room built up, and the noise levels rose when the word was passed round informally that HRH was running late. I suddenly recognised the tall man next me who I had never met. I started to engage Noel Odell in a conversation about what sort of things they were using in the 1920s, but I knew so pitifully little that I had difficulty in asking an intelligent question. Suddenly John Hunt came sweeping past us saying 'Philip has arrived, if he comes your way simply stick your hand out and introduce yourself'. As it so happened he did and after introducing myself as a supplier he made some comments about how tough mountaineering must be at such altitudes on Everest. 'Yes' I said, 'but nothing like as tough as it was in the old days. May I introduce you to Noel Odell who was on Everest in 1924 when Mallory and Irvine disappeared'. This then sparked Odell's famous description of his last sighting of the pair, with the tiny audience of myself and HRH Prince Philip.

In the intervening years these memories came back to me from time to time and maybe, just maybe, I subconsciously looked a little more closely into historical aspects of clothing and equipment. But not consciously, because there was little, indeed no time at all to pause in the relentless search for new and better ways of producing the innovations that my customers demanded. I spent the whole of the next 25 years designing and developing equipment, clothing and footwear for leading-edge mountaineers and polar explorers around the world. These included Joe Brown, Don Whillans, Dougal Haston, Chris Bonington, Reinhold Messner, Peter Habeler, Peter Boardman, Alex McIntyre, John Barry, Pat Littlejohn, John Cleare, Bill O'Connor, and Roger Mear, to name but a few. I steadily improved and broadened my outdoor skills and from time to time I was able to take up invitations that came my way to go on trips. In a period of seven years I seemed to demonstrate a rather Shiptonesque attitude and experienced almost every form of outdoor travel in all seven continents of the world: bike, kayak, dog sled, crampons, skis. These activities were almost an everyday part of my life and it wasn't until catastrophic problems hit my business that I realised how special it was. In the maelstrom that occurred I was thrown out on the other side, with no part to play. I realised that I had been lucky or perhaps greatly privileged to have had the opportunity to work with such a number of very innovative mountaineers. All of them had played such an important part in the development of world mountaineering activity in the post-war period. Nevertheless, here I was 25 years after meeting Noel Odell, out of a job, uncertain of the future, pounding away on my computer, trying to convince myself the new skills were essential, and every so often glancing upwards towards Striding Edge, a well-known ridge leading to the summit of Helvellyn. Down the line came an e-mail from a Mary Rose, at first glance obviously something to do with archaeology! This was a request for an interview about my earlier life and could I be available sometime perhaps?

'Yes,' I answered, 'but what exactly do you need ?' She had decided to write a book on the history of the outdoor trade, and asked if I would share my past experiences?

'Certainly', I replied, 'Anything else?'

She sent me a quotation from George Bernard Shaw about what was worn in the Himalayas in 1921, likening it to 'a Connemara picnic surprised by a snow-storm'. She asked me what I thought about it. During holiday periods in the mountains I do recall often wondering why Britain, as a non-alpine country, had produced so many mountaineers. There were no answers, because I wasn't researching the subject, and no one else seemed to know either. Asked the ques-tion as to what they might be wearing, I had only seen traditional pictures show-ing a row of seated expedition members, wearing their tweed jackets – just as Shaw described. But it seemed unlikely to me that this was all they had. After all I did have a very close contact with the cotton industry, living as I did in the heart of Lancashire, where just about every family had someone who was connected with or had been a textile employee. I replied that I really did not think that they only had Norfolk jackets and tweeds because there were many wonderful fabrics available in earlier periods, and indeed a much greater variety than today.

Our correspondence continued, steadily growing until towards the end of the three-month period we were corresponding daily. When the question came down the line 'Would you like to be the co-author of this book' we had still not met. However, my reply was immediate, unquestioning maybe even unthinking. And I said 'Yes of course'. Little did I realise how much work would be involved. In fact the work in the early period was a cathartic experience, but steadily step-by-step grew a new passion, an overriding pervasive desire to discover and understand the origin and evolution of all the different forms of equipment, clothing and footwear. A huge task, especially so since no-one had done any prior work at all.

Mary B. Rose

I was a student when I first discovered the outdoors and from the 1970s hills and mountains became vital to me. I vividly remember the top of my first Lake District fell in 1972 – Coniston Old Man. It was a wild windy day with the clouds parted to give a tantalising view. 'This is how I want to spend my spare time', I thought. More and more weekends and holidays were spent, first in the Peak District and then the Lakes and Scotland and further afield. Getting a job at Lancaster University in 1978 was just perfect. It was a young, unstuffy institution and it was within sight of the Lake District and on the edge of the Forest of Bowland – what could be better? Hills, mountains and wild places are where I am most content; they restore and heal as well as just bringing perspective. Moments of pure happiness can be a fleeting view on a wild day or pink tinted snow on a fading January afternoon or listening to distant deer while camping in Sutherland. I can remember precisely when I first had the idea for a book on the outdoor trade. It was in the Lake District, on Maiden Moor on a wet, windy spring weekend in 1995. Sick of a leaking waterproof and the smell of wet wool, I had just replaced my old jacket and pullover and I can remember saying to Tony, my husband, as we were blown along in the murk, 'Wouldn't it be great to write a history of gear? – I am sure no one's done it'. Then I began enthusing about how much fun it would be until I remembered I still had the massive millstone of a book on the British and American cotton industry to finish. And so the idea went on ice, filed away in the back of my mind for another four years. It was probably a good thing. Had I contacted Mike Parsons then, he might have been interested but, would have been too busy running Karrimor to give me more than an interview, and the year or two just after he lost the company would have been wrong too for all kinds of reasons.

As I struggled away to finish the cotton book I never quite forgot about my dream to write about my hobby. During the last round of research, one dark cold day in January 1999, I was waiting for the archivist to bring me some files. I began idly flicking through a catalogue for the Co-operative Holidays Association (CHA) and it contained a note of some clothing advice for 'Lady Ramblers' for 1910, who were told to avoid wearing stays if they wanted to breathe and it rekindled the idea. Six months later the final manuscript of the cotton book went off to the publisher and I heaved a sigh of relief. The choice was there – I could either go on writing about the cotton industry or family firms forever – the safe option – or I could see if I could turn a fantasy into reality. After a decent period of procrastination I decided to go ahead and started planning on how to do it and checking what sources might be available. This is what led me to Mike in January 2000. His name was on a list of people in the outdoor trade that a colleague had sketched out for me and, over a coffee, another colleague said 'If you want to write a history of the outdoor trade you should contact Mike Parsons – his Dad started Karrimor'. Having had several Karrimor rucksacks over the years this sounded a great idea, so I did, and it is one of the best decisions I have ever made. He was helpful from the start and apart from agreeing to an interview gave me an enormous range of contacts with all the names of key people in the trade over the last 40 years, including his rivals – a researcher's wish list. But what really intrigued me was that, from the beginning, he challenged my preconceptions and made me think that there was more to old gear than I had realised. He was of course right; my cotton industry work told me that Lancashire had indeed produced a massive array of textiles which must have influenced gear. Over that winter I kept in touch with regular progress reports and queries and the replies I got back became more and more interesting.

Certainly I had not thought initially about a joint book but, by the end of April, the idea kept popping into my mind and the more insights I got down the line the more I thought about it. But academics and businessmen do not usually write books together; we had never actually met; could it possibly work? The more I thought about what bringing together our two sets of skills and knowledge could do for the depth and scope of the book, the better the idea seemed. The crunch came in May when I thought I needed to track the main innovations in gear to make sense of my preliminary research. What Mike sent back in response confirmed what I already knew – that he would not only bring a lifetime of rich experience, but a bubbling enthusiasm which would be great to work with. I suggested that if he was going to put all that effort into answering my queries, would he like to collaborate on the book. I bit my nails and the answer came back yes and a week later we met up for the first time.

Our background and temperament could not be more different, but that is the secret of the success –passion for the outdoors and the history of gear provides the foundation of the arrangement. The project itself is all absorbing and fascinating to me because it is combined the study of innovation with research into my hobby. But, by working with someone who has lived and breathed the trade for a lifetime, I have learnt more in the last two years than in the previous twenty-two as an academic. Mike comes from outside my world so I have had to explain and question what I do and how and that has been a real plus. Mike has done the same and it has shaped our book. Yes, as a business historian with a deep interest in textiles and a passion for the outdoors, I could have written a history of mountaineering clothing and equipment. But at best it would have been two dimensional – 'competent but uninspiring' perhaps. By collaborating, I set off on a journey of discovery into outdoor sport and outdoor business without knowing fully how it would work, but with a hunch that it was the right thing to do. At the very least it has meant we have written something unusual and it has certainly been fun.

I enjoyed writing my other books, but this one has been different from anything else. Previously, when I wrote the history of people's businesses they were all dead and whilst I enjoyed piecing together their lives from letters and account books, there were many times I would have loved to have been able to ask 'Why did you do that ? What did you think of such and such?'. For the recent parts of this book I have been able to do just that – and not just ask Mike, but people across the trade, all of whom have been very helpful and friendly. Many of them have stayed in touch as the research has gone on and helped, commented and enthused. There has also been the fun of carrying out the archival research in tandem with Mike, who would be in Patterdale responding to my regular daily e-mails of what had turned up in the Alpine Club or the Royal Geographical Society or where ever I happened to be. And comments invariably had come down the line by the morning, so far from the usual quite lonely process I was getting feedback and suggestions. Once Mike even got an e-mail from me, when he was in the Alps, telling him that I had been shown the original 1936 Grenfell windsuit used by Ruttledge on Everest. He was as excited as I was and jokingly mailed back: 'Weather foul here. Marian and I could do with one each'! It has been these exchanges that have made the research come alive .

The richness of the interaction which has shaped the book and made it unusual has blossomed into further collaboration set to continue well beyond this book. Our way of working and the way it has enriched our ideas has coincided with growing efforts by Lancaster University Management School to build meaningful dialogues with business in the region. Our unique collaboration has attracted attention and Mike has just been made an honorary Entrepreneurial Fellow. Writing history is truly about the future as much as about the past.

Our Approach

Everest 1975. 'Camp 6 was a lonely place. Sitting wind-rocked in our summit box on the evening of 23rd September, Doug Scott and I talked over our day's work and planned for the summit push on the morrow. We were happy with our general condition, physical and mental, and also with our progress that day. The long traverse above the rock band towards the couloir, which led out of the face onto the summit ridge had been fixed with 1,500 feet of rope, all that we had for that purpose. It had been a long interesting day of climbing. Vertical rock steps, and delicate climbing on loose snow-covered slabs and much of the inevitable snow wading. The plan was to leave at 3:30 am and try to make the summit.

The night passed not too uncomfortably, and we were off at the scheduled hour. The rest of the summit is compounded into a blur of many memories, all still very positive in my mind. Long wearying snow slopes leading to the rock step in the couloir, defeat nearly taking us in hand here in the shape of the failure of my oxygen system. Penknife surgery finally solving the problem after all conventional methods had failed. Doug tiptoeing delicately for hours before getting through the rock, and then the steep and incredibly effort demanding snow slopes above. But our urges were always upwards and 3 pm. saw us on the South summit. Conditions were bad enough and it was sufficiently late for us to contemplate waiting until early morning before trying the ragged snows of the summit ridge. There was indecision in the wind, but a cup of hot water prodded us into trying a rope length on the final ridge. It wasn't good but it was fine conditions compared to what we had just emerged from on the face. Onward it was, going strongly, slowed briefly by a deep snowbound Hilary step and potential wind slab avalanche slopes above, onto an easy wind driven plateau and a summit sunset like we've never seen before. Three rolled into one as each cloud level lowered beneath the sun, and purple Everest shadow projected 100 miles or so out onto the brown plains of Tibet, giving relief to our saturated with whiteness eyesight. A place to linger, but not for us with a twilight descent to the South summit still waiting. This passed slowly enough, with hopes of a moon keeping us from thinking about a bivouac. But that night it remained forever hidden so it was over the cornice beneath the South summit, out of the now strong wind and into Tibet for the night.

Our home was a shallow ice cave, our means of warmth each other. The stove ran out after an hour. The oxygen had already gone, so we shook and rubbed and talked inanely keeping awake to prevent frostbite of the limbs and maybe permanent freezing of the brain. Thus passed the highest bivouac ever.

The no-warmth sunrise saw us rattling into movement, and warming slowly onto the descent. We both kept checking on each others and our own minds aware of the danger of lack of oxygen hallucinations. There were none, and in a mere three hours we were sitting once again in the still solid summit box and radioing the happy news to the others at camp 2."

Dougal Haston, Leysin, Switzerland, December '75.

The homecoming of an expedition is often an affair of highly mixed and strong emotions and this one, of Chris Bonington's 1975 Everest South West face expedition, was no exception. The ascent was a huge achievement, 5 previous expeditions of various nationalities had failed. The success of having got Doug Scott and Dougal Haston followed by Peter Boardman and Pertemba (and probably Mick Burke) to the summit, was overridden by Mick's death.

In my position as a designer and manufacture of outdoor equipment I had already supplied Bonington's Annapurna expedition. I asked Dougal if he would write me a few words about the ascent and the consequent notorious bivouac, but he was even more sparing with words than most other high altitude mountaineers.

'Dougal, do you think you could possibly add in something about the equipment? I asked. The following additional paragraph came back:

"It would be another long day, a very long one to reach the top and get back to camp six, perhaps that's why the bivouac sack and stove were among the items to be packed. The evening meal finished, the last thing to do before trying to sleep was pack our sacks. Doug was using the standard expedition frame sack, which had been specially made with three pockets in the back to take oxygen cylinders, and the special outside pocket to take the crucial demand valve of the oxygen set. Preferring a lighter frameless, padded back sack, I had modified the standard Karrimor Lofoten, with the help of Hamish MacInnes, who had fixed straps inside to hold 2 cylinders and cut a hole in the side to make the connection with the tube, and demand valve. This I had been using for the last two days with heavy weights, and with a high level of technical climbing. It felt good. Two oxygen cylinders apiece, the oxygen system, a bivouac sack, stove and spare cartridge. That was our back load. The climbing gear would go around our bodies. If there was a bivouac there would be no food. Just hot water; we didn't even have a spare teabag."

This was vital information and helped significantly with the next generation of rucksacks. However, in this case I was in a privileged position and could ask for this information. It is barely believable, the more so with time, that so little has been written about equipment,. This is especially so, considering the preceding years had seen an explosion of new equipment and devices, pushed along initially by the Second World War and by the expedition boom which followed the first ascent of Everest in 1953.

Dougal, however, was little different from the many generations who preceded him and the several who followed. Despite equipment appendices in expedition books, mountaineers and explorers have always been very sparing indeed with the equipment information when they wrote their accounts. I recall an equipment debriefing with one small leading edge Himalayan team, who frequently climbed together and went out to the Himalayas as though going to the Alps. On this particular occasion it became clear, to my surprise, that none of the four knew what the other was taking or was accustomed to taking. All they knew was that it worked when they climbed together. In other words, as Pete Hutchinson said, 'the best gear is invisible, it leaves you free to get on with the job in hand'. That was the inspiration for the title of our book. The story of gear has long been a hidden one and has never been told precisely for this reason. But the evolution of kit we take for granted in the mountains involves far more than just a technical understanding of what was used. Its evolution is not just a prop for adventure. It is the very essence of outdoor sport. Indeed we go so far as to link the emergence of mountaineering as a sport with the appearance of specialist producers and equipment.

Quite apart from a reluctance by climbers and explorers to tell the story of their gear, tracking the evolution of clothing and equipment for extreme environments is quite difficult to research. This is partly because most of the most familiar items of kit have historic origins. When men and women attempted to climb Mont Blanc in the eighteenth century, there was no mountaineering equipment. Instead, they took clothing and equipment which was in daily use in mountain regions. It was clothing and equipment which had evolved as part of life in mountainous or extreme regions and was just taken for granted and certainly was not worth studying. Darwin's *Origin of the Species* and the later *Descent of Man* changed all that when it exploded the religious myths surrounding the Garden of Eden. At first sight this seems a strange digression in a history of mountaineering. But this work was soon to stimulate archaeological and anthropological work on the everyday life of ancient man. Of the equipment currently used for mountain sports, only the bicycle could be reasonably described as a modern invention. Everything else from breathable clothing, through the rucksack, to the ice axe, crampons, skis and kayaks have their origins thousands of years ago. They have been adapted and improved by modern sportsmen for their particular needs.

Detailed archaeological research, stimulated no doubt by Nansen's polar journeys in the 1880s and 1890s, began to reveal that his modes of travel, ski and kayak were truly ancient. By 1920 painstaking work, using cave drawings and carvings demonstrated that skis and kayaks had been used some 4000 and 2000 years earlier respectively. But many years later one particularly dramatic discovery preserved in ice unlocked the key to the way late Stone Age man lived and dressed in the alpine regions. In 1991 two German mountain walkers, on the border between the Austrian Tyrol and the northern Italian region of the Sud Tyrol, found a human body in the glacier ice and alerted the Mountain Rescue Service. By chance two well known mountaineers, Reinhold Messner and Hans Kammerlander, were passing and they hacked the body out of the ice, unaware that it was the body of an ancient man, frozen in time 5000 years ago. He became known as Oetzi, after the Otztal valley in which he was found. He is now housed in his own museum in Bolzano in northern Italy.

Ten years of detailed research showed just how well he understood his environment and how little that we use is actually new. He was very well-equipped and had all the essentials of the modern mountain traveller, along with his bow and quiver full of arrows – for both hunting and personal protection. While the look of his clothing was a bit strange, everything else was rather familiar and astoundingly advanced.

His boots were filled with a special sweat and moisture absorptive grass, chosen by Nansen, Amundsen and other Polar explorers right up until the early part of the 20th century and is still used by Lappish (Samoyed) peoples today. It was not until the footwear innovations of the 1953 Everest expedition that any better form of insulation was devised. He had a backpack, a basket carried with a band over his head – a technique familiar to Himalayan travellers today. The same techniques for carrying a pack were known throughout alpine Europe and in parts of the Western Isles of Scotland until the 1930s and 1940s. Of course, he also had his fire lighting equipment which was crucial to survival. Important too, was his equivalent of the Swiss Army penknife: flint sharpener, a bone awl, a stone knife in a wooden handle, together with a variety of stone blades and of course the vital spare sinews for repairing his clothing and boots. He had previously suffered from frostbite something which, despite all our technologies, still happens today. His fur clothing was warm and effective for his alpine crossings, but at lower altitudes would cause him to overheat. But there were plenty of fastenings, meaning the clothing could be easily ventilated. Oetzi also had a lightweight, breathable waterproof cape. This was made of grass and, to ensure that it was durable, he had left the roots of the grass attached to the lower end. Oetzi did not use what we describe as textiles for his protective clothing or shelter. This had begun in China around 3000 years ago when silk weaving was first developed. Silk came to be used for all types of lightweight gear, from tents and clothing to ropes in the late nineteenth century and was the true forerunner of many high quality, high performance fabrics.

If skis, kayaks and protective clothing were all part of normal existence for stone-age man, crampons had to wait until the Iron Age. The skill of the blacksmith closely tracks the introduction of the horse from Asia by the Greeks and the Romans. It was probably just as natural to make special horseshoes for gripping on ice as it was for human feet. Certainly spiked shoes can be seen in some Roman friezes and make the earliest crampons 2000 years old. That then leaves the ice axe and the bicycle. In the beginnings of mountain craft a standard wood axe was used. However as the first early reports in the Alpine Club Journal of 1864 commented 'the axes still used in Chamonix can only be used for cutting steps when going upwards, (by using a horizontal swing of the axe of course) and one therefore one has to return exactly the same way

9

which no self-respecting mountaineer will wish to do'. The design was changed so that the blade was fixed in a transverse manner and in the very similar way to the wood craftsman's adze. This is the tool for creating a smooth surface before the wood plane and still used today. The only significant piece of outdoor sporting gear to be invented relatively recently was the bicycle. Like all the other items of gear, it was very much part of daily life in the late nineteenth and early twentieth century. It relied on vulcanisation of rubber and the invention by John Boyd Dunlop of the inflatable tyre and was a truly modern invention.

The origins of familiar pieces of equipment were obscure and that has made for difficult research. But identifying and interpreting precisely what was worn can be more complicated than it appears. This is because it is remarkably hard to get behind the 'official view' of what was worn. Clothing represents cultural short hand. Until the very recent past, indeed until the 1960s, clothing was how you categorised people, how you judged their position in society and their respectability. Clothing was a language and, as such, held messages and hidden meanings which could only be deciphered within a national, historical context. Simply looking at pictures of what was worn, say on nineteenth century Polar expeditions, by nineteenth century women climbers or by the 1920s Everesters may not be enough. Drawings, etchings or photographs often convey the public image of dress and may demonstrate all the trappings of respectability, when the reality was very different. Drawings of Polar explorers in full naval dress, of women climbing in long skirts or photographs of George Mallory and Sandy Irvine in their tweeds and Norfolk jackets, en route for Everest, need considered thought. They may be giving impressions for public consumption that need careful questioning and setting in a wider context. This has made the search for what was worn by previous generations of mountaineers challenging, but also intriguing and intensely rewarding.

Mountains and wild places provide the backdrop for our book but, far from being hidden, the story of gear and the innovators hold centre stage. Gear becomes 'the toy(s) that outdoor people use' and it helps to define and is refined by the activities for which it is used. We trace how, through time, the emergence of new sports and outdoor activities encouraged innovations which, in turn, moved enthusiasts into new areas and across new boundaries. People as much as products lie at the heart of this process and we focus on the development of 'communities of knowledge' which have developed through time in different sports and in different regions of the world. Most of the key gear innovators – whether the nineteenth century pioneers or designers in late twentieth century outdoor companies – have also been active sports people or explorers. They have had to be able to understand what was needed and what could be improved and also to build an informed dialogue with potential customers. We show the way that, prior to the emergence of numerous specialist firms, pioneers designed and improved their own gear – working alongside craftsmen to develop 'the right pattern'. Often the design was not quite right and could be disastrously wrong as witnessed on some desperate bivouacs in the Alps in the nineteenth century.

Most books concentrate on either polar exploration or mountaineering. But this is an artificial divide because the two histories are intimately intertwined. The challenges are similar and indeed polar exploration was one of the inspirations for a generation of early mountaineers. But the ties are even closer, for eventually polar explorers and mountaineers created overlapping 'communities of knowledge' which affected product evolution, through the people involved. That said, different nations experienced varying conditions – climatic, social, political and economic. This had an impact on the way outdoor activity was approached, the tools that were developed, the kit designed and the capabilities evolved. Consequently an Alpine climate demanded a different approach to winter sports from a Scandinavian one. Even before global warming meant that snow was a rarity, the caresses of the Gulf Stream have made for a temperate British climate. Nor are the British a natural mountain nation for, in comparison with the Alps, the hills of Snowdonia, the Lake District and Scotland are mere pimples. This meant the British certainly lacked the natural instincts and skills of mountain people or those who lived close to the Arctic circle. Set in this light it is amazing that Britain produced any mountaineers and explorers at all. They were activities for which – in contrast to other nations – they were peculiarly ill –suited. Yet for a comparatively short time – up to the First World War- they appeared to dominate both activities. From then until the successful ascent of Everest in 1953 Continental European climbers were developing techniques which quite outstripped those in the UK. This is now relatively well known, but what is far more obscure is the extent to which this story was intertwined with equipment – both hardware and clothing.

Innovators are people who design, develop and apply new, practical solutions. In our book this has been applied to clothing and equipment for exploration and mountaineering. We are not interested in every single piece of new clothing and equipment used on every journey, expedition or outdoor sport. Nor are we interested in every single innovator or every innovative company. Through the compelling history of the evolution of exploration, mountaineering and outdoor sport we have chosen to look at innovations which have really made a difference, the genuine platforms of innovation, that have also been linked to changes to the activities. We see innovation as a process and an interaction, not an isolated event. And it was a process involving people, fallible people and is set against the shifting backdrop of history. But we believe that innovation is more than anything about learning – about how to respond to changes or promote those changes. It is also about assessing risk, not just in the conventional sense, but in the sense of choosing which bit of kit or combination of gear to take on a trip for greatest safety, in a given set of circumstances. We are also interested in attitudes – why some approaches to equipment and clothing are favoured in some periods or among some groups of sports people and not others. You may not agree with our interpretation but we have tried to make sense of a complicated story. That is what history is about, making patterns out of apparent chaos. But we hope to surprise you and as a taster we have identified some myths, there are many more embedded in the book:

1) *Mallory and Irvine were dressed for their Everest expedition 'as if for a tea party in Connemara surprised by a snow storm.'* This is one of the most enduring images in mountaineering history and one of the most misleading. What did they know about layering, how good were 1920s windproofs, how were they tailored, what was the design of the boots?

2) *Victorian women climbed in skirts.* A bit like the misconceptions about the 1920s Everesters and their Norfolk jackets, we all have images of women climbing in skirts. But when we think about it – they could not have done so, or not on anything remotely difficult. Most women climbers and those men who have thought about it know the stories of women taking their skirts off to climb in trousers or knickerbockers or buttoning them up. But the charade that was acted out, the reasons for it and the extent to which for women mountaineering was a hidden world in which every imaginable taboo was broken, has remained obscure.

3) *Edward Whymper climbed the Matterhorn in 1865 looking like a refugee and wearing a single strap rucksack.* This is again the popular image and doubtless stems from the controversy relating to his fabled and notorious descent. As with Mallory and Irvine and the Victorian women, photographs may deceive and another one, rarely reproduced, shows him as he would have been when he was active, young, fit and with a two-shoulder strap pack. This is much more the image of the tough young climber and the designer of the most enduring mountain tent design and other items of equipment.

4) *The British invented mountaineering.* Certainly the British dominated the so called Golden Age in the middle of the nineteenth century – as the first industrial nation they had the wealth and leisure to do so. But they lost the lead and it passed to the German speakers. Herein lies a fascinating equipment tale which helps us re-tell the story of interwar and indeed post war mountaineering. We explore how the 'games' climbers play are indeed linked to the 'toys' they use.

5) *Arnold Lunn brought skis and skiing to the Alps and was the founder of Alpine skiing*. We show how it was Nansen who was the inspiration for skiing outside Norway and the Austrians who spread it world wide. When we look at the way skiing spread by this route to North America a fascinating equipment story emerges.

6) *'Modern Lightweight Equipment'* We challenge the throwaway phrase of many modern outdoor journalists and show that for much of the twentieth century gear got heavier. The Victorians and the Edwardians were the true lightweighters and we look at silk tents weighing just 14 oz, silk ropes and lightweight rucksacks with loads of as little as 6.5 pounds for an Alpine summit.

7) *The hob nailed boot* is often used as the incorrect and derogatory term for the nailed climbing boot. We look at the art and science of nailing and dispel any idea that this was a primitive form of footwear. We look at the origin of nails but also at the complexity of nailing patterns and how and why they developed. We look at the strengths of the nailed boots rather than assuming they were inferior. For the early ice climbs, crampons were unnecessary because nailed boots were very effective

8) *The shift to the rubber moulded sole- the Vibram- was for grip.* We challenge this and demonstrate there was another consideration – frostbite. We investigate how the Vibram was developed – especially during war-time and the benefits it brought.

It is certain that in a work of this kind which has no precursors, we will make some errors and omissions. If you have knowledge or personal experiences which you think maybe relevant we would be most pleased to hear from you; please e-mail Mike at:

mike@KIMM.com or Mary at: **m.rose@lancaster.ac.uk**

Alternatively through our website: **www.invisibleoneverest.com**

CHAPTER 2
The History of Polar and Snow Travel

'Scott died because he was reaching for the moon', declared Roger Mear.

'A film company called me to ask my views. (There is a film being made based on the old theory that Scott was foiled by unseasonably bad weather.) I just told them Scott was an early day Neil Armstrong.' Roger had naturally been consulted because he made the first repeat of the Scott route to the South Pole in 1986.

'But don't you think that not having dogs was a substantial disadvantage?' I asked with some surprise.

'Not really' said Roger, 'using skis and man hauling can undoubtedly take you further than dogs' I had called to see Roger to renew a friendship which included participating with him on a couple of cold trips, to K2 base camp in winter and Antarctica. I had taken the opportunity to ask for advice on my polar chapter and on the long drive home I reflected on what Roger had said. I was quite perplexed that Roger's opinion seemed to be quite at variance with the practice; following the First World War all expeditions to Antarctica used dogs and the popular perception is that Scott failed because he didn't use dogs. It also contradicted my own, admittedly tiny experience, both with dogs and in polar regions.

One personal incident had left a lasting impression on me. It occurred in 1992, in Sarek, Sweden. John Noble, who had several years of dog handling experience with the British Antarctic Survey, had invited me on a 350 km dog trip through Arctic Sweden. As the trip progressed I became more familiar with handling the dogs and instead of shrinking from the chorus of 35 dogs howling as we touched the first chain each morning, I began to enjoy it. I had my own team of 5 dogs, and never before had I had such a huge animal responsibility. I had to ensure that I knew every dog by name so that I could find the harnesses and fit them on. Knowing the positions that each dog preferred was important too, because of their likes and dislikes of other dogs. When I chained them out in a long line, as temperatures plunged to minus 35°C, to ensure that there were no fatal fights I always felt slightly guilty as I went into a warm hut or tent. I would cut up the frozen meat and ensure each got a reasonable share. All this became part of my routine. On one particular morning I was sharing an eight dog sled team with John and he said, 'I would like to get some pictures, hold on until the other teams have moved away and until I have moved ahead to a good position'. One by one each of the other five dog teams pulled away and my dogs became more and more frantic. They were howling, pulling, tearing, desperately trying to join in what nature had taught them to do best, chasing and hunting the other dogs. I reached down for a second to adjust my skis, maintaining what I thought was a firm grip on the top rail of the sledge, when crack, the cord tethering the sledge to the tree snapped. Away went my dog team, hunting the lead team, seemingly

Dogs and Sleds, Sarek Sweden.

dancing over the deep crystalline snow on their wide paws, leaving me to grovel along on un-waxed skis. But they were probably travelling at 20 kph and all I could manage in the deep snow was about 3kph. I caught up with my dogs, red-faced from exertion but mainly embarrassment, only when they had caught the leading team. The chase was now over and sorting out a snarling, biting, fighting tangle of 2 dog teams took a long time.

If nothing else this merely proved how much faster dogs can travel on snow than I could, but Roger used the word 'further' not faster. So how then could I equate my experiences with Roger's views? I tried to make sense of this conundrum by looking back at the history and statistics of polar exploration and travel. How had equipment innovation contributed to exploration and the evolving sport of polar travel? Surely a table of distances covered by all historical journeys, when set alongside all the detailed methods of travel, would answer these issues clearly? With mountaineering the issue of ethics was an important one and had significant influence over and even control of the innovation of equipment. Each nation contributed differently in different periods according to the self perceived 'rules of the game'. Ethics surely would not play a part here in Polar regions?

Overview

Broadly speaking the understanding, practice and equipment needed for polar travel and living has evolved over 6 main periods: prehistoric, Viking, British North West Passage, the heroic or innovation period, post war scientific and finally the new polar game beginning in the early 1990's.

SPRI Collection

Bill O'Connor Collection

Left: Return of Atkinson Party, January 29, 1912. The use of sail had by this time been in practice for nearly 100 years *Right:* Wind power, the Para-kite revolution in modern polar travel.

The pre-historic period tells the story of the origins of skis, sledges and toboggans. In the Viking period came the first recorded accounts of the use of skis. There was some interchange between Nordic people and the Eskimos, although for many centuries following that the indigenous people of Greenland were entirely isolated from Europe. This ended in the fifteenth century when interest in finding the North West Passage formed the precursor to the British naval period and the infamous Franklin expedition of the 1840s and the Nares expedition of 1875. Then began the innovation period/heroic age when knowledge and experimentation reached a peak in the late nineteenth/early twentith century. The Americans Peary and Cook and Scandinavians, Nordenskjoeld and Nansen competed for the North Pole and Amundsen finally made the whole NW passage journey and then won the battle for the South Pole against Scott. In parallel with the development of mechanised travel, polar travel with dogs continued until they were excluded from Antarctica in the late 1980's. Finally the Norwegians again revolutionised polar travel in 1996; not this time using dogs but grasping the synergy offered by communications and wind power technologies emerging from the late 1980s.

Pre-history and Overview of Indigenous Peoples

The story of successful polar living and travel is tied to an ability to understand and respond to an extreme environment, by working with it rather than against it. In modern parlance it can be seen as 'multi-skilled', combining the art of survival with sledging and kayaking and, in some regions, skiing. The Arctic had supported human life for thousands of years before European explorers ventured north. The Inuit in Arctic Canada and Greenland and Inupiat in Alaska are just two of the peoples commonly referred to as Esquimaux or Eskimoes. The Samoyed, who frequent an area stretching from Northern Scandinavia to Russia, are well known as reindeer herders and known as Lapps in Scandinavia. The

J. Arthur Bain

Nansen learnt his Kayak skills from the Eskimos whilst over wintering in Greenland, after his successful crossing in 1888.

Aleut Indians who inhabited the chain of islands extending from the Alaskan coast towards Russia are another important group. They understood their environment by an instinct born of thriving in what, to most Europeans, was a deeply hostile world. Through an evolving and holistic process of adaptation they developed skills, clothing, tools, and hunting techniques, modes of living, diet and methods of transport ideally suited to their frozen world, so that they were perfectly acclimatised to life around and within the Arctic Circle.

Clothing was made of a variety of animal skins – including bear, wolf and seal and they hunted from light, fast, manoeuvrable boats. These were called 'man's hunting boat' or the kayak whilst the women travelled in the umiak, a much larger slower boat resembling a coracle. They used skin tents in the summer, but in winter their insulation came from a combination of the snow itself, made into blocks to form igloos, body heat, and from skins laid on the floors. Sleeping was on a high shelf where the air was much warmer. Light, on the other hand, came from simple lamps burning either blubber or seal oil passed along a long wick. Their clothing, with its multiple layers of animal skins, each carefully chosen for its particular qualities in a particular position and weatherproof layers, brought insulation but little breathability. Outer layers had simple belt fastenings which could be opened quickly to avoid perspiration from exertion building up and freezing. Heat is the enemy in the arctic.[1] They also devised snow goggles made of antler moulded to their facial contours and with narrow slits to prevent snow blindness. Washing was in urine, as was the tanning of animal skins. In the nineteenth century they invited visitors to sleep with their wives, which must have surprised Victorian travellers, but it was very necessary genetically. Indeed some of the early explorers have known descendents in Arctic regions.

Travelling on the sea ice, in winter, involved the use of dogs to pull sledges and, as with their clothing, this reduced chilling and conserved energy, since the alternative – man hauling – was both exhausting and sweaty. They lived near to their hunting grounds and had no need to cover great distances in contrast to the explorers. Seeking conceptual objectives, such as the North Pole where there was no land but only drifting sea ice, was the invention of geographers and explorers and probably incomprehensible to Eskimos at the time. Dogs of different breeds are widely used for transport in all arctic regions. Huskies are found wherever Eskimos live and are vital to winter travel. Dogs have a totally different cooling system to horses and men. The wolf and the dog originated from cold areas of Eurasia and do not sweat through the skin, only through the tongue and paws. When you leave them out at minus 35°C they curl up with their nose under their tail and if it snows, all the better, they are then covered and protected from the wind. Man and horse have hot country origins and sweating, (which causes cooling) is the killer of the arctic. Had man had the same physiology as the dog, there would be no need for breathable membranes in our outerwear, but we would all speak with our tongues hanging out! However, sweating has been man's constant problem and therefore a manufacturer able to accommodate such a fundamental need would have a market indeed. From the early nineteenth century it became the outdoor clothing manufacturers' 'holy grail' and is still so today.

Eskimo modes of transport were energy efficient and so was their diet; the food was rich in protein and was eaten raw, which conserved essential vitamins.[2] Those people who lived within the Arctic and pre polar regions did not always follow the same travel techniques. Whereas Eskimos travelled by sledge, Samoyed (Lapp peoples from Scandinavia through the northern areas of Russia) used skis at least from 4000 BC. There is some evidence to suggest that the West Coast Greenlanders had close connections with Vikings and may well have encountered skis. When in 900 AD Eric the Red set up colonies on the west side of Greenland, he was either a great optimist or just being economical with the truth, when he gave the land its name. However, a mini ice age started around 1310 and as the crops failed in Europe, so Greenland became progressively more inaccessible. The weather and the ice pushed the Inuit people south, and it is possible that after the skirmishes and the mixing of genes, they became acquainted with skis. One of the key reasons that they did not persevere with skis was the almost total absence of wood. The early Eskimo sledges were made of whatever was available, such as whale bone or rolled seal skins, and these materials were almost impossible to make into long thin flat skis. The Samoyed, however, lived in the subpolar zones and had access to trees. The Greenland Eskimo gave their name to the anorak, the Alaska Eskimo the parka. The Aleuts had an amazing garment which was both waterproof and breathable. Called the kamleika, it was made from dried seal intestines, stitched together and the seams sealed. To check the seam water proofing, arms and neck were tied and the garment filled with water.

The Viking Period

Nordic people had first visited Greenland in 982 AD when Eirik Thorvaldson (or Eric the Red) explored either Cumberland Sound or western Greenland. This brief interlude aside, the Inuit Indians were entirely isolated from Europeans and the Europeans from them, until the wave of exploration, mapping and navigation that followed Columbus's discovery of the New World in 1492. The first written account of skiing is in the Viking "Sagas", where several kings are described as being superb skiers. In 1206, during the Norwegian civil war, two men on skis carried the infant heir to the throne 35 miles to safety in the middle of winter. This historic event is celebrated today by the annual "Birchleg (ski) Race" or 'Birkebeiner' over the same route in Norway; so called because the men wrapped their legs in birch bark to keep them warm and dry. The Vasaloppet Cross Country race (90km) held annually in Sweden, honours Gustav Vasa's ski trip in 1523 when he raised an army and beat the Danes who were then in control of the country.

The British Naval Period 1600-1875

Nineteenth century British Arctic exploration had it origins centuries earlier when the quest for a short cut to the Pacific via the North West Passage began. Columbus's voyage had been encouraged by the need of the Spanish to find an alternative route to Asia as more and more of the Near and Middle East became dominated by Islam. This was the beginning of a search, which soon involved the British and which continued sporadically for the next 500 years.[3] The dream of a short cut to the Pacific was driven by economic imperative and the irrationality of rivalry between European nations. Many of those who worked for the British Hudson Bay Company doubted the existence of a viable route, a view confirmed by James Cook who, in the 1770s, found his way blocked by a giant barrier of ice. The Admiralty accordingly abandoned exploration for half a century and were anyway embroiled in the Revolutionary and Napoleonic Wars from 1792 until 1815.[4] But peace with the French left an over-manned Navy and numerous redundant officers. The search for the North West Passage was resumed with evangelical zeal, considerable public interest and great loss of life. It was masterminded by John Barrow, Second Secretary to the Admiralty who championed Arctic exploits as combining new scientific knowledge with potential commercial benefits which enhanced British prestige. The coincident break up of a part of the polar ice cap made voyages through these waters easier.[5] Set alongside the experience of the previous 200 years it served to confirm the Navy as the driver of British polar exploration effectively until the First World War. Even when the British Government ceased to fund expeditions, after the Nares expedition of 1875-6, naval influence and tradition remained important –

with implications for the planning, the conduct and equipment of expeditions and for their leadership. The return of the British Navy to the Arctic began in 1818 with Ross's abortive quest for the North West Passage. Exploration continued with almost an expedition a year until John Franklin's fateful trip in 1845-8. Virtually all the expeditions have been described as flawed and under-resourced. But the Franklin disaster was the culmination of this folly and ended with the loss of the entire crews of both the ships Erebus and the Terror, when all 129 men perished. The obsession with the North West Passage was replaced by another, ever more publicised one – the search for Franklin. The discovery of relics of Franklin expedition by John Rae in 1853-4 was confirmed by Leopold McClintock in the closing years of the 1850s. This marked the end of an obsessive era, and travel across the ice became a crucial feature of the search. The English began sledging in the 1820s and 1830s but it was from the searches for Franklin that many of the traditions of English polar travel were born.

The so-called 'naval period' was certainly marked by mistakes and error, but this period of exploration saw both equipment innovation and a sustained building of knowledge, both among explorers and also their suppliers. Additionally they were able to draw on the fruits of the industrial revolution as they equipped their expeditions. When Franklin made his second trip to map 1000 miles of Arctic coastline in 1825, he was perhaps the first man to take an air bed made of rubberised cotton or 'MacIntosh'- though how useful he found it is not clear. But not all innovations taken on these early polar trips were trouble free and some proved killers. Parry was an early user of processed foods, taking a selection of canned soups, from the Rotherhithe company, Donkin and Gamble. The trouble was that although canning had been patented in 1811, 7 years later no one had invented a can opener and on the expedition cans had to be broken open using a mallet and axe. By the 1840s canning was becoming more normal and John Franklin took 8,000 'tins' of meat, vegetables and soup, supplied by London merchant Stephen Goldner under the Goldner patent. It was lethal stuff and much of the meat was inedible. They contained a hidden killer for lead solder was used to seal the tins. Relatively recent autopsies on the remains of three of Franklin's men detected lead poisoning although hunger, scurvy, and frostbite were probably the dominant factors.[6]

The British had plenty of men, unlike the Americans who, when joining the Arctic search for Franklin, had the greater need of dogs because of lack of manpower. Disease also played its part, many expeditions, British and American, would have liked to use dogs but were prevented from doing so because the animals died of disease.

In one sense Britain's early industrialisation was an advantage for these naval explorers – it brought wealth as well as innovations. Especially after the

Napoleonic Wars, when the links between the military and industry were exceptionally close, it brought an awareness of technological changes and new developments which might make survival and travel easier. But it may also have helped foster a sense of the superiority of British methods, techniques and people which became embedded in culture even before the Victorian age. When combined with an almost overwhelming sense of propriety and the importance of image – especially within established institutions like the Navy and in so many elements of Victorian life- this may have limited the extent to which British explorers learnt or were prepared to admit they learnt from the Eskimos. That dress is a fundamental cultural statement is hardly contentious, but this idea has rarely been applied to aspects of functional clothing. The British certainly seemed more squeamish about identifying themselves with indigenous people through the wearing of furs – much more so than mid- nineteenth century American explorers who, perhaps as a reflection of their Frontier-shaped social values positively relished it.[7]

Certainly once British naval explorers began to leave their ships and to cross the ice they observed Eskimos practices, traded with them, copied them and used their clothing. Between 1829 and 1833 John and James Clark Ross searched for the North West Passage. There is ample evidence that the John Ross party traded extensively with Inuit Indians for clothes such as Inuit dresses, sealskin jackets, boots, gloves and animal skins. The Inuits received European goods including knives in return. But what is fascinating were the lengths the British Navy were prepared to go to disguise their reliance on native dress. 'Traditional' Naval standards had to be maintained at all costs and for as long as possible men were inspected in their 'best' cloth uniforms. Ross talks in embarrassment of the situation after four years when his men were now 'dressed in the rags of wild beasts, instead of the tatters of civilisation'.[8] Even more telling are the illustrations of the expedition, where drawings show Ross's men in full naval regalia conversing with 'primitive' Eskimos with their spears. A more blatant attempt to give a public image of British superiority over 'uncivilised' people, with dress as a symbol of respectability would be hard to find.[9] Ross became reliant on indigenous people for clothing because his expedition lasted 2 years longer than intended. But on the majority of British expeditions in search of Franklin rigid dress codes were imposed and publicly maintained. These expeditions attracted considerable publicity, which may well have led to a desire to maintain appearances. Function was undoubtedly eclipsed by appearance and Naval officers were reluctant to deviate from the codes laid down by the Admiralty in London.[10] The naval tradition was for expeditions to be as self-sufficient as possible and to go out to the Arctic fully equipped as though for a military campaign. This was in turn, supplemented by the shipboard workshop of craftspeople and sailors, whose skills became so well honed on long voyages, that they often took up these trades on return home.[11]

Initially much was inadequate and better suited to temperate than polar climate. However, even in 1820s there is evidence of some evolution and adaptation to develop clothing specifically for the Arctic, with fur lined jackets. In addition there was clearly experimentation with English textiles including rubber proofed cloth usually known as 'Macintosh'. Similarly again in the 1820s cork was tried for the soles of boots to improve insulation. But the primary initiatives came during the search for Franklin and in 1857, Alexander Armstrong commented that special clothing had been developed for polar exploration consisting of:

'One complete suit of blue double milled box cloth, boots stockings, boot hose comforters mitts and caps all of excellent quality and well adapted for Polar service'.[12]

There were complaints as Collinson recollected of his 1850 voyage:

'Clothes generally supplied by the Admiralty (are) not very satisfactory: not good enough material and badly made' and included a wide range of textile items.[13]

But the story of Naval influence and Victorian propriety inhibiting the use of Eskimo clothing among mid nineteenth century English explorers can be taken too far. Not all English explorers fell under naval influence and John Rae is a prime example of a Victorian explorer who recognised how well adapted the Inuits were to their environment and who embraced their methods. Rather than being the head of a vast, London supplied expedition, Rae was not an English naval man, but a Hudson Bay Company doctor, who originally hailed from Orkney. He organised relatively lightweight, small expeditions and, in the 1830s, surveyed nearly 2000 miles of the Canadian Arctic. Twenty years later he discovered the remains of the Franklin expedition. He was also perhaps the foremost European exponent of Inuit methods of travel and survival.

'His everyday suit was a fur cap. Large leather mitts, with fur around the wrist, lined with thick blanketing and moccasins made of smoked moose skin, large socks with thongs of skin stretched across the soles to prevent them from slipping. He also wore a light cloth coat with its hood and sleeves lined with leather, a cloth vest and thick moose skin trousers, all of which were 'neither so heavy nor so warm looking as the dresses commonly used on a cold winter day in England. In addition he carried 'a spare woollen shirt or 2 and a coat made of the thinnest fawn skin with the fur on, weighing not more than four or five pounds to put on in the snow hut...'[14]

Yet Rae's appreciation of Inuit methods did not stop with dress for he embraced dog sledging and, unlike the Naval forays into dog driving when they harnessed them in rows, he adopted an Inuit style fan. This was safer for crossing crevassed or melting sea ice. He also observed and followed the practice of coating runners with ice.[15] The only means of 'waxing' or sealing wood runners at the time was wood tar which in low temperatures would not slide.

The irony is, that Rae had so little impact on English polar practice. As a Hudson Bay employee he had first hand experience of the climate and by trading with and learning from the Inuits, gained insight into their way of life. But it was Francis Leopold McClintock, the captain of the yacht, *Fox,* who confirmed the fate of the Franklin expedition and, from his experiences, became known as the father of English sledging. That he developed knowledge and an understanding of Arctic travel is indisputable but that he was taken seriously and his advice immortalised while Rae's, with its deep empathy with Inuit life was forgotten, is interesting. It would be too simple to say that while McClintock was a Navy man, Rae was not and so his insights, experiences and methods were taken less seriously.[16] But with his Hudson Bay Company base he was far from the seat of Naval power in London, and thus excluded from expedition organisation. Leopold McClintock's early experience had been gained with James Ross in 1849. But his ideas have been distorted with time. Whilst he lacked Rae's natural empathy with the Eskimos, he learnt much from them and recognised the value of both dogs and fur clothing, if it was Eskimo made. He confirmed that since sledges were mainly man-hauled:

> *'In the Government Searching Expeditions we gained no experience of snow houses, and but little of sledging with dogs, yet that little was sufficient to convince us of their value. For instance, during the spring of 1854, our only team of dogs was kept constantly at work, and without counting occasional short trips, they accomplished in 60 days' travelling, 1830 miles, affording an average rate of thirty miles... On several occasions they performed the distance of sixty miles between the Assistance and North Star.'[17]*

He went on to provide two pages of detailed description of dog driving and estimated that with dogs travel distance would probably be 25% further.

Unlike Rae though he did not use furs extensively, but instead described his clothing system as:

> *'Soft warm woollen articles under a cloth which is impenetrable to the wind, and is commonly known as box-cloth; and this again under a suit of closely-textured duck overalls, as snow repellers.'[18]*

The choice of textile, rather than fur clothing, may in part have been influenced by naval dress codes, but McClintock outlined practical and functional reasons saying:

> *'It will be noticed that furs are not used. Although they are very warm and agreeable, when in good condition, to sit in, to sleep in or even to work in, where they can be dried each night before a fire; and although they have generally been used hitherto, yet they*

SPRI Collection

SPRI Collection

Left: Lieutenant Evans in Burberry Windproofs. *Right:* Evans and Green making fur skin Sleeping Bags, May 16, 1911. 'Never an explorer until you have eaten your weight in hair' was the saying.

> *have been deliberately set aside for such dresses as I have described, because we have found that they check the escape of evaporation, they more readily absorb moisture, are more difficult to dry and shrink much when wetted and frozen. I speak of such furs as are commonly procurable in this country. Those which have been dressed by the Esquimaux and North American Indians are much better suited to our rough work'.[19]*

The origins of modern layering systems lie in the much maligned nineteenth century British naval expeditions. On the Nares expedition of 1875 hand sewn canvas windproofs were added. In the 1880s Nansen incorporated a hood in the style of the Eskimo anorak and, in the 1890s used the new Burberry gabardine which proved to be better as a windproof fabric. These ideas were embraced by the 1920's Everesters and of course are still followed today.

There are several clues here which explain McClintock's choice of clothing. He recognised the quality of clothing made by indigenous people, but clearly the Naval habit of collecting supplies at home rather than in the Arctic may have been an influence here. However, survival in polar regions is holistic, rather than just being based on one element of equipment. Fur clothing was ideal for dog sledging, but too warm for the massive effort of man-hauling and merely caused condensation and freezing. The comparative virtues of Eskimo style animal clothing remains controversial and much depended on the quality of tanning and the time of year the animal was killed. In addition, each part of an animal has different qualities and attributes, something fully understood by the Eskimo. Westerners quite simply could not gain thousands of years of understanding in just a few decades. Perhaps the most telling thing of all about animal furs in clothing and sleeping bags was the expression, "never a polar explorer until you

have eaten your weight in hair".
Depending on the quality and the
thickness, the skin always began to
shed hair after a period.

What is interesting is how
selectively McClintock's 'Arctic
Sledge-Travelling' was used by later
explorers who seemed to ignore what
he said about dogs and indeed furs. It
was apparently Robert Falcon Scott's
bible as he planned the *Discovery*
expedition 1901-4 and he quoted him
verbatim in *Voyage of the Discovery*.
The source of some of the distortion
came undoubtedly from Sir Clements
Markham – who as a midshipman on
the *Assistance* with McClintock in
1851 was impressed by the image of
man hauled sledges setting out from
the ship and by the whole ethos of
the Franklin search expeditions. He
was an arch naval traditionalist and
also McClintock's biographer, with

J. Arthur Bain

Nansen often skied with his wife, who had to buy boys clothing to get trousers to fit. Strangely the picture appears to show him using one pole whilst he was one of the early exponents of the 2 pole technique.

the perfect opportunity to fuel his myth. As President of the Royal Geographical Society, Markham was to have a major influence on the planning and equipping of British Antarctic expeditions before the First World War.[20]

The ill fated Nares expedition of 1875-6 marked the penultimate milestone in the building of the 'British naval tradition' of polar exploration. It prepared the way for the ultimate naval trip, Scott's ill fated attempt on the South Pole in1910-12.

There were two great myths in this period, which often served as inspiration. The first, which was held strongly by John Barrow, was that there was an open north polar sea. This might sound either naive or even some political ruse to drive his own ends. But there was some rationality to the thinking. Soundings had brought up samples of dead coral which of course only lives in much warmer seas. Darwin's theories had not yet been published, so there was no understanding of geological timescales. The second myth was that Greenland had an inland area which was a green fertile oasis and this view was held by the Swedish explorer Nordenskjoeld. These were arguably delightful ideas to help ensure that newspaper readership remained high and so these myths did not die an early death.

M. Parsons Collection

Ancient meets modern: Original raw-hide construction techniques mixed with modern wooden/PTFE laminates used on a Nansen sled at Dogsled.com Cambridge UK.

The Innovation Period 1875 -1914

Food, stoves, clothing, footwear, sledges, skis, skins, sleeping bags, tents, kayaks and special boats were all areas ripe for improvement – so Nansen certainly thought.

He seldom merely used the best practice or best existing product, but improved upon them and often with inspired innovations. In doing so he became known as the father of modern polar travel. When his years of exploration ended he became Norway's first ambassador to UK and after the First World War earned a Nobel peace prize for his work on repatriation of prisoners of war.

His sledge, which is still in production today, was an improvement of a design recommended by the American Adolphus Greeley, based on a Chukchi Siberian model. The Nansen burner (actually a heat extractor) was also based on a Greeley device and his silk tent was built on a recommendation by a Danish explorer. He learnt to paddle a kayak whilst he was in Greenland for the winter after his crossing. The typical Greenland kayak was unsuitable for being carried for many days across sea ice on a sledge and would not hold enough equipment. Therefore, he modified it so that it was shorter and broader of beam. For his Greenland ski travel he attempted to design a skin which would both grip and glide. However, he reverted to longer straighter skis for his attempt to reach the North Pole, (choosing to ignore the 1868 revolution in skis which was shorter skis with a side cut to enable turns to be made) to make crossing crevasses safer and co-incidentally provide more grip. For his clothing he combined the very best techniques from the Eskimos and the British. For less cold conditions he created a new windshell jacket with a Lancashire-made fabric marketed under the name of Thomas Burberry. By designing the jacket from this new fabric, with an integrated hood, he further developed the layering system. But it was the design, construction and 3 year Arctic expedition of that very special boat called the *Fram*, which was the greatest single piece of innovation and possibly the greatest risk taken perhaps by any explorer.

> *"What he wanted was a ship with sloping sides and rounded bilges, completely smooth, rather like an egg cut in half. In this way the ice could not get a grip, and instead of being crushed by the floes she would rise safely under pressure. To traverse the Arctic Ocean it was originally proposed to reach the Bering Straits via the Suez Canal and Indian Ocean so she needed to be a good Ocean going boat but also of shallow draft for negotiating Siberian coastal waters."[21]*

He was told that these characteristics were mutually exclusive, but commissioned a drawing and sent it to Colin Archer, a Norwegian of Scottish origin and one of the four leading naval architects in Norway who were able to understand ship design theory. The nature of the contract was intriguing, because it gave the flexibility needed to complete the boat on time and to the correct quality level. There was a fixed fee for the design and building, whilst all materials and wages were paid by Nansen when requested. It was launched on time and there was only one moment on his expedition when there was a risk of the boat failing. This was due to the danger that the ice would open, allowing the boat to fall into the open water and then be crushed when the ice closed again. But the boat survived and was used again to sail to the Antarctic. When Nansen made the decision and said to Amundsen, 'you shall have *Fram*' it was a critical turning point for the organisation of Amundsen's successful South Pole expedition.[22]

For all the other products Nansen used his extensive network of contacts and correspondents, linked to his extensive reading, to provide his basic research platform. In order to enlist the advice of Nordenskjoeld, the leading polar explorer of the time, he travelled to Sweden unannounced. He sensed the pleasure an older person would feel in acting as valued mentor and in so doing demonstrated quite unusual qualities for a young man. His personal presence was always accentuated by his Jaeger clothing, which was regarded as most unconventional at the time. Jaeger camel hair clothing and sleeping bags became state of the art in this period. In later years Nansen's own openness made him the advisor of many later explorers, including both Scott and Shackleton.

Whenever he began experimenting he made a prototype which he would then test on a quick ski trip. Where the product was found wanting it was further improved and adapted. In other cases with so many craftsmen on the boat, the prototyping work could take place on board. This was unexceptional and very much the way the British navy, with their vast teams of workmen, also behaved. But innovation needs more than a full complement of craftsmen. It needs a much more open and flexible environment than the very structured organisation of the Royal Navy – which could stifle the imagination. Above all it requires leadership and persuasion, boldness, commitment and something else extra on top, the indefinable quality of instinct bordering on genius.

Nansen had all these qualities. His early passion in life was skiing. Breaking with popular mythology that all Norwegians are born on skis, he did not start to use these things until the age of 2 and he did his first jump at ten years old. In the Huseby race of 1881 when competitors were invited from Telemark (the home of the top skiers), Nansen finished seventh and was the best skier from Christiana. This was the period when, as in mountaineering, there was a debate as to whether skiing was a sport. 'Nansen unequivocally took the view that skiing was 'a means of travel' and should not run the risk of being 'turned into a performing art'"[23]

Mountaineers and explorers are often inspired by the accounts of other adventurers and the attempt by Nordenskjoeld, the Swedish explorer, to cross Greenland in 1883 certainly inspired and informed Nansen. Nordenskjoeld was not himself as skier, but had taken 2 Lapps with him in 1883. They travelled so they claimed a distance of 230 km doing the round-trip of 460km in 57 hours. They did not of course find Nordenskjoeld's hidden oasis, but only good flat fast skiing terrain as far as the eye could see. In order to prove that such a distance was possible in the time, a race was organised in the following year and the winner was the same Lapp who had penetrated the Greenland ice cap. His time for 200 km was 21 hours 22 minutes, in wet heavy snow. In one of those fortuitous happenings that seem to surround every significant new mountain route or polar journey, the American Robert Peary was diverted by other duties from repeating his attempt to cross Greenland. In 1886 he had covered about 100 miles eastwards from the Disko Bay. He was prevented from returning to complete the crossing in 1887 and Nansen grasped this window of opportunity. He was an expert skier, convinced the crossing could be done on skis, but he needed Arctic travel advice. For this he persuaded Nordenskjoeld, who was 30 years his senior, to act as his advisor and he took Lapp skiers with him. His expedition was put together very quickly and he left Iceland on June 4th,1888 having just been awarded his doctorate, learnt to speak the Eskimo language, developed and tested all his items, obtained a letter of credit from the Royal Greenland Trading Company (because there were no banks) and chartered a ship.

Getting ashore was the major problem because of ice. Starting with snowshoes for some days he eventually, after 17 days, changed onto skis as the snow and angle of slope became easier. This was just the point when the Lapps were despairing of ever getting onto skis which is what, after all, they had come for. For wax Nansen probably used only wood tar burnt in and sled dogs were not taken. Double poles were adopted by Nansen as was traditionally preferred by the Lapps in any case, in preference to the single pole. Between 1893 and 1895 Nansen took the *Fram* and dogs into the Arctic Ocean in an attempt to reach the North Pole. A new travel system was inaugurated; skis with sleds and dogs, plus kayaks for open water, all adapted by Nansen in Greenland from the Eskimos. This trip was exceptionally bold. Nansen's style of expedition was entirely different from anything which had gone before. Everyone else had ensured that they had a suitable line of retreat and expeditions were supported by depots of food and equipment. Nansen, in starting from East Greenland, where there was no habitation and no boats waiting if he failed, created a new lightweight and very bold style of expedition. The analogy is climbing an 8000 m summit in alpine style, (i.e. progressing up the mountain without depots/camps), something which mountaineers did not do for another hundred years. Indeed the inspiration for Roger Mear's unsupported 'Footsteps of Scott' expedition was Messner and Habler's ascent of Everest in 1978 without oxygen and in alpine style. It is more difficult to make an analogy with Nansen's 'Furthest North' trip, which lasted three years, but by relying on skis, sledges, dogs and kayaks and freezing his boat purposely into the ice he was breaking all of the established rules of polar travel. On his return he lectured in England, completing 45 lectures in 46 days. At the Royal Albert Hall where he spoke to a crowd of 15,000 people and was presented by the Prince of Wales with a special gold medal for Arctic exploration by the Royal Geographical Society (RGS).[24]

Amundsen was born in Norway in 1872 and when Nansen returned home from Greenland on May 30th 1889 a young impressionable 17-year-old Amundsen was amongst the 30,000 strong crowd. This experience was the route source of Amundsen's inspiration. After serving as a seaman on an Antarctic trip aboard the Belgian vessel *Belgica,* Amundsen finally succeeded in opening the north-west passage in 1902-3. Arriving at Beechey Island, Amundsen paid tribute to Franklin and his men, 'let us raise a monument to them, more enduring than stone; the recognition that they were the first discoverers of the passage.'

For his South Pole trip he used Nansen's boat the *Fram*. His improvements in equipment and techniques of course built on Nansen's innovations. From his own polar food experiences he realised that fresh food was critical and planned the time of his expedition to enable the team to live partly on fresh seal meat. He also realised that the cranberry was particularly good for health and had one of his expedition men collect and preserve a quantity of them for the journey. He perfected the use of dogs, improved sleds further and designed harness systems. Navigation by sextant was a long job, especially the calculation which could take as much as an hour per day. Amundsen's team used a pre-formatted system which speeded up their routine.

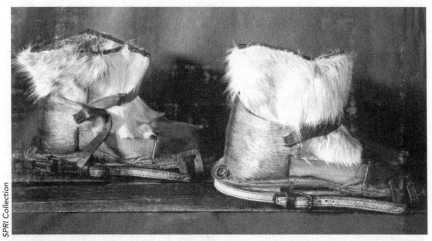

SPRI Collection

Finnesko (lit. Finnish shoes) were used for much cold weather exploration because their softness and flexibility helped warmth. To be used with skis however needed adaptation to give enough lateral stiffness.

For clothing and footwear Amundsen, like Nansen, had learnt from the Eskimos. But he adapted it further by making significant improvements in footwear. All satisfactory polar footwear use was based on original 'native' patterns, and was always soft and flexible.

This flexibility was the key to keeping feet warmer because circulation was not restricted. However, for these very extended ski journeys Amundsen wished to have more control of the ski. He considered the boot and the ski should be as one. His team made and remade the footwear in the long Antarctic winter three times over, to give the right combination of stiffness for the sole and flexibility for warmth. Inviting both the fruit preserver and the carpenter who made the winter quarters (which were transported to Antarctica on the *Fram*) to accompany him on the expedition was a visionary method of ensuring high quality of workmanship. If there were failings they would not only have to share the problem, but would be seen as the root source of it. This was about 70 years ahead of the quality circles which brought the Japanese into world leadership by the 1980's, but the philosophy is identical.

Amundsen was the first person to indisputably reach both poles. He attained the North Pole by airship in 1926.

Food and Drink as Human Fuel in Polar Regions

There is compelling evidence that Scott died in Antarctica in 1912, not from exceptionally bad weather but from the effects of scurvy. It is perplexing to understand why this should happen. Surely this problem had

SPRI Collection

Nutrition 1911 Polar style; Giving whisky to a pony that swam ashore!

been solved by Captain Cook on his voyages in the 1770's? The results of Lind's work on the use of citrus fruits to combat scurvy had been published in 1771 and the principle had been used in the Navy since the eighteenth century. Ironically Scott had been fed erroneous advice from Nansen, himself so careful of diet. In 1909, a seminal paper by Holst led to the discovery of vitamins by Casimir Funk in 1912. Holst had savaged Nansen's own doctoral research and Nansen responded in kind in a vitriolic newspaper article. At the same time Nansen advised Scott that scurvy came from tainted food, and it probably cost Scott and his men their lives.[25]

Northern American peoples have traditionally prepared special foods to sustain them through the winter. These were salmon or meat based with a very high fat content and were also mixed with wild berries. It was the Cree Indians who lived to the South of Hudson Bay who have given their name to what must be, in its original form, the ultimate balanced diet, *pimikhan or pemmican*.[26] and often used as explorers' rations.

The American physiologist W.O. Atwater determined the calorific values of proteins, fats and carbohydrates. between 1895 and 1905 This showed that the energy available to the body from eating, proteins, fat, and carbohydrate are respectively 4, 9 and 4 calories per gm. Polar explorers have almost always had a very high fat diet; the body gives the correct signals of its needs, By a very significant coincidence fat has more than twice the calories per given weight than carbohydrate. The slow speed of polar travel ensures that the body is able to 'burn' or metabolise fat, in contrast to the hard breathing runner who is burning all the glycogen from his muscles in two hours, hence "the wall". From this moment on, planning on a scientific basis was possible in order to minimise weight and maximise the number of calories; extremely

SPRI Collection

Meares and Oates at the blubber stove, 26 May 1911. Animal fats were still used to supplement paraffin in this period but fat burns with a very sooty flame, users became black after a short period.

vital factors when equipping an expedition for several months. Amundsen was one of the first to plan calories in the diet this way. However, as far as vitamins were concerned both he and Nansen used their long experience and careful observation of what kept men healthy in these conditions; fresh meat, lemon juice, and carefully preserved Norwegian cranberries.

Water, however, is the obvious prerequisite to food. Creating drinking water in polar and high mountain regions needs heat to melt ice or snow. Continuous polar travel, in very low temperatures, brought hydration problems of an entirely different magnitude to those in Alpine mountaineering or indeed the Eskimo way of life. Both sledge and especially ski travel, created much higher respiratory rates and hence dehydration levels. Limitations in fuels and stove design meant early nineteenth century polar explorers remained ship-based.

In the pre-history of man and stove, the lamp came first in 70,000 BC. Initially a hollowed-out rock was filled with moss or some other absorbent material previously soaked with animal fat and ignited. These were also developed into basic heating appliances, which were still used by the Eskimos in the first half of the twentieth century and indeed blubber stoves were still being used in 1912 by Western explorers to supplement their paraffin supplies.

Wood and other vegetable matter and animal fats remained the only fuels until winemaking and, more especially distillation processes, were developed by the Arabs about 2,000 BC and created spirits- the forerunner of the alcohol we use for stoves today.

Stoves used in early polar exploration burnt spirits (alcohol) and had multiple wicks by the late nineteenth century, in order to improve the heat output. However, the problem of keeping a wick trimmed was that, if not done regularly and precisely, some of the fuel was not properly burnt off and merely evaporated. Multiple wicks exacerbated this problem. In the 1880s Nansen read of the pioneering work of

Nansen and companions around his stove and Greely burner.

Adolphus W. Greeley (a U.S. naval officer involved in polar exploration) on stoves used in Arctic regions. His invention involved a peripheral flue system to absorb heat from the hot gas of the burner. This was highly effective in making the optimum use of the heat source, and water melting pans were wrapped around the primary cooking vessel for added efficiency. There have been several re-inventions of this concept, one being the volcano kettle of the 1960s, which could boil a pint of water with a newspaper. The Trangia cooker is the modern equivalent of the Greeley/Nansen burner.

The great breakthrough for polar exploration was the discovery of paraffin (oil) and the development of the pressure stove. Paraffin (otherwise known as rock oil) had been produced from shale for 20 years before the first successful oil drilling in Texas in 1859. However, it continued to be used in wick lamps and stoves, which did not extract all of the available calories from it, until a breakthrough by a Swedish engineer, Carl Richard Nyberg (b. 1858 Arboga, Sweden). By 1882 he had completed his first prototype of a vaporisation torch using petrol for fuel, called a soldering lamp or blowtorch. These first blowtorches preheated the fuel and projected the resultant vapour jet onto a circular spreader, which ensured the maximum air was used. Stoves, like humans need oxygen and the circular flame allowed more oxygen into it, a hotter flame was the result. A mobile source of heat for maintenance work was a boon to the entire world and the idea spread extremely rapidly.

In 1892 Nyberg branched out into the manufacture of paraffin stoves and the Primus stove was born. Nansen benefited from his habit of reading widely when, just before he left for his 'furthest north' trip in 1893, he saw a small advert in the paper for this new stove and responded. He had used alcohol for his Greenland trip and despite the modified Greeley device, suffered from 'arctic thirst'. The nature of this breakthrough for polar travel was quite simple, the distance which could be travelled for a given weight of fuel increased by the order of 60% due to the greater efficiency of the combustion process.[27] That is without considering the improved ability of the body when fully hydrated. This was a lesson which the British were to fully exploit in the race for the third pole, Everest. The Swiss, however, ignored proper hydration and it was a small but significant contributory factor to their 2 failures on Everest in 1952.

Tents

Weight and portability was a big issue and Whymper's tent from 1860s was actually a full porter load. (*see Whymper's engraving of Luc Meynet in Chapter 3*)

Whymper tent design established a high level of stability and wind resistance, and arguably was not improved upon for mountain purposes (polar tentage is another issue) until the arrival of the geodesic dome in the late 1970s. The 'A' poles which provided the basis for the stability of the design, were initially in bamboo cane with brass ferrules. Following commercialisation of the aluminium smelting process, in Germany in the 1880s, aluminium became increasingly widely used in all manner of outdoor equipment, including poles for tents. Rubber coated fabrics were already available and generally referred to as Macintosh and so, from the outset, Whymper's tent had a sewn in rubber coated groundsheet. Weights were around 22lbs (10kg).

Nansen for his "breakthrough" 44 day Greenland crossing in 1888 chose a very lightweight raw silk tent of 2.8 kg. The tent was made in several pieces, so that it could double as a sail for the sledge, while the ground sheet was left out because it picked up lots of ice and thus added weight.

Nansen also used a silk tent for his second great trip known as 'furthest north'" from 1893 to 1896, This was a much longer trip with much rougher ice and so the tent shredded long before he finished the trip. As a result, makeshift shelters using the sledges, kayaks and the remaining fabric were constructed. For the next thirty years, silk tents were used by mountaineers and for cycle camping, an activity pioneered by Thomas Hiram Holding in 1898. It is probable that Nansen's early use was a major influence. The next generation of polar explorers reverted to cotton – especially the windproof Burberry used for clothing. Speed of erection was critical and Nansen's tent erection time of 'three minutes for one man' was difficult to better and so eventually the pyramid tent became the polar model. Amundsen, Scott and Shackleton all experimented with and finally evolved a one pole tent which was initially square. This was then reconfigured by Amundsen, for his final successful journey to the South Pole, so that there was 'no corner to the wind'. This tent became known as the bell tent, with a circular floor plan and quite low walls. J. Russell-Jefferson invented the circular tunnel entrance in

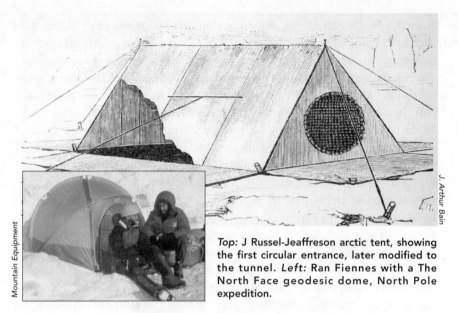

Mountain Equipment

J. Arthur Bain

Top: J Russel-Jeaffreson arctic tent, showing the first circular entrance, later modified to the tunnel. *Left:* Ran Fiennes with a The North Face geodesic dome, North Pole expedition.

1895.[28] The principle was followed by Amundsen, who said on his journey south, 'The arrangement of the door was on the usual sack principle, which is now recognised as the only serviceable one for the Polar regions'.[29] A sack was taken with the bottom cut out and then stitched into a hole cut in the tent.

F.G. Jackson (who met Nansen when the latter made his land fall in 1897) had a folding tent, rather like the hood of a cabriolet car, and it was probably this tent design which went with Shackleton to Antarctica.[30] The tent was much disliked because it was more difficult to erect, feeding poles through stiff canvas sleeves was quite awkward. It was not until after the 1922 Everest expedition, when Mallory demanded better tentage, that mountaineers embraced a tunnel entrance into the original Whymper design, This tent was called the Meade and is described at greater length in chapter 7.

But it was obvious from the earliest times that a rounded structure, especially if it were rounded in both floor plan and cross-section would offer not only less resistance to the wind but also more head room and living space. In 1950 Buckminster Fuller, the American architect, had been asked to design a 'production line house' to provide employment for unemployed aircraft workers in Dakota after the downturn of activity following the end of the Second World War. The principles of the support structure for the geodesic dome was that it used a pattern of tetrahedrons and octahedrons. The load bearing is carried on each of the self bracing triangles and is thus distributed evenly throughout the structure. This meant that, unlike most other buildings, there were no limits in dimensions and therefore a dome could be actually created over a whole city. A dome has, compared with any other shape, the maximum inner volume for the minimum outer surface. This has significant advantages in terms of heat loss, lower wind resistance, less fabric used. Putting the concept into tents was to take a further quarter-century and needed the arrival of many new materials, coil zips, aluminium poles and high strength lightweight fabrics. The breakthrough occurred in 1977 when Bruce Hamilton of The North Face company located in Berkeley California, got together with Buckminster Fuller and designed the Geodesic Dome. By this time materials had changed dramatically; lightweight coated nylon fabrics were used with a new grade of aluminium. This had a vital combination of characteristics of hardness and flexibility with a retained memory to spring back to its original shape. Coil zips had also arrived in the late 1950s and early 1960s while coated fabrics were just achieving high enough tear strength. This product created a genuine revolution in tent design and was one of the last great equipment breakthroughs. Very heavy pyramid tents remained in use for polar survey work and the pyramid has recently made a come back for adventure racers wanting to emulate Nansen's '3 minutes for one man' tent erection times.

Skis, Dogs and Sledges

Skis were used around 4,500 years ago, in northern Europe, around the time 'Oetzi' lived in the Alps. But there is no evidence of skis in Alpine regions until modern times. Snow shoes were in use from a similar period but tended to be found only in the areas south of permanent snows and on marshy areas in summer, where movement was as difficult as in deep snow. Conceptually the snowshoe could be considered as a kayak for the feet.

Sledges and toboggans (toboggan, n. Athabascan Indian word for flat bottomed sled) have also been used for thousands of years. The Neolithic hunter fishermen, who existed in northern Europe between Scandinavia and the Urals, were using sledges around 3000 BC and it is thought that these were pulled by dogs. Scandinavian rock engravings show sledges of around 2000 BC. When the British arrived in northern Canada in the quest for the North-West Passage, McClintock described the Eskimo sledges as, 'wretched little affairs, 2 frozen rolls of sealskins covered with ice and attached to each other with bones.' Stefansson noted that the Inuit in the Coronation Gulf area made sledge runners by slitting musk ox hide and freezing it like a plank. Nelson observed a small sledge with walrus tusk runners in the Bering Straits area;[31] 4 different types of sledge evolved. The Greenland sledge with its narrow runners, suitable for thin snow with an underlying hard base, was favoured by Peary the American. There was also the toboggan which was flat

Crevasse crossing in Arctic with Elisha Kane in the 1850s. Note the use of animal skins by this USA explorer.

bottomed and originated with the Athabascan Indians. The boat sledge has been used mainly in the broken sea ice of the arctic regions and probably first used by Parry in 1827 in an attempt to reach the North Pole from Spitzbergen. Finally there was the Nansen design, which had a number of advantages, not all unique to this design. These included the high raised hand rail which could be used to steer the rear end so the driver could step up and ride the sled. It was made without any screws, but with pegs using raw hide and kept as light and as flexible as possible. This meant that it would withstand very heavy usage without damage. Many different materials were used for shoeing the runners including ivory, bone, German silver, and of course water ice. The latter was a technique which many explorers picked up from the Eskimos; the runner was first covered with snow or even earth and then water was spurted from the mouth, the resulting ice being polished with a fur cloth. The Nansen sledge is still produced today in Cambridge for the British Antarctic Survey. It is no longer pulled by dogs, since their exclusion by agreement from Antarctica in the late Eighties.

While many have questioned whether it is humane to use dogs for polar travel, few challenged taking the horse, a totally unsuitable animal to the Polar Regions. Few if any have questioned whether it was humane to employ humans to pull sledges and the use of sails has been uncontroversial, although Nansen's Lapps were somewhat perturbed. McClintock, however, did question man-hauling when he said, 'all our sledges have been drawn by the seamen, and the labour of doing so has been most excessive'. Henry Kellett, leading a search for Franklin in 1851 said, 'I have been a long time at sea, and seen varying trying services, but never have I seen such labour, and such misery after. No amount of money is an equivalent... Men require much more heart and stamina to undertake an extended travelling party than *to go into action.* The travellers have their enemy chilling them to the very heart, and paralysing their very limbs; *the other the very contrary.'* Sir George Richards writing to Lady Franklin's niece said, 'there will never be any more Arctic sledge travelling I hope because there will never be anyone to look for again in those regions – I would confine anyone who proposed such a thing in a lunatic asylum, burn every sledge in existence, and destroy the patterns'.[32]

Thankfully the patterns weren't burnt!

Skis

The key problem for the skier is how to make the ski grip. The original prehistoric skiers solved the problem by having one ski, about 1 m shorter than the other, and covered with fur. Just before he left for Greenland, it was suggested to Nansen that he use sealskin. But he was not successful in getting it to work, despite soling the ski with German silver (nickel, copper and zinc) and cutting out a channel down the centre to insert the skin. Thereafter, Scandinavian skiers focused very much on perfecting the art of ski propulsion by means of waxes. Skins, by contrast, were preferred by the Alpine Europeans. The art of protecting the wood from humidity is as old as skiing itself and from this grew the wax which provided a grip. The first wax was probably made to the old Lappish recipe, a blend of tallow and wood tar, repeatedly burned into the wood base.[32] They probably put tallow on top and polished it. This wax provided sufficient traction to pull sledges on shallow slopes, but had very poor glide, important for races. In 1843 the first ski race was held in Norway, although the first commercial sale of ski waxes began among gold miners in Sierra Nevada, USA in the 1860s.

In 1868 Sondre Norheim, a young man from the Telemark region, broke all the jumping and cross-country records at a Nordic tournament in Christiana (Oslo). Prior to this, a single toe strap had been used to hold the ski on the foot. Norheim revolutionized skiing by adding a willow strap around the heel and contouring his skis, so that they were slightly waisted in the middle. The new binding and refinement of the ski shape gave greater control and manoeuvrability which meant faster running and longer jumps. The words, "Christiana" and "Telemark" were given to the new ski technique he pioneered. He is considered the 'Father of Modern Skiing'.

Wax and waxing techniques continued to develop, both to fulfil a commercial demand and provide competitors with significant advantages. The waxes being developed could be used on snow (but not ice) and increasingly gave a better rapport between the grip and the glide. The first ski wax advertisement was by Thranes in 1888 and was followed by the first ski wax patent by Emil Selmer in 1897. At this point, however, waxes were still more or less useless on 'transformed' snow (meaning changed from the crystalline structure to very wet snow or ice.) New solutions were keenly sought and, by 1910 a new type of very sticky wax, called Klister began to be used in competitions. Peter Østbye filed his Klister patent in 1914, and this was quickly followed by a patent covering the use of melted rubber from bicycle inner tubes mixed with tar to produce a second generation of Klister. Torgeir Bratlie of Oslo and Peter Kindal of Rjukein were the patentees.

Wax remained the standard method of grip for skis in Scandinavia, but for the steeper alpine terrain, something more was needed. The story of the first alpine ski ascents is told in the chapter on mountaineering equipment.

Skis and the Military

The military have been extremely important in establishing the ski as part of our sports activities. Norway showed early leadership and in 1716 ski troops were first organised. By 1733 Captain Emahusen had produced the first set of rules for ski-troops. In the early nineteenth century ski soldiers were still an important part of the Norwegian defence force. At this point they were using a single pole in one hand, rifle in other and skis of differing lengths, the short one with skins permanently attached and used to push and give traction and the other for gliding on. The need to carry a gun either for hunting or military purposes was probably an important reason for the use of the single pole.

The use of skis in the Alps was almost unknown before the publication of Nansen's book on the crossing of Greenland. However, within a very short period Zdarsky and Bilgeri were training large numbers of soldiers in Austria to move on skis. Whenever large scale training in skiing has been given by an army, then the practice moves into the civilian population within a decade.In 1902 skiing found its way into the French army; and Germany, Austria Hungary, Italy, and Russia also recognised the tactical importance of ski units for scouting, communications and patrolling. As early as 1891 a ski detachment of the 20th Russian Infantry Division performed a 10 day's march of 1,115 miles. In 1903 the *ecole militaire de ski* was established in France to train the *Chasseurs Alpins*. This school regularly held courses of instruction which lasted 2 months. At the end of the first month cadets were expected, in full marching order, to cover 60 km.

At the beginning of the Second World War, Finnish ski soldiers held back very much larger Russian forces because of their skills as skiers. Information[34] that the Germans were training special mountain troops for use in Alaska and in the Canadian and American Rockies encouraged the Americans to take mountain and ski warfare seriously and the result was the 10th Mountain division. This division became heavily involved in training and in the development of specialist clothing and equipment. But its impact lasted beyond the end of the war, for among US Army volunteers were often exiled top Austrian skiers, including Friedl Pfeiffer from St Anton[35]. At the end of one of the training sessions, his Army squad marched into a more or less defunct old mining town in Colorado, called Aspen. As Friedl walked into town he was struck by its similarity to his hometown, St Anton in Arlberg Austria. He vowed that if he had the opportunity to come back he would set up a new ski resort. This he did, and the training of thousand of service men to ski by many of his fellow countrymen, plus the investments by wealthy Americans who were passionate about developing Aspen as both a place of culture and ski activity created the world's largest ski market, the USA.

Post War Periods
Further Advances in the Waxes and Skins

Adhesive skins were first produced in the 1930's, called Sohm skins[36] which were glued on using a type of ski wax. They could not be easily re-attached during a trip and the glue came off onto the ski sole impairing glide. Tricouni the climbing nail manufacturer developed an ingenious Trima system which was in use until the early 1970s. This, however, needed the permanent fixing of a number of small keel like devices into the ski channel on the sole of the ski. Both systems had significant limitations. In 1968 Hans Fischli founded TÖDI-SPORT in Switzerland. He was convinced of the advantages of the old adhesive skins. He developed a new adhesive which remained with the skin when it was peeled from the ski and even better, was reusable many times before new glue needed to be applied.

This achievement was probably helped by the fact that by now ski bases were sintered (a technique of fusing a plastic powder into a microporous solid) and the new generation of waxes were polymer based ensuring much lower friction. From 1946 Swix introduced the second generation of ski waxes by utilising synthetics otherwise know as polymers. Yes even ski waxes were totally changed by the polymer revolution.

The Detailed Analysis of Historical Journey Times

This table, by putting polar travel in a long term perspective should provide the solution to Roger Mear's initial riddle about man hauled versus dog sleds. A study published in *Polar Record* in 1995 [37] throws less light on the matter than one would expect and this is simply because it is almost impossible to compare like with like. There are 3 entirely different questions; speed, distance and the nature of support ie the crux question of whether depots were laid in advance (as with Amundsen, Scott and Steger to the South Pole).

The study compared all explorers from 1820 until the present day and here is a small selection:

Explorer / Year	Dogs Vs. Man-haul	Total Distance	Time	Av miles/km	Comments
ARCTIC JOURNEYS					
Lyon (Parry) 1822-23	Man	130 Miles	15	8.5/13.7	NW Passage
McClintock / 1852	Dogs	1328 Miles	106	12.5/20.1	NW Passage
Rae / 1851	?	1060 Miles	39	27.2/43.7	NW Passage
Nansen / 1895	Dogs	235 Miles	40	5.9/9.5	Towards N Pole
Peary / 1909	Dogs	637 Miles	21	30.3/48.8	North Pole.
Peary / 1909	Dogs	306 Miles	8	38.3/61.6	8 days in final successful (?) push to North Pole,
Steger / 1986	Dogs			8.5/13.7	North Pole
ANTARCTIC JOURNEYS					
Steger / 1986	Dogs /Man			8.5/13.7	South Pole
Scott / 1902-03	Dogs	960 Miles	93	10.3/16.6	South Pole
Scott / 1911-12	Man	800 Miles	76	10.5/16.9	South Pole
Amundsen / 1911-12	Dogs	870 Miles	39	22.3/35.9	Return from South Pole
Amundsen / 1911-12	Dogs	62 Miles	1	62/99.8	Best day travel when depot laying
Amundsen / 1911-12	Dogs	870 Miles	55	15.8/25.4	To South Pole
Herbert / 1968	Dogs	1180 Miles	134	8.8/14.2	Traverse of arctic sea via North Pole
Mear/ Swan/ Wood 1985	Man	873 Miles	70	12.5/20.1	Scott's route to South Pole
Fiennes/ Stroud 1992-93	Man	1487 Miles	95	15.7/25.3	Traverse of the Antarctic continent
Ousland / 1996	Dogs	1767 Miles	64	27.6/44.1	First and first solo unsupported crossing of Antarctica.

Drawing conclusions from this information is both difficult and even dangerous but a few aspects stand out immediately.

1. *The conventional wisdom today is that the British naval explorers failed to reach their objectives e.g. South Pole because they did not use dogs. The table contradicts this conclusion and breaks one of the most entrenched myths.*

2. *Returning from the South Pole (which few have done), shows considerable acceleration of speed when using both dogs and skis.*

3. *Peary probably did not reach the North Pole; his last 8 days were not achievable. For this reason and because he had no-one with him to check his calculations his journey remained controversial. Few of his contemporaries and later explorers believed him. Jeannette Mirsky summed up the situation well when she stated: "plausibility is not proof; their arguments boil down to a simple matter of faith: do you believe or do you not? Cook, Peary, – their footsteps are as untraceable as their names would be if written in water "*[38]

4. *The acceleration given by the modern sail and the traction kite is hidden in these figures because only averages are quoted. Fiennes and Stroud using a modest amount of sailing technique had a achieved the most important thing of all, a vision of possibility, by crossing the Antarctic land mass. The first complete crossing of Antarctica, the longest unsupported journey in the world was completed solo by Borg Ousland, of Norway. Ousland set off from Baerkner Island on November15 1996, hauling a sled and supplies weighing 375lbs and the 1,767-mile took 64 days; there were no depots.*

Man as the Ultimate Machine

Only man can achieve a journey of this length; snowmobiles, tractors and all mechanical transport need refuelling and Antarctica has no fuel stations.

But how exactly was it achieved? This second polar travel revolution was again Norwegian. It was preceded by the opening up of the first civilian flights in 1987 by Adventure Network International (ANI), which landed on a blue ice runway about 680 miles from the South Pole and not far from Mount Vincent, Antarctica's highest mountain.

Equipment had got steadily lighter and more efficient over the preceding decade and a half. Evidence that modern skis, skins, waxes or sleds are contributing to distance was difficult to establish and so I decided to enlist Roger's help; "the three most important innovations in order of importance are: communication, traction kites, and GPS. Perhaps most important is the fact that there is a synergy between all of these three innovations when applied in polar travel, and it is that on which the revolution is based." As telecommunications become better and the support and emergency services linked to them, it becomes possible to cut food rations to within a few days of the estimated journey time, "because the button can be pressed if you don't make it." Borg Ousland who did have communications only took 75 or 80 days food for a trip he did in 64 days." Paradoxically it appears that,whilst this revolution is labelled "unsupported" it is based on communication which is effectively the ultimate in support, of "come and get me out of here" Roger Mear on the "Footsteps of Scott" 1986 expedition, where there were no radio communications; needed more margin and therefore took 120 days of food for a journey of 72 days.

Travelling under sail / parachute can add huge distances, 50-80 miles on the days it is usable. However, the new sail, the traction kite is a revolution. It is based on the paraglider (which had undergone dramatic improvements of

Tamang porter in Nepal with his headband in alternative position.

Bill O'Connor

performance; by measure of its glide ratio from the top of a mountain downwards the improvement was from 1:3 to 1:7 in less than a decade.) It can pull, without any wind, or with the wind in almost any direction. "The two-day crossing of Greenland will be achieved very shortly".[39]

Global Positioning System GPS, originated in 1973 but only reached "Initial Operational Capability" by late 1993. The first hand-held GPS receivers were manufactured by Magellan in 1989 and, while they sold for $3000 compared to just $300 today, this was clearly a breakthrough. When travelling by traction kite, the distances can be 100 miles or even more per day. Because one is using wind power it's like a sailing situation ie loosing leeway is the problem and therefore one has to recheck position very frequently. "When travelling by traction kite I used to keep my GPS running continuously," said Roger. "At the end of the day you could be many km off the line and so your GPS would give you automatically the next days bearing. When we were on "footsteps of Scott "we were still using a sextant at the time, although at walking speed we thankfully didn't need to recalculate position very often."

Perhaps what has been achieved, through the equipment which these pioneers created, is to make polar travel a more enjoyable experience and indeed almost open to all. A similar revolution to this occurred about 50 years ago. For several millennia man had been accustomed to carrying loads suspended by a single band either across the forehead or across the shoulders.

The Napoleonic Wars saw the revolution of the two shoulder strap pack. Until 1950 carrying all your food and equipment on your back was restricted to those with well-developed shoulders;trappers and hunters, blacksmiths and indeed tough mountaineers. Dick Kelty of California developed a new aluminium tube pack frame based on the original 'Trapper Nelson' wooden ladder model. One day he noticed that someone was supporting the weight of the load by pushing the ends of the protruding lower aluminium tubes into the pockets of their jeans. This led to the idea of the hip belt to support the weight. From this point on carrying all your belongings on your back became open to all and indeed it was declared as fun and called backpacking. Antarctic and polar travel appears to be similarly poised as backpacking was in 1950. Since 1987 a Scottish/Canadian company, ANI has been offering tourist trips to the South Pole. Once you are there your onward movement, on foot, skis, or with kites (but no longer dogs) is your choice, tempered by the logistics of the region and your personal skills.

Have an enjoyable sledge packing trip!

CHAPTER 3
Bivouacs by Candlelight
Equipping the Victorian and Edwardian alpinist 1850-1914

The Origins of Mountaineering and Outdoor Sport

One evening in November 1857, twelve English gentlemen met in London and agreed to form a club which would enable them to both find climbing partners and share information. The club was named 'Alpine Club' and was the first of its kind in the world. Climbing was a new and dynamic sport in the 1850s and activity had grown dramatically in just a decade. Between 1850 – when many Alpine peaks had not even been identified or mapped, let alone climbed – to 1865 most of the 4000m peaks in the Alps and all of those in Switzerland had been climbed. The Four-thousanders were the ultimate prizes for mountaineers and so after Edward Whymper's momentous ascent and descent of the Matterhorn – the last of the Alpine giants – the so called 'golden age' came to an end. Remarkably 60% of these first ascents had British climbers in the party and strong partnerships had already emerged between the professional guides and their clients and especially between the Swiss and the English professional classes. The English are not a natural mountain nation and lacked the natural instincts and skills of mountain people, or those who lived close to the Arctic Circle. Nor were they the first to start climbing in the Alps; that was left to French scientists and others who lived close to the Alps, while climbing began on the sandstone towers of Saxony early in the nineteenth century. Set in this light, it is amazing that Britain produced any mountaineers and explorers at all. They were activities for which – in contrast to other nations – they were peculiarly ill-suited. Yet for a comparatively short time – up to 1900 – they dominated both.[1] So why did the Alps capture English imaginations in the middle of the nineteenth century? Also when did mountaineering become a sport – rather than just the pursuit of scientific knowledge which involved climbing mountains.

In trying to explain this, there is an interesting analogy to be drawn with the Lancashire cotton industry – Britain's largest nineteenth century export sector – which was an entirely artificial transplant, as raw cotton could not be grown in northern Europe. The prominence of British mountaineers in the third quarter of the nineteenth century and of explorers through to the First World War, was just as unnatural. The link with the industrial revolution is not just metaphorical, because it created the wealth and freedom for those bold enough to travel and to climb. Britain, with Lancashire at its epicentre, was the world's first industrial society. It also lay at the heart of a vast empire which in the late nineteenth century was at its zenith. Industrialisation involved factories, technology and trade but it also created whole new classes of lawyers, accountants and patent agents. Added to this list should of course be the clergy. The bankers were already there of course, refugees from war torn Napoleonic

AC Collection

The earliest known photograph of mountaineers; c1850, but the people and location are sadly unknown

Europe, attracted to London as a great commercial centre. These so-called 'professional' classes became the new elite in society and formed the core of the newly formed Alpine Club. These people had the time and money to pursue their passions and their public school education had brought a growing emphasis on physical exercise and of course *games*. They became innovators, not merely in a new sport, but also in the very equipment that was needed to succeed.

The wealth that came from early industrialisation created a leisured elite, but of course there was more to the nineteenth century English love affair with the Alps, than just people having the time and money to travel to pursue their passions. As mountains became places to be admired, gazed upon and climbed by the wealthy, and travel became much faster and more comfortable, scenic tourism was born. For the first time individuals and particularly women, could travel extensively for personal reasons, without having to be a member of the military services.

It also became much easier to travel to Alpine areas. In the early nineteenth century moving around in the Alps could be a chilling experience – both actually and metaphorically – and needed a steady nerve. Robert Hyde Greg, the Manchester cotton magnate, wrote in his journal in 1817 that the scenery was magnificent and awe inspiring but, the casual nonchalance of his driver alarmed him too:

> *'The path was never more than eight feet wide often not six and very much inclined... Our driver, however, far from being alarmed either for himself or his precious charges kept nodding off all the way, only opening his eyes to flog his horse or when a jog told me we were out of the track'[2]*

Thomas Cook Archive

Railways began in England and opened across Europe and the Alps from the 1850's. The travel agent was a crucial innovation for putting together itineraries and ticketing. Thomas Cook was the first.

In a matter of thirty years the coming of the railways transformed travelling times to and from the Alps from days to hours, while Thomas Cook later helped to cut the cost. The first passenger railway in Britain, from Liverpool to Manchester was opened in 1831 and was the precursor of a rapid transport network; it spread first in Britain and then on the Continent from the late 1830s. In the 1850s railways extended to the very edges of the Alps pushed, it has to be said, by British engineers and finance. Railways and suspension bridges were invented in the 1830's and by 1851 it was possible to travel from London to Chamonix within 48 hours (by rail, navigation and diligence) compared with the 12 days it had taken previously to get from the North French Coast to Geneva before the coming of the railways.[3] By 1867 the rail network connected all the major towns around the Alps: Lyon, Basel, Munich, Vienna, Trieste, Verona, Milan, Turino and westwards into the Rhone valley following the Mediterranean coastline.[4]

Alpine passes had changed little since Roman times, save during the Napoleonic Wars when Napoleon used them for troop movements. Suddenly they became open to rail and road traffic. The Albula pass was a road by 1839, giving access to the Engadine, while the Julier pass opening northern Switzerland to the Engadine had a road from 1826. These dates indeed give us the clue to the very early British passion for the Engadine and St Moritz in Switzerland. The Bernina pass, from Pontresina – Poschiavo, giving access from Engadine to Tirano Italy, had a road by 1865. The Brenner pass was an old Roman crossing, by 1867 there was a rail route through the Arlberg by 1884 which brought much needed winter visitors to St Anton. By the 1920s this was home to the world's largest ski school.

Travel to the Alps from England began to get cheaper too, courtesy of Thomas Cook. In the 1840s Thomas Cook had pioneered mountain tourism in Britain by promoting rail excursions to Scotland. By 1860 his so-called 'Tartan Tours' had taken 50,000 people to the Highlands. But in 1862, unexpectedly the Scottish railway companies refused to issue any more tourist rail tickets and he was forced bring his trips to a halt. Ironically it was this blow which took Cook to the Alps for the first time for, as the Scottish route closed, the Continental one opened and with reliable rail services in Continental Europe he began to introduce a wider clientele to the Alps.[5]

But this development was anything but popular with the elite mountaineers who first went to the Alps in the 1850s. They were unwelcome 'tourists' damaging exclusivity. Whilst this was anything but mass tourism, it marked a subtle widening of those able to appreciate mountain scenery.

Changes in communications did not stop with railways. It became easier to travel, to get information, to plan a trip, to contact hotels. Progressively there were better postal services from the 1840s, the beginnings of steam shipping, of the telegraph and the opening of the Suez Canal in 1869 which drastically reduced journey times to India. The world quite simply became a smaller place. This meant that the English love affair with the mountains did not end with the Alps and by the First World War had extended to all the major mountain ranges of the world. As the Rockies, the Andes and the Himalays all became accessible English mountaineers continued the 'summiting' game they had begun in Switzerland and France. Douglas Freshfield, Honorary Secretary of the Royal Geographical Society and President of the Alpine Club summed the position up perfectly in 1893:

> '[The professional traveller] forms only a small proportion of the Englishmen and English women who, on business or pleasure, yearly extend their wanderings over the globe. One of the results of the rapid multiplication of lines of ocean steamers and railways in distant seas and far off countries has been it is easy for men of comparatively brief leisure to undertake and share in exploration in the course of a vacation tour. The goal of years ago has become the starting point...'[6]

Railways and communications did not make the English into climbers, but they made new areas accessible at a time when other forces were whetting middle class appetites for mountaineering.

Mountaineering was not initially a sport but was linked with science, geology and a fascination with climate. This could have been to disguise the fact that actually climbing mountains was a delightful form of escapism or more likely the scientists discovered this for themselves. But it began to be obvious that as the Himalayan explorer, Younghusband said, climbing mountains 'served no useful purpose.' This could well have been the origin of the public outrage following the Matterhorn disaster in 1865 – which included a plea from Queen Victoria to Gladstone that mountaineering should be stopped. There was nothing new about Englishmen being killed in remote and inhospitable places, after all 129 men died searching for the North West Passage across the Arctic region on the Franklin expedition just 20 years earlier. This had attracted national attention but not condemnation. What was different though was that there was some potential national commercial or strategic gain – however misguided – from the search for the North West Passage. There was none from climbing the Matterhorn. For the first time people were valuing experience over possessions – something increasingly common in the late twentieth century. But it must have been deeply unsettling in Victorian England.

Interestingly the publicity surrounding the search for Franklin and his lost crew during the 1850s, may well have been one of the crucial triggers which encouraged growing numbers of young Englishmen to visit the Alps. Certainly, the upsurge in English Alpine climbing in the 1850s and 1860s perfectly matches the Arctic search parties regularly featured in national press and the subject of exhibitions and lectures. It was certainly an influence on Victorian youth who were inspired by the tails of search for the ill-fated 1845 Franklin expedition and of McClintock's confirmation of the discovery of the remains in 1859.[7]

The Franklin mystery held the national imagination. Boys growing up in that period, who had been captured by the idea of adventure amid polar ice, were to learn as young men that the central mountains of Europe offered a field for similar adventure, in not dissimilar surroundings. Nor was it unnatural that they knew about the mountains at this time. The second edition of Forbes *Travels* (1845) was no doubt still lying about in the library, and fresh in their parents minds. Speers' account (1846) of his Wetterhorn ascent would still be remembered, and could easily be brought out of the cupboard. Under these conditions, men like Charles Hudson and Eardley Blackwell started their climbing before yet another wave of publicity occurred . In 1851 Albert Smith, the controversial and much criticised publicist of mountaineering climbed Mont Blanc. He saw that the time was right to arouse public interest in mountain adventure, and would not be without profit. His lantern shows brought mountaineering to the armchair traveller, among them a nine year old Douglas Freshfield. Albert Smith continued his public lectures for six years and stopped just one year after the foundation of the Alpine club.[8]

A Sport Emerges

Mountaineering then and today is a sport without a formal set of rules. Indeed, some would say it is not sport but a pastime. Instead of rules it has a very strong set of ethics , but ones which differ by type of rock, by region, by country, by mountaineering 'tribe' and even by altitude. How then, without formal rules, can we recognise the beginnings of a sport? Three criteria can be used instead: the growth of clubs, specialist committed suppliers, and recognised equipment standards. By 1864, one year before Whymper climbed the Matterhorn (which marked the end of the golden age) these were all in place.

The Alpine Club of 1857 was the first mountaineering club to be followed by others, often with rather different objectives. The OeAV (Austrian Alpine club) was the first of the European clubs, founded in 1862, followed closely by others and by the Christiana (old name for Oslo) Ski Club in 1866.

By the end of the golden age in 1865, such was the level of enthusiasm that a few firms began to specialise in producing mountaineering equipment. Arguably their decision, along with a growing awareness of the need for safety standards, marks the true birth of the sport.

The English may have been Alpine pioneers, but they were not the first gear specialists . The expertise to make mountaineering equipment resided in the Alps –after all climbers were using adapted versions of what mountain people took for granted. Also only those manufacturers located in what became mountain resorts, had any chance of achieving a reasonable level of business and the feedback which allowed them to improve and adapt their products This, combined with their own personal affinity for and an understanding of the demands of the mountain environment, was responsible for creating the famous alpine brands of today.

In a small Alpine village called Chamonix, in the valley of the Arve, a region still belonging at that time to the Duchy of Savoy was a family of blacksmiths called Simond. By the 1850s they had already been practising their craft for almost a century, and their products included ice axes for mountaineers. In 1861, having experienced a steadily increasing flow of English mountaineers, they decided to specialise entirely on mountaineering tools and were almost certainly the first company to do so. This was confidence indeed for mountain climbing may have been eclipsed by some other craze, though probably the Simonds could have just reverted to being blacksmiths. Climbers could now buy gear from craft workshops who were beginning to specialise. Simond was one of the first of many continental hardware manufacturers, Grivel was another. By the 1890s the Alpine Club listing of equipment suppliers highlights just how crucial these Alpine specialists were. But the 1860s saw another move which helped to define mountaineering as a sport. In 1864 safety began to be addressed for the first time, and the Alpine Club investigated the two most crucial aspects of equipment: ropes and ice axes. The testing which followed led to the setting of the world's first equipment standard. A red thread was inserted into all hemp ropes which met this standard. It was probably one of the most enduring standards and stayed in existence until the early 1950s, when nylon ropes replaced hemp. The work on ice axes led not so much to a specific standard but to a set of recommendations. Amongst these was the idea that the pick of the axe should have a curvature which corresponded with the radius of the arc made by the mountaineer's arm as he swung the axe to cut the step. In interesting contrast to the standard for ropes, the recommendations for ice axes were not followed and this radius was not really applied until the late 1960s, when Scottish mountaineering brought a new impulse to ice climbing techniques. This then is the beginning of the mountaineering we know, not for science, not for colonialism, not for Empire building, not for map making, not to guard frontiers, just for sport.

The development of technical equipment is reserved for a separate chapter. But if the Victorian Alpinist needed to go to the Continent to get much of their kit they often relied on their own designs, worked out and perfected by a craftsman, for more mundane but equally important items of clothing and equipment.

Modern mountaineers have to learn how to survive in extreme conditions both psychologically and physically. They need the protection of technologically sophisticated clothing and equipment to survive and perform well. Arguably the closer to the present we move, the more will have to be learned, because so much tacit knowledge has been lost. Our ancestors may have lacked much of what we deem essential in the mountains, but possessed a greater natural awareness of how to survive and move around on frozen or mountainous terrain. Many early climbers were intensely practical men who had a typical Victorian fascination with ingenious and extraordinary devices . They had sufficient wealth and leisure to pursue ideas which might make their hobby more pleasurable. They used what was available and improved and adapted it to meet changing aspirations and solve new problems, while their daily lives made them sensitive and aware of how to keep warm – certainly more so than we are today.

Modern climbers are constantly bombarded with information from suppliers, from retailers and from gear reporters, on a bewildering array of products. In the mid-nineteenth century, information may have been limited, but from the start tourists guidebooks to the Alps contained mention of stockists of equipment while the Alpine Club's publications, first *Peaks, Passes and Glaciers* from 1859 and from 1864 the *Alpine Journal* always included advice on equipment. Reading the personal experiences of mountaineers in this period is very revealing . These accounts – published in the *Alpine Journal* and in accounts of their travels – show a real appreciation, often tempered by wry humour, of how best to survive in the mountains. These men, while often public school and university educated, were highly practical men. They may not have been able to buy ready-made specialist equipment, but they had an understanding of what was needed and who to approach to help them develop it. They lived in the era of the Great Exhibition of 1851 – that celebration of inventiveness and the ingenious gadget. Moreover, many early mountaineers were scientists and some will have had links through the growing number of provincial scientific societies with businessmen able to help them.[9] Experience could also be shared relatively easily in the close knit world of the Alpine Club and in the Alps. New young climbers could find a mentor willing to share past years of experience – ranging

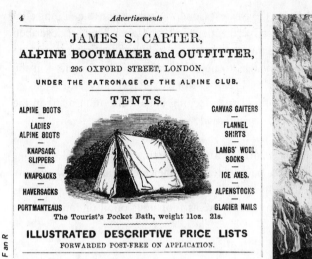

Left: 1867 Advertisement of James Carter : Alpine Bootmaker and Outfitter, London. Perhaps the earliest of all retailers who styled themselves 'outfitters'. *Right:* The Reverend Girdlestone, Guideless Climbing on the Sella in the 1860s.

from how best to stay warm, how to secure the most prestigious guides to where to buy gear. Just such a relationship developed between Francis Tuckett and the young W.A.B. Coolidge. Coolidge first contacted Tuckett at the age of 17 for advice on equipment and later referred to him as his 'Alpine Godfather'.[10] The highly personal flavour of the first of the series of Alpine Club exhibitions of equipment in 1887 reinforces this sense of a pool of mountaineers' knowledge and expertise. The collection of members' equipment, with advice on where they had used it and how they had improved it, was a long way from a trade show and indeed there were no firms represented.

By the 1880s more systematic information and advice was becoming available, however. Initially aimed to serve the needs of scientific exploration, the Royal Geographical Society had produced a series of *Hints For Travellers* since 1854. These volumes provided advice on what scientific equipment to take on an expedition but mountaineering equipment was ignored until 1883. Advice really only become insightful from 1893 when Douglas Freshfield – President of both the Alpine Club and the Royal Geographical Society- pointed to the key importance of mountaineering knowledge to the success of scientific expeditions.

This feature expanded in the 1890s, in parallel with reports and exhibitions from the Alpine Club, as well as some classic tracts on mountaincraft such as Clinton Dent's *Mountaineering* first published in 1892. By the 1890s specialist mountaineering equipment – made on the Continent- was available from a number of outdoor retailers in London . Of these the earliest was James S. Carter established in 1806, who was the earliest London shopkeeper to call himself a Tourist Outfitter.[11] His 1867 advertisement in the *Alpine Journal* described him as Alpine bootmaker and outfitter, and was probably the first in London.. Most clothing and equipment was to be found where it was made – in the Alps especially in Switzerland, Italy, Norway, Germany and Austria. However, tents and some clothing and sleeping bags were often made in the UK, often to order from a pattern and made in a workshop.

Keeping Up Appearances: Clothing and Sunburn

Since mountaineering was a new sport in the nineteenth century , few saw any need to wear special clothing or even adapt their everyday dress. It seems doubtful though whether many men were as foolish as one London dandy in 1819 who claimed:

'I endeavoured to ascend some mountains, but my stay-lace gave way, my Morocco boots burst and my dowlas trousers got wet through ....'[12]

This was the period when men wore corsets to enhance appearance – a practice soon to be followed by women – but they were hardly ideal for physical exercise. Men and women climbers of the 1850s simply wore what they would have worn for a winter's walk or for hunting or shooting – the origin of the much beloved Norfolk jacket and knickerbockers. Draughty houses meant that people had to dress warmly and when they travelled this was even more important. Unheated, horse-drawn carriages and walking or riding long distances, in all weathers, was accepted as a matter of course. The earliest trains had open carriages and were unheated. However, by 1842 Dickens talked of stoves on American trains and soon steam heating was introduced for first class travel in Britain and Europe. In such a world the clothes of the Victorian upper middle classes may have been fashionable, but they had to be warm. Indeed one of the earliest recorded uses of down clothing had nothing whatever to do with mountaineering, but was in the quilted eiderdown petticoats worn under women's crinolines in the 1860s.[13]

The early mountaineers knew of necessity how to keep warm and even if they used or adapted their country shooting clothing, this was well cut and well suited to the purpose. The Norfolk jacket was originally always made of woollen tweed and had numerous pockets – which were essential for climbing, whilst the close tailoring of a bespoke outfitter ensured an excellent fit.

Among the first generation of climbers was Canon Girdlestone – the Oxford cleric who was also a pioneer of guideless climbing . This engaging man was especially active in the 1860s, though was still to be found in Arolla in 1901. He left a lasting impression, for as one Alpinist recalled:

'what visitor to Arolla in the old days does not remember his spare figure, his breezy bonhomie and his habit of emptying his bath water out of his bedroom window, to the consternation of tea drinkers on the gravel below...'[14]

He was an eccentric and outlawed by the Alpine Club establishment for his reckless approach to guideless climbing. But he was extremely knowledgeable about how to survive in the mountains and how a mountaineer should be equipped. His advice on dress and on diet has some relevance even today. On clothing he was quick to point out that the many pockets *must* button up in case they filled with snow or to avoid the loss of the many odds and ends he carried with him. This was the era when cotton began to be used for everything from under-garments to fashion wear and work clothes. However, Victorian mountaineers seem well aware that it was chilling when damp and consistently used silk or wool for underwear and flannel for shirts. Staying dry in the mountains was another matter. Although Charles Macintosh had patented his rubber-coated waterproof fabric in 1823 it did not breath and was therefore horribly uncomfortable when worn for vigorous exercise. Girdlestone suggested that any waterproof should be of tweed as it was 'impossible to walk long in a Macintosh without oppressive heat.'[15] The other problem with the use of india rubber coating was that unless it was spread out to dry it would crease and perish; it also had a most unpleasant smell. However, occasionally British mountaineers would carry one. Mummery and his team had one waterproof garment between them on one particular wet descent and Lily Bristow was quite thankful for it. The Klepper Company of Rosenheim also made these sorts of garments during the nineteenth century. It was common for agricultural workers and carters or anyone working outside in the nineteenth century – and indeed into the twentieth- to use sacking to keep dry. Charles Boner who, in 1873 produced one of the earliest guides to mountain travel, advised would-be mountaineers to follow the lead of Austrian peasants who had centuries experience of the climate. He recommended:

'the purchase for 6 or 7 shillings of a 'Wetter Mantel' (weather cape). This is something like a carter's frock (with or without sleeves, but with is much better) reaching to the knees and made of Loden, a light yet warm, coarse brown stuff made in Bavaria and the Tyrol. It will prove waterproof for a considerable time ; that is to say the rain will run off its hairy surface without penetrating... It will do to put on in case of rain or when you get to the top of a mountain and are warm after your climb. Being light it may easily be carried in your rucksack....'[16]

Its waterproof qualities made loden popular with climbers throughout the latter part of the nineteenth century and it was widely available in the numerous outfitters which sprang up in the Alps with the growing popularity of climbing. It continued to be used by Austrian and German climbers right up to the Second World War in both the Alps and the Himalayas. Another alternative was oiled silk – also used for tents and umbrellas , and although a better idea than Macintosh being lighter and more durable it did crack and deteriorate with time.[17] Thomas Burberry patented gabardine in1879, cotton threads were proofed before weaving, making for the first time a breathable and tolerably waterproof fabric alternative to Macintosh.[18] Later developments to the weave of the cloth in the early twentieth century dramatically increased its wind resistance. It was a wonderful fabric for dry snowy conditions and immensely popular with early skiers. However it leaked in driving rain, so that being wet was an occupational hazard for mountaineers well into the twentieth century. No wonder Canon Girdlestone recommended taking an umbrella – which was also popular among the Bavarians for walking too and from the huts (and remains common in the Eastern Alps today) and all Alpinists favoured wide brimmed hats! These hats, which were almost the hallmark of the Victorian climber also gave protection from the sun and where the crown was high a small lump of snow could be inserted as a cooling device.

Keeping extremities warm and safe from frostbite was a problem for early mountaineers as it remains today. Again Girdlestone's advice on gloves shows genuine insight and what he describes sounds remarkably like an early mitt. He said that:

> 'Very warm gloves are to most men necessities, to save the fingers from being frostbitten, but through which it is possible to cling to rock and stock. A bag for all 4 fingers with a later pouch for the thumbs [i.e. he is recommending a mitt] answers best, as the fingers remain much warmer when not separated from one another; it should be made of hareskin, with the fur inside. The iron fastenings of the axe head to the stock should be for the same reasons cased in leather.'[19]

The leather insulation for the axe was truly revolutionary, coming around 120 years before appearing on modern axes. He also recommended gaiters to keep snow out of the boots. Twenty years later Clinton Dent, one of the Alpine Club's equipment experts wrote at greater length about clothing, and there were a growing number of mountaineering outfitters, in both Britain and in the Alps. However, if the range of what was available had increased by the 1890s much of Girdlestone's advice remained valid and the problems of developing suitable gloves continued. Certainly Dent was pessimistic about finding a glove which combined protection against frostbite with a decent grip for the axe. He also warned that wet gloves were worse than no gloves in high winds and severe cold.[20]

Any idea that the lack of modern sophisticated gear meant that the Victorians did not know how to keep warm is therefore just not born out by the evidence; they were both more knowledgeable and more adaptable than most modern climbers. In some ways Victorian climbers almost took clothing for granted. Unlike every other element of gear, which form the centre pieces of numerous *Alpine Journal* accounts of mountaineering epics, clothing – certainly men's clothing – rarely seemed worth mentioning. Clearly there was ample advice about clothing but clothes seem to have been 'invisible' for most mountaineers. They did not worry about being wet, they were used to it and in most other respects their clothing functioned well.

At sometime or another all climbers, especially if they are fair skinned or bald get badly sun or wind burnt. It is excruciating and one of the enduring images of poor Sandy Irvine , on the 1924 Everest expedition, is of the agony of sunburn and cracked lips when he complained at Camp IV of:

> 'A most unpleasant night when everything on earth seemed to rub against my face and each time it was touched bits of burnt and dry skin came off which made me nearly scream with pain' 21

Irvine had faced the drying wind and blazing sun of the Himalayas, against which the significant range of sun preparations then available were useless. His Victorian predecessors in the Alps suffered just as much and had to learn how to combat the effects of sun and wind, as no proprietary lotions were on the market. But they also had to face shocked relatives when they got home and not just because they were disfigured. It was an age when pale skins – for both men and women – symbolised class, standing and respectability, and only labourers or primitive people were weather-beaten or had dark skins. Even men were stared at if they were tanned – certainly among professional groups. Members of the all male Alpine Club were easy to identify simply because they looked so hideous as one member recalled:

> 'They wear extraordinary boots and still more remarkable head dresses. Their peeled, blistered and swollen faces are worth studying. Some by exercise of watchfulness and unremitting care, have been fortunate enough to acquire a fine raw sienna complexion. But most of them have not been so happy. They have been scorched by rocks and roasted on glaciers. Their cheeks – first puffed, then cracked – have exuded a turpentine like matter which has coursed down their faces like the resin of the trunks of pines. They have removed it and at the same time have pulled off large flakes of their skin. Their lips are cracked, their cheeks are swollen, their eyes are blood shot and their noses are peeled and indescribable.' 22

Not an appealing sight but a common one, in the best Alpine hotels in the summer and at Alpine Club dinners back in London.

Masks – eerie, sinister and downright dangerous – were one solution. Linen or preferably fine woollen gauze masks, with eye holes cut in them, were used from the early nineteenth century by men and women climbers. They kept off the sun and wind but transformed mountaineers into a strange alien species. More importantly they obscured vision, which could inhibit choice of hand and foot

Mrs Lizzie Le Blond in a mask typical of those used in the late nineteenth century by men and women to prevent sunburn, effective creams did not exist and tanned complexions were eschewed.

Alpine Club Collection

holds and made it difficult to wear dark glasses. John Tyndall, the mountaineering physicist, weighed up the pros and cons of masks on a trip in 1863 and opted to be parched:

> *'the sun was strong, its direct and reflected blaze combining against us. The scorching warmth experienced at times by cheeks lips and neck indicated that, in my case mischief was brewing ; but with the eyes being well protected by dark spectacles, I was comparatively indifferent to the prospective disfigurement of my face. Mr Sclater was sheltered by a veil, a mode of defence which the habit of going into places requiring unimpeded eyesight has caused me to neglect.'[23]*

Not surprisingly veils were not very popular and although one was still displayed at the 1899 exhibition, numerous noxious concoctions were also used to prevent and treat sunburn . Ladies were urged to try 'soured milk applied thickly at night and washed off with plenty of soap', but it cannot have been too appealing or practical in a hut or worse still a tent. Alternatives included cucumber juice, vaseline, glycerine, or cold cream.[24] Lanolin was an especial favourite and seen as a more natural protection:

> *'it is readily absorbed by the skin and is capable of combining with its own weight of water....which renders it more pleasant than other fats to use on the skin, especially when perspiration is present.'[25]*

None will have given much UV protection and some will have meant they basted gently in the sun. But they will have reduced some of the drying effects of sun and wind. It took the growing popularity of skiing and winter sports, especially after the First World War, to prompt the manufacture of sun and glacier creams.

Bivouacs By Candlelight (Planned and Unplanned)
Tents

Many early planned and unplanned bivouacs were under rocks or behind shelters constructed from boulders – a practice which continued well into the nineteenth century and which emphasises just how tough these early mountaineers were. Early expeditions involved a bewildering array of paraphernalia, bedding and provisions, without which no self-respecting scientific mountain explorer could travel. Nothing was easily portable and, where tents were carried, these were heavy – bear in mind that Whymper's special mountain tent weighed 18lbs – and bulky and were probably military style tents not designed for use on rock or snow or in strong winds. To move on rough, icy and slippery terrain could be painfully slow and exhausting for heavily burdened porters and cause potentially dangerous delays for parties at altitude. This happened in an attempt on Monte Rosa in 1820 when the exhaustion of his entire party, but especially the porters, slowed progress so much that Joseph Zumstein was forced to bivouac in a crevasse high on Monte Rosa (the highest undertaken at the time). He vividly described the mind and limb numbing effect of the cold when temperatures plummeted to –7C by 6.00pm. Cold and despondent they waited the arrival of the porters with tents and blankets and he captured the precise moment when hypothermia began to set in:

> *'I had committed the imprudence of clothing myself too lightly, because on my former expedition I had suffered from the heat. Already the cold so penetrated me that my companions perceived I was growing pale. I lost all energy, and an irresistible drowsiness stole over me. The experienced chasseur, Joseph Beck, feeling anxious about me, began to shake me to warm my blood and restore defective circulation, by which means he soon set me right again. Meanwhile the cold continued to increase and our perplexity was extreme... Only one acquainted with the upper ice world can appreciate the danger to which we were exposed...'*

Fortunately the porters arrived soon and they were able to protect themselves better from the cold . They lit a fire and used the tent as a cover. The party of eleven crammed under the tent and after somewhat dispiritedly eating 'capital soup'

Bivouacs by candlelight.

F and R

they all lay on their right sides 'covered with blankets and skins and packed close together in a row, to prevent being frozen in the night'.[26] The party failed in their attempt to climb Monte Rosa. However, this early bivouac highlights not so much the hazards of early climbing expeditions, as the resourcefulness of the mountaineers and their understanding of how to stay sufficiently warm to survive. It also demonstrates that whilst porters were the solution to the problem of weight, their bulky loads could lead to cold and anxious delays.

Writing in 1870 Girdlestone commented that, in the course of 70 glacier expeditions, without guides, he had slept out regularly to shorten a long day. He made light of any discomfort, taking it as a price to pay for enjoying the freedom of the mountains. After all he said, it was possible to stay tolerably warm and comfortable by making:

> 'vast brews of chocolate, mulled wine, by songs and the like, eking out thereafter nature's scanty coverlets with good Swiss blankets'.[27]

Nonetheless some of these spots were fairly uncharitable, even to an optimist like him, and he captured one such occasion in the Eigher Hohle, en route for the Eggischorn, especially vividly. This particular cave, although supplied with pots and pans and some damp hay to sleep on, was especially cold. Not only that but:

> '...our fuel was unfortunately very wet, and the fire, as soon as it had yielded enough smoke to fill the cave, went out. After the third or fourth trial, our perseverance was rewarded; we filled pan with snow, and set it on the fire to melt. Soon a fragrant jorum of chocolate was brewed; eggs were beaten into it, the bottle of cream we had brought was poured in and supper began.'
>
> Now came the dreaded bedtime; the small extent of our fuel forbade any attempt at keeping up a fire through the night, and the cold fog, chilled by the fast falling snow, filled the cave. We rolled as closely together as we could on the hay, and covered ourselves with the rugs, after reading aloud from a German New Testament.
>
> Peter and I smoked most of the night to keep ourselves warm. Pryce was no smoker, but nature generally balances advantages, for he was a snorer, as we learnt when he fell comfortably off to sleep. We two hardly slept at all....'[28]

It is all too easy to picture the scene, to sympathise with the stinging eyes from the smoke, to feel the rising dampness and chill , the stiffness and discomfort and to recall nights sandwiched close to snorers, who inexplicably always go to sleep first. This window on a Victorian bivouac highlights what was taken for granted, as a necessary part of mountaineering, before down sleeping bags, lightweight tents, portable stoves and sleeping mats. What this encouraged, in a number of Girdlestone's contemporaries and successors as in subsequent generations of climbers, was a series of efforts to find ways of making a night out more comfortable.

Three Victorians standout as both exceptional mountaineers and designers who contributed to making sleeping out more comfortable. Whymper and Mummery developed outstanding tents and Tuckett – the typical Victorian tinkerer – designed a revolutionary blanket sleeping bag. It is only possible to understand these men's innovations by placing them in the context of mountaineering in the period and of the personalities and pre-occupations of the men themselves.

The Whymper tent 1865 was already equipped with a sewn in rubber coated (otherwise known as Macintosh) groundsheet.

Although portrayed as a difficult, jealous and unforgiving man , Whymper was also a very practical one. Having been apprenticed in the family engraving firm, he was extremely practical. Instead he revelled in the design of serviceable equipment and in the mechanical technologies of the Victorian Age. He described the Fell Railway on the Mont Cenis pass with evangelical fervour. He was one of that breed of mountaineers, which include Mummery, George Finch and much later Don Whillans, who were able to assess, and develop equipment for mountaineering expeditions. Whymper's practical experience, as a trained engraver, gave him professional knowledge of the dialogue that takes place as a design is executed and this was reflected in the way he developed equipment. In this period, designer-climbers of necessity talked directly to the craftsmen, who were to interpret their instructions and had a deep understanding of the processes involved.

Whymper's controversial ascent of the Matterhorn secured him a place in the history of mountaineering but his tent, first used in 1862, proved to be one of the classic designs and was used by generations of mountaineers. Quite apart from the events of July 1865, his writings before and after the accident provide a wonderful snapshot of what it was really like to climb and sleep out during the Golden Age of Mountaineering and how he tried to improve the experience.

Seeing camping as an integral part of mountain travel, Whymper, like modern gear reporters, had strong ideas on what should be used.

He often designed and patented his own kit or adapted existing patterns for his personal use. He summarised his advice in an article entitled 'Camping Out', which appeared in the *Alpine Journal* in 1865, shortly before his fateful conquest of the Matterhorn . Predictably outspoken, he took issue with the idea that

Whymper's tent high on glacier at Col du Lyon.

bivouacing nights were 'nights of discomfort and often misery' feeling that 'camping out may be done in the Alps at high as well as low elevations with both pleasure and comfort', providing proper gear was used. He despised sleeping under rocks and in caves – favoured by so many of his contemporaries- and warned against making camp in the dark, in case of inadvertently sharing a hole with unwanted bedfellows. He had good reason for this, whilst human companions were probably unwelcome to this rather antisocial man, far worse could lurk in the shadows of a dark cave. One particular night left a lasting impression, or more accurately impressions. On his very first solo bivouac he thought he had found a suitable cave, lit a roaring fire and settled down warm and replete into his blanket sleeping bag. His contentment was very short-lived and he recalled:

> *'I dreamed I was a prisoner of the Inquisition; the tortures were being applied; priests were forcing fleas down my nostrils and into my eyes, and with red hot pincers taking out bites of flesh, now cutting off my ears, and then tickling the soles of my feet. This was too much. I yelled a great yell , and awoke, to find I was covered with a crawling mass of something. The something was ants; I had camped by an anthill, and after having driven the inhabitants to madness by scorching their tails, had coolly lain down in their midst. The moral is instructive; the hole may be perfect, but there may be something in the hole; don't therefore if you value your skin, make your camp after dark.'[29]*

One can only sympathise – no wonder he set about designing a suitable mountaineering tent – which was windproof , and crucially ant-proof. His first attempt was not entirely successful when it had its first outing on the Matterhorn on 29 August 1861. Adapted from a design by Mr Galton, whose *Vacation Tourists* had prompted Whymper to write his guide to camping out, this tent was intended for a high camp:

> *'it opened like a book , had one end closed permanently, and the other closed by flaps. It was supported by two alpenstocks, and the canvas sides were prolonged and turned underneath. Numerous cords were sewn round the lower edges, to which rocks were to be attached, and the main fastenings passed under the ridge and through rings screwed on the tops of the alpenstocks; these were secured by long iron pegs.'*

With the help of his guide he carried the new tent and other equipment, including his blanket sleeping bag to what looked like the ideal site, on a grassy site leading down to the Matterhorngletscher. Mountain tents need to be weather proof but critically also withstand strong winds. Many a prototype – including over a hundred years later the Whillans box which was whipped off Ben Macdui in a gale – have needed modifying after mountain trials. Whymper's was no exception, for the wind was so strong that the tent nearly blew away:

> '*exhibited a marked desire to go to the top of the Dent Blanche, that we had great fears for its stability. The wind which playfully careered about the surrounding cliffs, was driven through the gap with the force of a blow pipe; the flaps on which stones had been placed, would not keep down; the iron pegs would not stay in, and it behaved altogether in such an absurd manner that we were obliged to take it down and sit upon it.*[30]*

Through a process of trial and error he modified the design and was rightly delighted with the results. Whymper's experience with the first tent taught him that Alpine tents must be as portable as possible – since even in an era of porters and guides unnecessary bulk is a nuisance. They must also be strong and stable, warm and weatherproof. The new tent was the same shape and material as its predecessor (forfar [a type of canvas]), but lancewood poles which formed an A shape made the tent extremely stable. These were fixed at each corner and all tipped with a conical point of iron to penetrate the ground and fastened together by steel bolts – this dramatically improved its stability while other changes made it more wind and weatherproof and comfortable. It was 7 foot square and weighed 18 pounds cost just under 75 shillings (£3. 75p) and slept 4 people. He had developed one of the classic mountain tents which was still in the Benjamin Edgington catalogue a hundred years later. This was quite an achievement for a 22 year old tent designer who had only seen the Alps for the first time two years previously.[31]

By a combination of skill, instinct and an ability to learn and adapt, Whymper turned camping into an art form. In the most unpromising conditions he could assess a potential camp site and find ways of ensuring that he and any companions could survive and do so in relative comfort. This could involve altering or adapting gear whilst on a trip. In 1865 one climbing partner was especially impressed by Whymper's ability to make the best of the most uncharitable sites. Forced to camp below the summit of Mont Suc in the Mont Blanc Range he commented:

> '*The situation was not at first sight particularly luxurious; there was no cover, and the only shelter was afforded by a large rock which formed a wall on 2 sides. We should have fared but badly, only for Whymper's skill, who brought to bear on existing circumstances the experience of many Matterhorn bivouacs. Our plaids were*

soon sewn together and artistically disposed, with the assistance of our glacier cord into the form of a tent of snug and inviting aspect. We likewise numbered amongst our impedimenta that marvellous and necromantic not to say hanky panky, tin canister invented and patented by him. It contains in its bowels a complete 'batterie de cuisine' and every part of which, according to the position in which it is held, a saucepan, a coffee pot, gridiron, or warming pan. Its external envelope was soon singing and bubbling over our frugal fire with a puree of hot wine sugar, cloves and we agreed altogether that it might have been worse, much worse...'[32]

Whymper believed that the tent combined with a blanket sleeping bag and a mackintosh base and a portable stove transformed nights out on high mountains from profound discomfort to 'some of the most pleasant episodes of our lives'.[33]

The advice and the messages the tent conveys should also be set against what followed, when changing climbing needs and philosophies made differing demands on equipment. His tent, while portable, was bulky and he employed a 'tent bearer' Luc Mehnet. It became synonymous, first with guided climbing with porters in the Alps and with the large scale, porter supported expeditions of the Himalayas.

Fred Mummery, owner of a Dover tannery, was king of the bivouacs and all that was unconventional in climbing, and more generally. He was nothing like the stereotypical Victorian, but enjoyed life and mountaineering to the full and according to Smythe popped champagne corks as he went. He displayed none of Whymper's painstaking planning. Instead there was an inspiration, a humour, an exuberance and an enthusiasm not to say recklessness, which shaped his climbing, was reflected in his writing and also made him attractive to women. Arguably the greatest climber of his generation he became a magnet to a close knit group of friends – Norman Collie, Ellis Carr, Hastings, Cecil Slingsby, Godfrey Solly and of course, for a while Lily Bristow- who climbed together for the sheer thrill of it and from 1891 without guides.[34] Mummery far preferred camping high in the mountains to a nocturnal trudge out of the valley or back at the end of a long day. He sums up his feelings of distaste for:

'the horror of the valley of stones on a dark night were vainly conjured in their most hideous form. The utmost concession that aged limbs could obtain was permission to gîte high on the rocks above the lower fall of the Nantillon Glacier, I am aware that youthful climbers scorn gîtes and regard a night spent in plunging head first into deep and gruesome holes as an excellent restorative previous to a difficult ascent. I was once in full accord, but the rolling years have given strength to the arguments in favour of camping out; and now a shelter or a tent, a sheepskin mattress and an eiderdown bag are resistlessly attractive compared with an early start interminable stones and the torture of the folding lantern– that instrument from which 'no light, but rather darkness visible' is shed.[35]

Mummery's personal drive, vigour and sexual magnetism was not matched by his physique. He had the typical climber's thin, not to say spindly build,

Left: Whymper's tent bearer (tent weight around 25lbs), Luc Mehnet. It was custom in this period to have both guides and porters (some of whom were trainee guides). *Right:* Mummery Tent, showing use of ice axes as poles. The tent had no sewn in groundsheet as its predecessor, the Whymper tent. This tent was consequently much lighter but too drafty even for Victorian climbers. It had many subsequent upgrades and was in production until 1968.

which combined both agility and strength. But he was myopic and had a spinal weakness which, taken together, made stumbling around in the dark, carrying heavy loads a torment.[36] Naturally he disliked the discomfort and feeling a fool and this, as much as a philosophical preference for guideless climbing, helps explain his liking for lightweight gear. The Whymper tent just did not serve his purpose because it was too heavy. It also had a defect in the wet as he had found in the Caucasus in 1888:[38]

Whymper was the man who had blocked his election to the Alpine Club and so personal antagonism may have made him want to come up with something better than the Whymper tent. By 1892 Mummery had designed a lightweight tent which became another enduring classic. Combined with other sleeping kit, including eiderdown bags the Alpine Club saw it as essential for any climber wishing to sleep out above the snowline.

It was quite simply the mother and father of all lightweight tents, including many design features which persist today. Another A style tent, made of forfar and sometimes silk, at 6ft by 4 ft it was both smaller and lighter than the square Whymper tent and was designed for 2 or three people. Like Whymper he experimented with substituting ice axes for poles to save weight. But when early starts were needed this could be highly irritating. [38]

It catered ideally for Mummery's disabilities, but it also proved an important liberating force, opening up a range of new possibilities. The growing network of mountain huts did not attract him as an alternative to camping, because they were unguarded and so often dirty and quite simply too low. The tent allowed him to climb high and stay high and he first used the super-light silk version in

1892 on a trip with his friends Ellis Carr and Cecil Slingsby. They still used porters –who still struggled and slowed the party down- but the weight difference between the Mummery and the Whymper and between blanket and down bags is stunning as Carr's account shows:

> 'Mummery, Slingsby and I started at 4.00pm with the porter carrying the material from our camp. This comprised a silk tent of Mummery's pattern, weighing only 1.5 to 2 lbs; three eiderdown sleeping bags, 9lbs, cooking apparatus of thin tin 1.5 lbs or, with ropes, rucksacks and sundries about 25 lbs, in addition to the weight of the provisions. Though not unduly burdened the porter found the valley of boulders exceedingly tiresome, and in spite of 3 distinct varieties of advice as to the easiest route across them, made such miserably slow progress , often totally disappearing amongst the rocks like a waterlogged ship in a trough of the sea, that were forced to pitch our tent on the right moraine of the Nantillons Glacier...'

The tent was fine for three men, but it was not the softest or smoothest of spots for a campsite. Slingsby seems to have spent the night lying on a boulder, thrashing around most of the time trying to avoid it. While impressed by how portable the new tent was Carr – perhaps wondering whether this was one of Mummery's 'clever ideas' – was not entirely convinced by the lightweight tent. He commented with some scepticism that:

> 'the night was too fine and still to test the weather-resisting power of the material and as it was thin enough to admit sufficient moonlight to illuminate the interior of the tent, and make candle or lamp superfluous, we inferred that that it might possibly prove equally accommodating, in case of wind and rain. It was necessary, moreover, on entering or leaving the tent, to adopt a form of locomotion to which the serpent was condemned to avoid the risk of unconsciously carrying away the whole structure on one's back.'[39]

It is unclear whether they were using oiled silk, which may crack with cold, but which was soon almost universally used for lightweight tents. If they were not, Carr was right to be uneasy, but as a general design it was ideal and the tent, whether in canvas or silk, virtually became an emblem of high altitude camps until the 1950s. For instance, in 1903 on a trip to the Caucasus the likeable and amusing lightweight enthusiast, Tom Longstaff took:

> 'a very light silk Mummery tent, but with the improvement of a floor sewn in to keep out wind and snow. Our sleeping bags were of eiderdown, weighing under 3lbs each. Our climbing rope was of silk'.[40]

It is interesting that both Whymper and Mummery, while developing different styles of tent, had similar thought processes. Both for instance went round the tent with ice axe syndrome very much as modern design students insist on developing the combination of tent and pack frame. They were also bitter rivals and it is interesting that in 1892 both men's designs were adopted by Benjamin

Edgington the tent makers – one wonders whether this was intentional.

The tent designs of both Whymper and Mummery reflect more than just difference in weight. They reflect the sharp contrasts in the two men's attitudes to mountaineering and indeed in their personalities. Whymper was the pioneer of the large scale, meticulously planned expedition in the mould of Hunt and Bonington. In contrast, Mummery was the father of the lightweight, back of the envelope approach to mountaineering, when groups of friends team up and, with minimal logistical hassle, go to climb – his natural successors were Tilman and Shipton. Bill Tilman is still fondly remembered addressing the BMC conference in Buxton and the crowd was in raptures when he said that an expedition was not worth doing if it could not be 'planned on the back of an envelope. This inspired Chris Brasher to set himself up an annual trip from the 70's onwards, which all referred to as the OBOE club (on the back of an envelope) although each friend, to whom he delegated something, probably filled several envelopes!

For Mummery's friends the tent became inseparable from their shared experience and friendship after his death . Collie recalled, with a pleasure tinged with nostalgia, how he Mummery, Hastings and Slingsby slept out far away from civilisation he marvelled that it was not more popular – especially since the growing numbers of mountain huts built by various national Alpine Clubs were pretty squalid. He commented in some frustration:

> 'Why do not more mountaineers who take small tents to the Alps is always to me a mystery. For long ago most of the huts have become abominations, while the free life that is afforded by camp life adds a very great charm to mountain expeditions. having tried it so often in the Himalayas, in Skye, in Norway in the Canadian Rocky Mountains and Switzerland, perhaps I may be biased, but even if I never again had a chance of climbing a first class peak in the Alps, I would return there to live the lazy, delightful, disreputable life in a tent, near ice and the snows and the pine woods, to smell the camp fire lie on my back all day amidst the grass and the flowers, listening to the wind and looking at the sky and the great silent peaks. On the other hand, the idea of spending a month in Swiss hotels, arising in the darkness to wander forth in a bad temper, chilled to the bone, in order merely to finish off the remaining peaks of some district, so that I may say I had been up them all, and therefore never be bothered to return again [does not appeal].'[41]

Mountaineering conventions could be broken by the use of the Mummery tent but that was not all. Had climbing been less of a 'hidden sport' the tiny tent might have been banned as the scourge of Victorian respectability and as a potential marriage wrecker. Lily Bristow, one of the most outstanding of Victorian women climbers, joined Mummery and his friends several times in the early 1890s, sharing their climbs and also their tent. Fred Mummery and Lily Bristow were enthralled with each other if their writings are anything to go by – drawn together by a mutual love of mountains and a compatibility of climbing styles and abilities. Few of his contemporaries could keep up with Fred Mummery, but Lily Bristow could. After they climbed the Grépon in 1893 he pointed to the lie behind the notion of climbs degenerating into an 'easy day for a lady' for:

'...Miss Bristow showed the representatives of the Alpine Club the way in which steep rocks should be climbed and usually filled up the halts, during which the elder members of the party sought to recover their wind , by photographic operations. We congratulated the first lady who had ever stood on this grim tower, and then we listened to the voice of the charmer who whispered of hot and cakes, of jam and rolls of biscuits and fruit, waiting for the faithful in the Pic Balfour gap. There we feasted sumptuously and having bundled the cooking stove and other luggage into our knapsacks, we hurried to the easy ledges to CP and were finally chased off the mountain by wind, rain and hail.'[42]

Lily Bristow's letters are peppered with references to Fred who she thought:

'is magnificent, he has such absolute confidence, I never once had the slightest squirm about him even when he was in the most hideous places, where the least slip would have meant certain death, and there were very many such situations. It is a really big score for him to have taken me (and the camera) on such an expedition'.[43]

They climbed together guideless with friends and alone throughout that summer and that itself was exceptional. The tent made it possible and, depending on how you read their recollections, becomes almost a symbol of flouted Victorian morals and doomed romance. Ever the romantic, Mummery paints a cosy picture of the bivouac before the Grépon:

'few places can rival the narrow ledge of rock, with a precipice in front and an ice slope rising behind, where our tiny tent was pitched, and few setting suns have disclosed more gorgeous contrasts and tenderer harmonies than that which heralded the night of August 4 1893.Our party consisted of Miss Bristow, Mr Hastings and myself. Warmly wrapped in sleeping bags, we sat sipping tea till the smallest and laziest stars was wide awake.'

If Geoffrey Hastings felt a gooseberry he never said, but Lily made it plain in her letters that she had camped there before – alone with Fred Mummery – and commented on how cramped the tent was for three. It was nothing to the following night however when six rather than three squashed into the tiny tent. Lily was even charmed by this for:

'Everybody was wet through except myself, who was only partially so, as I was wearing Fred's short waterproof coat. We reached our camp soon after 11 pm ...Imagine six people in a tent which had been tight for three. Sleeping bags, tent and everything were of course sopping wet, but it was bliss and comfort after our experiences outside. Fred pulled off my boots and wormed me into a wet sleeping bag, and I lay down in the shallowest part of the pool and felt heavenly comfortable and warm. The other poor devils all had to sit up, as there was no room for them to lie down, and they must have been horribly cold and wet...'[44]

Whether Lily's family were alarmed by the messages in the letters and stopped her from climbing with Fred Mummery, or whether Mary Mummery became suspicious of how innocent their nights away in a tent really were, is not clear. For whatever reason the outings stopped abruptly – perhaps to the secret relief of Mummery's circle of climbing friends. Who would have thought of something as mundane as a tent being asign of moral turpitude? But it threw Lily and Fred forward into a world without Victorian constraints and respectability in the hidden world of the high mountains.

Sleeping Bags

The development of the first efficient, if heavy, mountain tent was left to Whymper, but the replacement of blankets with other, more effective coverings and the use of some kind of ground insulation was vital to comfort. Sheepskin sleeping bags were sometimes used but Francis Fox Tuckett, the Bristol Quaker and businessman and author of *A Pioneer in the High Alps*, was responsible for the systematic development and improvement of a blanket sleeping bag. Between 1856 and 1874, although his trips were liberally peppered with avalanches and lightening strikes, he and his guides climbed 165 peaks and 376 passes. Like many early mountaineers he saw climbing less as a recreation than as a 'scientific occupation'. He was the nineteenth century equivalent of the 'gear freak' and was an inventor, a tinkerer and an adaptor both of scientific instruments and of equipment for camping.

His fascination with the novel and the ingenious made him, according to one contemporary:

> *'a sight to see, being hung from head to foot with 'notions' in the strictest sense of the word, several of them being inventions of his own. Besides these commonplace things as a great axe-head and a huge rope and thermometers, he had two barometers, a sympiesometer, and a wonderful apparatus, pot within pot, for boiling water at great heights first for scientific and then for culinary purposes'* [45]

Inspired perhaps by Whymper's encounter with the ants, he even developed his Insect Puzzler.

His most carefully documented innovation, and one later applauded by Whymper, was a sleeping bag design which showed all the hallmarks of the way a practical mountaineer may evolve items of gear, improving them on the strength of their performance or malfunction on the hill. Like Whymper's tent the prototype, which was 'composed externally of Macintosh and lined with thick homespun Welsh Cloth' was not entirely successful when he first used it in 1861. The bag was certainly warmer than blankets, but the waterproof covering caused problems. Macintosh – like coated nylon in the 1960s and 1970s – was impermeable to moisture, so that while damp was kept out perspiration and condensation was kept in. Whymper sums up the disadvantages of Macintosh covered sleeping bags as uncomfortable because the fabric was impermeable and so caused chilling in the cold and overheating in the warm – quite apart from the unpleasant smell.[46] To rectify this he left the Macintosh on the under side but the upper side resembled a type of sleep suit made of a very dense scarlet blanketing with the trade name of Swanskin. Only the lower end of the bag was covered with rubber coated fabric. He first used it in 1863 on the ascent of Monte Viso , the easy but prominent peak in the Dauphine on the Franco-Italian border, and was clearly very excited by it as he described his new bag in great detail as follows:

> '[it opened] like a shirt front to admit the body, and provided with 2 arm holes for greater convenience and facility of movement. At the point where the upper surface of macintosh terminated a sort of bib or apron of the same woollen material commenced, and could either be thrown back over the feet if not required, or drawn up to the chin and secured by a button to each shoulder if greater warmth was desirable. A hood or capote also of woollen, but uncovered with Macintosh, to facilitate the escape of perspiration and confined air, and constructed after the fashion of Arctic headgear, completed the ordinary means of construction. Stuffiness, however, though a major drawback, might be put up with in the event of a night of rain or snow in preference to a state of more or less complete saturation; and therefore in order to provide against such contingency, I added a loose sheet of Macintosh, with button holes down each side, by which it could be attached to a corresponding series of buttons on the bag and thus render the latter impervious to water.'[47]

He had the bag manufactured for him by Messrs Heyes and Co, a firm of waterproofers in Bristol and the total cost, including labour and materials, was £3 6s 0d (£3.30). Although it was comparatively expensive the weight to insulation ratio was undoubtedly better than a blanket would have been and, at 8.5 pounds, it could easily be carried in a knapsack.

His party of four – including Croz the guide killed two years later on the Matterhorn – faced an uncomfortable night. They were perched precariously on a narrow ledge buffeted by a fitful wind and facing sub zero temperatures. They had no tent and only Tuckett a sleeping bag, though one of them used his sack as a makeshift bivouac bag. As a good Quaker, Tuckett's sense of fair play meant he genuinely worried about the ethics of expecting his guides to endure worse conditions than he did. Accordingly he lent his guides some spare clothing and a light windproof sheet. This was placed over a coverlet borrowed from a chalet to help keep them warm and Tuckett heated wine in his fabled wine boiler to provide a nightcap. Anyone who has spent a cramped night high on a mountain can identify with Tuckett as the long night dragged on:

'I meanwhile entered the bag, and planting my feet firmly against a rock to prevent slipping, endeavoured to compose myself to rest, but the intensity of the cold aggravated by the wind, combined with an uneasy position and the constant sense of being in motion downwards, proved too much for me; and after long and persevering efforts, I calmly abandoned myself to persistent condition of semi-conscious wriggling. The time seemed to pass very slowly, as usual under such circumstances... [he woke covered by an inch of snow] The prospect was anything but cheering and my feelings were nearly akin to the painful, that I confess the thought of having to hold out for some hours more was peculiarly unwelcome.'

Yet if it was a miserable night, it was a pretty good way to test a new sleeping bag and he was cheered with the thought that:

'Still though cold, I felt I could yet bid defiance to the weather, and any grumblings that tried to make themselves heard were silenced by the sense of satisfaction at the manner in which my bag bore the severe test to which it was exposed. A temperature of −2.5C as shown by a thermometer protected from radiation, snow, wind and damp, the worst possible combination in short, were all rendered endurable by its means, and this in itself was worth finding out at the expense of some personal discomfort.' [48]

Whether his guides were quite so happy this early sleeping bag test is unclear, but the design was good for those who could afford it.

Although comparatively heavy, Tuckett's design, or variants of it, was used by mountaineers throughout the nineteenth century and was made up, initially, by a range of suppliers to the original pattern. It continued to be recommended in the Royal Geographical Society's *Hints for Travellers* and by the Alpine Club in the 1880s and 1890s. There were some additions and innovations by the 1890s when:

'An ingenious bag devised by Mr Howse [which] consisted of a mackintosh sack, one longitudinal half being capable of inflation. Thus the camper might lie in luxury on an air mattress. Dr Frederick Taylor, who exhibited the bag, had used it during many seasons and found it was practical and easily carried.'

But the majority of bags were 'reproductions of Mr Tuckett's original design.'and were followed by such suppliers as Silver and Company and Jaeger. [49]

Indeed Jaeger camel hair fleece bags became firm favourites from the 1880s as a substitute for the original flannel. These bags offered better insulation, were more comfortable and, at 7lbs, weighed less than the flannel bags. Dr Jaeger's Sanitary Woollen System Company was founded in 1884 after Lewis Tomalin of London acquired the German rights of the ideas on the benefits of woollen clothing, laid down in Dr Gustav Jaeger's book *Health Culture*. Jaeger is now a prominent and exclusive fashion house, though initially they produced their woollen underwear as well as outerwear. But it was their supply of woollen underwear, mitts, stockings, puttees and especially their famed camel hair sleeping bags to explorers and mountaineers, which provided an important plank upon which the company could build their brand.[50] The Jaeger bag was still being advertised by the tent maker and camp outfitter, John Edgington and Co in 1921. However, while blanket bags endured for travel at lower altitudes, they were still comparatively heavy and the insulation properties were inadequate for higher mountain ranges such as the Andes or the Himalayas and on the Icelandic icecap or north of the Arctic circle, where increasingly down was a better option.

The use of down as an insulator has a long history and there is archaeological evidence of feathers and down in the tombs of the Vikings. Eiderdown was also habitually used in bed quilts and although at twice the price of goose down was very expensive. The 1849 promotional material of Heals, the London department store illustrates its powers of insulation as follows:

> 'The eiderdown used is of the finest quality and as it combines the most warmth with the least weight of any known substance together with its adhesive quality and freedom from stem or quill its advantage over every other article as a lining for quilts is obvious...'[51]

It was only a matter of time and changing demands, before this light and versatile material was used in the mountains.

Any sleeping bag is designed to insulate the body's warmth from the cold air outside by a non-conductor of heat. The combination of air and light eiderdown make for superb insulation far better than that provided by wool and with, far less weight. There were no manufacturers of down sleeping bags in Britain in this period. Mountaineers were advised by the Alpine Club, in their guidance for light camps, to have their bags made up for them to existing patterns.

> '1.5 lb of eiderdown suffices for a bag of the kind, measuring 5ft. 6 in. in length (longer would be better) and 2 ft. 6 in. in width at the opening, and closed at the foot by an oblong piece measuring 14 in. by 8 in. Heal and Son, 195 Tottenham Court Road, have the pattern for this bag. The weight of the whole complete is 2.5 lbs. A single bag, somewhat wider than the tent might be used to hold three men, and would doubtless be lighter than three separate bags. The bags can be wrapped in a Macintosh sheet, and that again enclosed in the tent ; the whole bundle (for three men) will only weigh 12 lbs.'[52]

Eiderdown bags were first used during the early 1890s, their combination of lightness and warmth making them synonymous with both the shift to more lightweight, guideless expeditions and with journeys to both the Andes and the Himalayas. Mummery was one of the first enthusiasts for eiderdown bags, which represented the perfect complement for his small, oiled-silk tent, for remote bivouacs first in the Alps and then further afield.

Maybe from prejudice or expense or the lack of any truly down-proof fabric, eiderdown sleeping bags only caught on slowly though many mountaineers regretted their omission. In a mildly shambolic, if ultimately successful crossing of Spitzbergen in 1896, Sir Martin Conway ruefully admitted to under-estimating the warmth of an Arctic summer- expecting it to be 'jolly cold'. His team ended up, as a result over-equipped with fur clothing and reindeer sleeping bags. Eiderdown sleeping bags would have been far better he admitted and set about explaining to any subsequent travellers how to procure some. They still were not commercially manufactured and the traveller he said:

> *'must be content with bags made of eiderdown quilt. One kilo of eider-down will suffice for a bag. The down may be purchased for about 30 kroner a kilo through Mr Mack of Tromso. It should be made up in England in a cover of woollen sateen of the kind you can get at the Army and Navy Stores, and doubtless elsewhere... a piece of thin rubber sheeting should form part of each man's pack; it will serve to keep the sleeping bag dry on the march, and for floor to the tent in camp.'*[53]

Unplanned Bivouacs

Planned nights out have a charm all of their own and are quite different from being benighted. Unplanned bivouacs are grim and whilst Lily Bristow's night out after the Grépon was cold, cramped and uncomfortable (especially for her companions), it was nothing like as unpleasant as a night perched on a narrow ledge without a tent, precious little food , with no stove and with wet clothes. Even allowing for the habitual discomfort of Victorian life and the climber's capacity for the understatement, these nights were purgatory. All mountaineers have their favourite bivouac stories and the *Alpine Journal* is full of them. Later no doubt these will have been embroidered and revisited at numerous Alpine Club dinners. They have all the qualities of mountaineering epics – discomfort , endurance and self-deprecating humour. L.W. Rolleston and Tom Longstaff were caught out on a trip to the Caucasus in the early 1900s. Dripping water had formed veerglass on the rocks on a particularly tricky section of a ridge and, at 14,500 feet they were forced to bivouac as darkness fell. As Rolleston recalled:

> *'Neither of us had been benighted before and up until midnight we endured the experience fairly well; afterwards we found it horribly cold, while clouds gathered and a little hail fell. We kept our feet from frostbite by putting them in the rucksacks together with the lighted lantern ; but when we tried to improve matters by adding our aluminium stove, we had more heat than we bargained for, and destroyed a rucksack and a pair of stockings. We should have been wiser to remember our Shakespeare:*
> > *'O who can hold a fire in his sack*
> > *Though shivering on the frosty Caucasus.'*[54]

August Lorria and the unconventional Oscar Eckenstein did not even have candles after their ascent of the Hohberghorn, when they spent the most uncomfortable night of their lives in sub-zero temperatures. On the ascent they had been warm in their Jaeger sleeping bags but, assuming that they would get down in the day, they had sent their porter back to the valley. Just whose idea it had been to leave their lantern on the moraine of the Festi Glacier, rather than take that little extra weight up the mountain, is unclear. But, in the fading light they were like squirrels, searching in vain for hidden winter supplies of nuts, and about as successful. They were soaked from floundering around in wet snow on a fruitless search, and without a lantern it was unsafe to continue, so they were forced to spend the night out. 'It was not a convenient place for a bivouac' remarked Lorria ruefully. It was in fact awful and they were lucky to survive without serious frostbite:

> *'Above and below us were sheer walls of rock. Eckenstein found a small shelf on which he could just manage to lie down, but I was only lucky enough to discover one where I could sit, for if I wished to lie down, the whole of my body save my feet head and shoulders hung over a steep gully in the rocks. To increase the discomfort of our position a cold north westerly wind began to blow. We had to resign ourselves to our fate, though I long rebelled against it, but any attempt to push on would have simply been most dangerous. We fastened ourselves to the rocks with our rope. Of course it was impossible to think of sleeping. As the night wore on it became colder; our upper clothing froze quite hard, the thermometer read –7C at 11.30pm. The cold pierced us to the very marrow, for it must be remembered that we were still at a height of 12,140 feet. It was in vain that we tried to keep warm by hugging each other as tightly as the limits of our prison permitted. Nothing would help us. My feet began to freeze till at length I took off my shoes as I usually do on a bivouac, and had not done this time simply because my feet were very wet and I had no dry socks with me. I wrung a good deal of water out of my wet socks and put my feet into my rucksack made of thin cloth. This scanty protection worked wonders; my feet gradually got warm again and that was a great thing under the circumstances ... Finally, after what seemed an endless time the long wished for dawn began to appear... Eckenstein had in some measure whiled away the time by smoking, and had warmed his hands on his pipe.*
>
> *This small consolation was, however, denied me as I am not a smoker.* [55]

Lanterns

Accidents, bad weather, underestimating the time needed for a difficult peak, all left climbers struggling through fading light at one time or another. Also then as now, early starts, to get on the snow before it softens, are an integral part of climbing above the snowline. Before the headlamp, it was an entertaining experience. Seeing in the dark certainly gets easier from habit and of course there was none of the brilliant modern street and domestic lighting we are used to. Electricity and the electric light bulb were Victorian inventions, but gas lighting and oil lamps remained the norm in homes until the twentieth century. In 1887 the Alpine Club announced proudly that their winter picture and equipment exhibition had been 'well lighted by a temporary installation of electric lighting' – highlighting just how unusual this was.[56] People in Victorian England were simply more used to the dark or to dim lighting in every day life than we are and so would have found seeing at night easier. However, climbing with candlelit lanterns was frustrating, cumbersome, sometimes dangerous and contributed to many unplanned nights out.

Lanterns, to protect candles, were used throughout the Golden Age of mountaineering and by the early 1890s continental folding lanterns were available. The best folding lantern was the Italian 'Excelsior Mountain Lantern' which had been adopted by the Italian Alpine Club and was available from both London mountaineering outfitters Hill and Sons and from such continental retailers as Knecht and Cie of Berne. A lighter Austrian version was available in Vienna but was not terribly robust. Mummery hated the folding lantern, declaring it useless – he may have been right but his poor eyesight made him loathe the distorted shadowy world of candlelit walking. A British 'Beresford Lantern', improved by Alpine Club gear expert Clinton Dent was available from Silver and Co in London, for use in camps. By the 1890s Meta – disgusting smelling methylated spirits in cake form- had become available while a few used petroleum lanterns. However, the shift from candles to more modern fuels was comparatively slow, perhaps because early models were even more unreliable than traditional lanterns.[57]

Sometimes lanterns were lost, forgotten or broken and Dent advised substituting a bottle with the bottom knocked out. Lantern light is dim and capricious and the cause of many a stumble, but there were ways of deploying it to better effect, as Dent explained:

> *'If there is only one lantern to a party of three, it is usually carried by the second man. Four or five persons will go much faster over rough ground if provided with two lanterns. If any member is unable to see well in the dull early light, he had better carry the lantern. The next best place for him is immediately in front of the man who carries it. It is often desirable to rope while the lantern is in use, as time is saved.'[58]*

Theory was all very well, but practice was quite different and scrabbling around on glaciers by lantern light could be a surreal experience, as Canon Girdlestone found in the Bernese Oberland in the 1860s:

> *'We left the [Guggi] Hut at 2.30 am and almost immediately found ourselves among the lower seracs of the Guggi glacier. Jumping crevasses and climbing over round icy towers and pinnacles, may be pure amusement in daylight, but when it has to be done on a dark night, by the light of two lanterns, separated by 100 feet of rope, it becomes exciting. The leading lantern disappears round a corner, then while you are*

endeavouring to ascertain whether there is a bottomless 'schrund to be crossed in front, or a precarious passage to be made in ice steps, a voice from somewhere says 'Come on; why don't you come on?...'[59]

It could be difficult enough when lanterns were working properly but often they did not and needed frequent relighting– a source of much resigned frustration. Combined with tiredness on difficult ground lanterns became a source of real danger . In the late 1880s Mrs Jackson, a relatively little known English climber, traversed the Jungfrau and Jungfrau Joch with her guides in winter and found just how tricky reliance on candlelight could be. The January day had been superb and, although cold, there was little wind. They reached the Jungfrau summit with comparative ease, pausing long enough to take in the view. But the winter day was short and the going tricky, noticeably slowing them down . In failing light the descent became a nightmare:

'Oh the weary descent of those rocks; they were not only very steep and very rotten but they were covered with snow in the worse possible condition, and the utmost care was needed to prevent a slip. To make matters even worse it was , by this time, quite dark and one of our lanterns obstinately refused to keep lighted, and our only remaining hope had to be continually passed from hand to hand to enable the one person then moving to see where the next step might be. We were all glad to reach the plateau on which the routes from the Jungfrau and the Jungfrau Joch join , but were getting very anxious about our chance of passing through the ice fall in darkness. One lantern can only light up a short distance in front, and the only other thing we had to depend on was a large torch, used I think for signalling; this would burn brilliantly, it is true but just for one half hour.'[60]

Forced to give up trying to find a route through, they gave up and spent a miserable night huddled in an ice cavern with a tot of brandy and little to eat, but raisins, cheese and Mrs Jackson thought there might have been a stray chicken bone to suck. When they woke the chimney they had been searching for was just twenty paces away.

Stoves and Cooking

Relying on lanterns made mountain travel difficult, but portable stoves, which began to appear before the end of the Golden Age, opened up new horizons. There had to be something better than a smoky fire in a cave – which anyway meant carrying up supplies of fire wood. In this period, before the Swedish Primus stove transformed both arctic and later mountain travel, mountaineers adapted a number of devices which ranged from the ingenious to the downright dangerous. Tuckett, the Alpine tinkerer, devised one of the earliest burners and had it made by a Mr Stevenson of Edinburgh and used it on his ascent of the Aletschorn in the late 1850s. The main peculiarity of this device according to Tuckett was:

Left: Camp on Mont Suc showing the Whymper burner. *Right:* Tuckett's beloved Russian Furnace, an early alcohol stove.

'the Russian Furnace the action of which is rather facilitated than impeded by wind, and is so powerful and rapid that snow pressed down tightly in an electro plated copper vessel holding about a quart, may by means of it be converted into boiling water, even at the greatest altitudes, in a matter of three or four minutes. This ingenious contrivance is, in principle a self acting blow pipe, vapour of spirits of wine being the agent employed.'

It was a revolutionary device and Tuckett was like a child with a new toy on the trip. He revelled in demonstrating to his guides and porters how easily it boiled water for soup.[61] The burner became known as the Rob Roy (after John 'Rob Roy' Macgregor, the canoeist) and was sold by Silver and Co for many years. Whymper incorporated this burner into his cooking set. It was attached to the base of an interlocking tower of pans, and carried tea, salt & pepper in the first instance and the top served as a pan with a set of interlocking tins which – taken together meant water could be boiled and tea or coffee carried without getting mixed up with pepper or sugar. This portable device eased dehydration and helped to make a night out comfortable, it was also far ahead of its time for it was hung in the tent, a practice which only became common a century later. What was needed though was a stove that was sufficiently light to be stowed in a rucksack and which might make an unplanned bivouac a bit more civilised. Nothing could be worse than trying make a brew with nothing but a couple of candles. But it was precisely what Fred Mummery, Norman Collie and Geoffrey Hastings tried to do when stranded for the night on a traverse of Mont Blanc in 1894. Amazingly they succeeded in melting snow and – taking it in turns to hold the kettle – got the water close to

CATALOGUE OF
EQUIPMENT FOR
MOUNTAINEERS
EXHIBITED AT THE
ALPINE CLUB
DECEMBER
1899

Alpine Club

Alpine Club Exhibition 1899. This is one of the few illustrations showing a climber wrapping his puttees. These were the predecessors of the gaiter and word and usage is of Indian origin.

boiling point. Then Geoffrey Hastings took his turn, almost drifted off to sleep and poured the hot water down Collie's back [62] Perhaps this was the defining moment which prompted Mummery and Hastings to design a lightweight burner weighing about 1.5 lbs later to be exhibited in the Alpine Club Exhibition of Equipment in 1899. However, at this exhibition the Primus stove combined with a set of aluminium pots pans and plates was, for the first time recommended by the Alpine Club as the 'best canteen for mountain explorers'.[63] It has been shown in chapter 2 just how crucial the Primus was to Polar travel; this advice from the Alpine Club marks the beginning of its use in mountaineering.

In Victorian households pans were made of copper and iron and were extremely heavy. Yet initially whilst some of the shelters and caves had cooking pots stowed in them, much of this heavy, bulky equipment had to be carried up by porters in the early days of mountaineering. Something more portable had to be a better idea and Whymper's cooking set was made of tin. The introduction of aluminium, for camp cooking utensils in the 1890s, was a major breakthrough. Because aluminium was far lighter than tin and did not corrode it became the norm well before the First World War.

In 1851 when the flamboyant eccentric Albert Smith prepared to climb Mont Blanc in a party of 40, his guides conned him into a provision list fit for several reasonable sized banquets. It included:

60 bottles of Vin Ordinare	*1 piece of beef*	*6 packets of sugar*
6 bottles of Bordeaux	*4 legs of mutton*	*4 ditto prunes*
10 bottles of St George	*4 shoulders of mutton*	*4 ditto raisins*
15 bottles of St Jean	*11 large fowls*	*6 lemons*
3 bottles of Cognac	*35 small fowls*	*2 ditto salt*
2 bottles of champagne	*6 pieces of veal*	*4 wax candles*
1 bottle of syrup of raspberries	*10 small cheeses*	*6 packets of chocolate*
6 bottles of lemonade	*20 loaves*	

Source: Quoted: W. Unsworth, *Holding the Heights* (London: Hodder and Stoughton, 1993), p. 59

It took 20 porters to carry all this and made Smith a laughing stock, though he did get to the top, where he had a nap – whether from exhaustion or over indulgence is not clear. By contrast in the 1860s Canon Girdlestone's day-time diet was spartan in comparison and, apart from a limited understanding of rehydration, has remained unchanged for nearly 150 years:

'For provisions to drink I usually take, if alone, half a bottle of cold tea, otherwise some common wine also. Many prefer to have their wine heated with spice, sugar and lemon before hand, finding that they can drink wine spice when unable to touch it otherwise....[as to food]... Cold mutton, salami (sausage) and bread with butter and honey or preserve to make it palatable under hot sun form a good basis. In addition a stick of chocolate is useful in the pocket in case of unexpected hunger, and a few prunes or raisins are almost essential for keeping my mouth moist in climbing....'[64]

Wine was synonymous with Victorian climbing. Some like Fred Mummery drank with exuberance and pleasure, while Francis Tuckett treated a bottle of champagne like a scientific experiment commenting that

'the vigorous leap of the champagne cork proved an interesting and agreeable confirmation of the diminished pressure indicated by the barometer.'[65]

probably in case anyone thought it was just for fun. But they all took wine of some kind, partly no doubt to cheer themselves in a miserable camp. Canon Girdlestone once cajoled a giddy and reluctant companion to continue along a tricky ridge, by opening one of the bottles of champagne he had reserved for the summit. Much of it was fairly disgusting and needed sweetening, heating and spicing – doubtless the origin of glühwiein which even inspired Whymper to develop a 'wine boiler'.

Obviously a night out or in a hut needed more substantial food as well as wine and this could be bulky. However, before Smith's ascent of Mont Blanc things began to change as the first convenience food appeared in the 1840s and 1850s. Certainly cooking remained very labour intensive, but packaged, processed and dried foods were developed. There had been a canning patent as early as 1811, but it really took off in the United States during the American Civil War 1861-5 with a growing variety of canned foods imported into Britain and Europe from the 1870s onwards. Dried and concentrated foods – many made in Europe- also began to appear as supplements.[66] Since soup was the mainstay of many Alpine meals, whether in huts or for camps, these new foods soon found their way into the mountains from the 1860s onwards. Liebig's extract of meat was developed from research by the German, Professor Justus von Liebig who founded Liebig Company in 1865 and became a particular favourite of Canon Girdlestone's. Ever enthusiastic for anything new Tuckett was also an early convert to convenience food. He

A selection of convenience foods shown at the 1899 Alpine Club Equipment Exhibition

PRODUCT	MANUFACTURER
Preserved, dried and pressed vegetables: *Hydraulically pressed and supplied in 1 lb. Packets, they soak to 10 times their original bulk*	**The British Preserving Company**
Extractum Carnis: *A most refreshing and nourishing drink may be made from the above by dissolving about a quarter of an ounce in boiling water, which will be sufficient for a tea-cupful. In pots 1 oz and 2 oz*	**Brand and Co**
Savoury Meat Lozenges: *Invaluable for Mountaineers who will find them substantial support. In small boxes.*	**Brand and Co**
Tabloid; Brand Tea: *Compressed and extremely portable, a convenient little case for 100 cups*	**Burroughs Wellcome and Co**
Saxin: *Most concentrated and palatable sweetening agent*	**Burroughs Wellcome and Co**
Edwards' Desiccated Soups	**F. King and Co**
Consolidated Soups: *These soups are most easily prepared, containing not only all the constituents necessary for a healthy life, but are presented in a most agreeable and inviting form, flavoured with the best condiments, requiring no addition whatever but water to make them into the most delicious soup and will keep for an indefinite time. Put in tins 2.5 inches long, with loose covers at each end, equal to 1 quart of soup*	**Portable Food Company**
Desiccated Vegetables: *These require no boiling, but simply soaking in hot water to make them ready for use and become perfectly soft and digestible. Being thoroughly desiccated these goods are not affected by the frost.*	**Portable Food Company**
Nelson's Gelatine and Liquorice Lozenges: *Invaluable to mountaineers, for they are nourishing and prevent thirst. The liquorice lozenge is recommended for soothing and moistening the throat*	**G. Nelson, Dale and Co Ltd**
Nelson's Soups and Beef Teas	**G. Nelson, Dale and Co Ltd**
OVO: *Desiccated Eggs will keep indefinitely*	**Supplied by G. Scriven**
Hipi: *A pure mutton essence possessing all the nutrient properties of first class essence*	**G. Nelson, Dale and Co Ltd**

Source: *Alpine Club Catalogue of Equipment for Mountaineers December 1899* p. 7

waxed lyrical about the delights Chollet's Julienne au Gras, a fairly unappetising looking block of dried vegetables.

First boiling water in his Russian Furnace this was sliced into it to make:

'a couple of quarts of really excellent soup and vegetables as a [soup]...The soup, both from the manner of its production and intrinsic excellence seemed to make a profound impression on my companions, who had I suspect, previously imagined the brown looking cakes, out of which the vegetables to spring into existence, like flowers from the conjurers hat, to be de Herr's supply of cavendish. Many an exclamation of surprise .. rose around me as the process of conversion went on...'[67]

These proved to be the first convenience foods to find their way into the mountains and were soon followed by many more, while firms like the Portable Food Company catered especially for campers. By the 1890s stews or soups could be pre-prepared, using potted meat, and placed in Silver and Co's self cooking tins and Bovril or Dr Koch's meat peptone were alternatives to Liebig. However proprietary dried soups – such as Lazenby's pea, bean and Julienne – were recommended as well as Edward's desiccated soup. All these needed soaking for around 15 minutes before being added to boiling water –so were much slower to prepare than a modern dried soup. But they helped reduce weight, though quite what nutrients remained is harder to tell. However, beef tea Lozenges – made by Brand and Co – were recommended as diet supplements and one mountaineer, G.P Baker, survived exclusively on them for two days. Other concentrates included:

'rations condensées accélératrices (formule du Dr Heckle) made by Gaucher, costing 3 francs a box and more commonly known as Kola biscuits have been found to delay the approaches of exhaustion'.[68]

The growing popularity of concentrates and convenience foods is reflected in the 1899 Alpine Club Exhibition, which lists a formidable array of products – some dubious, some probably disgusting but others possibly potential life savers.

Rucksacks

The two strapped rucksack first appeared during the Napoleonic wars and, whilst climbers were occasionally seen with one strapped haversacks these were not the norm in the Alps as the following description shows.

'For a pedestrian there is nothing like a rücksack. You can put much in it or little: a roll of bread or an apple or a roebuck. It is opened in a moment and closed in a moment. It lies well at your back, and coming down lower than a knapsack, fatigues less, as it makes less demand on your muscular exertion to carry it. Placed at the highest point of your body, and projecting forward at right angles with your back, a knapsack is the best arrangement that could be devised for

causing the bearer the greatest amount of fatigue. Carry but 10 lbs. a whole day in a soldier's knapsack and again in a rücksack and tell me if you find a difference. This said a rücksack is nothing but a square bag of coarse green canvas. The upper part or neck is open, with a cord running through it that it may be drawn together and tied. Just in the middle this cord is looped to 2 leather straps which pass over the wearer's shoulders and are fastened to the lower corners of the bag on each side. As it hangs just at the bend of the back, the lever like power exercised by a weight placed at the extremity of the body between the shoulders is in this case not exerted. The materials of which it is made not being stiff it adapts itself to the body, which is also a relief. It costs a mere trifle and it is to be had anywhere'.[69]

The Lightweight Revolution

The big time explorers had ships, horses, dogs and sleds, porters to carry their gear. It still had to be light although lightweight is a relative word. We think of lightweight gear as being a modern phenomenon – the consequence of new technologies, fabrics and designs. But as Tom Price, the one time warden of the Eskdale Outward Bound School in the 1960s, wryly observed, our predecessors were truly featherweight campers:

'We have, over the years been conditioned to believe a tent with half a dozen poles, a built in ground sheet and a flysheet all bristling with Velcro and weighing eight pounds, is still a 'lightweight tent'. We not only have to pay all that money. We have to carryover all the stuff as well. Yet over 50 years ago, J. Langdon and Sons of Duke Street, Liverpool, were selling a tent weighing 2.5 lbs complete, while [in 1905] T.H. Holding of Maddox Street in London was producing one of Japanese silk that weighed 13oz, to which one had to add poles and pegs...'[70]

This tent was part of Thomas Hiram Holding's Phantom Kit for the self propelled camper which he outlined as follows:

Tent	13 ounces	Down Quilt	1.5 lbs
Poles	15 ounces	Cooking Apparatus	1 lbs
Ground sheet	10 ounces	Pegs	10 ounces
Ground Blanket	8 ounces	Ridge Pole	Optional
			Total: 6 lbs

Even with the addition of personal kit and some food the load was a mere 12 lbs for the hiker or cyclist camper using Holding's kit.[71]

Holding's vision of lightweight gear came from outside mountaineering and, while his tent was also known as the Alpine Wigwam, it was probably too flimsy for Alpine conditions and lacked a sewn in groundsheet. But there were mountaineers – especially guideless climbers- who were dedicated to saving weight by the turn of the century. Some used silk ropes which, at 35 Swiss francs a kilo compared with 9 francs for a 30 meter long manila rope, were very light but very expensive. As a devotee of silk ropes Tom Longstaff

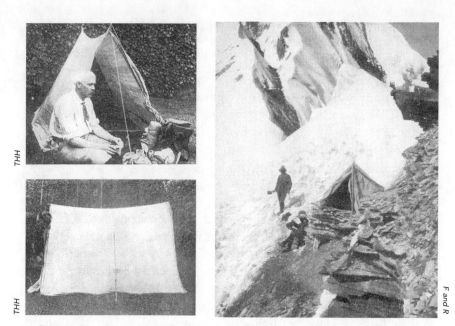

THH

THH

F and R

Left: Thomas Holding's Phantom Tent, weighing 13 oz.3.15 *Right:* Lightweight camp on Nanda Devi (1903).

was probably the first mountaineer to derive cachet from highly expensive performance gear. He cheerfully remarked in 1903:

'A silk rope is useful in many ways to the guideless climber. For instance it will obtain civility from haughty hotel-servants, and even guides themselves may be beguiled into conversation by its means ; if they will ask its price the owner's respectability is at once established, and he is put down as mad, and not merely a mean person.'[72]

Two other enthusiastic guideless climbers were W.T. Kirkpatrick and R. Philip Hope who personally designed gear for their trips to the Alps in the early 1900s. Perhaps, as contemporaries, they were influenced by Holdings' ideas or maybe common beliefs on the attractions and practicality of lightweight travel were just coincidental. They did make some of their own equipment and sought out the rest from specialist suppliers at home and on the Continent. But they were not commercial manufacturers, and instead their long climbing partnership gave them plenty of opportunity to fine tune their kit. Relying on porters only as far as the huts they adapted and improved items for their own use with the prime aim of making their loads as light as possible. Kirkpatrick advised:

'Extra clothing and other necessary equipment can be reduced by careful selection, and by considering every ounce, and even fractions of an ounce, to a very light weight. As an instance of the minute consideration we have devoted to

the matter of weight, I may mention that one year, when were trying to find the best holland covering for a rucksack, I received a small pattern from Hope, with the weight marked in grains and compared with a sample which I had sent him. His sample was a grain or two lighter than mine and was promptly adopted.'

Everything was meticulously weighed and adjusted, especially the rucksack, which was home made and went through a long evolution until it weighed just 8.75 oz for a trip in 1903. Two years later they made the following further adjustments:

'...we carried rucksacks made of Burberry's thinnest gabardine and weighing 6 oz each. It is not absolutely waterproof, but the jaconet bag, weighing 1 oz keeps one's extra clothing dry. This worked well and saved nearly 2 oz.'

Everything they took was carefully chosen for its combination of lightness and utility, with combinations of light Shetland wool and silk and everything compact and portable. Their truly minimalist kit kept them warm on 'the coldest days' and made them legends in their lifetime. For their walk to the hut they carried just 9lbs to which of course they added an axe, crampons and a rope; for a summit bid they carried only 6lbs.[73] Their choice of kit was an art form. But the choice of lightweight gear was also a safety issue for Nansen and his Polar trips and among later generations of climbers looking to get up and off challenging faces as quickly as possible. Finding the right balance between weight and safety and hence risk lies at the heart of modern Alpinism and is looked at in a later chapter.

Thomas Hiram Holding , London tailor and pioneer cycle camper, was not a mountaineer though he occasionally did some hill walking. His first passion was canoeing. As such he contributed much to the development of specialist equipment in Britain, but he came from a quite different tradition from the Alpinists. The Victorian mountaineers camped to allow them to climb high and stay high. But 'in the early 1860s, camping for pleasure was an exceptional indulgence, and those who followed it voted freaks.'[74] In the 1860s John Macgregor created an enthusiasm for the 'prehistoric' sport of canoeing. A contemporary of Francis Tuckett, Macgregor or 'Rob Roy' saw portable camping as a means of enhancing his enjoyment of his sport. Like Tuckett, Macgregor used the Russian furnace which he helped to popularise and which for many years bore his name. That the newly formed Alpine Club was the model for the Royal Canoe Club, which he founded in Putney in 1866, leaves open the intriguing possibility of whether the two men knew each other.[75]

Macgregor can be classed as a true 'pioneer' innovator and he was Thomas Holding's major inspiration. Holding's passion for an outdoor life began when, in 1853 as a nine year old boy he crossed America with his parents, before railroads had penetrated much beyond the Eastern seaboard.[76] Not

British Library Collection

John 'Rob Roy' Macgregor, c 1860 in his canoe on the rapids of the Reuss,Switzerland. He pioneered canoe travel and took his rigid canoe to the headwaters of many European rivers by train and diligence.

surprisingly this left an indelible impression with young Thomas and gave him a taste for outdoor living, which never left him through adolescence and his apprenticeship as a tailor in London. Fired by Macgregor's writings he purchased a canoe and made his first long distance canoeing trip in Scotland in 1877 and spent most summers on the waters of English rivers, with a further trip to Scotland in 1886. He loved camping and it was infectious, attracting friends tempted by his, for the period, quite outrageous schemes. He took up cycling in the 1870s and the idea of cycle camping gradually took hold of him and simmered gently for many years until the coming of the Safety bicycle in 1885 and he was the pioneer of it. [77]

Holding believed that camping could and should be comfortable and was obsessed with making it so. In 1887 his tent and lightweight kit won first prize in the Royal Canoe Club's camping competition.[78] Had Holding stopped there he would have been remembered as a pioneer 'lightweighter' who designed kit for his own purposes – much as Macgregor and Tuckett had done before him. Instead he became a legend in his lifetime and he sold his products, manufactured by sewing machine in his tailoring workshop, to a growing number of cycle and pedestrian campers to whom he also provided patterns and plans for self manufacture.

His background was different from men like Tuckett or Kirkpatrick and Hope for he was a tailor – indeed one of the most influential tailors of his generation. As author and editor of numerous cutting manuals and journals, including *The*

London Tailor and Record of Fashion, he was also an able teacher and ran a school of tailoring. Like so many twentieth century outdoor innovators, enjoyment of sport gave him a practical understanding of his products. As one of his contemporaries, W.J. Pearce wrote in 1909 for cycle camping:

> *'light must everything be... even those very essentials that are usually so heavy –stoves, pots and pans. Away with the heavy canvas for the softest and strongest materials possible. The tent must receive our first consideration.'*[79]

This sums up the needs of this sport (and canoe camping) perfectly – everything should be compact and attachable to part of the frame of the bicycle. They were sentiments reflected in everything Holding designed, from his tents, to his Baby Primus to the lightweight So-Soon pans and the panier bags to carry them all in.

Only the relatively wealthy could use the Holding Phantom Kit because silk may have been light, strong and extremely 'packable', but it was very expensive and was only 'for the man who has it in his power to spend £3 to £5 for a tent' – the equivalent of a complete set of clothes for a mill girl in 1910 and more than a week's wages for a clerk or a civil servant.[80] Not surprisingly Holding never manufactured these in any volume. Instead prospective campers could use the detailed patterns included in his *Camper's Handbook* – rather like the Heals' patterns for down sleeping bags used by Alpine climbers. He resembled some of the pioneer mountaineers in that he was looking for craft solutions to the practical problems posed by his enjoyment of the outdoors. However, he was far more than an inventor for, as an established craftsman, he made his own tents. As a vigorous organiser of cycle and cycle-camping clubs, he was able to penetrate a far wider market than the mainly bespoke craftsmen who interpreted the designs of the Victorian Alpinists.

CHAPTER 4
Broadening Horizons
Women's Climbing Dress in a Hidden World

'The slopes of the Breithorn and the snows of the Weiss Thor are usually supposed to mark the limits of ascents suitable to the weaker sex – indeed strong prejudices are apt to be aroused the moment a woman attempts any more formidable sort of mountaineering. It appears to me, however, that her powers are, in actual fact, better suited to the really difficult climbs than to the monotonous snow grinds usually considered more fitting. Really difficult ascents are of necessity made at a slower pace, halts are fairly frequent and, with few exceptions, the alterations of heat and cold are less extreme. Snow grinds, on the contrary, usually involve continuous and severe exertion. Halts on a wide snow field are practically impossible, and the danger of frost bite in the early morning is succeeded by the certainty of sun burning at midday.'

Mary Mummery, the author of this observation, was quite clear that women excelled at intricate climbing but found that most men failed to appreciate this saying that:

'The masculine mind, however, is with rare exceptions, imbued with the idea that a woman is not a fit comrade for steep ice or precipitous rock, and, in consequence holds it as an article of faith that her climbing should be done by Mark Twain's method, and that she should be satisfied with watching through a telescope some weedy and inver-tebrate masher being hauled up a steep peak by a couple of burly guides, or by lis-tening to this same masher when on his return, he lisps out with a sickening drawl the many perils he has encountered. Alexander Burgener, however, holds many strange opinions; he believes in ghosts, he also believes that women can climb. Nonetheless it was with some surprise that I heard him say 'You must go up the Teufelsgrat...'[1]

And she went with both enthusiasm and agility. It was rather a sad irony that Mary Mummery was soon forced to give up climbing from ill health, leaving her husband free to climb with Lily Bristow and break just about every Victorian taboo. It was Lily Bristow who taught 'the men of the Alpine Club how to climb steep rock' during the ascent of the Grépon while, with some of the earliest down sleeping bags and Mummery's silk tent they slept out far from Victorian respectability. These stories provide a wonderful backdrop to the charade of nineteenth century women's climbing dress, where impressions masked realities in the 'hidden world' of mountaineering. It was a world where women climbers (certainly English women), if they were illustrated at all in the earliest days, were shown in crinolines, graduating gently through long skirts to the knee length 'frill' in the years before the First World War. The public impression of women climbers was of a gentility and comparative elegance, which was not too far removed from conventional views of Victorian dress and behaviour. After all dress was cultural shorthand for class and status, conveying the wearer's position in society. The pioneer naval polar explorers had preferred the outside world to see them in formal garb, even though they wore furs to stay warm. Similarly early women climbers and certainly their families transferred English value systems, as symbolised by clothing, to the Alps. It was an image that was quite at odds with climbing to a high standard and yet this was precisely what a minority of women did, their achievements obscured by a cloak (or maybe a skirt) of respectability. Comparing the public and private worlds of the top female mountaineer, before the First World War, reveals a complex charade where they only *appeared* to follow dress codes whilst privately flouting them along with many other conventions – as soon as they were out of the valley. The sheer practicality of climbing difficult, technical routes means that few modern mountaineers would be that surprised that this was the case. But the story of how and why women went to such lengths to conceal what they did, gives intriguing insights into the contradictions faced by early female climbers in the nineteenth and early twentieth centuries.

The Public Image

Middle class women in particular were expected to conform to an ideal of womanhood which, by combining purity and refinement, seemed to make all but gentle exercise, let alone anything as energetic as climbing, out of the question. Clothing is a mirror on social values and attitudes and Victorian ladies were apparently:

> 'trapped into inactivity by layers of under garments, encumbered by ruffles lace and bows and 15 to 20 lbs of material hanging to the ground from a constricted waist and encased in a portable prison of tight corsets as an exquisite slave – it stopped them engaging in any activity more vigorous than a sedate stroll.'[2]

With clothing came status, so that lavish and extravagant dress became a sign of a leisured and genteel lifestyle in Victorian England.[3] Consequently from a purely practical point of view the progress of women's sport became inseparable from dress reform, which in turn accelerated female participation in physical recreation.[4]

Growing interest in the history of women's sport before the First World War has focused primarily on the so called 'rationalised sports' pursued by middle class women. Women's enthusiasm for tennis, cricket, swimming, golf and hockey was linked to expanding formalised education and had a liberating effect. Of all the sports Victorian and Edwardian women engaged in, cycling has had greatest attention and symbolised metaphorical and physical freedom, and not just for middle class women, but across a wide social spectrum. Sport itself impacted on the design of sportswear and none more so than with the bicycle:

'The bicycle liberated women from their actual and symbolic encumbrances of long skirts and tight lacing. The new forms of dress designed for the bicycle – shortened skirts, divided skirts, knickerbockers, skirts with elastic insets and bloomers of rational dress allowed women a new physical independence and symbolised their revolt against restrictions. With the bicycle, women appropriated two unprecedented forms of freedom – bodily and spatial mobility.'[5]

Women climbers were not numerous enough to capture popular attention in the same way as cyclists- there were just seventy-two members of the Ladies' Alpine Club as late as 1925.[6] Anyway since theirs was a largely hidden sport – undertaken far away from the popular gaze – it had less political significance. Nevertheless the public image of female climbers was uncompromisingly proper.

Our vision of what Victorian middle class women wore to climb is derived from photographs, drawings, literary accounts, advertisements and books on mountaincraft. Climbing was anything but 'womanly' in the classic Victorian sense and was quite unlike the 'gentle and respectable' games deemed suitable for women. It could not have been more different from croquet which was played at home one handed 'in order that womenfolk might be able to guard their complexions from the sun, a game of frills and fancies of petticoats, giggles and maidenly blushes'[7]. Climbing was a physical, outdoor activity which took women away from nurturing and the family and could leave them sunburned and wild looking, contradicting all norms of respectable behaviour. Common sense dictates that to climb also involved fundamentally breaking dress codes. Yet this is not the public image of the Victorian or Edwardian female climbers, who in the most extreme cases were shown wearing at worst a crinoline and certainly a long skirt, which might just show the ankles. Certainly a few like Mrs Le Blond or the American Mrs Bullock Workman were photographed wearing frills – the short ugly skirts that began to appear around 1900 – but they were the exception.

The crinoline was an extreme fashion and public images gave way to supposedly more practical tweed skirts with flannel petticoats. In 1889 lady mountaineers are advised to:

'have your gown tailor-made or if you prefer to patronise a dressmaker, as plain in cut and finish as possible and be particular not to let the skirts be made heavier than can be helped....Let the skirts be as short as possible to clear the ankles. Nothing else is permissible for mountain work, where one must face bogs, deep heather, thorny gorse and must not stumble into the hem of ones garments on the face of a rocky precipice. I must however draw the line at the modern feminine costume for mountaineering and deer stalking, where the skirt is a mere polite apology – an inch or two below the knee, and the result hardly consistent with a high ideal of womanhood.'[8]

The myth of climbing in skirts was also perpetuated in the small amount of advertising material portraying female mountaineers, most notably that of Burberry. Thomas Burberry opened his shop in 1865 and patented his famous gabardine in1879. This fabric was produced in Lancashire for Burberry and with consistent improvement to make it windproof was ideal for cold climates. It was initially used for Polar exploration but was ideal for winter sports and mountaineering. Unlike Jaeger, Burberry was a conservative firm and the only bifurcated garment in their sports range was a voluminous aviation dress which could be 'easily divided and vice versa'. For mountaineering right up to the First World War they advertised the 'airlight, untearable Burberry climbing gown' and its long skirt. Its comparative lightness and water resistance made it an improvement on tweed, but it was hardly practical in other ways. At between 8 to 10 Guineas, with 2 guineas extra for a silk lining, it was also easily one of the most expensive.[9]

Skirts were often described as being adapted with buttons and tapes. There are many descriptions of Heath Robinson type devices involving tapes and buttons which were used to adjust the skirt for climbing. In 1838, when Anne Lister climbed Vignemale, she wore capes, cloaks, shawls and petticoats with tapes and loops to allow her to hitch up her skirts. [10]

After her tour of Monte Rosa in the 1850s Mrs Cole advised:

'Every lady engaged on an Alpine Journey should have a dress of some light woollen material, such as carmelite or alpaca which, in the case of bad weather, does not look utterly forlorn when it has once been wetted and dried.

Small rings should be sewn inside the seam of the dress and a cord passed through them, the ends of which should be knotted together in such a way that the whole dress may be drawn up at a moment's notice to the required height'.[11]

This was very much the design recommended in 1883 by Mrs Blair of the Dress Reform Society:

'Red Brown. Short skirt, with tabs and buttons, and elastic to shorten the skirt at will. Narrow trousers to fasten on flannel circular band. Loose, pleated bodice with waist band. Stocking –suspenders from waist. Flannel skirt with under wear, weight, 4lbs 9 oz. Hygienic boots'[12]

The use of tapes, buttons and ties remained the received view of how women 'managed' long and voluminous skirts in the 1890s. In 1892 Clinton Dent, apparently under advice of two female climbers, described a particularly complicated device for a skirt with a circumference of some 3 yards:

'When climbing the skirt must, whatever its length, be looped up, and therefore it is easy to have a skirt which in the valleys or towns does not look conspicuous. For looping up the skirt, the following plan is effective. An extra belt of strong ribbon is put on over the skirt which is then pinned to it in fish wife style. The length is arranged according to the requirements of the occasion. One safety pin attaching the two sides and another fastening the back, the hem being pinned to the outer belt do the work...some employ loops and buttons for shortening the skirt...'[13]

BURBERRY Outfits.

To withstand the severe strain of climbing, and to make provision for rapid changes of temperature, Mountaineers require garments constructed of especially manufactured textures.

BURBERRYS weatherproof materials, woven and proofed by Burberry processes, are just what the Mountaineer requires and when made into outfits under expert advice, the climber enjoys to the full his hazardous pursuit, with an assurance of all the comfort possible.

BURBERRY MOUNTAINEERING GOWN.

The BURBERRY outfit displays the utmost economy in weight, with phenomenal durability.

Proof against rain, sleet, wind and cold, yet retains perfect self-ventilation. Practical in form and perfected by inventions that preserve absolute limb freedom.

Full particulars and patterns of the materials that experience has shown to give the best results, write for **BURBERRY-PROOF CLIMBING KIT.** Post free on application.

BURBERRY MOUNTAINEERING OUTFIT.

Burberry Climbing Gown. This was 11 years after Jaeger began advertising knickerbockers for mountaineering. From *Fell and Rock Journal* 1907-9.

Anything less practical than a skirt of this size is hard to imagine. But it was hardly surprising that Victorian women climbers – supported no doubt by their husbands and brothers made strenuous efforts to ensure that they appeared to be climbing in skirts and not trousers. Middle class values demanded that they should; to do otherwise and to display the outline of the legs, was deemed immoral. But censure was not just on the grounds of morality for, if upper and middle class women did not wear trousers or 'breech' their skirts, working class women and performing women undoubtedly did. So trousers were a class issue as well as a moral one.[14]

The Wigan pit brow girls (photographed in their work trousers) are a well known example of be-trousered Victorian working women, which deeply shocked respectable society in the 1860s. But there were other more apposite examples – those women who, like the Filey bait girls, climbed for a living. Harold Munby – barrister, poet and 'benign pervert' – described bait girls on the Filey coast in 1868, who were highly proficient and enthusiastic rock climbers. He recalled:

Flamborough Bait girls Molly Nettleton and Sally Mainpiece with breeched skirts. They enjoyed climbing but it was part of their work.

'I went out at 9.30 and through the village and across the fields to Brial Head. Following the path at the edge of the great chalk cliff, I came to the point from which in the autumn and winter weather I have so often seen the Flambro lasses climb the rope. And then, looking down I saw the new rope, my gift and Molly's treasure, hanging from the stake and going down the whole height of the cliff, to the broad platform of table rock at the bottom... [250 feet below]

Towards 11 o'clock, however, two bait girls appeared near the foot of the cliff, striding and swooping among the wet seaweed. Both were breeched up to the knee... at the height one could not hear their voices; but I saw them clamber up to the base of the rock, and there Molly seized the rope, tried it with her own weight and began to mount. Hand over hand, sticking her toes into the crevices of the chalk wall she went up, as easily as one might walk upstairs, and having thus climbed about 50 feet, she turned round and with her back to the cliff worked her way along a level ledge that just supported her heels to an over hanging point. There stooping forward as coolly as possible, she hauled first her full basket and her fellow's, which the girl below first ties to the rope end. When the baskets came up, she just loosened them, and hoisted them up, with one hand, upon a broader ledge above her head: then, grasping the rope again, she climbed up to it and sat down.... [after they reached the top] ... they began to run Molly first, head foremost down the dizzy slope of rock, until they both disappeared over the edge of the cliff wall below. I, the man of the party, was left in a ridiculous position; a useless spectator of these vigorous athletics.'[15]

Trousers were also worn by women in circuses as by two French velocipedists (early cyclists) in 1869. These girls:

'were drest as men in jockey caps and satin jackets and short breeches ending above the knee and long stockings and mid length boots. Thus clad they stepped forth unabashed into the midst and mounted their 'bicycles' each girl throwing her leg over and sitting astride on the saddle. And then they started, amidst cheers pursuing one another round and round the hall, curving in and out, sometimes rising in their stirrups (so to speak) as if trotting, sometimes throwing one leg or both legs up whilst at full speed: and after riding do, with all the skill and vigour of young men, for a quarter of an hour, these girls halted and dismounted and made their bow amidst thunderous applause.'[16]

Bear in mind that women who climbed were very much from the genteel classes. Born the 'delicate child of wealthy parents' Elizabeth Hawkins-Whitshed fits the image of the Victorian 'lady' perfectly and was the personification of elegance. Twice widowed, she is better known as Mrs

Aubrey or Lizzie le Blond who had a stunning climbing career spanning more than 20 years from 1881, and was the driving force behind the formation of the Ladies' Alpine Club in 1907.[17] But, if she broke with convention by climbing, she was very much the child of her era, and wealth brought her the leisure to spend summers and winters in the Alps. So cosseted had been her background that she admitted in 1928 that when she set off with guides to try and climb Mont Blanc in 1882 at the age of twenty-one:

'Never till that moment had I put on my own boots, and I was none too sure on which foot should go which boot. It is difficult for me to realize now that for several years longer it did not occur to me that I could do without a maid.'[18]

For a woman of her background to be known to wear trousers would be a massive break with class, convention and rejection of position. The treatment of early women cyclists highlights the opprobrium and hostility faced by be-trousered women. As one woman remembered:

'It's awful. One wants nerves of iron and I don't wonder now in the least so many women have given up the Rational Dress costume and returned to skirts. The shouts and yells of the children deafen one, the women shriek with laughter or groan and hiss and all sorts of remarks are shouted at one, occasionally some not fit for publication. One needs to be very brave to stand all that.'[19]

Women's Climbing Achievements

If the numbers of women who climbed were small, their achievements before the First World War were considerable and quite at odds with their public image of refined dress. In 1871, six years after Whymper's first ascent, Lucy Walker climbed the Matterhorn, the first woman to do so, her exploits prompting *Punch* to publish the tongue in cheek poem 'A Climbing Girl':

'A lady has clomb to the Matterhorn summit
Which almost like a monument points to the sky;
Steep not very much less than the string of a plummet
Suspended, which nothing can scale but a fly.

This lady has likewise ascended the Weisshorn,
And, what's a great deal more, descended it too,
Feet foremost; which seeing it might be named Icehorn,
So slippery 'tis no small thing to do.

No glacier can baffle, no precipice balk her,
No peak rise above her, however sublime.
Give three times three cheers to intrepid Miss Walker
I say, my boys, doesn't she know how to climb!'[20]

She was not the first female Alpine mountaineer by any means, for Mont Blanc was climbed in 1808 by a local girl. This was perhaps the earliest mountaineering publicity stunt, for local Maria Paradis was virtually carried up the mountain by her guides to publicise her refreshment stall. Other early women included Henriette d'Angeville who, in 1838, climbed Mont Blanc with guides and porters and every comfort known to men (and women), while in the same year Anne Lister made the first tourist ascent of Vignemale in the Pyrenees.[21] Lucy Walker was, however, one of an admittedly small number of pioneering Victorian women, who climbed with guides and relatives to a consistently high standard in the Alps during the second half of the nineteenth century. Between 1858 and 1879, in the company of either her father or brother and their guide Melchior Anderegg, she made 72 ascents of major Alpine peaks and crossed numerous high cols. This included a first ascent of the Balmhorn (3799m) in 1864.[22] Contemporaries of Miss Walker included the Pigeon sisters who between 1869 and 1876 climbed 63 peaks and crossed 72 passes. In 1869 they completed the second crossing from Riffle to Alagna over Sesia Joch with guide Jean Martin and a porter; on the first crossing by two Alpine Club members in 1862 it had been described as a 'most daring exploit'. On this trip one of the sisters went last in order to provide protection for the porter. Four years later they made a traverse of the Matterhorn from Breuil to Zermatt.[23] Then there was American Miss Breevoort, who with her nephew W.A. Coolidge, her dog Tschingel and guide Christian Almer swept through the Alps in the late 1860s and early 1870s. Their successes included a first ascent of the Pic Central on the Meije in the Dauphine in 1870 followed the next year by a first ascent of the WSW ridge of the Eiger rounding off in 1874 with the first winter ascents of both the Wetterhorn and the Jungfrau.[24] Isabella Straton was another woman to make her mark in the Alps in the 1870s climbing with her friend Emmeline Lewis Lloyd and guide Jean Charlet. In 1876 with Charlet, Sylvain Couttet and Michel Balmat she made the first winter ascent of Mont Blanc. Described later by Lizzie Le Blond as one of the greatest women climbers of her day, the unassuming Mrs E.P. Jackson had a formidable record. It included a first ascent of the Weissmies and the West ridge of the Dom in 1876 and 1878 respectively. In January 1888 she completed a winter traverse of the Jung Frau including an overnight bivouac.[25]

In the 1880s and 1890s there was also of course Mrs Le Blond who made numerous winter and first ascents mainly with her guide Josef Imboden. She also pioneered 'manless' climbing, making a traverse of Piz Palu. *Alpine Journal* editor E.L. Strutt summed her up as a 'highly skilled climber who had extraordinary judgement which had 'never been surpassed in any mountaineer, professional or amateur, of the so-called stronger sex.'[26] Katy Richardson equalled Lizzie Le Blond's skill as a climber and in one week in 1882 completed the first traverse from the Zinalrothorn to Zermatt via the Weisshorn, Matterhorn and Monte Rosa with Emile Rey.[27] Fred Mummery enjoyed climbing with women and introduced his wife to the Alps in the late 1880s, where their ascents included the first ascent of the Teufelsgrat which she described vividly in her chapter in her husband's book. [28] Lily Bristow's short but brilliant career in the Alps was also of course largely linked to Fred Mummery and she completed one of the first known female leads on a major route on an ascent of the Petit Dru.[29]

One of the most outstanding female climbers was Gertrude Bell a highly gifted and educated woman. Her stepmother described her as a 'scholar, poet, historian, archaeologist, art critic, mountaineer, explorer, gardener, naturalist, distinguished servant of the state.' During 1901 and 1902, this extraordinary woman carried out an impressive number of new routes and first ascents with her guide Ulrich Fuhrer and his brother Heinrich. [30]

Gertrude Bell's contemporaries were the Pasteur sisters with numerous first ascents to their credit while in the years before the First World War several other Continental women climbers developed a formidable record. They included Mlle Heiner, Eleonore Hasenclever and Frau Kasnapoff. The two most notable female American climbers in the years before the First World War were Annie Peck who climbed and travelled widely in the Andes, while Fanny Bullock Workman made a first ascent of Pinnacle Peak in the Himalayas reaching 22,500 feet in 1906. In 1910 Australian Freda du Faur became the first woman to climb Mount Cook.[31]

All these women are well known as the pioneers of female climbing but Georg Gernert's listing 'Frauen als Bergsteiger 1760-1925 reveals many many more climbers with first ascents. There was for instance Jeanne Immink from Amsterdam who completed several first ascents in the Dolomites in the 1890s. Ilona and Rolanda Eötvös from Budapest, who were active in the Dolomites in the years leading up to the First World War. Outstanding among these 'lost' women has to be the almost unknown English woman Beatrice Tomasson who, between 1897 and 1903, completed some eight first ascents including the formidable south face of the Marmolada in July 1901. Quite how someone with such an exceptional record was ignored by the climbing establishment in England remains a mystery. It seems a shame that although her photograph does hang in the Alpine Club in London it remains hidden in the basement next to the bunkhouse.

A number of forces – which differed from country to country – brought these women to climbing. These ranged from improved education and the development of physical education within it, especially after 1880 in England, to a small number of women who, like Gertrude Bell, attended university. It was through their families that many women came to mountaineering in this period, the enthusiasm of fathers, brothers and husbands bringing them to the Alps for the first time. This

Women on a glacier c 1890, these were tourists rather than serious climbers.

does bring into question our perceptions of Victorian family life and the constraints placed on middle class women. In 1894 Lady Greville commented

'It is scarcely necessary nowadays to offer an apology for sport... women cheerfully share with men, hardships, toil and endurance, climb mountains, sail seas, face wind and rain and the chill gusts of winter'.[32]

Interestingly though, while they were happy for their daughters, sisters and wives to climb, the Alpine Club establishment did not admit women until 1975. Dress codes were slow to change for all female sports and it remains to be seen how, despite them, some women were able to climb to such a high standard. They were not strolling up Box Hill on a Sunday afternoon or even taking a guided foray onto the tip of an Alpine Glacier. They were climbing to the limit and yet the public image remains that they did so dressed in a genteel way. However, the hidden world of climbing made it easier for them to break taboos and conventions than in virtually any other sport.

All Was Not What It Seemed: The Private Reality in a Hidden World

Trousers are the logical garb for climbing and essential for those climbing to a high standard. This is partly for ease of movement, but also for safety. Victorian photographs are a particularly poor guide to what women actually wore to climb. Certainly many women who were photographed in the Alps were wearing long skirts, but this does not show that they were climbers or even, when they appeared to be making a complex manoeuvre, that this was the reality. In the first place there are numerous photographs of the women who 'wandered round the picturesque parts of Swiss valleys... or were occasionally allowed on the safer parts of glaciers' close to the judging eyes of respectability.[33] They certainly wore long skirts and their images have parallels with modern 'tourists' who visit the Lake District, Scotland or the Alps on a car or coach tour, venturing out in unsuitable clothes and footwear. What these images do *not* do is reflect clothing and equipment used by an active sports person, which at the very least would be muddy or show signs of wear.

Active Victorian climbers were understandably shy of being photographed in their climbing breeches – certainly before 1900 – and maintained a 'public' image posing on rocky paths and outcrops in their skirts. In any event portraits of mountaineers, until the replacement of glass plates by roll film and the pocket camera –respectively introduced in 1889 and 1898, were necessarily contrived and rarely taken on mountain tops, simply because of the bulkiness of the equipment. Even then, it was not until the interwar period that good quality small cameras became readily available and widely used. Many early photographs of mountaineers were then taken by local photographers who took shots of groups as they set off, with women respectably dressed in their skirts. Mrs Le Blond made it plain that taking a photograph when she started climbing in the 1880s was cumbersome and contrived:

'Dry plates had come into use only a short time before and hand cameras were unthought of. We who photographed had set up our cumbersome machines on tripods and, perhaps in a high wind grasp a ballooning piece of velvet and attempt with half frozen fingers to turn ice screws while we adjusted the focus. '[34]

'Touching up' a photograph is not just the product the digital age and could turn a posed event into a sporting image. One German photographer described how he 'doctored' a photograph of Dutch climber Madame Jeanne Immink who was ironically wearing knickerbockers and who appeared to be making a very complicated move. When asked many years later how she managed to maintain her hold, given the length of exposure using glass plates, the photographer replied:

'Beyond zat corner I haf a guide viz a rope; on zis side of her I haf anozzer guide, viz a rope. Zen I make mein photograf and zen I ob-lee-der-ate ze rope!'[35]

This makes all posed photographs showing women climbing in skirts equally suspect.

Common sense and a knowledge of the demands and safety requirements of climbing as a sport dictates Victorian women could not have climbed to a high standard had they worn crinolines or even Clinton Dent's skirt with its 3 yard circumference. The idea that they climbed in crinolines is quite simply ridiculous. These dresses had skirts with a circumference of as much as 5 yards supported on an internal wire frame. In an article in *The Englishwoman's Domestic Magazine* 'Peachblossom is advised not to attempt the climbing of stiles in a crinoline for the task is impossible'. In that case imagine had 'Peachblossom' been tempted to try any serious mountaineering![36] However,

Alpine Club Collection

The idea of women climbing in crinolines was ridiculous though on this trip M stowed a copper tea pot beneath her crinoline.

for modest walking in the mountains, crinolines had their uses, as one account in the *Cornhill Magazine* for 1863 suggests:

'M. had a weakness for performing all her excursions in a roomy crinoline, and it had been an amusement to A and G., the whole time to watch the peculiar forms into which the inflated petticoats were driven by the superincumbent weight of the copper teapot, slung under the skirt of her dress'....[37]

Wide hooped skirts were not only impractical for mountaineering they were downright dangerous. Indeed full skirts of any kind were a hazard precisely because they could blow up over the wearer's head. This is exactly what happened to Félicité Carrel, daughter of the guide Josef Carrel, who would probably have reached the summit of the Matterhorn in 1867 – 4 years ahead of Lucy Walker: *'had the wind not assailed her petticoats too roughly'.*[38] She had the consolation of having the col where this happened named after her.

Long trailing skirts could also dislodge lose boulders and rocks and be a danger to the rest of the party. Indeed Katy Richardson narrowly escaped serious injury when a rock, disturbed by her climbing partner's skirt, crashed onto her. [39] In addition, the sheer weight of such skirts, especially when wet were a major hazard. In the 1850s before the publication of *A Lady's Tour of Monte Rosa*, Lizzie Bourne died from exhaustion and exposure, on Mount Washington in the White Mountains in America . There were 47 yards of fabric in her dress and when a search party found her body the soaking layers of cloth weighed around 60lbs. [40] Tapes, buttons and loops that supposedly made the skirt so adaptable could be a nuisance too. After a particularly difficult day Mrs Brevoort complained in the 1870s that:'My dress plan too, has failed, and descending snow slopes the snow enters the rings and stuffs up the hem and makes me heavy and wet.'[41] Many years later just before the First World War, the potential hazards of wearing skirts, however adapted, were perfectly summed up by Julian Le Grande:

'The difficulty with a skirt when one gets in higher regions, the wind literally catches it and turns it into a balloon, very often blinds its wearer, impedes progress of the climber and becomes most dangerous. Even fitted with many elastics like a cycling skirt and attached round the legs it is without avail against the wind which one must encounter in high altitudes.'[42]

Nonetheless skirts may not have been without practical uses in high mountains when women were bivouacking. The skirts, which they consigned to rucksacks while climbing, will almost certainly have been useful as camouflage devices when carrying out bodily functions, as still happens today in some areas of Asia.[43] There were also some dress modifications which may have eased toilet arrangements for women in the mountains. For instance, one 1909 illustration of ladies winter-sports underknickers in the catalogue for Och Brothers of Montreux does suggest a buttoned gusset flap, which may have helped. Three years later W. Bocher of Munich were advertising women's skiing and mountaineering 'pumphosen' or knickerbockers which show a buttoned rear flap which can only have had one purpose. [44] But more research is needed to see how, if at all, garments were adjusted to cope with the perennial problem of going to the toilet on a long climbing trip.

Alpine Club Collection

Henriette d' Angeville, who climbed Mont Blanc in 1838 and was the second woman to do so. She was the first woman to be shown wearing knickerbockers under her skirt.

For climbing trousers were the practical solution and were being used in the mountains remarkably early. In 1838 Henriette d'Angeville wore Scottish tweed knickerbockers under her skirt when she climbed Mont Blanc and may well have removed the skirt. These very early trousers will also have been partly for warmth, although under-drawers were introduced in the 1820s they did not always have gussets.[45] A tiny number of women wore trousers under short skirts or even trousers on their own even in this period. One was the first female Norwegian mountaineer, Therese Bertheau, who shocked Christiania (Oslo) gentlemen, in the mid 1860s, by letting her skirt fall to expose that she was only wearing trousers.[46] In 1873 Annie, Edward, May and Tom Westmorland climbed Pillar Rock in the English Lake District and both girls were photographed wearing knickerbockers.[47] However, for English women certainly, the public image until 1900 was that if knickerbockers went into the mountains they were for extra warmth rather than the woman should remove her skirt to climb. Clinton Dent's 1892 advice is especially coy in its mention of trousers:

'Knickerbockers of waterproofed cloth lined with flannel will probably be found best, and though a little heavy, are a great safeguard against a chill when sleeping out.'[48]

What he omits to say is that they were used without a skirt for climbing, yet this was precisely what did happen, simply because this was the only practical solution.

Referring explicitly to Dent's chapter in *The Girl's Realm* published in 1899. E.M. Symonds complained:

'In the volume on Mountaineering in that generally up to date series, the Badminton Library, ladies are recommended to wear a skirt of ordinary walking length, to be looped up when necessary and an underskirt (if desired), as well as knickerbockers. It is difficult to understand how any really stiff climbing could be accomplished in two skirts the weight of which alone would be a serious tax on a woman's strength. Then there would be the risk of getting 'hung up' on projecting rocks, or sweeping down stones on other people's heads; while the case of a bad slip or a fall into a crevasse, the fact of the legs being entangled in skirts would add very greatly to the difficulties of recovery or rescue. Whatever the books may say, it has been the custom for years among ladies climbing in the Dolomites and other rocky districts, to discard their skirts as soon as they reach the scene of action, and only resume them when they return to civilised regions.'[49]

This view was echoed by Mrs Le Blond reminiscing in 1932:

'Dress in those days was not such a problem as it might be supposed, for except that one wore a skirt over one's knickerbockers, the costume when this badge of respectability was removed did not differ greatly from that usually worn today.'[50]

The implication is that by the 1880s and 1890s, however women climbers were portrayed publicly, when they were in the high mountains they wore trousers for practical reasons. There are numerous stories of mishaps when skirts were left on summits only to be retrieved by unfortunate guides. But sometimes efforts to maintain the charade of respectability took on the character of a French farce, as when Lizzie le Blond lost her skirt after a long day. She vividly recalled:

'I had an awkward experience connected with climbing dress .. having left my skirt on top of a rock with a heavy stone to keep it in place, a big avalanche gaily whisked it away before our very eyes, as we descended that afternoon. Unwilling to venture across the couloir so late under the hot sun in search of it, I came down just as I was till close to the village where I remained concealed behind a clump of trees while Imboden fetched a skirt from my room at the hotel. I had carefully explained to him exactly where he would find a suitable one, but to my horror, he appeared after a long interval with my best evening dress over his arm ! There was nothing for it but to slink in when he gave the word that all was clear, and dash up to my room hoping I should meet no one on the stairs.'[51]

Compared with other sports where, apart from the brief flirtations with bifurcated garments in the 1890s, skirts remained the norm until after the First World War, female climbers could be far more radical over their dress.

Right: Knitted Corsets, the Jaeger alternative to rigid corseting. from the Jaeger catalogue 1896.

"MELITA" AND "VICTORIA."
PRICE 6/-

This was because, once they left the valleys, certainly in the Alps and when they travelled further afield, they entered a 'hidden world' and broke numerous taboos. They engaged in 'unwomanly' activity with gusto, skill and sheer enthusiasm. Miss Muriel Dowie said as much in a paper to the British Association at Leeds on her recent tour of the Carpathians in 1890. Dressed smartly in a tailored costume she said she had:

> *'in those far hills no fear of Hyde Park before her eyes, she shed her skirt and bestrode her pony in all the glory of knickerbockers; and when tired of riding, she took off her sandals and walked the mountains barefoot.'*[52]

"ECONOMIC" NURSING CORSET.

The contrast between Lizzie Le Blond's public and mountain persona was even more striking than Murial Dowie's. Compare the posed photo of the wealthy, bejewelled, young society woman with the image of her climbing all day 'like a child' and then bumping down a mountain pass on an early safety bicycle in the 1880s, after a hard day's climbing. In her mountaineering memoirs she recalled:

> *'I found [my bicycle] very useful for the beginnings and endings of climbs. To jump on a bicycle after being on foot for twelve or fifteen hours was a restful change of exercise and a quick way of covering the remainder of the way home... The only brake provided was a plunge brake on the front tyre which could not be used incessantly and for long descents back pedalling became too fatiguing. So when dropping down thousands of feet by means of a series of zig zags and curves, one resorted to another method which, however soon became illegal. Breaking off bushy branches from the last pine trees met with on the upward way we carried them to the top of the pass, and as soon as the descent became severe each tied their branch to the long piece of rope and let it trail behind. The roads were... dirt roads so each member of a bicycling party strung far apart was visible only as swirling cloud of dust'.*[53]

Wearing trousers was the visible element of dress code to be broken in the mountains, but removing corsets and stays was both radical and essential. Nothing was more constraining of physical activity and the strength needed for climbing, than that symbol of Victorian womanhood the ubiquitous corset. These encasing prisons constrained women's waists and breathing and weakened their back muscles, becoming part of their bodies and their minds. Corsets were manufactured for babies, girls, sleeping and pregnant women and even sportswomen, including mountaineers. Indeed as one set of guidance notes for intending mountain walkers pointed out while:

'Tight bodices are fatal to breathing power… so are stays but if you are used to them you had better keep to them as you do not get proper strength in your back in a week to enable you to do without them.'[54]

Certainly some women, such as Emily Hornby, who was a regular visitor to the Alps between 1873 and 1896, did climb in stays and worried about the danger of removing them. Her corset was of some practical use though because she made it into a money belt.[55] But Emily Hornby, whilst enthusiastic and energetic was not climbing to the same standard as women like Lizzie Le Blond, Gertrude Bell or Lily Bristow. It is very doubtful, had they remained corseted, that they could have developed sufficient strength and agility to complete their more difficult and sustained ascents. However, the cult of Jaeger underwear, first marketed in 1884, did help free women from the tyranny of tightly laced corsets. There is no evidence one way or another to confirm whether they shifted to this healthy form of underwear. But it would in any event have been vital for warmth and insulation, rather than the by then fashionable but chilling cotton and they were firmly advised to wear either silk or wool next to the skin. Undoubtedly they would have known of Jaeger clothing, as the company regularly advertised in climbing periodicals.[56] A compromise seems to have been a knitted corset made as short as possible.[57]

In the 'hidden world' of the high mountains, therefore, Victorian women could reject normal codes of dress, provided they made sure that no one, other than mountaineers, knew about it. One inevitable effect of climbing in this period was, however, sunburn which was very uncomfortable and also socially unacceptable especially for women and very difficult to disguise. Only female labourers – such the Wigan pit brow girls, one of whom was described as 'a very comely woman… complexion golden brown with brilliantly rosy cheeks' – were tanned. Indeed one male commentator in a rather patronising article specifically warned women:

'Climbing is very bad for the complexion. I would not dare in the pages of The Woman at Home to describe what I have seen in the way of damaged complexions on mountainsides. Lanoline may do something; masks may do more, though at the time they are distractingly hideous. But I think it must be laid down that any really eager mountain climber must be content to part with at least one skin. That leaves I believe six: so it is no final argument. But the process of departure is not beautiful. A skin will last longer if you avoid snowfields, but the circuit will often be unconvincing to the male members of the party. Still rocks are far less damning to the face, though they have a way of taking all the skin off your fingers.'[58]

Since a passive lifestyle was a hallmark of class and gentility for women (and men) it is no surprise that they were prepared to go to extraordinary (and largely ineffective) lengths to protect their skins with masks and potions.

Respectability went far beyond dress and appearance and English female mountaineers broke virtually every other social taboo– including chaperoning –

before the end of the nineteenth century. A shocking part of mountaineering in the late nineteenth century (certainly from the point of view of those at home) was for women to bivouac or sleep in mountain huts without a father, brother or sister as chaperon. But many of them did just that although some of the male climbing establishment did not relish it, especially the rather straight laced Clinton Dent, who openly derided the notion. The 1890s was a period when a young upper middle class women could not 'visit a friend two or three streets away, walk in the park attend a tea party, play or concert or even church unaccompanied.'[59] To contemplate sharing a tent or a bivouac with a man or men was just plain outrageous. Lizzie Le Blond wryly remembered that:

'...occupied with the joy of sport, I invariably set out quite unconcernedly with my two guides, and remained unaware of the enormity of my behaviour till my book revealed it to a very early Victorian grand-Aunt, who declared that I had shocked all London...'[60]

The contrast is even more striking for Gertrude Bell, one of the most outstanding climbers of her generation. In 1891, when a student at Lady Margaret Hall Oxford, she had written guiltily to her stepmother Florence Bell that she:

'...had driven home alone with a young man in a hansom cab. I don't think many of our watchful acquaintances saw me on Sunday, it was a streaming afternoon, I felt sure you wouldn't like it, but you know I didn't either'[61]

Eleven years later on an epic and potentially life threatening bivouac, on the Finsteraarhorn in 1902, Gertrude Bell, her guide Ulrich Fuhrer and his brother Heinrich were stranded for a second night by bad weather, failing light and tiredness when they were unable to light their lantern. In a letter to her father Gertrude recalled using her discarded skirt as a makeshift windbreak in a vain effort to light their matches:

'It was now quite dark, the snow had turned into pouring rain, and we sank six inches into the soft glacier with every step. Moreover we were wet through; we had to cross several big crevasses and get down the sérac before we could reach the Unteraar glacier and safety. For this we had felt no anxiety having relied upon our lantern but not a single match would light. We had every kind with us in metal match boxes but the boxes were wet and we had not a dry rag of any kind to rub them with. We tried to make a tent out of my skirt and light a match under it, but our hands were dripping wet and numb with cold – one could scarcely feel anything smaller than an ice axe – and the match heads dropped off limply without so much as a spark.'[62]

They spent a dreadful night in pouring rain huddled together on their three ice axes their feet in rucksacks all three suffering frost-bitten hands and feet. Gertrude's toes were so badly affected that at least one had to be amputated – ending her climbing career. The climb itself was an exceptionally demanding route for the period. That they survived at all was attributed by Fuhrer to

Gertrude's determination and courage.[63]. This kind of experience was not uncommon for top women climbers, yet broke so many normal Victorian conventions and remained firmly hidden from respectable society. It is even harder to imagine how, away from the mountains, Lily Bristow could have shared a tent alone with Fred Mummery as she did in 1893 or Isabella Straton could have married her guide, Jean Charlet. Yet this is precisely what they did.

English social norms and dress codes were not universal and a process of change that began before 1914 gathered pace thereafter. Continental and American women were generally more relaxed about dress and the bloomer suit was far more popular for cycling, especially in France before 1900, than ever was the case in Britain.[64] Different social values must have played a part, for there were far more illustrations of Continental than English women climbing in trousers and even posed pictures of women like Madame Paul Franz Namur who, in 1908 it was claimed always climbed in masculine dress.[65] Italian women, were accepted as members of the Italian Alpine Club from its inception, also openly climbed in trousers and seemed happy to be photographed as such. For most female climbers their functional clothing was just that – a practical rather than a political matter. A few were active feminists and of these easily the best known was the American, Fanny Bullock Workman who, in 1906 made a first Ascent of Pinnacle Peak in Kashmir at 22,600 feet with guide Cyprien Savoye and a porter. Normally with her husband, she travelled widely in the Himalayas partly by bicycle, her tea kettle strapped firmly to her handlebars. A keen disciple of female emancipation, her dress in public was extremely conventional. She was not especially radical in the mountains either and advised:

'For peak climbing... a short scant skirt reaching the knees is the most practical. On difficult rock or snow ascents this is easily removed and given to the porter and one continues in knickers only.'[66]

The often complicated nineteenth century compromise between appearance and practicality, which led so many women to disguise their functional mountaineering clothing, was beginning to break down even before the First World War. Plain speaking, American Anne Peck, who climbed extensively and successfully in the Andes in the early twentieth century, was perfectly open about what she believed women should wear to climb – trousers – and was unashamedly photographed in them. She thought the kind of compromise chosen by Fanny Bullock Workman, and indeed Lizzie Le Blond to judge by the photographs, was hideous and she was right. It would be hard to find a more awkward mix of styles, and one ironically almost identical to that worn by labouring women. As she said:

'A scant skirt barely reaching the knee and showing the knickerbockers below, such as some ladies have worn is as unbecoming a costume as could be devised;

and for a woman in difficult mountaineering to waste her strength and endanger her life is foolish in the extreme'.[67]

Though even she admitted to putting on her normal skirt before re-entering her hotel.

The sheer wildness and roughness of the Southern Alps led Constance Barnicoat, who crossed Copeland Pass around Mount Cook South Island New Zealand in 1903, to favour trousers. Walking and climbing in New Zealand is, even today, wilder and rougher than the Alps. At the turn of the century, when Constance made her guided crossing, she faced trackless moraines, glaciers, numerous river crossings and dense virgin bush. As she said:

Alpine Club Collection

'Skirts, even the shortest, are almost impracticable in such places, the mountains being very steep and almost pathless, while the moraines on the Mount Cook side are some of the worst imaginable. Two young Englishmen staying at the Hermitage, both trained mountaineers, said they had never known a place so destructive of boots and clothes, that Switzerland was nothing to it. Whatever boots you

Constance Barnicoat equipped for the Copland Pass, Southern Alps, New Zealand.

have seem to be run through very quickly, while on those moraines you never keep nails very long. I promptly sent for proper boy's boots, the heaviest procurable, with very thick soles, which I had well nailed and generally rigged myself out as much like a boy as possible, with a while wool 'sweater', knickers and puttees to my knees. Except in such dress the guide flatly refused the risk of taking ladies; and he was perfectly justified. I wonder if anyone realises until they try it, the freedom of being without the tempestuous petticoat? Whatever arguments may be urged against boy's dress for a woman anywhere within range of civilisation, those arguments do not hold good in the wilds such as we went through, where absolutely not a soul was to be met for days, except our own party. A real boy's dress is, in my view, far preferable in every way to a compromise such as the so-called 'reformed' costume.'[68]

In some ways, of course, her open advocacy of 'boy's dress' is precisely because the wilderness of South Island New Zealand was an even more hidden world than the Alps. However, that she felt able to say it publicly and, like Annie Peck be openly photographed, marked quite an important step forward.

A major turning point for women climbers in England was the establishment of the Lyceum Alpine Club – soon to be renamed the Ladies Alpine Club in 1907. Excluded from the Alpine Club and from most provincial clubs- with the exception of the Fell and Rock Climbing Club of the Lake District, women climbers for the first time had an organisation dedicated to their interests. Being based at the Hotel Great Central in London it was desperately refined – reflecting the public rather than the hidden world of women – and membership was tiny.[69] However, one of their earliest and most widely publicised events was in May 1910. This was an exhibition, organised by Mrs Nettleton and Mrs Le Blond, of clothing and equipment for women mountaineers. Well publicised and drawing national press attention, it conveyed publicly what women needed and used for mountaineering. It gives an intriguing snapshot of how far the development of clothing and equipment for women had progressed and the extent to which they were prepared openly to declare their preference for functional climbing gear.

Far from hiding their use of male clothing members of the Ladies' Alpine Club openly displayed it in that most conservative of venues, London and pointing to the need for light and serviceable gear, a report in the *Morning Post* declared:

'A very becoming costume has been adopted consisting of a coat of the sport type adopted by men, knickerbockers, puttees and solid boots with nails and other projections on the soles and a hat of a smart Alpine shape. When parties of women face the risks and hardships of ascending a peak, and even of expeditions lasting some days from peak to peak, it is necessary that their equipment should be workmanlike before everything. They carry their tents with them for sleeping out at night... There is a silk tent for example weighing only 16 oz quite waterproof and folding into so small a space that it can be put in the pocket. The minimum weight and the maximum of protection are necessarily aimed at in the fabric used for dress and shelter, and the materials prove that manufacturers have gone far to meet these needs.'[70]

Lightweight camping did not appeal to everyone though and 2 years before the expedition Mrs Le Blond preferred a touch of luxury in her camps in Norway:

'[Our] tents are of Whymper pattern made by Messrs Edgington of Duke Street, London Bridge and have proved all I could wish. They are absolutely waterproof, are commodious and are quickly erected. In them we have portable bedsteads with thin hair mattresses, pillows and sheets. The washing basins and buckets from fetching water were of Willesden canvas.'[71]

Women may have been totally clear about what was the best attire and equipment for climbing but outside the 'hidden world' amazement and prejudice continued right up to the First World War as one member of the Pinnacle Club reminisced:

'Just before the War, people on the road near Ogwen would walk backwards for quite a long way, in astonishment and mirth at the sight of my sister and me in our corduroy breeches.'[72]

By the Ladies Alpine Club Equipment Exhibition of 1910 the public image of clothing, certainly for top female mountaineers was changing, although the 'frill'/trouser combination remained the option preferred by the majority of English climbers in this period. Even male authors of mountaincraft manuals acknowledged that whilst skirts were normally worn in the valleys, they should be removed for a climb, and that women should do so for safety's sake if for no other. Thus C.E. Benson's rather patronising comment gives an interesting insight into changing attitudes and a growing preparedness to 'go public' on women's mountaineering dress:

'There must be no superfluous fullness about the skirt, and it must be as light as possible, if only out of consideration for the man with the rucksack, for into that it must go at the foot of the climb. Some ladies cling inanely to the artificial trammels of society, in the shape of a skirt while climbing. It is perfectly futile ... and the skirt will certainly cling insanely to the rocks and quite probably get irremediably torn off.' [73]

A number of small retailers and manufacturers began to take the needs of women's climbers seriously. In the case of lightweight tents and camping paraphernalia displayed, women were of course using what had become available for climbers generally. Their sports clothing was another matter however. In the nineteenth century women relied on their tailors and dress makers to help them adapt clothing, especially from field-sports and develop a suitable outfit, including jacket, knickerbockers and trousers and tailors' cutting manuals give a good guide to what designs were available. Those of Thomas Hiram Holding, tailor, editor of *The Tailor and Cutter*, pioneer cycle camper and founder of both the Camping Club and the Cycle Touring Club, contain very early descriptions of women's sporting clothing. In 1885 he wrote that:

'The Norfolk Jacket is still to great extent worn by ladies accustomed to travel and to participate in sports. I have seen ladies wearing it as they climbed with Alpenstocks the mountains of Wales: I have seen it in wear on the lochs of Western Scotland.... In the nature of things it is not what we may term a dressy garment, but it is at all times both ladylike and becoming, provided that the material be well chosen, that the garment be cut with style and made to fit with accuracy. If too loosely cut, if ill fitting or if ill chosen material or if ill made it is a discredit and by reason of its marked appearance a decided eyesore.'

But it his discussion of women's trousers – predictably not illustrated- which is especially interesting. In 1885 he pointed out that:

'It has now for a number of years been the custom for all ladies who go hunting, or who take horse exercise to wear trousers made of cloth or other stout warm material. I consider the fashion a good one, both from a sanitary point of view, for decency and comfort.' [74]

The big problem though for any tailor, opting to make women's trousers or breeches, he warned, was the impossibility of taking accurate measurements. Combined with the inevitable prejudice and taboo, this meant in practice few tailors were prepared to experiment with female trousers.

Some women certainly had skirts turned into trousers, if those belonging to

Style C.

LADIES' CLOTH KNICKERBOCKERS.

For Cycling, Golfing, Mountaineering, &c.

Made in Style H, closed, to fit into the waist.
     „   „   O, open,   „   „   „
                with waistband.
     „   „   C, closed, to fit below waist.
Prices according to Material—ask for patterns.

	Small.	Medium.	Large.
Waist, Style H & O ...	25 in.	28 in.	31 in.
„ „ C ...	27 in.	30 in.	33 in.
From ...	7/6	8/6	9/6
Camelhair Fleece ...	18/6	20/6	22/6

KNICKERBOCKER LINING.

To button inside Knickerbockers.

Light Natural, undyed...   ...   .   4/9

Style O.

Jaeger Collection
Westminster City Archive

Jaeger catalogue 1896. Ladies' cloth knickerbockers, 1896.

Amy Mounsey Wallis are anything to go by and they also bought boys' clothing.[75] Looking back to before the First World War, Jane Inglis Clark of Edinburgh and founder in 1897 of the first Scottish ladies' climbing club recalled that: *'...boys' tweed suits were the only available outfit for women'*.[76] The one British firm which did advertise women's knickerbockers as early as the 1890s was Jaeger with its close associations with the Rational Dress movement. However, given the greater popularity of knickerbockers for cycling and their use under skirts for skiing on the Continent, it is likely that many women bought their outfits while abroad. However by 1910 and the Ladies' Alpine Club Exhibition a firm called Thomas and Co, described as well known ladies' sporting tailors were producing very stylish knickerbocker suits.[77]

Other specific female designs, presumably as part of the trouser 'charade' were skirts which converted into capes. An even more versatile version with the name 'Universalrock für Damen' was advertised by W. Bocher of Munich in 1912 and could also be turned into a sleeping bag.[78] Boots may have been less of a problem although Jane Inglis Clark complained that she could not get suitable nailed boots in Scotland. However, James Carter the Alpine Bootmaker and Outfitter of Oxford Street London advertised Ladies Alpine Boots in the *Alpine Journal* in 1867 and continued to do so throughout the nineteenth century.

Alpine Club Collection

Tailored woman's climbing breeches, from Thomas and Co, 1911, the type of outfit displayed at the Ladies Alpine Club Exhibition in 1910.

A Changing World After the First World War

When women returned to the Alps and to climbing at the end of the First World War dress codes had changed for ever. The War had created a need for more functional clothing for women and for those working in munitions factories and on the land, trousers were widely used. After the war skirts for everyday wear became shorter and shorter, while during the 1920s and 1930s, trousers and, even more revolutionary, shorts began to be worn for women's sport. Recalling pre -war days Jane Inglis Clark commented:

> *'It is almost impossible for the girl of today to realise the great difficulties that had to be overcome by women in those early days of climbing.'[79]*

This is not to suggest that all dress taboos were swept away over the four years of the war, or that custom was the same for all mountain sports and for all classes. Rather, while maintaining respectability was *the* non-climbing concern for women mountaineers before the First World War, afterwards, certainly for the upper middle classes, dress just was not worthy of much discussion. A good barometer of how controversial an issue is in any sphere, is the number of column inches devoted to it. In the 1920s and 1930s neither the *Ladies' Alpine Journal* nor the *Pinnacle Club Journal* contained a single article on clothing, other than those retrospective ones by women like Mrs Le Blond, recalling past difficulties and dilemmas. Moreover both journals contain numerous photographs of women in climbing breeches during the 1920s and 1930s, and not one elicited a single comment.

That trousers became the norm for climbing and winter sports is clearly illustrated in the clothing catalogues of the period. For its ski range, Burberry, that bastion of pre-war decorum, shifted its advertising focus from women in swirling skirts for climbing and skiing to stylish, body hugging trousers.[80] It is a view confirmed in the *Gamages* catalogue 1926-7 which advised its lady winter-sports customers:

> *'Skirts if worn should be short, and the custom of dispensing with them, certainly for skiing, although never on the ice rink is growing. In 1926 there was plenty of evidence of increasing popularity of trousers instead of riding breeches'.[81]*

In the same year top female skier, Dame Kathleen Furse, reassured women that:

> *'The normal wearing apparel at a winter sports centre consists of trousers or breeches instead of skirts so no one need be*

LADIES' ALPINE CLUB
1925

Alpine Club Collection

Front Cover of Ladies' Alpine Club Journal 1925 – trousers were no longer an issue for Club's members by the interwar period.

shy of appearing in them the first day out. So long as clothes are simple and serviceable they call for little comment, but they should be well cut and of a suitable material. [82]

But even in the more liberal 1920s, which was after all the decade British women got the vote, the significance of the 'hidden world' did not entirely vanish nor did all taboos about women in trousers disappear. Bifurcated garments may have been accepted for sports and leisure and become increasingly fashionable for evening wear in the 1930s, but they were not normal everyday dress for women before the Second World War. [83] There were also significant class differences and while the upper middle class members of the Ladies Alpine Club, the Pinnacle Club and the Ski Club of Great Britain were blasé about wearing trousers, the mainly fell walking members of the Co-operative Holidays Association (CHA) were not. It was not just that their sport was less dependent on trousers, but these mainly lower middle and working class women often faced far stronger parental constraints as to what was 'respectable' than wealthier women. Recalling the 1920s one CHA member said:

'Preparing was great fun – hiking boots and woollen stockings (which were replaced by woollen socks when away from Mum's prying eyes!). Girls did not wear shorts – good heavens the very idea – and trousers just weren't the thing, so a good heavy skirt was the order of the day. My mother never realised they were really divided skirts. [84]

Although by the 1930s, when the hiking and cycling craze was in full flight and breeches and shorts more normal for all on the hills, women continued to be harassed. According to one pioneer youth hosteller who wore shorts:

'We had several people stop their cars and take snaps of us. We also had abuse hurled at us for being hussies and showing our knees. [85]

Until the mountaineering outside broadcasts of the 1960s climbing and mountaineering remained a secret and hidden sport, a world in which to escape from the trammels of respectability. The conflict of the images of Victorian women climbers and the reality of what they achieved are only intelligible in this context. Much was obscured, covered up and hidden from public view and women's clothing was just part of it. The camera colluded in the posed and artificial image of what happened – just as polar artists had done earlier in the century. Even male climbers were rarely seen dishevelled, sweaty or dirty as they often must have been. We have a view of what we expect from Victorian England but to understand what was really worn, women's climbing dress has to be set against sporting practicalities. To appreciate the imperative of concealment, sport and clothing have to be set in their social context. It was generations before the climbing establishment came to accept women climbers and even longer before manufacturers identified a market niche and began to make clothing and equipment designed specifically for women.

CHAPTER 5
Widening Participation and
the Market Place, 1890-1939

L.L.Bean, Eddie Bauer, Sporthaus Schuster, Blacks and Ellis Brigham are today among the world's most well known outdoor retailers and all were started in the early part of the twentieth century or during the inter war period. Something was clearly happening to encourage this kind of retailing development, much of it also linked to innovative outdoor products. But variations in the development of outdoor activities between countries meant that the patterns and experience were markedly different. L.L. Bean and Eddie Bauer are today perhaps America's two best know outdoor retailers and they have much in common. Both were started by outdoor enthusiasts who were also designers; both had mail order catalogues; and both were major wartime suppliers. In 1911, L.L. Bean of Freeport Maine field tested a hunting shoe – the Bean boot- and twelve months later launched a four page mail order sheet – encouraged, perhaps by a new US parcel post service. It was ideal for rural Maine and to reach out of state customers. Selling by mail order catalogue had its origins in the rural United States as the only way to reach a large, dispersed domestic market. It was pioneered by E.C. Allen and Aaron Montgomery Ward in the 1870s and evolved to an art form by Sears Roebuck in the 1890s.[1] Bean opened his first retail store in Freeport in 1917 and his business boomed during the 1920s pulled along by rising demand in the 'Prosperity decade' of the 1920s. Sports of all kinds flourished in the 1920s and this was the basis of Eddie Bauer's Seattle business selling tennis rackets. He did not move into the outdoor trade until the 1930s following a brush with death on a winter fishing trip. This inspired him to look seriously at alternatives to wool for insulation and he settled on down. In 1936 he took out a patent for down clothing and the Skyliner down parka was launched – the first to be produced in the United States. Both men's businesses survived and indeed expanded during the Depression of the 1930s, but what really built their reputations were their wartime military contracts. L.L.Bean designed boots and equipment for the military, his hunting background giving him a strong understanding of insulation. Bauer produced some 25,000 flight suits and a quarter of a million down sleeping bags and, alone among suppliers was allowed to display his brand label – a massive advantage in product awareness post war. They both gained a bulk market during the war and this provided a vital springboard to post war retailing development.[2]

The origins of Sporthaus Schuster, were very different. The firm should be seen against the background of the late nineteenth century development of mass mountaineering clubs in Austria and Germany, of the rise in Bavarian climbing in the years before 1914 (to be discussed at length in chapter 6) and the growth of winter sports in the Eastern Alps. August Schuster of Munich was founded in 1914 and became, not merely the leading climbing equipment retailer in the German speaking area, but perhaps the most important retail climbing equipment brand in the world in that period. Products included ski bindings, tents, clothing, crampons and axes. Never has a retailer branded such a wide range of goods and this represented the vision and drive of the founder. The brand- ASMU was created in the early 1920's after the name of the founder August Schuster Munchen and continued until the late 1960's. Many of the first public announcements of new climbing equipment appeared in the Schuster catalogue. During the period of the 1930s they were strong supporters of Paul Bauer's Himalayan expeditions, much innovation and customisation work having been done in their workshops. Schuster continues today as Sporthaus Schuster.

These are just examples, for there are many others round the world, like Paddy Pallin (Australia, 1930) or Aux Vieux Campeur (Paris 1941). But what they highlight is that the widening of the market for outdoor products and the types of products developed, was linked very closely to national conditions and to the way in which outdoor sports and activities developed. This was also true in Britain where a widening of participation in outdoor activities, from cycling to fell walking to climbing was not matched by the emergence of a mass market. Nevertheless this period did spawn some world class retailers – including Blacks and Ellis Brigham – which were also moulded by the conditions of the period.

A Widening of Outdoor Activity

Cycling became immensely popular and fashionable in Britain following the invention of the safety bicycle and the pneumatic tyre in the 1880s and their progressive improvement. By the 1890s cycling had changed from being the sport of eccentrics to a fashionable craze:

'So large had the patronage of the bicycle become that it had been reported many businesses were menaced, notably the tobacco trade, the piano forte and the hatters and tailors were crying out.'

So complained a bemused Rossendale Free Press in 1896 no doubt reflecting a reaction mirrored countrywide.[3] A vast cycle manufacturing industry grew up very quickly in the West Midlands. By the peak in 1897 it

Carrying equipment on a penny farthing was impossible; just 12 years after the appearance of the safety bicycle Thomas Hiram Holding invented cycle camping with his trip to Connemara. The 'baby' primus (inset) was specially designed to be fitted onto the bicycle frame using a special clip.

employed over 42,000 people compared with just 600 in 1881.[4] Thomas Holding helped to popularise cycling and the related, but much less popular, cycle camping by establishing a number of clubs. He was founder of the Bicycle Touring Club in 1878 (the forerunner of the Cycle Touring Club CTC), the Association of Cycle Campers ACC (1901) and the National Cycle Camping Club NCCC (1906) and, like his enthusiasm for outdoor living, his inspiration for club organisation came from Macgregor's success with the Royal Canoe Club. [5] By 1899 the CTC had 60,449 members and there were numerous local clubs, although at first only the middle classes could afford £20 or £30 for a bike. However, by the end of the 1890s a combination of falling prices, a large second-hand market and hire purchase arrangements brought the bicycle within reach of clerks, office workers and the skilled working class. Price cutting and foreign imports meant that by the outbreak of the First World War cycling was a sport for everyone. Tom Stephenson, the working class access activist, paid 30s 0d (£1.50) for his first second hand bike in 1910.[6]

As a specialist craftsman Holding never served a volume market in the way that Blacks' were to do in the 1930s and the overall scope of his business was comparatively limited. His tailoring brought him military connections, so he knew about tents – and he knew about the shortcomings of what was available and only the silk Mummery, produced by Benjamin Edgington from 1892 was lightweight at 1.5 lbs to 2 lbs. He also drew on North American style tents of the kind he saw on his boyhood journey. With a catalogue called *Refined Camping* he aimed at the pockets and attitudes of the heavily middle class ACC and NCCC which merged to become the Camping Club of Great Britain 1910 with 1012 members.[7] Yet this was nearly ten times the size of the Alpine Club and he was quick to grasp the very real commercial opportunities they offered. His own personal gear was state -of -the -art, but never viable for more than a few lucky individuals. Silk tents – like silk ropes for climbers – were prestigious, highly prized items for the cycle camper, but were well beyond most people's pockets. Cheaper, light and durable substitutes for silk were essential if he was to sell tents in any volume. His position as a prominent tailor was a help here, as he had links with fabric suppliers who developed cloth to his own personal specification. By 1909 there was a remarkable range of these of varying weights and capabilities which could either be bought by the yard direct from Holding for self manufacture or could be used for particular tents manufactured in his workshop.[8]

A lawn substitute made especially for him was Allene which apparently 'stood a 24 hour downpour in August without a flysheet'.[9]

Combined with other more standard cloths this allowed him to supply a range of designs with tents of differing weights and prices to order. A startling array of types of pole mainly in bamboo were available and, like his predecessors Whymper and Mummery, he experimented not with an ice axe but with a pole that could be used as a walking stick.[10]

Holding was interested in perfecting the entire kit and so went far beyond tents to include stoves, cooking equipment, carrying clips and paniers. Indeed as the originator of the cycle bag he was the first to identify the need to carry on a bicycle. But easily the most significant for the lightweight camper were his modifications to the Primus – presumably in collaboration with London based Condrup who were the sole distributors. He began experimenting with them in 1893 – just a year after they became commercially available and concluded that they were immensely powerful stoves which were just too heavy and cumbersome to be carried on a bicycle. It took him:

> 'three years to get a smaller size – 5 inches across – made and then it had projecting legs. So I devised a second model and had the feet set right underneath, the projecting pump shortened and changed the valve from the side to the top, christening it the 'Baby Primus' which is the best of all the Primus models . Still pursuing my Spartan notions re compactness, space and solid packing, I designed the So-Soon pans for taking the Primus stove inside...'[11]

Holding had a lively and engaging writing style and, like John Macgregor and the Alpine pioneers, his enthusiasm and personality spilled over into his books. *Watery Wanderings* and *Cycle and Camp in Connemara* became classics, appealing to middle class men and women, intent on escaping from domestic routines. The charm of his writing is partly because he tells his readers what camping was really like – that canoes could sink and tents collapse or could be awkward to erect. In *Watery Wanderings* the first day and night could have been a disaster because the canoes were overloaded and nearly sank because his friends had not quite grasped what he meant when he told them to travel light. Pitching the tents was also complicated and frustrating. [12]

Nothing swayed Holding's faith in the pleasures of camping provided that everyone remembered that :

'that the lighter the weight and the smaller the bulk, the happier will the canoeist be... if he intends to stay in a hotel or seek shelter in a house, there is small need to take anything but his bacca box and cane; but if he goes in for camping, and therefore for enjoyment and independence, for economy and health and for self reliance – all these things being inseparable from camping – he must necessarily take that which will protect him from inclement weather and keep up temperature during the cold hours of the night'[13]

Not for him the grim bivouacs of the Alpinists and even Rob Roy's habit of sleeping rough in outhouses could be avoided he believed if gear was compact and light enough.

Holding was an exceptionally good journalist able to bring his experiences to life. But, by applying this skill commercially in his catalogue and, indirectly through *The Camper's Handbook*, he pioneered techniques of 'relationship marketing' based around the clubs he had founded – though personality clashes often caused him trouble. He progressed from offering instructions on tent making for CTC members, to providing an illustrated list of appliances and equipment available from Maddox Street to AAC members in 1904. This was a forerunner to his own highly personal and informative catalogue in 1905. *Refined Camping* differed from those produced by specialist outdoor retailers, like Hills and Co or their continental equivalents, because it did far more than provide prices and technical specifications – although these were there too. It offered practical advice based on Holding's own experience and was aimed directly at fellow or aspiring enthusiasts, in the clubs he had founded. It was a highly personal document – almost a journey of discovery – through which he identified directly with his customers. He told them about his hopes and how he had developed his products, and showed how they were based on his own practical and sporting understanding. He was quite clear that since nothing truly lightweight was available that his mission was to achieve this. But he aimed to encourage customer loyalty too saying:

'...[in originating] my reform of camping appliances, I fixed on the highest attainable quality as essential to lightness, neatness and durability. To attain all

this, I pay higher wages than my imitators... Notes and illustrations... bring such original things as I have designed and which I believe are best as they are certainly the lightest [and most] up to date...The prices are the lowest compatible with the above conditions... When I made cycle-camping possible I found nothing, adaptable to it, and therefore designing and actually making or instructing others to make such things as would suit the sport...'[14]

The catalogue is interspersed with photographs of his designs in use with detailed practical guidance, with pride of place of course going to the Phantom Kit (described in chapter 3).[15]

Holding then was not a faceless retailer or manufacturer, he was a specialist who projected his personality and experience – in a light conversational way – to his customers. It was a style of marketing that was mirrored later in the Black's catalogues in the 1930s. But, outside the United States, there were few other equivalents before those of Graham Tiso's – the Edinburgh outdoor retailer, those of Tony Lack at Pindisports and Mike Parsons' Karrimor Technical Guides, all in the 1970s.

Thomas Holding, therefore, created a demand for lightweight camping gear and soon others followed him. By 1910, the London firms of Gamages of Holborn, Popes and Sports and Games all carried lists of lightweight tents and equipment, while schisms within the camping movement encouraged changing supply arrangements . [16] In 1906 Holding had parted company with the ACC, setting up the rival NCCC and losing his direct access to the ACC market, a move which led the ACC into manufacturing. The ACC set up a Supplies Committee to source items at discounted prices and a 1909 editorial of *Camping* emphasised that the ACC (by then the Amateur Camping Club following an amalgamation with the Camping Club which catered for pedestrian and motor campers) saw supplying gear as a key aim.[17]

Still a co-ordinating body rather than manufacturers, the ACC had a catalogue and offered similar kind of advice to that found in Holding's *Camper's Handbook.* But the rivalry between ACC and Holding rapidly became openly commercial and thoroughly nasty. Holding was sole supplier to NCCC, and ACC refused to carry Holding's advertisements in *Camping* declaring his tents were 'not in any way superior to those offered by the Club'. Holding irritably dismissed the ACC as 'a petty trading company'. [18]

It was only a matter of time before the ACC moved into manufacturing in its own right and this followed in 1911 with the establishment of its Supplies Department, which published its first catalogue in 1914 and included all kinds of camping equipment. In 1919 the ACC became the Camping Club of Great Britain and Ireland and a separate Society for manufacturing equipment – Camp and Sports Co-operators was born, soon to have the trade mark Camtors.

Even before the First World War the prosperous middle classes did not have the countryside or the new outdoor sports to themselves. From the beginning of the industrial revolution industrial workers had walked in the countryside for pleasure. But walking or rambling (as it was more often known in the UK) as a distinct recreational activity became increasingly popular during the late nineteenth century. This was especially so from the 1870s, when the Saturday half holiday with pay became firmly established in Lancashire. Rambling and cycling, from the industrial towns and villages bordering on the Pennines, were more than recreational pursuits. They were part of wider political and social movement linked to the socialist Clarion Clubs on the one hand and to churches, chapels and the temperance movement on the other.[19] There was also a synergy between rambling and cycling as the majority of cyclists abandoned their bikes in the winter months when the condition of country roads – then often just a combination of rolled stone, gravel dirt and sand – made walking an attractive alternative. Clubs proliferated from the 1870s onwards especially in industrial Lancashire and Yorkshire– starting with the Liverpool YMCA Rambling Club in 1874 and by the end of the century most manufacturing towns and districts – including Manchester, Burnley, Colne, Nelson, Blackburn, the towns and villages of Rossendale and of course Sheffield had their rambling clubs. The West Pennine Moors and the Yorkshire Dales were popular, but the Derbyshire Peak District, with its gritstone edges and wild, boggy moors were accessible from most of the main industrial towns. As a result this area became the heart of a hard pre-First World War rambling and climbing movement. It was here that the tradition for long distance walking – which eventually culminated in the opening of the Pennine Way in 1965- began.[20] Set alongside the massive explosion in cycling, as there were more than 8000 members of Clarion Cycling Clubs alone by 1913, this marked the beginnings of mass participation in outdoor sports.[21]

Wakes weeks – when all cotton mills closed – were the norm in Lancashire by the mid nineteenth century and holiday clubs and cheap rail transport had spawned tawdry, glitzy Blackpool with its instant entertainment. By the late nineteenth century the 'rational holiday', and a constructive and healthy use of leisure, became an alternative to the rival 'unhealthy' and decadent attractions of the seaside resort. This was certainly the philosophy behind Thomas Arthur Leonard – the Colne Congregational Minister- and the Co-operative Holidays Association. He founded it in 1893 to 'provide [affordable] recreational and educational holidays [for working men and women] by purchasing or renting and furnishing houses and rooms in selected areas.' At 22s 6d (£1.12p) for a week at the Newlands Centre in the Lake District in 1913 this was less than a week's wages for the average worker. Hiking was the most popular outdoor activity – although some centres also included climbing. Membership grew rapidly from just 268 in 1893 to 14,000 in 1911 when there were 40 centres including six on the Continent.[22]

Quasi-military youth movements – including the Boy Scouts, the Boy's Brigade, the Church Lads brigade, the Girl Guides and the Army Cadet Force all took off during the late nineteenth century and Edwardian period. With their fixed camps they helped to foster an early enjoyment of outdoor living and activities. Of these easily the most influential was the Boy Scouts founded by Baden-Powell in 1908, prompted by embarrassments of Mafeking during Boer War. Baden Powell believed that recruits to the British army were both morally and physically unfit to fight and Scouting was his response. It was a remarkable success and took the world by surprise. It had over 152,000 members by 1913 – though the heaviest concentrations were in London and the Home Counties, rather than the industrial north. [23]

The mainly middle class lightweight cycle campers were wealthy enough to purchase specialist gear of the kind supplied by Thomas Holding before the First World War, and upgrade it as they became more experienced. But for the vast majority of working and even lower middle class sportsmen and women, even the cheapest lawn Holding tent represented three quarters of a week's wages. Even had they been able to afford such luxurious equipment, there were very few outdoor retailers outside London although there were a growing number in Manchester.[24] But these served the specialist Alpine market rather than the general British outdoor market. The majority of walkers, cyclists and climbers in the industrial north were largely innocent of the availability of specialist lightweight gear or clothing, even if they had thought it necessary – which they generally did not. Most walkers and cyclists from the industrial towns – whether middle or working class wore everyday work clothes and their appearance after a long day could have prompted the following:

'What are these,
So wither'd and so wild in their attire
That look not like inhabitants o' the earth
And yet are on't'[25]

Cecil Dawson from Manchester was one of the pioneers of long distance walking and was by all accounts a 'hard man'. On one of his first expeditions, from Llandudno to Manchester, he set out with a male companion accompanied by a party of well wishers in a pony and trap. He was too fit for them and first the companion and then the pony dropped out with exhaustion ! His favourite area was the Peak District where in 1906-7 he developed the Marsden to Edale traverse which ,when frozen in winter, remains one of the best long distance walks in the Peak. But he had little, if any specialist equipment . He was one of the first people to avoid rotting boot leather by using the cheap gym shoe for fast walking on acid, peaty ground, although in winter, nailed working boots were needed. He did not even bother with a rucksack but:

> *'managed with poachers pockets fitted all round the inside of the coat. At the start of a week's tour we must have looked like escaped umbrellas.'* [26]

In this period the Peak was also the home of a breed of climbers quite different from their wealthier and more travelled counterparts in the Alpine Club. The gritstone crags became a playground for the northern working man, who developed rock climbing as a sport in its own right rather than as mere training for the Alps. Men like Stanley Jeffcoat from Buxton and Siegfried Wedgwood Herford – a Manchester engineering student brought gritstone climbing to its technical maturity and dressed distinctively:

> *'Gone were the flat cap, the gaiters and the Norfolk jacket. [Old photos show] white pullovers were now in vogue and the heavy woollen balaclava was becoming standard winter headgear. The general tendency to lighter clothing was symptomatic of the change from grip and pulling to stepping up from friction to balance as the basis of technique and from chimneys to open faces as the typical style of climb...'* [27]

was an adaptation in dress prompted by sporting needs but involved little purchase of clothing as all items could be handmade.

The pioneer Peak walkers and climbers were urban dwellers rather than working class. Not surprisingly the rest of outdoor enthusiasts had even less – whether clothing or equipment. Stella Davies is in no doubt that the middle class dress reform movement, which so shocked polite society in London in the 1890s, was not mirrored in working class Lancashire before the First World War. Women she said:

> *'...were too modest or too hard up to buy special clothing, not sufficiently go ahead sartorially...'* [28]

But there was one innovation which suited everyone's pockets – both physically and financially –the Primus stove. Used for the first time on a real expedition by Nansen for his 'furthest north' trip with *Fram* in 1893-95 and all Polar explorers and some mountaineers and adapted by Thomas Holding for cycle camping – this bit of kit enjoyed a far wider popularity. It played a starring role in Lancashire warehouse worker, Stella Davies' early meetings with her future husband Bill. He would turn up at one o'clock at the warehouse where she worked on a Saturday, accompanied by a friend, to cycle out into the Pennine moors. Once there the friend would 'make himself scarce' and 'equipped with a Primus stove, enamel mugs, food and tea' the couple could spend a night in a cottage near Grindleford. The Primus continued to play a central role after their marriage and seems to have been the only piece of specialist gear they possessed . She recalled that in 1918:

> 'our anxiety over our child was lessening, the infernal nuisance of baby-bottles was at an end and the war looked as though it was drawing to a close. We took a fortnight's holiday. Packing child, Primus stove , kettle and frying pan and clothes into the pram we walked across Cheshire, up the Langollen valley, over Cerig-y-Duidion pass and up the Conway to the Welsh coast'[29]

This really sums up the spontaneity and the toughness of working class walkers in this period who thought nothing of walking 30 or 40 miles on a Sunday.[30]

But it was an enthusiasm that was innocent of special clothing or equipment. Unlike today, working clothing was functional, warm and durable and was designed to withstand the elements.

The Interwar Craze for Hiking and Camping

The First World War marked a fundamental break in most outdoor sports, but the interwar period witnessed an unprecedented hiking, cycling and camping craze, which reached its peak during the depression of the 1930s. As the table below shows membership of clubs and organisations grew dramatically and new ones like the Ramblers' Association and the Youth Hostel Association were established in 1930 and 1935 respectively

Outdoor Organisations 1930-38.

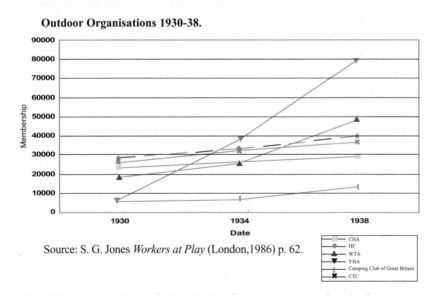

Source: S. G. Jones *Workers at Play* (London,1986) p. 62.

In 1931 it was estimated that during fine summer weekends there were approximately 10,000 ramblers and fresh air seekers in Derbyshire alone. Youth organisations were also more and more popular and membership of the

Scouts peaked at nearly 462,000 in 1933.[31] These figures underestimate just how many people were enjoying the open air in the period, however. Even in the era of the club there were many casual hikers, cyclists and campers who either could not afford subscriptions or who were not attracted to the existing clubs. There were some class differences as Richard Hoggart observed:

> *'In the thirties the craze was for hiking and though that seemed to me to affect the lower middle classes more than others, the working classes went on to the dales and hills and moors, which luckily are not far from most large towns. If hiking is not markedly typical of working class people, then cycling is.'*[32]

Climbing also became increasingly popular in the period, with a new breed of climber – the unemployed workers of the main industrial centres such as Sheffield, Manchester and Glasgow and they founded their own clubs.

L. M. S. & G. W. JOINT Rlys.

Delightful Combined Rail and Walking Tours

Ask at the Booking Office at LIVERPOOL (Landing Stage), BIRKENHEAD (Woodside), or ROCK FERRY for Pamphlet of ————

WALKING TOURS IN WIRRAL

giving a choice of 28 combined Rail and Walking Tours at

CHEAP FARES.

The Route to be taken on foot and the approximate distances are indicated in each case.

DOGS MAY ACCOMPANY PASSENGERS AT CHEAP RATE.

**Out by Train—
Walk across Country—
Back by Train.**

Superintendent's Office, Shrewsbury, June, 1929.

J. RATCLIFF, Superintendent.

F and R

Railway advertisement for LMS and GW Joint railways offering cheap tickets for walkers on the Wirral. As many as 10,000 per day were going in to Peak district on similar offers.

The dramatic upsurge in outdoor activity built on nineteenth century enthusiasms and was a reaction against the First World War. It can also be explained by a combination of increasing leisure and living standards for those in work, with enforced idleness for the unemployed and a widely shared faith in the benefits of physical activity. Standard hours of work fell from the pre-war 54 hour week to 48 hours in 1919 and, for those in work, the average weekly wage almost doubled from £1.60p in 1913 to £3.50 p in 1938, while prices spiralled downwards through the late 1920s and early 1930s.[33] This left more disposable income for leisure activities while gear itself became cheaper. By 1932 a brand new Raleigh bike cost just £5 or 9s 6d (47.5p) per month on hire purchase. Equally low price railway deals, underpinned by advertising aimed specifically at the rambler encouraged more people into the countryside.[34] The upsurge in activity was also inseparable from the Access Movement, the Mass Trespass of 24 April 1932 and the establishment of the Ramblers Association as a pressure group. Over a number of years owners of shooting rights on moors bordering urban areas – though interestingly not elsewhere – became more and more restrictive of access to rising numbers of hikers, planting signs threatening prosecution or worse, so hiking became a political as well as a leisure activity.[35] It is interesting though that proximity to urban areas fuelled the access problem for there were no such conflicts either in North Wales or the Lake District. These areas remained too remote for the weekend influx of hikers – but fundamentally for those urban dwellers who found their environment alien many wild places remained an escape – a balm against the unpleasantness of city life and the uncertainties of unemployment.

Just how you were affected by the Slump from 1929-32 depended very much on where you lived and what you did and Priestley's vision of three Englands in the 1930s sums up the position perfectly. If you lived in Lancashire with its cotton industry, in Sheffield with its steel industry or Glasgow or Tyneside with shipbuilding and had worked in one of those industries, you were likely to be worse hit. The Slump spawned a new group of mountaineers in Scotland and the Peak District who were very like the Munich group of climbers in Bavaria to be discussed in chapter 6. Rich only in time they bought little gear, hitched, walked and biked to the crags rather than using public transport and poured their energy into perfecting new climbing skills. These working class climbers could neither afford nor wanted to be part of the established clubs and formed their own. In Scotland these included the Ptarmigan (1929), the Creagh Dhu Mountaineering Club (1930) and the Lomond Club (1932). The Craigh Dhu, in particular developed a reputation for hard climbing and its members almost all lived on Clydeside and had previously been employed in either the shipyards of Clydebank or the Singer factory. Cost of living agreements drove many wages down in those areas dependent on the staple industries. But, if you lived and worked in the Midlands with its expanding motor industry, or in the Home Counties with services and consumer goods in the 1930s you would have actually become better off throughout virtually the whole of the 1920s and 1930s.

Interwar Innovation

In contrast to some of the Continental climbing hardware developments, the interwar period did not see many truly revolutionary changes in clothing and equipment in the UK. However, the growth of consumer income did encourage manufacturing and retailing changes which made it easier to buy reasonably priced gear, often on 'easy' hire purchase terms. Certainly, compared with the growth of the outdoor trade after 1960 choice remained limited. However, the expansion of Blacks, which combined factory manufacturing with its growing number of retail branches and a mail order catalogue, was inseparable from the hiking and camping craze and represented the beginnings of a shift away from the small scale specialist suppliers of the nineteenth century. Multiples had emerged in a range of sectors, including ready made clothing and boots and shoes before the First World War with companies like Burtons and Freeman Hardy and Willis. The replacement of bespoke tailors and shoe makers by mass retailing was a direct consequence of a combination of the late nineteenth century spread of the sewing machine and widening consumer markets.[36] But Blacks was a new departure for the outdoor trade. In addition a number of department stores began to stock outdoor gear with Harrods and Selfridges in London favouring ski clothing and equipment and Lewis's of Liverpool and Manchester proclaiming that 'In this great store you can get everything for Camping and 'Hiking'.[37]

Thomas Black founded a sailmaking and chandlering business in Greenock in Scotland in 1863 and this craft firm made hand-sewn sails for the neighbouring port of Glasgow. Even in the 1860s the coming of the sewing machine and steam shipping meant that, without changes, the firm's days would be numbered. By 1904 the second Thomas Black recognised that without diversification the firm would fail. His inspiration to move into tents came from America, on a trip to Kansas City, where he saw a firm making canvas marquees and decided to change both Blacks product and production methods. He installed sewing machines, replaced craft workers with cheaper female labour and began producing large tents for the army and for functions, in competition with firms like John and Benjamin Edgington. Inevitably business boomed during the First World War, when the firm supplied a range of tents and other large canvas items.

Like Thomas Holding, the Black family were enthusiastic campers whose first experience of outdoor living came in North America . Back in Scotland the family – including future inter war Chairman Crawford Black – regularly spent their summer holidays under canvas. As with so many outdoor retailers and manufacturers this gave them both an awareness of the potential commercial opportunities of camping and an understanding of their customers. The firm began manufacturing lightweight tents after the First World War and these were sold through their ship chandlery business. As the camping craze gathered pace during the 1920s, they began to expand and opened showrooms in Glasgow and larger manufacturing facilities at Greenock. It became a limited company in 1923 and opened its first London premises in Grays Inn Road five years later. Crawford Black took over the company in 1930 – the same year that the company supplied 4,700 tents for the millennium celebrations of the Icelandic parliament. Two years later the first *Good Companions* catalogue was produced.[38] In the outdoor trade most manufacturers and retailers were producing purely informative catalogues before 1914 though of course Thomas Holding's was much more discursive. Similarly, London based Gamages had special catalogues covering a wide range of goods, including outdoor clothing and equipment , before the First World War. By combining a manufacturing and retailing base with a wide ranging catalogue, offering reasonably priced goods, Blacks represented a major departure in the British outdoor trade during the interwar years

Even though there were relatively few outdoor brands, Crawford Black did not have the market to himself. Apart from long established firms like Benjamin Edgington, an important competitor was the Camp and Sport Co-operators (the successors to the Supplies Department of the Camping Club of Great Britain) whose trade mark Camtors was registered in 1924. The society had opened a factory in Grays Inn Road in 1926, offices and show rooms two years later and a branch office and showroom in China Lane, Piccadilly in Manchester in 1929. A new factory was subsequently built in Acton in 1931 and Grays Inn Road closed and in many ways this marked the peak of Camtors' activities.[39]

Camtors' first and most enduring innovation was the Itisa tent, developed in 1919. This lightweight, single pole tent weighed just 1lb 3 oz and was the perfect tent for the growing number of pedestrian campers of the interwar hiking craze. But since it was awkward to put up, it was unsuitablefor mountaineering.[40] In the 1930s they also made a range of rucksacs – based on Bergans Norwegian designs with the slightly jarring names of 'Camwegian' and 'Torwegian and several types of sleeping bag. [41]

Camtors' established market in the Camping Club of Great Britain and Ireland made it potentially quite hard for Blacks to break into the outdoor trade. But it was no accident that the firm became synonymous with the hiking and camping craze and Camtors did not. Crawford Black set about occupying the cheaper end of the mountain tent market and was also quite simply more successful at marketing In addition Blacks were prepared, by 1937, to offer easy terms which were consistently rejected by Camtors.

The distinctive Good Companions trademark with its rucksack, boots and Guinea Tent was the epitome of the era, with the name almost certainly drawn from J.B Priestley's popular novel. The catalogues – with their rich colour covers- were highly readable, offered far more than just price and product information. They combined details of what was available in Black's stores with a mail order service so a wide range of gear for Scouts and all types of campers, hikers and mountaineers was described in detail.[42] But the catalogues were also thick with articles by members of the outdoor movement and by editors of outdoor magazines, reflecting Crawford Black's personal enthusiasm for outdoor living and growing range of contacts. Lt Commander J.M. Kenworthy's (associate editor of *Hiker and Camper)* opening article 'The Camping and Hiking Outlook' is a period piece:

'The Camping and Hiking Movement is thoroughly in tune with the spirit of the times. Everyone feels the necessity of economising, and there is no way of getting so much enjoyment for so little money as to walk on one's own feet and carry one's own equipment on one's own back. So perhaps, high taxes and slack business will be a blessing in disguise for our movement...'[43]

Slightly patronising and 'improving' in tone with, of course, due deference to the manufacturers, one can almost hear the modulated tones of BBC English aimed clearly at the respectable lower middle class readers of *Hiker and Camper*, in which Blacks of course advertised, and who became Blacks' main customers. Like Thomas Holding before him, but lacking a personal club base, Crawford Black forged links with a number of the growing clubs though the catalogues. With blatant cheek he included an article by L. M Wulcko, the Vice Chairman of the Camping Club of Great Britain and Ireland (the prime market for Camtors) in his first catalogue. Entitled 'Practical Suggestions for Hikers and Campers (Pedestrian)' this outlines what he saw as the 'essentials' of clothing and equipment for both hiking and camping, including shirts, the interwar craze for shorts, a small rucksack, appropriate footwear. His ideal kit for the lone camper weighed between 15 and 20 lbs.

He went on to describe camping kit, emphasising the need to combine lightness with durability and comfort with portability.[44] Probably to avoid any controversy with Camtors, apart from a reference to the Bergan rucksack, Wulcko gave no commercial advice and indeed warned against too many gadgets, personally preferring improvisation. But the article was an effective marketing device for Blacks for, by containing a range of articles of this kind – the first issue contained others on planning a week-end hike, motor and motor cycle camping, Ordnance Survey maps and hiking and camping for women- the catalogues were far more widely read than a mere price list would have been. This of course encouraged the purchase of Blacks' merchandise – whether of their own manufacture or that from other companies sold in their shops or offered in their catalogue.

Camtors were no match for this kind of sophisticated marketing and their advertisements were lame, defensive and traditional in comparison as this 1935 example illustrates:

'For a quarter of a century we have resolutely maintained an uncommonly high degree of quality in the manufacture of equipment for camping or mountaineering. By doing so we have achieved a high position in the esteem of those who cannot afford to be other than good judges of equipment.'[45]

Nor were Camp and Sports able to compete with Blacks on price. In 1935 their 'Norwegian 'style rucksack the Camwegian retailed at 37s 6d (£1.87 p) which was precisely the same price as Blacks charged for the genuine Bergan.[46]

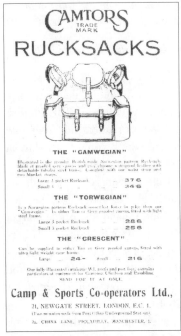

CAMTORS
TRADE
MARK

RUCKSACKS

THE "CAMWEGIAN"

Illustrated is the premier British made Norwegian pattern Rucksack. Made of proofed grey canvas and grey chrome waterproof leather with detachable tubular steel frame. Complete with one waist strap and two blanket straps.

Large 3 pocket Rucksack 37 6
Small " 34 6

THE "TORWEGIAN"

Is a Norwegian pattern Rucksack somewhat lower in price than our "Camwegian". In either Tan or Grey proofed canvas, fitted with light steel frame.

Large 3 pocket Rucksack 28 6
Small 3 pocket Rucksack 25 6

THE "CRESCENT"

Can be supplied in either Tan or Grey proofed canvas, fitted with ultra light weight cane frame.

Large ... 24 –   Small ... 21 6

Our fully Illustrated catalogue W.J. posts and post free, contains particulars of complete Camping Clothing and Rambling.

SEND FOR IT AT ONCE.

Camp & Sports Co-operators Ltd.,

21, NEWGATE STREET, LONDON, E.C. 1.
(Two minutes walk from Post Office Underground Station).
2a, CHINA LANE, PICCADILLY, MANCHESTER, 1.

Camtors advertisement for rucksacks from the *Wayfarer's Journal*, 1935.

In the 1920s and 1930s Blacks developed a number of lightweight tent designs including the Good Companion the Guinea and the streamlined 'improved' Tinker which was designed specifically for wild camping to rival the Itisa. The lightest of these was the Guinea Minor (which actually cost 12s 6d (62p) rather than a Guinea 21s 0d (£1.05p) and weighed 3.25 lbs. In addition, in 1933, almost certainly after supplying tents for the Icelandic millenium celebration alerted them to the eider colonies of eastern Iceland and to the delights of 'live eiderdown', they began manufacturing a range of down sleeping bags. They were not the first UK firm in this market- this was reserved for Manchester based Robert Burns five years earlier. But their sleeping bags became more widely known through their catalogue. Prices reflected the weight to warmth ratio and the degree to which they could be compacted and of course the expensive eiderdown bag was easily the warmest and lightest bag in the range as table below shows.

Table 1 Blacks Sleeping Bags 1933

Name of Bag	Rolled dimensions	Weight	Price
Icelandic eider down bag	9.5 inches by 4.5 inches	2lbs	47s 6d (£2.37p)
Special super-down lightweight	12 inches by 6.5 inches	2lbs 8 oz	35s 6d (£1.77p)
Feather-down	14 inches by 7inches	4lbs 6 oz	28s 6d (£1.42p)

Source: 1933 Thomas Black and Sons (Greenock) Limited *Good Companions Catalogue*, p. 36

These, along with their mountain tents gave them an opportunity to enter the specialist expedition market – both polar and Himalayan, which of course they exploited in their advertising.

The combination of modern factory technology, a growing market accessed through clever marketing and declining raw material costs (especially for

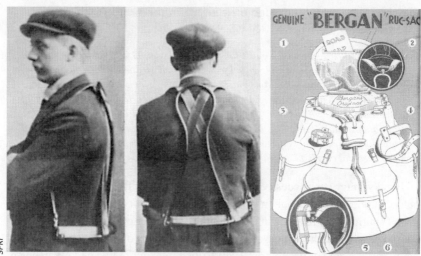

SPRI

Left and Center: Bergan with the carrying frame of his pack, 1909. *Right:* Bergan advertisement, 1937. Note the distinctive features which made the Bergan so sought after, note the early cord lock, which was used thirty years before anyone else.

textiles) during the Great Depression, enabled Blacks to manufacture own brand outdoor gear – primarily tents, rucksacks and sleeping bags. They sold these at relatively low prices alongside a growing range of other branded gear and a slot in a Blacks' catalogue, even in this period, was important to some key manufacturers. Of these easily the best known and most prominent was the Norwegian company Bergans – producers of best quality rucksacks in the interwar period.

According to the advertising material the Bergan Rucksack was 'universally conceded to be the most practical of all appliances for carrying a load'. Through the interwar period this carefully crafted canvas, leather and brass pack, with its hollow steel frame became a status symbol – the ultimate rucksack of the time. [47] It was no accident that a barely disguised Bergan is part of the Blacks trademark nor that Bergans received two full pages of advertising space in the catalogue – Blacks gained from being associated with such a quality product, while Bergans got access to a volume market.

Blacks strategy for building a broad customer base was quite subtle for there was a variety of kit to meet differing depth of pocket. Alongside Bergan rucksacks or the high priced Grenfell jackets, there were cheaper alternatives but without any suggestion that one was inferior to the other. Customers were not stigmatised with any sense that one kit was the poor relation but 'individual likes and dislikes vary so widely that we can do no more than merely suggest suitable outfits for the lone camper'.[48] These kits both undercut Camtors though they had the undoubted edge on weight. In the same year Camtors had advertised an 'Eleven pound' Kit which was:

> 'a special ultra-lightweight outfit for pedestrian campers, weighing 11 lbs and including the following items: a rucksack, 'Itisa' tent, featherweight groundsheet, four section bamboo pole, stub plate, twenty-four 5-inch Duralumin pegs in a wallet, down filled sleeping bag, Primus stove, water bucket, washbasin, canteen of aluminium saucepans and frypan, knife, fork, spoon and tin opener in a wallet, Bandalasta plate and mug, butter box, tea infuser, one large and one small provision bag, a lightweight down pillow and a condiment box for pepper and salt...The total cost is £7 16s 0d (£7.80p).'[49]

Blacks' interwar success exemplified the stage in the development of the outdoor trade when innovation was coming from firms combining factory based manufacturing with retailing and distribution. However other types of innovators co-existed, some linked to the specialist craft traditions of the nineteenth century while some were similar to post 1960 British innovators like Mike Parsons of Karrimor, Pete Hutchinson of Mountain Equipment and Gordon Davison of Berghaus. The first group included craft based manufacturers who, like Robert Lawrie and Ellis Brigham, moved into retailing while in the second was Robert Burns who used factory methods and an understanding of processes to reach both high performance and general markets. Like their Victorian and Edwardian predecessors these men had a passion for and an understanding of the outdoors. There was also a final category in this period – the Haythornthwaites of Burnley – who were not gear makers at all but who, with Grenfell cloth , occupied the position in textiles that W.L. Gore came to in the 1970s and 1980s. They produced a windproof, shower-proof gabardine which toppled Burberry from its monopoly of high performance, breathable, sport fabrics. They were not particularly outdoor enthusiasts but, based within Lancashire's long standing cotton traditions, they understood textiles. All these firms had close links of one kind or another to the interwar hiking and camping craze.

There are a still a collection of beautiful, hand crafted, burnished and beloved boots in the basement of the Alpine Club. These were made by Robert Lawrie, the Burnley cobbler who became to Alpine boots what Bergans was to rucksacks. Born in Lancashire 1902, Rob Lawrie learnt his trade in his father's boot and shoe business . A keen climber, his early life was inseparable from the outdoor enthusiasms of the Pennine Moors. In the 1920s and 1930s, while still at the small Family Boot and Shoe Merchants, Market Boot Stores, Burnley [50], he made a range of outdoor footwear for both climbers and hikers. In 1934 W.T. Palmer, author of the *Complete Hill Walker* quoted Lawrie's hints on hiking footwear, born of his long experience of the moors surrounding his home town, but also reflecting his strong preference for leather (which were after all the basis of his trade) as opposed to rubber soles:

'For moorland tramping and footpath and road walking, shoes are generally found most comfortable. They allow full freedom of ankle movement, and generally are cooler to wear. The question of rubber soled footwear is very much an individual affair, as there can be no doubt that people can wear rubber soled shoes and suffer no ill effects. It will generally be found, though that 95%, and probably more cannot wear rubber or composition soles over long period with any comfort. The reason for this is that the non-porous substance reflects the natural moisture (which should escape through a leather sole) back to the feet again, causing an excessively moist foot and thereby causing blisters through friction.'[51]

'We don't sell boots we fit them' remained Lawrie's philosophy throughout.

These were the origins of one of the best known mountaineering boot makers of his generation and a man who became an institution in his lifetime. It was not easy for a boot-maker from industrial Lancashire to break into the exalted Alpine Club/RGS supply chain – after all James Carter the London Alpine Boot-makers had been advertising their patronage from the Alpine Club since 1867.[52] But he achieved it on the strength of making a pair of boots for Ray Greene for the Kamet expedition. This almost certainly helped him gain the 1933 British Everest Expedition contract for 30 pairs of boots for porters, plus some high alti-tude boots for the Europeans [53] He could not believe his luck and milked the suc-cess for all he was worth. By December 1933 he had a new letter head and gone was the humble Market Boot Stores replaced with 'exclusive Alpine supplier'. In the window he displayed Dr Ray Greene's Kamet boot – an enormous boot for a giant of a man.[54] Burnley had given him the skill and knowledge to custom make boots for outdoor activity but was hardly a Mecca for alpinists. In 1935 he moved to 38 Bryanston Street, Marble Arch London specialising in 'Climbing and Skiing Boots and Equipment'. He wanted to be boot maker to the Alpine Club and capture the specialist end of the market, which remained heavily London based and he succeeded. His distinctive, custom made, boots literally lasted a lifetime and Charles Warren was still wearing those Lawrie had made for him, for the 1938 British Everest Expedition, in 1982![55] He offered a personal

F. E. Brigham

F.E.Brigham shop front.

service, remembered fondly by Bob Lawford, the current Alpine Club photo-librarian. A climber since 1937, Lawford recalled that it did not do to be in a hurry when you visited Lawrie's shop:

> 'He had a fine array of equipment and if he was about it was a case of sitting down and having a chat – last thing he wanted to do was sell you a pair of stock boots . Oh no, they must be made to measure and, having sold them to you, he would look after them as long as possible and if you liked the boots he would resole them and nail them according to your preference, he really did take a keen interest in what he sold.'[56]

Lawrie effectively became an 'institution' and his election to the Alpine Club, after the Second World War, was for his contributions to mountaineering as a businessman –even though his climbs in Switzerland, Austria and France would have qualified him. This was an interesting move for the Alpine Club where, in the nineteenth and early twentieth century, those in 'trade' or like Arnold Lunn with a professional interest in mountaineering were usually 'black-balled'.[57]

The other Lancashire-based mountain boot maker, whose career began in the interwar period was F.E. Brigham. Like Lawrie he was highly skilled and knowl-edgeable about boot-making and his customers' needs but Brigham's story could not be more different. Whereas Lawrie forsook his Lancashire roots for the exclu-sivity of London, Brigham's base – psychologically, temperamentally and practi-cally – remained firmly northern. Lawrie's style and designs reflected the tastes of the Alpine Club but Brigham served the climbers and cyclists of the Peak and Pennine moors.

If they had their own choice
all rock climbers would
say

'let it be a Bobby Burns
Rucksack, this Xmas'

THE man who tackles difficult climbs knows
the benefits of having a really good rucksack. He knows just exactly how it should
be made to be useful and yet comfortable, and
that's why he immediately says 'let it be a Bobby
Burns Rucksack' because he realizes that it is
the finest Rucksack on the market

PRICES as illustrated 18/6
TWO SIDE POCKETS ... ... 16/0   BUY DIRECT FROM
ONE MIDDLE POCKET ... ... 13/6   The "Actual" MAKER
          DELIVERED   AND SAVE MONEY

ROBERT BURNS
THE MAN WHO MADE "SLEEPING OUT" SAFE FOR DEMOCRACY
5, LEVER STREET.   MANCHESTER

Alpine Club Collection

Right: Robert Burns, Manchester clothing and equipment manufacturer. 'The Man who made sleeping out safe for Democracy' – linking his product to the Access Movement.

Yorkshireman, Frederick Ellis Brigham opened a boot-making shop in the Harpurhey district of Manchester in 1929. He was a boot-maker who loved cycling and held the 100 mile speed record. His first products were cycling and running shoes and he branched out as an 'Alpine boot-maker' before the Second World War.[58] Boot-making went on in the cellar below the shop and Bob Brigham recalls growing up in the 1940s behind the specialist shop which:

> *'was not much larger than the cellar. It was lit by a 100 watt bulb hanging in the window with another in the shop itself. The only climbing equipment available was ex-army surplus. The only socks were hand-knitted Harris Tweed wool; the only weatherproofs were camouflaged drill anoraks and sticky gas capes (which had a hump on the back to take a rucksack) and of course there were boots and more boots. In fact the shop walls bulged and overhung with towering rows of boot boxes, for my father has built up a good reputation for knowing all about boots.'[59]*

It certainly was not Marble Arch and customers were northern urban dwellers not the Saville Row elite. But like Lawrie, Brigham understood both his product and his market and liked talking to his customers. In the 1970s old customers recalled 'old man Brigham's' advice and the way he would produce just the right rucksack, from a tangle of goods in the cramped shop. [60] In the changing post war world, after F.E. Brigham's death, the shop moved to Cathedral Street, Manchester. With close links to gritstone climbing, through the Brigham brother Bob and Ellis, it became a source of innovation, while Robert Lawrie became a testament to a bygone age. [61]

Another Manchester innovator was Robert Burns, but he was a manufacturer and did not own a shop. But like them he was a keen outdoor person. A member of the Manchester Rucksack Club from the 1920s he was described as a man 'of courage, integrity and inventiveness with a sincere love of walking and climbing'. He was self-educated, sometimes outspoken but had a massive energy and enthusiasm which was reflected in his clothing and equipment.[62] Like so many outdoor innovators, he had an acute appreciation of what was needed and how it should be made. Precisely when he set up in business on his own is unclear but his Wanderlust rucksacks began to be advertised in 1927. This rucksack was not framed and at 21s 0d (£1.05p) was only just over half the price of the Bergan and was much lighter – though lacked both its crafted sophistication and the kudos. He had originally designed it for his own needs, declaring in an advertisement:

> 'The man who goes camping, trots the bogs of Bleaklow and Kinder and climbs the rocks of Tryfan and Scafell has need of a reliable rucksack. Such a man designed and made one for himself... he has now become a busy man. The necessity for thoroughly dependable slinging caused him to devise an entirely new method of attaching the slings, and this method for which a patent application has been registered is embodied in the Wanderlust Rucksack.'[63]

His own career as a bog trotter clearly gave him an affinity with the access movement which he unashamedly used in his advertising material. Indeed, access could be a commercial opportunity. In 1931 E.R. Buck and Sons, a firm with which Burns was connected, organised an exhibition of their Bukta brand rambling and camping gear at Whinnats, near Castleton in Derbyshire to coincide with a Ramblers' Demonstration.[64]

From his factory base, first in Lever Street and then in Hanover Mills both in the Piccadilly area of Manchester, Burns was, like Brigham, serving northern urban dwellers who loved the outdoors but could not afford high priced gear. He was an important British pioneer of lower price factory- made down sleeping bags and indeed 'cosy rapture sleeping bags' meant he was the man who 'made sleeping out safe for democracy'. [65] Like Lawrie this was the foundation from which he served the high performance market of the Himalayas in the 1930s – a story to be told in full in chapter 7- and he too supplied Smyth's Kamet expedition.[66] By 1937 Burns was a registered trademark and he advertised having supplied tents, sleeping bags, rucksacks, padded clothing and mountain stretchers to a range of high profile expeditions. [67] This made him almost certainly the only down clothing manufacturer in the UK – though it was beginning to be made in both the United States and France by the end of the 1930s. Despite developing such customised goods he remained firmly northern based, because he needed to stay close to his manufacturing roots and the skills which surrounded him.

So far all the innovators have been outdoor enthusiasts but Walter Haythornthwaite, the originator of Grenfell cloth, was not especially. He was more interested in Missionary work and attended a lecture by Sir Wilfred Grenfell – the Labrador missionary in 1922. Grenfell had found problems using furs because they were heavy and perspiration could lead them to freeze. He needed a light and breathable cloth. Quite why he ignored Burberry is not clear, but he struck a chord with Haythornthwaite who from his base in the heart of cotton Lancashire set about designing a new windproof gabardine:

> *'special yarns were obtained, the looms strengthened and weaving the cloth was a difficult job. Dyeing it was worse, for a cloth had been produced to repel wind and weather, so it also repelled the dye.'*[68]

Grenfell acknowledged receipt of the first bale in August 1923 and was delighted writing:

> *'I have tried filling it up with water and it doesn't come through, and it is so light and windproof it seems to me a solution to our problem of tackling the cold winter – and with its necessity for running at times up hills and at others 'sitting on', so that one does not sweat and freeze.'*[69]

This marked the beginning of a high performance fabric called Grenfell which replaced Burberry as a windproof for high altitudes [70] during the 1930s and was used for top of the market jackets for golf and hiking. In 1932, when Blacks first advertised 'Grenfell' jackets for hiking they retailed at 31s 6d (£1.57p) while a standard gabardine jacket was just 18s 0d (90p). But Grenfells were a bit like Lawrie boots and were indestructible, indeed as a fellow Burnley man Lawrie was a great fan of Grenfell jackets and did much to popularise them with members of the Alpine Club. Bob Lawford never climbed in anything else and recalled buying one from Lawrie's London shop fifty or so years ago which he still used in 2000.[71]

But for many of those who went into the hills in the 1930s a Grenfell jacket was a distant dream. Arthur Breakell, a Skipton post office worker, keen fell walker and member of the HF and CHA from the 1930s chuckled when asked if he remembered Grenfell jackets: 'Oh yes, I remember them, they were marvellous but I couldn't afford one.'[72] If someone who stayed in a fairly well paid, clerical job and became progressively better off during deflation of the 1930s could not buy a Grenfell, there was little hope for those industrial workers who were unemployed or on short time through the depression. He did have a Bergan though and that is telling, because a good rucksack had become a priority with almost all serious walkers and climbers. You could get your working boots nailed and many of the Glasgow and Peak District climbers wore their work overalls, but a decent rucksack for many seemed a complete necessity. Eric Byne tells of the weekend bivouackers in Derbyshire during the 1930s:

> 'The bivouacker... was a direct product of the slump conditions. For lack of money
> he would walk into the Peak on the Saturday to bivouac under a hedge or among
> boulders or in caves, lime kilns and haystacks. Such weekenders were numerous and
> could usually be recognised by their superior equipment, often bought after
> considerable sacrifice over long periods. Because it was necessary to carry a
> Primus stove, paraffin, cooking utensils, a weekend's food, sleeping bags and some
> spare clothing, it was also necessary to have something strong to put them all in.
> The Bergan rucksack, with its strong light, duralumin frame, proved ideal for the
> purpose.... None of them could afford proper climbing gear. They climbed with all
> sorts of boots, studded with many varieties of nails and often wore workmen's
> overalls or cast off plus fours, purchased for a song in the city's rag market. A good
> rope was a rare treasure, and worn out ropes were passed down and used until the
> very threads curled up in disdain.'[73]

In addition climbers were increasingly using gym shoes which could be
bought for 10d (under 5p) from Woolworths.

Harry Griffin, climber, journalist and for more than 50 years *Guardian*
diarist recalls his early climbing clothes at the beginning of the 1930s:

> 'A handful of us ..making an ascent of Coniston Old Man nearly 70 years ago – half
> a dozen young men in clinker nailed boots, wearing untidy old clothes, balaclava
> helmets and motor cycle goggles and using long wooden shafted ice axes.'[74]

And they were all in well established careers in the 1930s. Griffin did have
one luxury though – it was a pair of Lawrie boots in 1931 to replace his
government surplus ones. These boots were the most comfortable Griffin ever
owned and were custom made and were even dearer than a Bergan or a Grenfell
as Lawrie's ranged from 39s 6d (£1.97d) to £3 10s 0d (£3.50p) in 1933.[75]

From Thomas Holding onwards there was then a changing breed of innovator
in Britain who did not just consider what they personally needed but who pursued
the commercial possibilities of their development. But what this chapter has
revealed is that they did not reach a very large market and there was certainly not
mass consumption of all but the cheaper goods. Blacks had some impact certainly
– if W. Russell Flint is anything to go by their largely khaki shorts and shirts
amounted to a uniform for hikers in the 1930s.[76] More gear was certainly
available – especially for the mainly middle class campers, but the majority
neither owned nor seemed to want specialist gear. The pre-First World War
lightweight revolution was not really sustained and it would have been surprising
if it had been. Thomas Holding's gear was state-of- the-art and required
expensive special fabrics and workshop skills. The interwar period saw factory
made products and lower prices but it just was not possible to manufacture
cheaper tents to the same specification and tents actually got heavier. In Britain
the manufacture of high performance gear was focused on production for

Himalayan peaks and was concentrated on tents, rucksacks and cold weather clothing – but developments had virtually no impact for the majority who walked, climbed or cycled in this period. It was to take a range of social, economic changes and shifts in the focus of mountaineering and other outdoor activities, for a wider market to be reached. This is looked at in a later chapter.

CHAPTER 6
The Origins of Familiar
Climbing Techniques and Equipment

Karwendel, Tyrol Austria, May 1982

I arose at my leisure, content with the previous day's ski tour, enjoyed breakfast, picked up my skis and my pack and walked the 200m to the nearest snow. I put my skins on immediately, because the terrain started to rise quite quickly and wax would not hold. I pressed on, the familiar rhythmic hiss, hiss of the skins working in time with my thoughts. After three hours the Falken hut came into sight and, after that, the huge limestone wall, Laliderer, unfolded in a breathtaking panorama. 'There must be hundreds of rock climbing routes here', I mused.

'Don't get too close to the wall, but otherwise there is no avalanche danger', said Herman as he advised me on the solo day tour the evening before.

Yesterday had been a typical early ski tour start, as we drove through the foothills from Munich, crossing 2 custom posts, first German and then Austrian into a closed valley, always wondering what such apparently meaningless customs posts were for. We continued up through the beautiful Ahornboden (Maple Grove) looking so green and so different from when I normally came, on my skinny skis in mid winter. Taking skis out of the bag, Herman, Otto and Hans stared at my Telemark free heel skis, quite unfamiliar to them, and I began to wonder if I was making a silly mistake. The ascent was no problem, skis off at the niche, ascent to the summit, returning to the moment of truth, the descent. The snow was the worst 'porridge' I had ever encountered. Even Otto did not find it easy. My Telemark turns worked as well or badly as the alpine skis, to their surprise and my huge relief. 'I have never seen such skis since I was a young boy' said Herman 'this is history over again' I certainly sensed a sort of history amongst these mountains. But I did not realise then that I was at the very heart and birthplace of so-called technical climbing. Nor did I know that I was also in the region where the Norwegian snowshoe (which later became known as the ski) was transplanted into Europe following Nansen's ski-crossing of Greenland and the publication of his book in Germany in 1891. The very skis which I used on my ski tour had a 'free' heel and originated in Nansen's time. But they were rarely seen outside Scandinavia, so great had been the impact on technique of the 'clamped down' heels (introduced by Johannes Schneider in the Austrian Arlberg in the late 1920s. By the late 1970s, however, there was a revival, beginning in USA, which I had identified because of my involvement with Nordic ski distribution.

Front cover of Mizzi Langer catalogue, Vienna, c 1890's.

The memory of the trip and experience of many similar ones was especially significant for this book. Herman Huber[1] was the boss of Salewa the Munich climbing equipment company and the inventor of two 'breakthrough' items, the adjustable pressed steel crampon, and the tubular ice screw He also commercialised the Fritz Sticht belay plate.(the first practical mechanical means of holding the rope in the event of a fall) These items were certainly important to me commercially, I was their UK distributor, but I had no idea then just how important they were in the whole history of mountaineering innovation. Otto Wiedemann was a Bavarian mountain guide with responsibilities for training new aspirant guides and retailer training for Salewa. I was in Munich almost every month and took every opportunity offered by Herman and his team to go into the local mountains, for which I will be forever grateful.

Twenty years later, when I was researching this book. Herman accompanied me to the DAV (Deutsche Alpenverein/German Alpine Club) library. We arrived at the Prater Insel, the island in the river in Munich and as we walked to the entrance of the wonderful building Herman said 'I remember vividly as a boy of 16 coming here to help find and dig out all the bits and pieces from the ruins after the Allied bombing raid.' He paused and then looking me straight in the eye and said 'I don't happen to remember if that particular raid was American or British bombers.' I swallowed and then not surprisingly simply could not find any suitable words of reply, but was left with a feeling of admiration for the facilities of the DAV. Its origins were quite different from the English Alpine Club with it social elitism, though more like the British Mountaineering Council (BMC). From the start DAV was open to anyone with an interest in the mountains and now has over 600,000 members and 300 huts and a marvellous library which proved invaluable for our research.

Before completing the chapter I decided that I ought to fill some practical gaps in my knowledge and get some hands-on experience of some of the routes in the Dolomites and Kaisergebirge. It was also a rather good way to celebrate my 60th birthday with friend and British UIAGM guide, Bill O'Connor. We drove the length of the Alps three times, dodging weather and exploiting every window of opportunity. Bill's amazing knowledge of the Alps and our non-stop discussions about climbers from the past and their routes enabled me to get much closer to the subject. It even added something to the climbing. After many months of research the picture began step-by-step to clarify itself.

This is the story of 'the big wall game', taking the most direct routes up the steepest mountain faces. This is the origin of and, indeed, the driving force behind the innovations which created the style of climbing familiar today. Double ropes, harnesses, karabiners are all part of the picture as are the safety devices such as the piton, later the nut and still later the bolt, followed closely by camming devices. Alongside these are many 'invisible' innovations, including the means of keeping warm and dry, clothing tents and sleeping bags which acted silently in support and are largely covered in other chapters. Footwear is however so much part of the climbers technical tool kit that it is dealt with in this chapter.

The Story Begins in the Early 1800s

Already by 1811 the German educationalist and gymnastics founder Jahn[2] had installed the first public "gymnastics garden/place" near Berlin. His concepts and ideals had a lasting influence on both health and the active use of ropes. They possibly paved the way for the very early start of rock climbing around Saxony near Dresden, in a climbing area called the Elbsandstein. Climbing in this area is extraordinarily tough ,with some 1,200 sandstone towers of a maximum height of 80m, smooth rounded surfaces and plenty of "off width" cracks. The Saxons were a tough tribe, indeed the Bavarians, say of them that you have to kill them twice before they are dead'. They needed to be tough , for the climbing was quite unlike anything available in the Alps. From the 1840s – a decade before the so-called Golden Age of Alpine climbing- the Saxons began forging extraordinary routes. By 1916 they had reached the equivalent of UIAA[3] (Union Internationale des Associations d'Alpinisme) grade of 6+ (Elbsandstein grade 7c, British E2.5c, USA 5.10c) and by 1920 certainly UIAA grade 7. (British E3.6a USA 5.11b)

These were probably the most technically demanding climbs completed anywhere in the world and protection was minimal, but beginning to evolve. By 1915 the Saxons in the Elbsandstein made an overhand knot in rope slings, so that the knot could be jammed in cracks like a modern 'nut' and the loop used as a runner. Indeed when the first British nuts were introduced into

Germany, by Salewa in the late 1960's, they were hailed as an update of the original Saxon idea.

The Saxons' climbing techniques and fierce motivation drove them around the world with first ascents in many major mountain ranges by men like Hans Meyer, Oscar Schuster, Walther Fischer and the most famous of all the Saxons, Fritz Wiessner. Their techniques were closely linked to the Saxon sandstone rock, whilst their code of ethics was exceptionally strong. For these reasons the innovations which occurred in the limestone areas of Bavaria and Austria by the turn-of-the-century could not have occurred in Saxony. Climbing games vary with the character of the climbers, the region and the type of rock and a second group of innovators was centred on Munich the capital of Bavaria with very easy access to the limestone mountain's immediately to the South. The Bavarians have a long tradition of independence and this was reflected in their climbing techniques and attitudes.

Knotted sling used in Saxony from 1915 to 1928.

Herman von Barth was one of the early pioneers and made the first ascent (walking up the escarpment) of the Laliderer (where I started my story) in 1870. His style was somewhat different from the usual understated British manner; 'Whoever climbs with me must be prepared to die' he proclaimed, making his contemporary British climbers a trifle uncomfortable. If only Don Whillans could have been present his one line response to this would surely have been worth hearing. Some of the very early pioneers from before the First World War were still alive in the 1960s and Herman Huber knew some of them personally. In a recent interview, he vividly summed up the difficulties they faced:

> *"In the Northern Alps, Northern limestone ranges, such as Wilder Kaiser, Wetterstein and Karwendel, where rock climbing was fairly highly developed around 1910, new routes were hardly feasible without improved protection, and one of the forefront climbers of that period, Otto Herzog, I knew personally and he was nicknamed 'Rambo'. He was one of the forefront climbers who [gave] thought to how to protect our climbs and he got the great idea, when he watched Munich bricklayers at work, heaving up buckets with concrete or other construction materials everything by hand, as it was done at that time, heaving up on a rope, and they clipped the rope with the Fire Brigade's Karabiner to the bucket and this was the idea. Why do I not do this? It works, it's in the house construction, it is already used and the Fire Brigade also has Karabiners, so I clip it".*

Herman added further personal information about Herzog; 'Otto was a communist and after the 1919 revolution in Germany (which almost took Germany as it did Russia) when the Communists were ousted, Otto was hidden by his friends to save him from being assassinated The great thing was that his right wing political enemies saved his life by hiding him away, as he was their climbing idol'.[4]

Another of these Munich climbers was Hans Dulfer, (1893 – 1915) who has variously been described as; a climbing genius, a milestone in the development of rock climbing, a phenomenon, a star in climbing heaven, by his biographer, Fritz Schmitt (1985). He was not responsible for the introduction of individual pieces of equipment but he was the innovator of many techniques and routes. Either he or Tita Piaz is credited with the innovation of the lay back technique; the Dulfersitz (known as the classic method in UK). It was the first method of descending a rope without using the sailor technique of gripping the rope with the feet. It is rarely ever used today, polymer fibres will not stand for this sort of heat treatment, and few would know how to execute it. Certainly the combined use of the equipment and techniques and a good eye for routes created a series of fantastic climbs during the years 1911-14, before he was killed on the Somme in the First World War.

The third group were the Austrians, centred on Vienna with relatively easy access especially to the huge towers of the Dolomites to the South. In the climbing context Vienna and Munich were often referred to as "schools", probably because of their outstanding influence, They also had a limestone range, the Gesause, to the west of Vienna. Of these climbers the most important were Paul Grohmann (1838-1908), Paul Preuss (1886-1913), Hans Fiechtl (1883-1925 and Tita Piaz (1879-1948). They had their own codes, ethics and styles and, as a result developed distinctive techniques and often equipment. Paul Preuss , for instance had exceptionally strict ethics and he believed he should be able to get down anything he could get up. He was dedicated to solo climbing without the aid of ropes or other devices and he was not alone –however the context of this ethic needs a little interpretation. With the equipment and techniques of the period the leader was almost totally unprotected and a fall would usually mean death. Abseiling may sound a safer option than down climbing but probably not in those days, because the abseil route would be unknown and require quantities of pitons. Climbing without rope in this context therefore is not quite as reckless as it would appear when compared with the alternatives. He climbed 1200 routes – 300 of which were solo and 150 first ascents. He died climbing the north face of the Mandlkogel in 1913. Others in the group did use safety aids and contributed to their development.

For instance, Hans Fiechtl, (1883 – 1925) a Tyrol mountain guide and blacksmith, created the standard piton design, which was available through

Left: Munich climbing retailer Heinrich Schwaiger catalogue c 1902. **Above:** Folding bicycle used to reach the mountains and cross passes c 1902, depicted in Schwaiger catalogue c 1902.

until the 1960s. His finest climbs were accomplished with Dulfer and Herzog.

Angelo Dibona, born Austrian in 1879 and became Italian after the First World War when South Tyrol was handed over to the Italians. He began his experimentation with pegs and rope techniques in the limestone area Gesause, just west of Vienna in 1910. Herzog had pioneered pegs in his attempt on the Lalider and Dibona's successful ascent of the major wall was probably his greatest technical achievement. However his two routes in the Dauphinée are significant, the first ascent of the South face of the Meije the heart and of course the pinnacle which bears his name, Aiguille Dibona

Tita Piaz (1879 – 1948) was one of the earliest Austro-Italians to establish new routes prior to World War I and he was known as the 'Devil of the Dolomites'This was partly because of the boldness of his climbs and for his anarchic approach to all forms of government. His autobiography contains stories of him tearing along at great speed during the night on his motor bike, taking out a couple of hens and having a brush with a cow.

However, generally speaking the Italians did not start to make their mark until the early 1930s.Emilio Comici, (1901 – 1940) was very noteworthy of this period. Born in Trieste another town which has changed its nationality more than once, and perhaps not unnaturally considering the geology of this area, his earliest sport was caving. In 1929 he started the first climbing School in Italy.

Comici had a tremendous physique and in whatever type of physical activity he had focused he would have excelled. He chose to develop so called artificial types of climbing, mastering and developing the use of double ropes with alternate tension, the use of stirrups, and continuous use of these to take a line 'as the water drops falls'.

But the interests and skills of the Saxons, Bavarians and Wieners were not merely focused on rock and alpinism. They adopted a multi-sport approach to the outdoors and ski, kayak and bicycle became integrated wherever possible into mountain activities. The origins of cycling in Britain have been traced in chapter 5 and it was every bit as popular in Germany. The practice of riding from Munich into the long Bavarian/Austrian valleys was common; bicycles were hidden behind rocks or bushes awaiting the climber's return and continued well into the twentieth century. A folding bicycle already existed in the Heinrich Schwaiger catalogue of 1902 (Munich). With this particular folding bicycle innovation it was clearly possible, ice axe in hand, to have much more freedom of adventure, by taking your bicycle with you. Popular myth has it that the sport of mountain biking began in California in the late 1960's! Instead it was in the Alps more than half a century earlier.

Kayaking was also increasingly popular and unlike the English canoe pioneer – who had used the cumbersome rigid canoe – they soon had folding canoes. This breakthrough invention was made in 1905 by Alfred Heurich, a German architectural student. It was manufactured under licence commencing in 1907 by Klepper of Rosenheim, Bavaria. The Klepper Company was a supplier of various textile products, rubber coated waterproof jackets, and later tents for Paul Bauer the prominent leader of German Himalayan expeditions in the 20's and 30's as outlined in chapter 7.

Nansen's book, *The First Crossing of Greenland* was published in German (Auf Schneeschuhen durch Groenland) in 1891 and within a decade climbers were accessing rock climbing areas in winter by ski and made some early significant ski journeys . These included the traverse of the Oberland, by Paulcke and Schuster's first ascent of a 4000 m peak (Monte Rosa). This multi-sport approach to mountain travel differed significantly from the English tradition whereby people were either climbers and went to the alps in summer or were skiers and went in winter. There were a few notable exceptions who did both.

Society too seemed to differ somewhat from that in England. Without wishing to paint a picture of an egalitarian society, lawyers climbed with blacksmiths, who climbed with musicians, who climbed with university professors. Of course elite sectors began to emerge and the academic climbing club, focused on Munich was founded in the 1890s. The academic clubs were the key driving force in the Himalayan exploration beginning in 1929.

Germany was already emerging by the 1880's as the second industrial nation in the world and had already surpassed England in at least one key measure of industrial progress, steel production. Although the Germans were not the inventors of the aluminium extraction process, they were the first to commercialise aluminium production in the 1880s and this began to influence the development of outdoor equipment By the end of the century aluminium was already appearing in a whole variety of products for the outdoors, plates, cooking pots, utensils. It was, however, another 40 years before aluminium alloys appeared in climbing equipment. The first bicycle frame was made of this metal in 1896, by an American company made and licensed the 'Lu-mi-num' to the UK. But the idea was ahead of the metal's capability at this point.

While technical climbing was progressing apace in the Eastern Alps, the French were less obsessed with mountaineering than either the Germans or the English. Certainly there were many famous French guides. They were more obsessed with the bicycle and the world's first cycle show was held in Paris in 1869. It was in this period that the French passion for cycling emerged and by 1903 the world's greatest sporting event, the Tour de France was born.

The multiple outdoor skills developed in German speaking countries affected more than just the progress of mountaineering, it created a recognisable market, which in turn proved a stimulus to a number innovative retailers. The Alpine Club of London, in its groundbreaking exhibition of climbing gear in 1892-3, listed 95 suppliers and the majority of these were largely concentrated in the German speaking areas of Bavaria, Austria and especially Switzerland. Of the 95 retailers noted 19 were supplying food stuffs and the remaining 76 equipment of varying types. Some of these are still trading today including, Witting of Innsbruck, (the name changed to Sportler in 1996) Rodenstock of Munich (spectacles), and Lafontaine of Paris.

Heinrich Schwaiger was listed for Munich though Schuster of Munich was not. Founded in 1914, this retailer became not merely the leading climbing equipment retailer in the German-speaking area and was to become the most important retail climbing equipment brand in the world in that period,. As discussed in chapter 5 this brand – ASMU was created in the early 1920s, after the name of the founder **A**ugust **S**chuster **MU**nchen and continued until the late 1960's. Many of the first public announcements of new climbing equipment appeared in the Schuster catalogue. During the period of the 1930's Schuster were strong supporters of the Paul Bauer expeditions and carried out much innovation and customised work in their workshops. Schuster continues strongly today, although the ASMU brand has disappeared.

A crucial area of climbing innovation and every bit as closely linked to the progress of the sport as technical hardware was footwear. Boots were normally

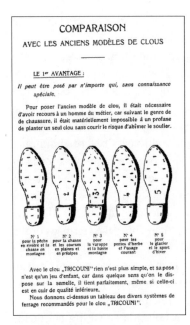

Tricouni Nails, Advertisement made in Geneva by Felix Genecand.

nailed –a practice which dated from Roman times. Very often the nails were used to protect the expensive leather and give the footwear longer life. This same principle was used when 'irons' shaped like horseshoes were fitted to wooden clogs in many areas of northern England until the 1950s. Climbers began at a very early period to customise the patterns of their nails. John Ball, the first president of the Alpine club, is the first recorded instance (Sept 1857) of a climber modifying his nails, "stopping for half an hour to screw in his points" whilst en route to the summit of Monte Pelmo in the Dolomites.

Félix Genecand, a jeweller by profession and passionate climber based in Geneva, Switzerland, designed a new type of boot nail and nailing system in 1912 which was a performance breakthrough. This was because he was able to harden nails for the first time by making them in 2 pieces. The hard gripping part was brazed to the softer malleable part which was attached to the boot by a transverse double nail. The hardened steel nails were aligned with the periphery of the toe of the boot. so giving the boot and the climber the ability to grip a much smaller hold, even to a small pebble. Additionally the nails could be fitted without the specialist help of a cobbler and ensured greater length of life. The name he gave to these nails was the affectionate nickname given to him personally by his climbing friends, "Tricouni" after the climb of the same name in the Salève near Geneva. Nailed boots were not only very effective on wet, lichenous or ice covered rock, but were better than today's moulded rubber soles. For many alpine climbs of the day, crampons were unnecessary because nailed boots were perfect on nevée slopes and good in ice steps. This very effectiveness arguably slowed down the progression of crampon development and usage.[5]

The critical issue with this type of footwear was insulation, because nails were perfect for conducting heat away from the feet. It was customary practice for alpine climbers to select boots large enough to be used with two pairs of socks. For Himalayan climbing the sizing was increased to allow three pairs of socks. However, simply adding more pairs of socks could not solve the problem and there were many attempts to improve boot design. These included

Left: 'We aim to advise on and modify equipment at modest prices' Vibram shop advertisement 1939.Vitale Bramani (used a combination of first and family names to create his trading name, later to become one of the best known brands in the outdoor/footwear world) was a wood carver and these skills were possibly used to prototype his first soles. *Right:* Vitale Bramani himself (standing right).

efforts for 1924 Everest expedition, Dyhrenfurth in 1936 and finally the Italian **Vi**tale **Bram**ani who developed what is now known as the Vibram sole in 1936/39, (the word VIBRAM being a combination/compression of the inventor's first and second names).

Rock climbing boots and shoes with various soles, rubber, (as plimsoles in UK) rope, transmission belting (as in Manchons in Germany) felt (as in pedule da arrampicata in Italy) were already in use around 1900. These shoes were often sold with the double function as hut shoes. No such footwear appears to have been sold by the British specialists and could only be obtained only from the Continental suppliers before the First World War.

The Manchon appeared in the of 1914/15 Sporthaus Schuster catalogue, and became the most famous climbing shoe at this stage. To help me understand this shoe rather better, Herman Huber once again came to my aid;

HH: The advertising slogan (of the thirties) was really interesting;

Kletter leim ist uberholt (climbing glue is unnecessary)

Seit man den Schuh mit Manchon sohlt (since one has shoes with manchon soles)

MP: So how good was the friction of this boot?

HH. Manchon was a transmission belt felt, designed for the purpose of giving high friction. However it was not so good actually. I heard a story from top climbers, one was Ludwig Gramminger, a famous mountain rescue man, a very close friend of mine. I learnt some of the old traditions from him. He told me that before very difficult crux moves, it was sometimes the practice to piss on the sole to make it wet and give it more friction for limestone climbing.

MP: Because this is slightly acidic you mean?

HH: Yes, but the boot should not be too wet but just damp.

MP: I learnt this technique in 1966 with old cable (ski) bindings where the thread is frozen and you shorten the cable to climb and then to go down you had to release the screws so the cable went around the lower loop.

HH: Yes of course when you have the uphill position it must be shorter.

MP: So we had to piss on the screw to unfreeze it.

HH: Very effective idea! I had the same problem, but I didn't think about it.

The Beginnings of Climbing Protection.

After the Napoleonic Wars the rope was adopted (as indeed was the two shoulder strap rucksack) as the standard safety support for mountaineering. From this point on there were 2 very strong influences on mountaineering safety behaviour. The first was the way in which the German tradition in gymnastics influenced the use of the rope. One branch of it had an alpine offspring the Munich based DAV 'Sektion Turner-Alpenkränzchen', (Alpine Gymnasts section) . This section still exists today. Similarly Otto Herzog was a strong 'Turner' (gymnast) and a member of the elite section of DAV Bayerland. [6] During the 1920s and 1930s British mountaineering writers occasionally made mildly deprecating comments about 'gymnastic' climbers in Europe. The root cause of these comments lay in differing British sporting traditions. Certainly the British strong tradition of gymnastics using ropes and beams in schools which only finally disappeared in the 1960s. If there was any gymnastic influence in British climbing, before 1900, it would have been quickly extinguished afterwards because of the strong influences of the literary aesthetes, most of whom did not consider that they were taking part in a sport. According to George Finch 'Mountaineering is not a sport, but a way of life'. Others considered they were participating in a craft and all the instruction books were about 'mountain craft'. The Navy certainly had strong traditions with ropes and, even today, at a UK public demonstration of naval personnel, amazing rope demonstrations can be seen. The British Navy were heavily involved in polar exploration through until the before First World War and Scott's fatal expedition. But their involvement with mountaineering was minimal. It is perhaps for these reasons that the rope was perceived and indeed used differently from in Germany.[7]

The second strong influence on the development of protection came from several thousand years of guides operating across the alpine mountain passes. As the new leisured classes arrived in the Alps in the nineteenth century, this created new needs and expectations. The development of technical and safe climbing methods was not separate from the 'rock engineering' that was done

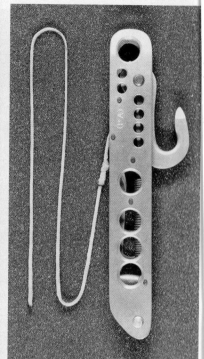

Front cover of Mizzi Langer catalogue, Vienna, c
op Right: Pierre Allain's decrocheur – 'sword of
s'. *Middle Right:* The first Brailsford nuts – the
ions of the British mountain hardware
turing industry. *Bottom Right:* MOAC and an
ottom Left: Doug Scott, Everest South West Face,
owing Karrimor box tents (first used in Patagonia)
oved critical to success on the Annapurna and
ace routes. Mountain Equipment down clothing,
by Pete Hutchinson.

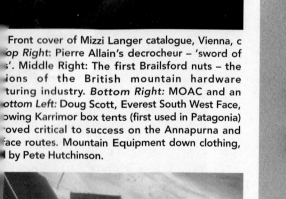

to allow 'safe passage' in the mountains, whether for walking routes or to allow guides greater safety (or to broaden their market for less able clients!). By 1900 the DAV had 100,000 members and resources to build mountain huts and the access paths to them. Each accident or problem brought some improvement to the path or road or the bridge. It became a priority to create a 'safe passage' especially across the passes and it was this which perhaps inspired the use of pitons in the mountains. To protect the growing number of DAV and OEAV (Austrian Alpine club) members between huts, on very steep parts steel cables and even steel steps, were laid into the rock. One of the earliest examples was the Zugspitz (Germany's highest mountain 2,964m) traverse, essentially a walking route. These steel cables passing through steel eyebolts on the walkers' traverse of the Zugspitz and elsewhere could have been the inspiration for a 'mobile lightweight system', which could be carried up the mountain as a team progressed. From this point began a long divergence in attitudes between the different climbing nations which led eventually to considerable friction.

Before the karabiner: Top shows the 'picture hook' piton. Below was known as the 'ring hook' piton.

Around 1900 in the German speaking areas there was a very broadly skilled mountain community, with a very rapidly improving rock climbing standards. For them the most appropriate safety rule had to be 'the leader shall not fall' – for he would be killed if he did. Many of the German and Austrian climbers of this period died before the age of 30. Many were climbing solo, that is without partner or ropes.

The second person could of course be protected to a small extent by the practice of holding the rope in the hands, but only of course if the leader was able to attach himself securely to a rock flake. This became more difficult as climbs increased in severity and this is where pitons come into the picture, enabling a lead climber to attach himself in places without any rock flakes.

From 1900 the first pitons, were the so called 'picture hook' type. They were simply a means of creating a replacement for the all-important flake, which held or protected the leader's rope, as he moved away from the belay. There were two versions of this, the forged version and the one made from a length of angle iron, with a short fold called the Mizzi Langer haken.

Up until this time, the basic abseil method had been to use the feet as the

Original Abseiling

Dulfersitz (now known as Classic).

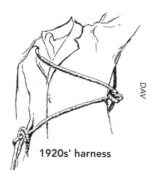

1920s' harness

DAV

Edward Whymper's single rope technique. He referred to this as a modification of a dodge all climbers use. The alternative to this was the far less secure grappling iron.

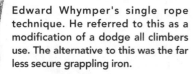

Karabinersitz

breaking method, and hands as a means of keeping upright, rather like a gymnast or indeed a sailor. This would have been Whymper's method and he also devised the first way of bringing the rope down after him.

Jean Esteril Charlet, (1840-1925) the French guide, is credited in 1876 with developing the next step in technique for descending a rope, where the rope was taken around one leg and the body.[8] (It is now known to Americans by the French word 'rappel' and to the British by the German word 'abseil'). But it was the Germans who grasped the concept and incorporated it into climbing technique. Because of this, the new method was referred to as the Dulfer-sitz (after Hans Dulfer) and known as the classic and still taught in UK until the early 1960's. An early device (still a possibility today if the one finds oneself without harness) called the 'karabinersitz' uses a rope or tape sling with a karabiner to form a figure 8 round the legs.Its application could be hazardous though and Toni Kurz died on the Eiger in 1936 when his knotted rope jammed in the karabiner.

From these techniques developed a method of traversing otherwise impassable areas of rock ,by first climbing higher and then abseiling at an angle to get to the desired place. This is known as a pendulum.

By 1900 roping up for glacier travel had a recommended technique, enabling a party of two to proceed with safety. The second man had a back loop for hauling his partner from a crevasse and additionally his waist loop was also passed over the shoulder, forming the very beginnings of the climbing harness.

Surprisingly late, in 1931, Dr Karl Prusik of Vienna introduced a method of ascending the rope itself. Immediately useful in crevasse rescue, observers at the time saw that there was a possibility for a mechanical device, but it was to

Alpine Club Collection

Top Left:
Farthest
Right: Fro
Cycle and

Top Left
1890's.
damacle
founda
manufa
Acorn.
1975, s
which
Everest
designe

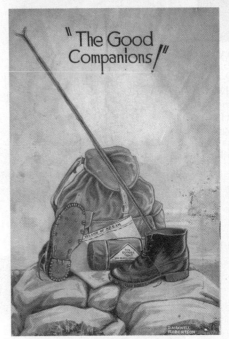

Bottom Left: Good Companions Trademark. This shows the Guinea Tent (the price when first offered) A Guinea was worth 21 shillings (£1.05p). Bottom right: Good Companions Front Cover, 1934.

Mountain Equipment

Marathon MK II

'KARRIMOR', Avenue Parade, Accrington BB5 6PR, Lancashire, England

Top Left: The Karrimor Marathon II tent using the first fabric to improve tear strength after coating. *Top Right:* Don Whillans with ME down clothing and sleeping bag. *Bottom Left:* Early Berghaus catalogue showing Peter Lockey on the Haute Route. Bottom Right: Front cover of Mizzi Langer catalogue, Vienna, c 1890's.

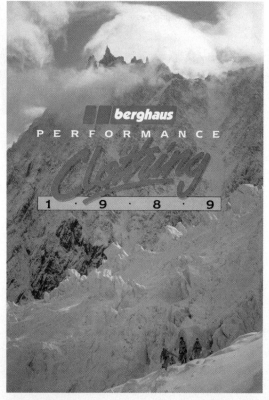

In the 1980s Berghaus emerged as the U.K.'s premier mountain clothing brand.

Canvas smock from the Nares 1875 Expedition, probably the origins of the multiple layering system we know today.

The SATRA boot as used by Hilary on the right still has the stretch outer boot attached, Tenzing is using his Swiss full overboots from the previous year, over his SATRA boots.

be more than 30 years in arriving, with the Salewa Hiebler prusiker and the Swiss Jumar. (It was the latter which was to help open the post 1960's Yosemite big wall climbing game by enabling the second to use Jumars for ascending the rope, instead of climbing.)

By 1910 pitons had evolved from the open sided 'picture hook' style to include a welded ring, the ringhaken, or ring piton, through which one of the 2 ropes was passed. This so obviously impeded the movement of the rope that an answer was needed. Within a very short time this arrived in the way of a small snap hook which had been introduced probably a good hundred years previously by the military for unclipping their musket shoulder straps, as they fixed their bayonet. The karabinerhaken (lit. Musket hook) was also widely used as a hook for tethering animals, hauling buckets of material on building sites and by the Fire Brigade, the inspiration for Otto Herzog. The French word Mousqueton, meaning a musket is the accepted French word for karabiner). The Kong Company s.p.a. (family Bonaiti) in Italy have been making these devices since 1830 but it was probably not until the 1930s that climbing specific devices emerged. What is curious, however, is that this same snap hook did not appear to be available at all in the UK until ex-army karabiners were released after the Second World War. The Fell and Rock Climbing Club (of the English Lake District) did an interview with a well-known Lakeland climber, Sid Cross before he died in the 1990s. He described his 1930s techniques, when karabiners were either unknown or unavailable. He would cut his previous year's hemp rope and tie off into sling lengths, threading onto each a large bull ring. The climbing rope was pre-threaded through the rings and each sling merely lifted off his shoulder at an appropriate flake.[9]

Pitons were also developed in this period and Hans Fiechtl, a Tyrolean blacksmith soon transformed the early square bar pitons into thin blades for easier penetration. They had an eye which also lay against the rock to improve strength under load. Pitons were still being sold under his name, Fiechtlhaken in Germany until certainly the late1960s and the design principles still hold today.

The Stripsenjoch hut in the Kaisergebirge opened in 1902 and presumably the demand was huge because it was tripled in size by 1905. A distinct turning point in climbing technique came about in 1908, which Tita Piaz noted in his autobiography.[10] By 1908 just about everything was 'climbed out' and every little pinnacle, chimney, minor pimple, and every ridge had its own conqueror who had given it a name'. At this point began the assault of 'the next last great problem', the West face of the Totenkirchl. The Munich climbers sought out Piaz,as probably the hardest climber of his generation, to lead their rope team and created a climb which is still today grade5 or 5-. He recalled how there was

O'Connor's Collection

Mike Parsons on the 1912 Dulfer / Schaarschmidt Route September 2002.

much celebration that Sunday evening in the Hofbrauhaus in Munich.

As the standards rose and the length of routes increased, there became less and less chance to find a natural and continuous line the whole of the way up. It was at this point that the additional techniques of the pendulum, and the tension traverse, with their use of pitons and karabiners began to come into play.

Pitons were in use probably from the late 1800's for fixing abseils points (as indeed they were in Britain, but later banned). They were to protect the ascent of a big alpine face for the first time in 1911 when Angelo Dibona led Guido and Max Mayer up the north face of Laliderer in Karwendel, Tyrol. Herzog had attempted the same but been beaten back by bad weather.

In 1912 George Sixt and Hans Fiechtl narrowly escaped death in a terrible night retreat on the Fleischbank Ost Wand, Kaisergebirge, Austria. I can understand the seriousness of their situation having done this route in 2002 with Bill O'Connor. The action of untyeing and pulling the rope through after the second tension traverse seemed to give a serious committing twist, 'it's upwards for sure from now on' said Bill 'we can't ab' off here, the sections below are overhanging' Fortunately the rain held off until we were descending the cable protected walking route in the dark, but if...!)

One week after Sixt and Fiechtl's narrow escape, Hans Dulfer and Werner Schaarschmidt succeeded. This was the first combined use of pitons, karabiners, double rope, involving the tension traverse technique for crossing 'blank' rock. (A drill was taken but not used). This tension traverse became a regular technique and was utilized on the Hinterstoisser traverse, an otherwise impassable section, on the north face of the Eiger. However, once on it there is no way back and the Hinterstoisser traverse resulted in several deaths when bad weather forced a retreat.

During the 1920's as it came to be realised that with the use of pitons and linked karabiners it was easier to hold a falling climber. The rope, which had until then been simply held in the hand, was taken around the shoulder, tensioning from the hip. The start of 'artificial' climbing in the same period, saw the use of stirrups (or 'etriers' as the English language absorbed the French). These also arguably gave the shoulder belay more impetus, because the lead climber often needed tension on alternate ropes. (Although made to a standard, the Alpine Club 'red thread' being the first in 1864, these ropes had

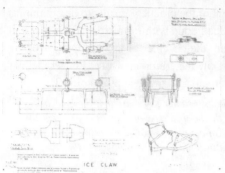

ICE CLAW

Grivel Collection

Right: Eckenstein at the competition he ran for cramponing. The images on the left show the Eckenstein Crampon.

very little elasticity to absorb the energy of a fall as with today's ropes and attaching oneself to the rock would simply have imposed a terrible shock load on a falling climber).

Enter the Ice Men.

Oscar Eckenstein was a founder member of the Climbers' Club. He was known as a blunt tactless character who was contemptuous of the establishment but commanded respect from others. Alistair Crowley wrote , "Eckenstein was the noblest man I have ever known. His integrity was absolute."[11] He climbed and went on expeditions together with Conway, Mummery, Compton (the British artist who lived in Germany), Martin Lindsay, Norman Collie, and others. He was a British railway engineer of German origin and designed a new 10 point crampon between 1908 and 1912. He approached Henry Grivel of Courmayeur with his design who was rather doubtful, but realised that this Englishman had the money to pay for the work to be done.[12] This crampon created a new method of climbing without step cutting, and effectively provided the foundation for all crampon technique to follow. To prove its effectiveness he organised a race, 'concours de cramponeurs'.

In a remarkable article in the *Climbers Club Journal* of June 1907, Arthur Andrews outlined all the reasons why crampons should be used, in other words to create a new rule, or at least dispense with an existing one, that is 'crampons shalt not be used'. This article is a highly persuasive analysis which deals with all possible objections to use of a certain type of equipment. [13] At its heart lies the key to why the British were left behind by Continental climbers in this period – differing ethics and climbing traditions. Andrews pointed out:

> *'While in the case of rock climbing true climbers have discountenanced pitons, iron pegs and fixed ropes, etc. except in so far as they have been really necessary for the safety of an expedition, ice has never been granted any quarter'.*

After a further a quarter of a page of examples, he established that the use of crampons is 'not a question of ethics but of the practical results to be obtained'.

He outlined the experimentation he had done with Professor J B Farmer and Mr J.C. Morland and Mr O. Eckenstein, the designer of the crampon, over the previous four years. His description of how the crampons worked is very telling in terms of how bad crampons really were prior to the Eckenstein model:

'The spikes are also arranged in a different manner to ensure that the heel spikes shall touch the ice in all cases before the boot in descending. In ascending, the front spikes touch the ice before the toe of the boot, and in traversing to the right or left the side spikes are so placed that they naturally bite the ice before the side of the sole can touch it.'

He then set out to prove: '(a) that it is possible to walk with a feeling of security on slopes up to 50 degrees. (b) That the fancied security is a real one'. The rest of the article outlined four years of experimentation and even contained the counter argument to those who might say that carrying crampons weighing 2.5 lbs was a waste of energy. "Crampons are so much more efficient that because of the time saved, one may omit certain extra gear." (Implying bivouac gear) [14]

Crampons were indeed gradually adopted over the next two decades but pitons and karabiners, were not . Amongst the early writers of instruction books; Claude Benson in 1909, George Abraham in 1907 and Harold Raeburn in 1920 all referred to pitons being used in descent but never in ascent. E.A.Broom climbed the South Wall of the Marmolata in 1906, he came across 'small pitons, which were of course, useless for ascending' so could only be supposed to have been fixed by a former party with a view to possible descent.

C.F.Meade's comments in the late 1930's, showed a complete lack of any technical understanding, but not unnaturally a lack of sympathy, with the German developments because of the rise of the Nazi party. The world was at war when he wrote;

'it seems as if the present phase in the evolution of mountaineering has evoked a new type of climber adapted to an environment that has become more and more exacting in consequence of the so-called exhaustion of the Alps. This new type of climber, proud in his skill in the use of hammers, pegs, rope rings, balustrades, stirrups, slings and pulleys, finds a new source of joy in a mystical worship of danger as an end in itself, so that he considers even the most foolish feat praiseworthy, as long as courage, skill and endurance are displayed in performing it. In the sinister shadow of the Eigerwand the votaries of the strange cult have sought their Valhalla.'

He went further to say;

'60 hand forged pegs with rings attached were a heavy burden. Twenty of them a foot long, were for use on ice walls, and 40 of a shorter kind were intended for hammering into crevices in the rock face in places where otherwise hand holds would be lacking.' [15]

It can be seen ,therefore, that the style of climbing described in this chapter was not practised by British but indeed was totally misunderstood by them. They had focused their activities on the snow summits of Switzerland, and everything beyond which was still a virgin summit. Good relations and sometimes superb partnerships with Swiss guides had certainly been a contributing factor to their retention of step cutting.

After the innovative period of Mummery (d1895) this was the last time British mountaineers were at the leading edge until 1954 when Brown & Whillans arrived in Chamonix with gritstone techniques, but perhaps more importantly, not knowing what they were not supposed to do. British mountaineering focused on the 'Summiting game' around the world, ignoring, even abhorring the quest for more and more difficult and technical alpine north face routes. This Summiting game, pursued to the exclusion of all other mountaineering 'games', did eventually culminate in an amazing first ascent of Everest by the British in 1953, which should not have happened if one makes judgements by studying climbing form over the previous two decades.

Until the Eckenstein crampon, ice axes had been rather long and always used double handed. At this point with the Eckenstein technique, axes were shortened and often held by the head, using the point of the shaft as the balancing (third) point of contact with the ice. Pictures of the day indicate that this technique was indeed the very origins of what which became known as flat foot or 'French technique'. Armand Charlet (1900-1975) the French guide developed it into almost an art form. Working in Chamonix at E.N.S.A. (École Nationale de Ski et Alpinisme) Charlet, followed by Andre Contamine, taught the technique to the world. The Bavarians, however, did it their way.

In 1923, Bavarian Willo Welzenbach repeated the Dulfer route, which had become the test piece for aspiring climbers. One year later, an older colleague, Fritz Rigele aroused Welzenbach's ambition with the idea of doing the north face of the Grosse Wiesbachhorn. [16] At this point, ice climbing technique had still not moved onto really steep ground and Rigele observed, 'even with such aids as the Eckenstein crampon and shorter axe 75 degree steep ice could not be mastered.' Ice climbing obviously needed rethinking and he had had the idea of an ice peg following a misunderstood conversation with Herman Angerer in 1922. Benighted on the Schrammacher North West face, Angerer had hung his lantern on a peg, driven into a rock crack at the edge of an ice slope in order to allow him to see where to cut further steps. Rigele misinterpreted this to mean that he had actually banged the peg into the ice. However, he tested prototype ice pegs with Georg Bilgeri and was delighted when they froze so solidly into the ice. For his first climb with Welzenbach he had three pegs made to his own specifications, about eight inches long and amazingly with a 'rectangular box cross-section', the steel being harder than for rock pegs. The birth of this new technique, and indeed completion of a significant new face route on ice, the Grosse Wiesbachhorn in 1924, should be described in Welzenbach's own words:

'The first of several pegs was hammered into the ice. Step after step and hold after hold were carved out of the cliff. Our numb fingers grasped these thin nicks, and slowly we eased our bodies upwards. Metre by metre we were forcing the route and all the details remain clearly imprinted on my mind; directly above me Rigele still clinging to the ice. Cautiously, so that the swinging action of his ice axe did not unbalance him, he cut one step after another, working his way upwards in the manner of a complete master. I paid the closest attention to every movement of my companion. Uneasily I watched the rope running out, praying above all that it would reach the next stance. But it was not long enough and just a few metres below a ledge promising deliverance Rigele called on me to follow. Gingerly I moved upwards testing each step deliberately while it required a supreme effort on Rigele's part to hold out on his tiny stance. Suddenly he yelled frantically 'hurry, hurry, I can't stand here any longer.' One thought only flashed through my mind: 'God help us if he falls now'. I hastened up to the next peg, grabbing the running belay and relieved the situation by calling out, 'carry on.' Immediately he continued upwards and soon disappeared from view behind an ice rib rising at the right-hand edge of the recess in the face. Just a few more metres, then the crux was overcome, and he shouted down jubilantly, 'climb when you're ready.'[17]

The angle of this ice bulge, which was the crux pitch was estimated by Welzenbach as 75-80 degrees in his report for the annual journal of the Munich academic Alpine club. Welzenbach was well known for his factual accuracy, his personal notes often being used for guide book descriptions.

Sadly this route no longer exists, history melting into oblivion with the onslaught of global warming!

This was the breakthrough, the fusion of rock and ice techniques which took the newly developed rope protection techniques and the new way of using crampons, with shorter axe of course, into the Western Alps. Over the next 12 years, despite a lay-off of three years with a serious illness which left him with a weakened arm, Welzenbach climbed a further 13 major north wall routes, the shortest route being the 600 m Grossglockner North face with rock of grade 4 and ice up to 65 degrees. Dent d'Herens, Lyskamm, Grosse Fieschhorn, Aiguille des Grand Charmoz followed by eight others. [18]

He climbed just about everything, except the North Face of the Matterhorn and of course the Eiger. The ice and rock pitches on these routes were, in many cases, steeper or higher grade than the Eiger. These routes were not only the proof that the Eiger was possible, but of course the root source of the inspiration. What was different about the Eiger was the huge subjective danger and its growing notoriety.

Before his death from hunger, illness and cold on Nanga Parbat in 1934 (leader Willy Merkl), Welzenbach climbed very extensively throughout the Alps, repeating many of the key routes. His comparisons and overview enabled him to propose a new grading structure for alpine routes. The guidebooks from the beginning of the early 1900s had been superceded and could not absorb the new levels of difficulty. The grading structure he proposed was eventually to become the UIAA scale.

Willo Welzenbach had grasped, both literally and metaphorically, the rope and safety techniques which had been introduced by Dulfer, Herzog, Fiechtl, Dibona and Piaz, and transferred them to the Great North faces of the Alps using his partner Rigele's innovation, the ice piton.

It is for these outstanding innovative achievements that Willo Welzenbach is known as the 'father of modern Alpinism'.

The 'Bare Knuckle Fight' (Mid 1930s – mid 1950s)
The Techniques Existed But Not the Clothing and Bivouac Gear

The 1930s was the most serious, boldest and most highly publicised climbing period and it has never been equalled. The rapid acceleration of techniques, following Dulfer and Welzenbach, meant that the 'last great problems' were achieved before warm and waterproof garments and bivouac gear had been developed to match the conditions. This factor alone , underlined the seriousness of the climbs.

The fanfare that surrounded the so-called 'last great problems', the Eiger North Face, Grande Jorasses, Cima Grande, was clouded by political overtones which often obscured the achievements. This is how German climber Rudolph Peters described clothing and hemp ropes in his book, 'Die Norwand der Grandes Jorasses' (1935). *The North Wall of the Grandes Jorasses*:

> *'Our retreat was decided. I was abseiling down into the spindrift and on arriving at the end I left the rope free for Rudi (Haringer). When he arrived I had fixed the next ice piton and so we went on down in monotonous sequence. For a long time we had been completely soaked and then our clothing froze to form a hard shell. The ropes had turned into heavy cables, which became more and more difficult, making the abseiling infinitely painful. Always there was the uncertainty of being able to find a stance after the next 40m, if not then our fate would be decided. If I were to slide off the end after some frightful period of clinging to the ropes, knotting the frozen rope (ends) being impossible, my companion would have to share my fate. For half an hour I have been penduluming back and forth over the iced up slabs, at the utmost end of the rope, until the piton found its place somewhere. We were caught in a desperate game with death, our lives being simply the table money in a game of roulette'.*

He went back one year later and made the first ascent, with Martin Meyer.

In 1930, shortly before Willo Welzenbach died on Nanga Parbat, Laurent

Grivel, a guide and equipment manufacturer from Courmayeur in Italy introduced the first 12-point crampons. Facing inwards and in a forwards direction was now possible, instead of zigzagging one's way up by cutting steps or using the sophisticated body angulation techniques, which were by now so well loved by the French. Long debates began on the differences between the two systems and styles and continued for many years.

Herman Huber tells the story of the origins of these crampons and their usage:[19]

> 'It is not clear when 12-point crampons arrived in Germany, but Ludwig Gramminger (head of the Bavarian Mountain Rescue and innovator of several products including the famous 'tragsitz' – the seat on a cable which saved lives in 1957 when Corti was plucked off the Eiger) had an extra two points welded onto his Stubai 10 pointers by the time of the 1936 Eiger rescue. This was when the Bavarian Mountain Rescue went to try to help two Bavarian climbers Toni Kurz and Anderl Hinterstoisser who died on their attempt on the Eiger North wall. During this period Austrian climbers experimented with making crampons rigid along their length, to enhance performance, but the idea was not commercialised at this point. Heckmair of course two years later on succeeded on the Eiger and had 12-point crampons'

Indeed Heinrich Harrer, writing in his book, *The White Spider* said:

> 'just before the rocks separating the second from the third ice field, I looked back, down our endless ladder of steps. Up it I saw the New Era coming at express speed; there were two men running – and I mean running, not climbing – up it. Admittedly, practised climbers can move quickly in good steps; but for these two to have reached this point quite early in the morning was amazing. These two were the best of all the 'Eiger candidates' Heckmair and Vorg – wearing their 12 point crampons. I felt quite outmoded ...'

In contrast to the very rapid uptake of the new German technical climbing methods. the diffusion of innovations in clothing and bivouac equipment was very slow. Ideas did not move quickly across national boundaries in this period and British and French clothing ideas did not reach Germany. Down clothing appears to have been unknown among German climbers even though experiments began in Britain in the 1920s with George Finch on the 1922 Everest expedition as outlined in chapter 7.

Pierre Allain and Vitale Bramani were even more significant for innovations which were directly sparked by cold experiences in the mountains.

Pierre Allain (PA) began to think about new bivouac equipment , in 1931, after a very hard night in a crevasse on "La Dent Parachée" (Vanoise) with Robert Latour. [20]

His newly created down jacket was used in conjunction with a short length sleeping bag (which he referred to as a 'pied d'éléphant' or elephant's foot). 'La

Grande cagoule' was literally 'a large cowl' fitting over the down filled jacket. Alternatively in case of an unplanned bivouac and no down equipment, the long cagoule could be pulled down over the knees and feet when in a crouch position. When used in a full length sleeping position, a half length inflatable mattress silk provided comfort and insulation from cold rising from the ground. In order to achieve a very light, but durable product PA imported from Japan some ultra-lightweight silk. This comprised two layers of silk which was cleverly cross laid "on the bias" to create a very high tear strength and the rubber coating between the two layers made it not only totally waterproof but also air holding. From this fabric he made his short inflatable mattress weighing only 400 g and of course his first cagoule.

After his first trials on a first ascent of the South Face of the Fou he wrote in *Alpinisme et Compétition*, in the chapter "L'Arête Sud du Fou":

> *'Here, we are totally equipped. The bivouac has become bourgeois, the risk has become security. The Bohemia makes way to the Organization.' 21*

This was indeed a sophisticated way of disparaging his own inventions. However, he was rather premature. His equipment was not commercialised in the French market until after 1945 and unknown in Germany until 1955. Then it was directly imported by Schuster of Munich.

After his 1933 ascent of the South Arête of the Fou Pierre Allain then went on to create twelve premières, beginning with 1934 West ridge of the Pic san Nom, South Face of the Meije, South Face of the Corno Stella, 1935 East Face of Caïman .

The French succeeded in climbing the first 8000er, Annapurna, in 1950.The great achievement of this trip was to find the route to the base of the mountain, without prior exploration. Maurice Herzog's team did not include Pierre Allain. However in a rather uncomfortable pre-summit bivouac (the precursor of two desperate post summit bivouacs where they were badly frostbitten) he was able to muse 'good old Pierre these (sleeping) bags are superb'.[22] But just what sort of man was Pierre Allain?

Herman Huber had met him during the course of business. Salewa was, in the late 1960s, already exporting considerable quantities of aluminium ski poles to France. A visit to Munich was arranged for the French retailers and amongst this group was Pierre Allain. A rapport was quickly established between these two mountaineers. Herman rated him perhaps above all other innovators saying, that if he ever had his time over again and had to choose an innovation collaborator it would be PA.

But it is Stephane Pennequin, the passionate climbing historian who had the memorable experience of meeting him in his fully operational workshop before he died.[23]

S. Pennequin Collection

Pierre Allain at work making Karabiners at the age of 88.

When Pierre Allain's book *Alpinisme et Competition* was reprinted, Stéphane Pennequin produced a wonderful article:

Do you believe in Father Christmas?' I certainly do! I met him in September 1992 in his workshop somewhere near Grenoble. With a secret smile he switched on each one of his four machines right in front of my astonished eyes and superb tools began to appear; the sort of tools that alpinists use in their never-ending quest for the summits.

And his real name? My Father Christmas is Pierre Allain.

If Isaac Newton or Kingdom Brunel should ever meet him one day they would no doubt have a real lesson from the Maestro concerning these machines. Today these are real treasures of alpine industrial heritage, brainstormed, designed and assembled piece by piece, 40 years ago by Pierre Allain himself.

These machines, under the sole control of Pierre Allain, the maestro of ingenuity and minutiae, produced karabiners in 22 operations and three minutes, with a capacity of 30,000 karabiners per annum. To occupy himself in a retirement of little prosperity, Pierre Allain had founded his tiny enterprise in the cellar of his house, in Uriage, in 1963. The organisation could be assured of all functions, from chief engineer to sweeper-up, as well as secretarial support; from PA himself. In addition to being the formidable climber which one knows him to be, this leading light of the rock world certainly illuminated the conservative world of climbing equipment'[24].

But, like most inventors not all of his developments were commercially successful. Certainly his aluminium lightweight Karabiner was taken up very quickly but this was not true of his descendeur. After a first prototype in 1947, in the form of a cross, Pierre Allain launched the Trident on the market several years later. It encountered a certain reticence amongst the traditionalists who preferred to continue to 'burn' their clothes using the traditional abseil method. An early demonstration of his new device was given by PA at Montenvers, sometime between 1943 and 1945, and he was accosted by the arch opponent of innovation and head guide, Armand Charlet with the question;

"What is that gadget you have there"?

"It's a descendeur" PA replied

'A descendeur? A rappel is something which one does with the legs or one doesn't do it at all!'[25]

But the tool which remained the most controversial was his 'décrocheur', a simple mechanism which allowed an abseil descent using only one rope. Once the weight of the abseiler was taken off the rope, this gadget unhooked itself automatically, the whole then dropping together. Climbers are well accustomed to living alongside calculated risk but they never accepted this concept, which had the feeling of descending with the Sword of Damocles close to one's neck! However, having used his descendeur some dozens of times, Pierre Allain was the proof of its security.

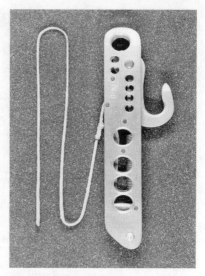

Pierre Allain's decrocheur – 'sword of damacles'.

Driving his research ever further, he conceived and tested in the field an even more astounding piece of apparatus. A gadget linked with the décrocheur this took the form of a ploughshare which enabled one to abseil from snow.

This was not all, for hidden in the bottom of a drawer in his workshop was a prototype, a nut, the result of his restless innovative spirit. Surely one must ask, if Pierre Allain in his alpine achievements, as a real aesthete, demonstrated a really pronounced taste for excellence, this unique prototype was the work of the purist who had a vision of real clean (piton-less) climbing. As Stephane Pennequin commented:

> *'If nowadays the name of Pierre Allain no longer resonates as a benchmark for the new generation of climbers, it should be remembered that even the least well equipped have a minimum of three climbing tools/articles of which PA is the creator; the aluminium Karabiner, the abseil device, rock boots, not to mention the down jacket and cagoule. For these, we mountaineers should be forever thankful'[26].*

Winter ascents of alpine face climbs were beginning in the 1930s, but the attempt by Vitale Bramani in 1935 on Punta Rasica, Bregaglia, was an autumn attempt to repeat the July 1935 route. The weather turned to snow and understandably they moved slowly, having left nailed boots and sacs at the base, descending with felt soled boots was difficult. Bramani spent one night out and got down for the rescue. Many of the others spent two nights out. A lot were badly frostbitten and five died.[27]

Left: Boot nailing and rubber patterns. **Right:** Nordica Ski boot with rubber sole. Rubber soles were already used for ski boots from the early 1930's, sometimes combining nails. This boot was 1939/40.

Vitale Bramani was already trading under his name linking first and last names together by 1937.

Such a serious accident and loss of friends became a motivating factor to develop a new product ,which was not only better insulated than the nailed boots, but would be as good on rock as the felt soled 'pedule'. Rubber soles had already been used on ski boots since the early 1930s, sometimes with a few Tricounis added on the edge if necessary. Vitale Bramani developed the first rubber sole moulded to imitate the shape of nails in conjunction with Pirelli. This was done in stages and necessitated some innovation in boot construction. With leather soles, stitching through all layers was possible. Rubber made this much more difficult. The first attempts left a peripheral track of thinner rubber to enable the stitching to go through, but this is quite unsatisfactory from a climbing point of view because the studded profile did not go all the way to the edge.

New adhesives were needed and these were eventually supplemented with brass screws. A local military climbing school in Aosta was the first to show interest, partly because they had operations in Russia. Indeed the military were in the most need of this innovation because armies, from Hannibal onwards are incapacitated by cold weather.[28] Napoleon, for instance marched on Moscow in 1812 with half a million men. The countryside before them was stripped of food and those who did not die of hunger died of cold in the famous retreat. The temperature dropped to -40°C and less than 20,000 men returned. Hitler repeated Napoleon's experience, before moulded rubber footwear was available. Certainly none was available in Germany for the first ascent of the Eiger in 1938. In November and December 1941, 10% of the German army of 100,000 men suffered frostbite of some kind, and there were 15,000 amputations. Moulded rubber soles for Army footwear went into production for the USA army early in the war. The arguments for the product were clear and

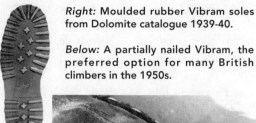

Right: Moulded rubber Vibram soles from Dolomite catalogue 1939-40.

Below: A partially nailed Vibram, the preferred option for many British climbers in the 1950s.

overriding; apart from the extra insulation, the lack of noise was also a factor. In 1947 Commando soles were introduced by the British ITSHIDE Rubber Co Ltd who were:

> *'contracted to supply to the Ministry of Defence hundreds of thousands of pairs of Commando soles for the manufacture of boots for the armed forces during the Korean war'.*[29]

In choosing their footwear mountaineers had more considerations than the army, they needed a combination of versatility, insulation and grip, which the new soles provided. They also brought advantages for manufacturers. The 5 main Italian boot manufacturers in 1939/40 each offered between 6 and 12 and different nailing patterns on their boots.

Changing to 'Vibram' moulded rubber soles reduced the need for such variety and thus cut costs. Lucien Devies and Giusto Gervasutti made the third ascent of the N. Face of the Petit Dru in August 1937 and this is regarded as the first occasion on which Vibrams were used on a major ascent. Devies commented in 1970 'Their invention was a revolution in the development of Alpine equipment, and we did not fail to proclaim their merits in that summer of 1937, but at first our praises were regarded with scepticism'.[30] Lionel Terray also tells the story of how a pair of Vibram soled boots were smuggled to him by Gervasutti across the high mountain frontier during the war period. Ricardo Cassin was another early user and made the first ascent of the 800m North face of the Leschaux in 1939 using Vibram soled boots. The information grapevine was working, in the western Alps at least.[31] Even so, the full transition, from nails to Vibrams for all users in all countries probably, took around 20 years. Some climbers in Britain and Switzerland continued with the 1930s practice of having their Vibram soles partially nailed.

But the hopes of achieving a single boot to do the job of two were short lived under the pressure of rapidly rising rock climbing standards. Pierre

Allain, was already experimenting with hockey boots in developing a rock boot design, just as Ken Ledward was to do in the 1960s, in research which ultimately spawned the KS-B (as described in chapter 8). The first rock boot with smooth friction sole was created in 1947 and called the PA of course.

Let There be Light: the 1950s to the Present Day

As life began to return to to normal after the Second World War, a new light started to shine on mountaineering activity -literally.

The folding candle lantern, first described in chapter 3 continued to be used from the early days of Edward Whymper. Ascending in the early hours was bad enough, but descending was awful, if not impossible, because the lantern did not have a beam or a handle to help direct the light. Acetylene lamps had been used by cyclists from the 1890s and by cavers from the 1930s. These lamps produce a significant amount of light and were often manufactured with glass lenses to create a beam of light. However calcium carbide, the chemical which produces acetylene, is nasty stuff and best avoided. More inhibiting, however, is the fact that it needs water to create a chemical reaction and, water is normally frozen early in the morning in the Alps. Enter the battery. Its first use in severe conditions was on Everest in the 1920s, but its length of life and output capability in cold conditions was very limited. A French company 'Pile Wonder' (literally 'wonder battery') produced the first battery operated headlamp although Candle lanterns were still in use until the mid 1950s.

However, it was a French caving equipment company, Petzl which developed this basic idea. Their products dominated the headlamp market for the next thirty years, until the field opened up again in the late 1990's. Then lights were developed using computer screen technology, the LED, which significantly reduced the power consumption and the demand on the batteries.

If the headlamp transformed Alpine climbing from the 1950s, the impact of synthetic polymers should not be understated. The first natural polymers were silk and rubber. The chemistry to understand polymers was developing strongly through the 1920s and 1930s and the key patents were taken out just before the Second World War. Their impact on outdoor equipment was arguably even greater than on our everyday lives. All manner of tents and clothing evolved over a thirty year period, helped considerably by first the zip and then the touch and close fastener. The safety aspects of climbing with ropes were simple. The rule had always been 'the leader shall not fall' and it was changed to 'he must fall if he is to improve' because of the development of numerous safety devices.

Climbing hardware innovations continued to pour out of Germany. The early 1960's were vintage years with the Schuster P. Hübei climbing helmet in the late 1950s. Fritz Sticht's rope brake or plate, was commercialised by Salewa along with the tubular ice screw and the adjustable crampon followed, later in 1972, by the rigid crampon in collaboration with Chouinard. The Salewa crampons were first produced in Munich in winter 1961-2, and they were a breakthrough from the old hand forged, individually sized crampons to a single adjustable size, using modern rolled steel and press stamping techniques. They were the first to be easily adjustable, rather than having to be made and custom fitted at the supplier's workshop. More critically, for the upcoming front pointing/ 'piolet traction' technique, the front section physically linked the two points together giving a much higher strength. By design they could be switched from climbing boots to ski boots very readily, but this size adjustability was also popular with retailers and users. This was because hammers, vices and blacksmiths and blow lamps were no longer needed.

Here is the personal story of Herman Huber, the innovator of this crampon. Like so many of the innovations discussed in this book, it shows the way in which a climber's understanding was crucial to equipment development and the way this, in turn, impacted on technique.[32]

HH: *'Basically the idea was based on something I and my friends needed, which was a crampon which was adjustable to mountaineering boots in summer and ski boots in winter. Because I had commercial experience selling existing forged crampons I was also conscious that this same adjustability would also be some commercial advantage.*

MP: *So how did Salewa make the transition to hardware from leather goods?*
(Salewa means Sattler and Leder Waren; Saddlery and leather goods)

HH: *Herr Liebhart, the Salewa General Manager at that time, he was General Manager of both Salewa Companies, Salewa Decorations and Salewa Leather Goods Factory, (which then already was evolving to Salewa Sports Goods), and he was ready because he had a wide enough view to invest in a metal goods production. He had seen our success in the mountaineering market in general and now was the time to do something with crampons. We had been buying crampons from Felix Ralling in the Stubai valley for some years, when suddenly he sent out an announcement to REI who was the distributor in USA, 'I am 73, don't send me any more big orders'. From a personal meeting following Ralling's 'send me no more orders letter' I was convinced I can no more count on this man and his production companies.*

For the time being we had to switch more to Stubai but they were more expensive, and not so much liked on the German market, more complicated in administration, not flexible enough to my feeling, so for the time being, around 1959, we bought more Stubai crampons'.

MP: *He had no successors?*

HH: *No not directly, but his wife had a son from another marriage, who should run the company later but he was still studying, and there was a production manager and good Technician/blacksmith, who happened to be my climbing partner, Fritz Muller. (I climbed the North face of Cima Grande with him) Salewa was about hiring him to come to Bavaria. But Fritz just had married an Innsbruck girl and started to build his house in Stubai, so it turned out to be impossible family wise, and I had to look for another opportunity. In the meantime I had to develop my crampon idea to the end, although being no engineer I thought that the blacksmiths technique, which I had seen many times, was a thing of the past.*

MP: *So how did you eventually find the production source?*

HH: *We used an existing Salewa supplier Gabriel Gauting. An independent, small workshop and they made the metal inlays for Salewa ski poles, stamped thin, 0.5 millimetre, we bought hundreds of thousands. He was not an engineer by profession, but in the old days he was a good tool maker. So we also could use him to make my Salewa crampon tools but Salewa had to invest in the stamping machinery because he had no money. We also participated 50% in the company. One day, with the excuse of having a ski holiday, I took Gabriel Gauting to see the production of Felix Ralling. I don't know if this was unfair or not but we even were offering to make modern tools for Ralling, wondering what his answer would be. He said 'no, whatever new tool, I want nothing'.*

The product was developed but the first delivery was a disaster, with poor heat treatment. At Gabriel Gauting we did not have our own heat treatment unit of course in the beginning, so we needed a treatment company and they didn't take much care. The crampons were pre sold of course in Germany to Sport Scheck who has an important catalogue. You know what that means when a new product is in a catalogue and you cannot supply? The crampon parts were burnt in the heat treatment, hundreds of them; it was fortunately only the heel parts. So I was in this heat treatment company three days myself checking each single piece, with the Rockwell hardness tester, throwing away, or not throwing away. I badly needed some to supply to Sport Scheck and others and it was a nightmare. We knew then we must install our own heat treatment as soon as possible, but this took time.

MP: *And market success?*

HH: *It was most amazing that, Edouard Frendo, (a French wholesaler and of the Frendo spur) bought 3,000 pairs of Salewa crampons and then Charlet copied our design. We had a Patent in France but it was amazing we won against the French attorney, and Charlet had to stop making this copy of the Salewa adjustment system.*

Our first business with the UK was when John Jackson of Jackson and Warr (later within the Blacks Group Greenock), showed up. He was the first man to buy Salewa crampons for the UK Market, maybe 150 pairs or something but he wasn't interested in 12-point and we supplied only 10 pointers at this point.

Later in the 1960s Graham Tiso (Tiso started his retail operation in Edinburgh in 1962) came along and took over the distribution for the UK.

The German innovations were not just in hardware. Nylon ropes, hawser laid were probably first used by the American 10th division and a small amount of these in olive green colour emerged after the war. Schuster started with a German-made laid rope (made in East Germany by Lützner, before the infamous wall was constructed) and of course bearing the ASMU brand. Another German company Edelrid produced the first Kernmantel rope in 1956, although the French had already experimented with nylon from around 1954.[33] John Cleare has vivid memories of the appearance of nylon ropes:

'We used hemp as a matter of course in 1951. My mentor – Bertie Robertson the great fell-runer – had a younger brother who was an academic at Queens / Belfast – and he came over to join us for a few days in Wales at Easter '51 ...with a new nylon rope!

We had seen one in operation a few days earlier on Sylvan Traverse on the Milestone (my second day's climbing) – a large party with this brilliant white line joining them. When we crossed their path it turned out to be "baby" nylon and we were amazed. When Billy R. turned up with a nylon rope three times as thick – full weight – we got very puzzled. But it was so nice to handle. Then in the summer holidays Tony Smythe turned up with a new three-quarter weight nylon rope and promptly took a big leader fall on Holly Tree Wall. I held him but he'd have died. ....all the way down Idwal Slabs... had it been hemp. So in the autumn term, age 14, I wrote my mother to try to get one – full weight – from nice Mr Lawrie – for my Christmas present. It cost £7 and they were in very short supply because of the Korean War. Then of course we always – from '57 until I guess the early 60s – took out 500 feet or so of three-quarter wt. Viking to pay for our alpine season. Donald Snell (Chamonix retailer) would buy it off us – usually in the form of credit which proved invaluable. One year the credit ran out but such was the good will that Donald wouldn't let Smythe and I traverse the Jorrasses without ice pegs and made us up some for nothing... which in the event saved our lives'.

The nylon laid rope was, however, very short lived and an alternative construction, which had been known for a very long time, came into being by 1960. Because the Germans were the innovators of this construction in nylon it has since born in the German name, Kernmantel, meaning that there is a sheath around the core. The British manufacture did not evolve into this new construction , probably because the market was seen as too small and the product needed properties quite distinct from sailing ropes, which needed to be completely without stretch. By contrast, climbing ropes needed the right amount of stretch in order to absorb the impact of the falling climber. In 1968 DAV founded a safety commission soon to be extended internationally by UIAA. This commission was responsible for co-ordinating the standards of all the interrelated climbing hardware; rope, karabiner and harness. The UIAA were responsible for devising the categories of single rope, half rope and twin rope, and developed the 'number of falls with 80kg' and maximum impact force criteria.'[34]

There are also definitions of the permissible elongation, sheath slippage, ratio of core to sheath, knotability (the ease with which knots are tied), the maximum impact force for certain masses and fall distances, the number of falls which must be held, the weight per metre.

Harnesses also have a strong German influence when, from the 1920s, the rope was usually tied around the chest. An additional length was taken across one shoulder and some climbers extended it across two shoulders. Following this practice Edelrid/Salewa had, by 1965, created a chest harness still from rope. Later the military parachute harness was the design model for the German climbing harness. However, in the same year,1965, Tony Howard had designed a leather harness with leg loops for use on the first ascent of the Troll Wall, itself a significant turning point in British big wall climbing.[35] Later, Howard teamed up with Alan Waterhouse to design and produce climbing gear based on their knowledge of webbing and chockstones. In 1970, Paul Seddon joined the team to form Troll about the time Don Whillans arrived at Troll's door and developed a harness for Annapurna South Face. This was the first harness using nylon webbing, although the Americans had used nylon webbing extensively to create, by knotting techniques, all manner of harnesses from a simple 'Swami' belt to a full harness. Putting them together was something of an Indian rope trick. All this was the beginning of another big equipment debate. The safety commission led by the Germans argued strongly for the full body harness whilst the British-American thinking backed the Troll/Whillans concept of the waist belt harness with leg loops.

The superiority of the full harness was fully provable in theory, but it was less than convenient in a mountain context when adjusting clothing layers and going to the toilet. The British design gradually became the accepted international norm. But not until the problem of the Troll/Whillans harness, with its potential to 'neuter' male climbers, had been solved!

The 'Natural Protection' Revolution and the Nut as Springboard

The Second World War changed many things in many countries. Britain and the mentality and aspirations of its working-class population were amongst them. It was almost as though a whole new variant of Homo Sapiens Britannicus had been mutated. This new breed came from the factories, the shipyards, the steel furnaces and called a spade, a shovel. They wanted nothing to do with the Alpine Club, took the best training possible and set up their own club, the Alpine Climbing Group (ACG).

Peg bashing in quarries,
Second nature to blacksmiths,
Swinging in etriers,
Pulling on aid,
The whack and dangle brigade in Europe do this,
So why not us,
Jamming fists in cracks,
Climbing in the rain,
Not knowing what they were supposed NOT to do,
Strutt who? Two fingers.
Froggies? We'll show 'em.
The Gerry's?
Guess they have done a bit,
Lets go see!

Brown, Whillans, and a host of others were in this new generation, they were the ones who wrote their book and went on the TV and became famous, but there were hundreds like them. Hamish MacInnes, Tom Patey and John Cunningham were Scots but from the same mould and if anything had two axes to grind, against the aristocrats and the English.

John Brailsford was typical of this new breed. He was an orphan from Sheffield and, after making an acquaintance with the outdoors as a scout (and later through Outward Bound) was apprenticed to a Sheffield steel company, where it was more than the steels that became tempered and hardened. He remembered a hard lesson vividly:

'As an apprentice I was given the job of forging twelve pairs of tongs for the foundry. They were used to lift hot metal moulds apart after casting had been completed. Tongs were paid at the rate of two shillings and sixpence per pair in 1953, about twelve and a half pence in current cash. I had been given an assistant, a man of some 59 years, and it was my responsibility to pay him. For each £1 that I earned, he received eight shillings or 40% of the total. We were allowed to book thirty shillings per day. Thus, twelve pairs of tongs equalled one day's pay.

We started early, 7.30 a.m. prompt, the hammer driver was prodded into action and Ellis and I got stuck in. At the end of the day, 12 pairs of tongs lay by my anvil and I cycled home, and then went to night school.

At 7.15 a.m. next day I clocked on and went to my hearth where Ellis already had the fire going and had made my tea. Such was the craft structure in those days. I then noticed a neat pile of short lengths of steel by the anvil.

F***! The short bits had been 12 pairs of tongs.

I sat down with my tea, fuming mad but helpless.

When George Henry Ratcliffe, the foreman smith, came on his round I was still sitting there.

'What's up, John'?

'That bugger is', I said. 'He's chopped a whole day's work there but what is far worse, the old devil is right, I can do better'.

George Henry knew my back ground as an orphan; my aunt lived next door to him in Ecclesfield. He made me an offer I couldn't refuse. I could remake the tongs to the best of my ability and Noble's satisfaction. If they were perfect, he would sanction my payment and let the previous days pay stand. I made my tongs, my pay and regained my self respect'.

These and many similar experiences made him the tough, but fair taskmaster he became to the around 3,000 students, first at the secondary school, followed by Loughborough University and as the head of outdoor education at Bangor. He finally became the training officer for the British mountain guides, where arguably, the concept of an apprenticeship in the training of a guide still has much to be commended. John had a vision in 1973 that the British could be guides to the same standard as all alpine guides. He pursued this vision setting up training for the British guides at Loch Eil centre, where Richard Grant gave him great support. His background as a blacksmith was to prove important to the final acceptance of the British guides into the UIAGM in 1977. This was because he shared the craft background of so many guides in the Alps.

Natural protection, the concept of the removable 'nut' instead of the piton which had to be hammered in, came from the British practice of threading the rope around a small rock which was naturally jammed in a crack. This obviously required first the leader and then second to untie and then retie onto the rope, which was clearly hazardous. In order to avoid this the obvious thing to do was to insert your own piece of rock. The first recorded occasion was in 1926 on Piggott's climb, and one of the most famous occasions was in 1954, on the West face of the Aiguille de Blaitière, by Joe Brown and Don Whillans. The next improvement came in the late 1950's when nylon rope slings were appearing and the practice began of stiffening these slings (for easier passing around chock-stones) by boiling in sugar solution. Rather than carrying a piece of rock, an engineering nut was a reasonable alternative. Many climbers worked in engineering workshops and collected nuts from work or even from the Snowdon Mountain railway line. The threads were then removed from the inside of the nut and the nylon cord tied through it. Exactly who was the first person to execute this is unclear, but certainly every climber of this period knows the person who did it, and they are many!

But the man who created the first manufactured version of the nut is John Brailsford. He was still teaching craft at Allestree Woodlands Secondary School, Derbyshire when in 1961 he made 'The Acorn' the first manufactured nut, which he turned on the lathe. He sold this prototype to Roger Turner Mountain Sports, in Nottingham.

Left: MOAC and an Acorn. *Right:* The first Brailsford nuts – the foundations of the British mountain hardware manufacturing industry.

The following year, the product was improved considerably in terms of its ability to fit into cracks and hold. This required a completely different process, aluminium die-casting, to produce the double wedge shape, but the minimum quantities required made Roger Turner hesitate. John therefore approached another mountain retailer who he knew very well, Bob Brigham. At this time Bob had teamed up with a British mountain guide called Peter Gentil. Peter had left J.E.B. Wright's 'Mountaineering Association' to set up a joint operation with Bob, offering **MO**untaineering **AC**tivities (hence MOAC). In this period, mountaineering was primarily a summer activity and Gentil and Brigham were looking for something to do during the winter and manufacturing hardware was a good option. The nut was called the MOAC after the company and the first six protoypes were sand cast in Derby. Bob Brigham found a firm in Manchester who sand cast 2,000 as a first run, and these were fettled and holes reamed by hand by Peter Gentil. The next batch was die cast, still from John's patterns.

John was also the supporting master craftsman for several other manufacturers. These included Clog, where he made all the prototypes and was 'paid handsomely' by Denny Moorhouse. He also received a royalty from Mo Anthoine's Snowdon Mouldings on the Curver ice axe for many years. Many individual climbers in the early Seventies who were urgently in need of a new axe with a curved pick willingly paid him 4/6d (0.24p) to have their old one altered and re-tempered.

From this point onwards new ideas proliferated, on the back of the nut. Within a decade this became an explosion with just about every nation contributing to some new shape or idea. Stephane Pennequin, the Frenchman who has made it his passion to study and collect every type of nut estimates that there are possibly 500 different variations! There are, however, only a very small number of important steps of improvement. This is an exciting story which has been the basis of several new hardware businesses in the UK. These Businesses include MOAC, Peck, Parbat, Troll, Clog, DMM, and Wild Country. The climbing nut therefore was the springboard for a new industry. It was a relatively easy manufacturing process to experiment with before venturing into products like axes, crampons and karabiners which needed in depth knowledge of complex tempering and hardening processes. It was also the spring board to higher standards of climbing in Britian where standards had arguably been constrained because of lack of protection, but subsequently reached startling levels by the early 1980s.

Not all new companies began with nuts. The spread of climbing created an emerging market for all kinds of equipment, and a wave of complementary innovations. Many, coming from Germany and France, could usually be copied, including belay plates, descenders, ascenders, climbing helmets and tubular ice screws to name a few. But another factor was at work which provided a stimulus for new hardware companies and this was the development of Scottish ice climbing using front pointing, in conjunction with the curved picks of two axes.

The potential to reduce the size of the nut, to go into a smaller crack, was limited by the need for a rope or tape to be threaded through the nut. This problem was solved quite quickly, in 1964 by Trevor Peck of Leicester, who developed and commercialised a range of sized nuts, the smallest of which were wired, hence much smaller. There was also the additional advantage that the stiff wire extended the effective length of the users arm, giving more opportunities for placements. Trevor Peck ran a hosiery business in Leicester and had become a passionate climber relatively late in life. The business certainly had some success but faded away when he delegated the hardware business and it did not survive his death. However, the products proved internationally influential in an interesting way. In 1966 Royal Robbins, the pioneer of many first ascents in Yosemite California, purchased a set of Peck nuts from Joe Brown's retail store in Llanberis, North Wales and proceeded to use and enthuse about these items in the USA. Significant articles appeared in USA climbing magazines in 1967 and in the Patagonia catalogue in 1972, which made a considerable impact on their acceptance there.

In the meantime Denny Moorhouse, a gardener by training, had returned from Bavaria, where he had worked as a labourer and could, converse and swear fluently in the local dialect. He had a good knowledge of Dolomite climbing areas and had climbed the Schmid Krebs route on the Laliderer wall. Maybe his extensive experiences in the Dolomites gave him an affinity for hardware. On returning to the UK he formed his first company Clog, in 1966,

Patagonia Collection

"Yvon Chouinard, founder of Chouinard Equipment (later to become Black Diamond) and Patagonia, working his drop-hammer forge in the 1960s."

with Shirley Williams. It was in her garden shed in Deiniolen, North Wales and produced a sized set of nuts that were 'state of the art' for a long time. He followed these up with every type of gear imaginable. His contribution to and influence on the British gear making scene was immense. He is a multiple entrepreneur, first with Clog followed in 1980 by DMM (Denny Moorhouse Mountaineering) and then finally in 1995 ISC, International Safety Components. His off the wall humour and his 'wizard' outfits, which he would wear occasionally at the trade shows, were all part of the colourful British scene, and are sadly missed. 'Climb now work later' was the company advertising slogan, very appropriate in the 1970's, a period of high unemployment which also arguably helped raise climbing standards. It was also a philosophy shared by many of the new hardware manufacturers, who began gear making to finance their real passion –climbing. Mo Antoine's view of Snowdon Mouldings – the business he founded with Joe Brown- fitted this pattern for he wanted 'to run the business but not be run by it'. By the 1980s :

> *'JB helmets have been sold to climbers all over the world as well as to NATO and the FBI and Snowdon Mouldings [had] grown and grown...But the principle [remained the same], climbing first, money second.'* [36]

At the same time, across in California the seeds had been sown. There was already a strong base of hardware innovation, John Salethé an émigré Swiss blacksmith had pioneered Yosemite climbing and the making of hard steel pitons. Yvon Chouinard followed and his hardware, made on location with a mobile forge, was the foundation for Great Pacific Iron Works (GPIW) which later (after a bizarre court case where the company was sued when a climber did not do up his harness after taking a pee) became Black Diamond. The tradition here was to leave the route bare of pitons, removing them as one climbs. The concept of the Fiechtl piton was absorbed and continued, but the blade shapes were significantly different producing a host of different configurations, all with interesting names, Leepers, (after Ed Leeper) RURP's (realised ultimate reliability piton) and Bongs (the sound as they hammered in) and even Harding's 'bat hook' were all part of a Yosemite climbers gear rack.

In 1974 Doug Scott commented:

> 'Now in Britain a move is afoot to reduce the pegs on aid routes so climbers can come along and put in their own chocks... Providing practice grounds for the "clean" ascents of big walls all over the world. Perhaps in the not too distant future, continental climbers will apply this "clean" climbing to the Alpine and Dolomite rock routes'.[37]

The search was definitely already on for something which would be effective in the Yosemite environment, where parallel cracks are the norm and it is devilishly difficult to get a wedge shaped nut to stay in place . In the early 1970s, Mike and Greg Lowe, the founders of Lowe Alpine, (prolific innovators in a wide variety of product areas from soft packs to crampons to camera bags) developed two new types of nut, based on a constant angle cam, one of which was sprung loaded.

Nature produces a constant angle spiral quite naturally although engineers, especially ones with computers, find them rather tricky. In 1973 the Lowe Brothers sold three of these devices to a Yosemite climber, Ray Jardine. As an aerospace engineer he understood the concept but, when he tried them, they fell out of the crack leaving him unprotected. He asked if they would like some information on how to improve the effectiveness but the conversation did not go anywhere. In 1974 he set about producing his own devices and worked for months in his climbing friend Bill Forest's (an American hardware manufacturer) workshop. His first prototype did not have a finger trigger to release the spring, so he selected a relatively easy route, where he could find a stance which allowed more or less both hands free to enable him to wriggle the new device into a crack. He felt instantly that it was the solution. The following spring he took a first set of working prototype 'Friends' (the spring loaded camming device) and at the end of the season did an ascent of 'The Nose' in a record time of 20 hours, a significant reduction from the previous best time of three days. It was clear that he had a really good product but for six years he worked to steadily improve prototypes, swearing each of his small number of partners to absolute secrecy. Mark Vallance had worked and climbed with Ray Jardine at Colorado Outward Bound School in 1973 and was introduced to 'Friends' in 1975, at the base of Washington Column, Yosemite. Ray handed him a No.3 Friend. Mark pulled back the trigger and inserted it into a crack. 'How did you know, who told you, who told you?' was Jardine's immediate concerned reaction, assuming that the secret had got out of the bag. Mark smiled and said, 'no one, but it's obvious isn't it? And a partnership was born although neither knew at the time. The natural development would have been for Bill Forest to make the 'Friends', but he did not believe they would take off and wanted to make one of the components in cast alloy.

Ray knew that this would not do the job; the alloy just was not up to it. Before Mark left the USA he asked Ray to send him some 'Friends' for his own use. Ray remembered this and it became clear to him that Mark was convinced about the product, unlike the Lowe Brothers and Bill Forest. One-day in 1977 Mark received his long-awaited 'friends'. With it was an offer from Ray Jardine for the world wide exclusive manufacturing licence. He was stunned. It arrived at a point in his life when he was unhappy in his work, but also had family responsibilities. He was married with a one year-old daughter to support. During the summer of 1977 Ray came over to the UK for two to three months at Mark's expense and they worked together finding subcontractors who could make all the components. At this stage the company was called Wild Mountain Workshop – although absolutely no workshop existed.

'I couldn't see how, at that stage, I could arrive at a price which I thought climbers would pay. Suddenly after several months, I found a supplier at the right price and extruded aluminium in relatively small quantities. In November 1977 I gave up my job and by January I had changed the company name to Wild Country. This is something I had thought carefully about; the name had to be suitable for the US, which I always perceived would be my major market. My break-even for the first year was to sell 3,000 Friends; at which point I would be able to support my family. In reality I achieved this target within six months and distribution in 15 countries all without any advertising whatsoever.'38

Mark Vallance had also been working on nut designs and developed two different configurations; one a barrel shaped wedge and the other a double concave wedge, for use on the pin scarred cracks of Millstone Edge as early as 1975. It was not until 1979 that, having been asked by UK climbing stores to produce a range of nuts, the idea suddenly became clear, he should integrate both convex and concave curves into one device. This was the birth of Wild Country 'Rocks' which Mark patented only in the USA – nuts had not yet become popular in Alpine areas. Chouinard Equipment produced a curved nut radiused in 4 different directions, an idea covered by Vallance's patent but rejected by him. Vallance fought the ensuing patent battle in a David and Goliath contest and was forced to grant Chouinard a licence when he ran out of money, but not before he had established his willingness to defend his patents.

The Return of the Icemen

By the late 1940s the potential for further ice routes in the Alps, given existing techniques, seemed to have been exhausted. There was a young Swiss climber called Erich Friedli who, in the late 1950s,repeated all of Welzenbach's Oberland climbs, in remarkably fast times. He used front pointing techniques and an ice dagger in the each hand, to avoid the step and hand hold cutting which had still been necessary for Welzenbach's steepest routes. He also climbed solo; not a viable new technique for many people to follow.

From the 1950s and into the 1960s leading climbers from all nations were beating a path to Yosemite Valley California, to play on the magnificent rock walls. Cheaper air travel created an exciting international flavour to climbing and contributed to the breaking down of barriers. Eventually as all the major lines were done, the leading edge climbers turned their attention to ice. Yvon Chouinard, with partners Doug Robinson and Doug Tompkins were very innovative. Yvon had been in Chamonix and wanted to have an axe with a curved pick but had to rely (as so many English speakers did in the 1950s and 1960s) on the personal help of Donald Snell, the Chamonix retailer. This was to help him persuade the Charlet factory to make, not only a curved pick axe, but one as short as 55 cm. The pick curvature, of course, was that which corresponded with the arc of the axe swing. This had been the recommended specification of the AC equipment committee of 1864, (yes **1864**) but the pick had become straightened because it was always guides, often themselves blacksmiths, who determined the designs of ice axes. They did not want a curved pick because, when cutting steps, this stuck in the ice, But this was precisely what Chouinard was now trying to achieve. If working with one in each hand he could now grip the ice with four points of contact, two axes and two crampons. The first time he used this was in the winter of 1967 in California. Strangely this new technique never acquired an English descriptive name, possibly because the arrival of the use of 12 point crampons was late and therefore relatively close to the introduction of the double axe technique. Later the Germans called it, 'zug-technique' and the French, 'piolet-traction'. Within a short while for the English and the Scots, it was just 'front pointing', was there any other way?

Together with Tom Frost, his partner in the hardware business Chouinard designed an alpine hammer and rigid crampons. These rigid crampons broke easily and the product was withdrawn until he found a suitable manufacturing partner, Salewa of course. The Salewa/Chouinard crampons became available in

1972. When Chouinard and Tompkins arrived in Scotland in the winter of 1970 there had already been much dialogue between them and Graham Tiso (already Salewa UK distributor) and Herman Huber of Salewa in Munich. The arrival was extremely timely because Scottish climbing had been emerging from more than a decade of evolution. Scotland is an unusual, and often frustrating climbing environment. Because it is low-level, close to the sea and Gulf stream the temperature fluctuates rapidly, above and below freezing point. The best place to find good winter climbing conditions therefore is in the gullies, which are protected from warmer winds and sunshine. Sometimes to the frustration of both climbers and skiers the snow in the gullies has been protected from temperature fluctuations and is not suitable for climbing. However, the open ski slopes can rapidly attain a condition known as 'boilerplate'.

Scottish climbing had always had its winter exponents, Norman Collie in the 1890s and Harold Raeburn who before the First World War did classics which bears his name. It was not until the 1950s, however, that the leading edge again shifted back to Scotland's winter climbs. Tom Patey was quite prolific and very bold but he was no great innovative technician. Hamish MacInnes on the other hand was, and was equally prominent on the west side with climbs on Ravens Gully (1953) Rannoch wall and Clachaig gully. Together with Patey and Graeme Nicol he made the first ascent of Zero gully, Ben Nevis, the first of the big gully climbs in 1957.

In 1958, Jimmy Marshall (climbing shop owner in Aberdeen) teamed up with Graham Tiso to do the parallel B gully on Lochnagar, something which Graham was always pleased and proud about. Jimmy dominated Scottish climbing for a period and Robin Smith and Dougal Haston were amongst the many that benefited from an apprenticeship with him.[39]

John Cleare describes the ice scene by winter 68/69; 'Under Johnny's (Cunningham) instructions the fellows at the Lodge (Glenmore Lodge Aviemore Scotland) were de-tempering their axes, re-bending them and re-tempering them in the workshop there which was when I first met Johnny and re-bent all my axes.'

When Chouinard arrived in Scotland ,MacInnes had already created his 'Terrordactyl' climbing axe with a tubular aluminium shaft. The pick was not radiused but simply dropped at an angle, so the arm action was rather more a pull down technique than swinging it through a radius. There was always much discussion as to which was the better tool, the MacInnes dropped pick or the Chouinard radiused pick.

John Cunningham and Bill March from Glenmore Lodge did the first Scottish ice climb without cutting steps, Hell's Lum in the Cairngorms. Cunningham had experimented with front pointing techniques whilst working for British Antarctic Survey (BAS) in Antarctica, in the 1950s and 1960s before returning to Scotland. Chouinard and Tompkins caused a stir by completing a direct finish to Ravens Gully and repeating a climb called 'The Smear' in Glencoe in one and a half hours instead of the previous five and a half. Doing my first ice climbing under Ian Clough's instruction (just before his fateful trip to Annapurna) we took an easier line just so he could watch the American pair in action. According to John Cunningham's biographer it is possible to pinpoint the start of snow and ice front pointing precisely it was in the:

'winters of 1970-1, when nights in the staff wingwere made hideous by mysterious comings and goings and the sound of hammering late into the small hours. It was the time when everyone's favourite axe underwent a metamorphosis, first a softening by heat, then some bending and shaping to the required angle... followed by some tempering.' [40]

It was a period of frantic experimentation with techniques and with gear with ever more bizarre tools appearing, only to be discarded. This included the Whillans Whammer which could open cans, act as a screwdriver, be used as an abseil device – in fact almost anything except be used as an ice tool. On a climbing week with Ian Clough I had a prototype of a Whillans 'Whammer' and it became rather clear on that day that this was not an inspired innovation. Even for hard drinking climbers, an integrated beer can opening tool was no real alternative to a curved pick. Chouinard not surprisingly agreed, but hastily added that some might consider him biased. Don had gone out to work for him in the USA working the forge, but they had fallen out. Over the next decade the Scottish climbing scene was very exciting, many climbers from all over the world came to understand and experience it. It in turn gave a stimulus enjoyed by climbers, manufacturers and retailers alike which will be discussed in detail in chapter 8.

Back in Europe:

'in 1969 the leading spokesman for ice climbing in France, Andre Contamine, wrote in the journal La Montagne. 'The 'piolet ancre' is one of the most useful techniques of the Alpiniste. It permits him to cover ground on the steepest slopes without fatigue or difficulty. It is the key to cramponing French style.' Two years later the Austrian climber Wastl Mariner (head of the Tyrol Mountain rescue and originator of several items under the Marwa label, karabiners, boot soles, crampons.) wrote in the same journal; 'the most natural technique anatomically and the most secure and sparing of energy, is to advance on steep ice on the front points of 12 point crampons, called front pointing'. He went on to criticise the French technique as unnatural and difficult to learn. This caused an absolute furore at the ENSA (Ecole Nationale de Ski et d'Alpinisme) in Chamonix when rebellious students posted the article on the bulletin board!' [41]

Finally the French recognised the difficulty and paid a visit to Scotland. In 1973 Cechinel and Jaeger climbed the North Couloir of the Petit Dru using the radiused pick tools. The following year new drooped pick ice tools were produced by Simond of Chamonix. The transformation into the new technique was fully underway, everywhere.

The next equipment development occurred when the Lowe Brothers created Footfangs, the new style of crampon, in 1978. The original prototype was produced by fitting ski edges directly to the boot sole. After negotiations with both Salewa and Camp of Italy, the latter won the contract for the production. This design further increased the rigidity of the crampon, but brought to a close to the period when one crampon design was applied to all types of climbing. From then on crampon designs became more functionally focused and less and less a multi function tool. Exactly the same happened with ice axes when in 1986 Grivel introduced the first curved shaft axe.

Warm clothing was followed by warm footwear and better shelter. German Himalayan expeditions had used front pointing quite early – along with two hand tools – a short ice axe and an Eisbeil (with a hammer head for ice pitons).But the first time a British expedition used this combination was on the Annapurna South Face expedition in 1970. It was also the earliest use in the Himalayas of cellular polymer materials, which were cellular foam but unlike all of the cheap foam beds available at the time, the cells did not connect. This meant that the materials were lightweight, flexible, waterproof and made excellent insulating material. The first product produced from this material was the Karrimat. Also produced by Karrimor on the Annapurna expedition were closed cell neoprene over-boots. At this point in time boots were still leather with felt inners. In 1968 an American engineer called Bob Lange developed an all plastic ski boot which created a whole new set of problems and opportunities. Within a few years the Italian manufacturing industry had grasped the concept but used a different process to produce plastic boots. By 1978 Koflach, an Austrian company had produced a successful rigid plastic climbing boot. Initially it was supplied with felt inners and then quickly they grasped the opportunities for the closed cell form material offered for inner boots. The Plastic boot became almost totally universal for alpine use for more than a decade, until change began again; a lighter product with a more natural feel for the foot.

The final word goes to the 'Future of Mountain Sports' congress[42] organised by the German and Austrian Alpine Clubs. It reached a stirring climax in a passionate address by Chris Bonington when he delivered 'The Tyrol Declaration' in Innsbruck on 8 September 2002. The working congress was made up of over 100 experts, official representatives, and world class climbers and mountaineers. The congress had been opened with a series of short addresses, including Reinhold Messner. He invoked the *spirit of Mallory* by reminding the congress about climbing *'by fair means'*. Messner stressed the need for self reliance for safety and self restraint to protect the heritage of mountain sports

Yosemite veteran Tom Frost put it most succinctly by describing the dichotomy that exists between the ethos of 'leave no trace' and the freedom to 'do whatever you want'. Frost highlighted the need to properly identify the problem, the cause, a solution and a means of implementation, which gave valuable guidance to the five working groups. Alex Huber said:

"Mountain sports have a future, but they also have a history...today climbs are being done in the 'plaisir' style, but old routes from earlier epochs are being retro bolted under the disguise of redevelopment. This shows a lack of respect both for the accomplishment of the first ascensionists and for the diversity inherent in mountain climbing – and it causes a rift in the climbing community."

The use of various types of aid has been a topic of debate since the last century. Paul Preuss insisted on the total rejection of all technical products, including the use of the rope; and while his example was rejected by those climbers who wanted to be survivors, his doctrine is being rekindled in certain modern climbing schools. Note also the situation in Bohemia where pitons, chocks and magnesium oxide are prohibited, and where, nevertheless, climbers attain a high degree of proficiency. Inevitably every generation has a tendency to question the ethics of its predecessor.

To quote Ricardo Cassin:

'The young must be given the right to use new means to carry on their personal experiments. Of course all methodological changes have their basis in that eternal desire to improve, which characterizes those persons who seek the unknown'.

CHAPTER 7
The Obsession with and Race for Everest
1921-1953

This 1924 base camp photograph captures the myth of the Norfolk jacket. Notice, however, the zipped pockets on Sandy Irvine's Burberry windproofs.

'A Connemara picnic surprised by a snow storm' was how George Bernard Shaw summed up the appearance of the 1921 Reconnaissance Expedition to Everest and it is very much the modern popular image. Mainly posed photographs – often on the approach march – project an almost universal impression of brave but misguided men in Norfolk jackets and knickerbockers, and it is all part of the romance of the Everest story. That in the 1920s British mountaineers went off to climb the highest mountain in the world dressed at best as for the Alps in summer, is in keeping with the idea of the 'gifted amateur'. When Conrad Anker found George Mallory's body in May 1999, just below 8230m on the north face of Everest, this inevitably led to renewed speculation about whether he and Sandy Irvine actually climbed the mountain in 1924. Anker doubted it, partly on the grounds of the technical difficulty of the upper reaches of the mountain which he saw as being beyond the ability of the pair, who were innocent of interwar advances in technical climbing. His other reason for scepticism stemmed from the inferior clothing and equipment he found. Leaky oxygen cylinders were undoubtedly a problem and the breaking weight of hemp is far less than nylon rope. But he found the clothing and footwear pitiful in contrast to modern clothing. He pointed to the single leather nailed boots, two pairs of hand knitted stockings, long underwear and puttees and seven or eight layers of silk, cotton or wool and fur-lined flying helmet. The contrast with Anker's own gear on his own summit day could not have been starker as he recalled:

> 'I had on two layers of fleece, a synthetic woollen parka, and a full down suit with wind-resistant surface. On my head a knit hat and the built in down hood on my jacket. On my feet, thick nylon boots insulated with closed-cell foam, with gaiters built in to keep snow out of the ankles. The suit alone provides three to four inches of insulation, which is a lot more than all seven or eight of Mallory's layers combined...'[1]

It would be nonsense to deny the impact of nylons, synthetic polymers, plastics and alloys on the design and capabilities of outdoor gear (and the sportsmen and women who used them) in the last 50 years. Those innovations form one of the central themes of this book. But it is very easy for the superiority of hindsight and a faith in more recent designs to distort the interpretation of the past. Anker's reaction to the clothing was instinctive and perfectly natural, but was Mallory really that badly equipped and did he feel inadequately clothed since there were no signs of frostbite? To appreciate what it felt like to be a 1920s Everester, it is necessary to understand what was known about survival in extreme environments and how that knowledge developed. Just as Thomas Holding foreshadowed the modern enthusiasm for lightweight camping, it may be that the combination of design, fabrics and tailoring went a long way towards ensuring tolerable comfort, even at high altitude.

Innovation and knowledge are close bed fellows and much depended upon what you did and who you knew. This applied both to climbing and to the development of equipment and British and Continental European climbers were playing different games for much of the first half of the twentieth century. The Austrians and the Germans were pioneering big wall climbing in the Eastern Alps and the Dolomites and developing technical aids like karabiners and pitons for protection and light felt-soled climbing shoes.[2] British mountaineers had begun with a summitting game in the Western Alps during the 'Golden Age' and, from 1880, extended it to the other mountain ranges of the world, when Whymper travelled to the Andes. It was only a matter of time before the Himalayas were added and Everest became the ultimate summit or the holy grail. It was an obsession which was to cut Britain off from the main developments in technical climbing for more than a generation. It also reinforced the division between the visible face of the climbing establishment, deemed to be 'officer' material for Himalayan expeditions, and the largely invisible urban and working class climbers of the Peak District and Scotland, for whom even a trip to the Alps was a wild dream. Since clothing and equipment are the toys climbers and outdoor people used, developed and improved in response to need, it comes as no surprise that British gear makers were not involved in manufacturing aids like pitons and karabiners before the Second World War. But the quest for Everest had its own effect – on innovation in clothing, in tents, in sleeping bags, in footwear – as a community of knowledge developed among mountaineers and between climbers and the manufacturers.

Survival in extreme climates was not new. Discussion of polar exploration has shown that by the time men and women were visiting the world's highest mountain ranges there already existed a bedrock of understanding – some of it deriving from the eskimoes. Interpreting and building on that knowledge varied significantly and it was the Norwegians, Nansen and Amundsen who perfected the art of polar travel by the First World War. British explorers such as Rae and McClintock appreciated the lessons of eskimo living and travel before 1850, but it was not until after the Scott debacle of 1910-12 that the significance of that knowledge was fully appreciated in Britain. [3] Nevertheless a bedrock of polar experience did develop and continued to build after the First World War and since at least some mountaineers – like Martin Conway – also went to the Arctic, there was some early synergy between polar exploration and mountaineering. In addition, suppliers of mountaineering clothing and equipment – like Benjamin Edgington, Burberry and Jaeger – were also at the forefront of supplying the major Polar expeditions. So dialogues with explorers about designs and innovations were repeated and reinforced by those with mountaineers and doubtless retold on journeys and in Himalayan base camps.

The Royal Geographical Society (RGS), founded in 1830, was synonymous with nineteenth and early twentieth century British Arctic and Antarctic exploration and with the quest for Everest, 'The Third Pole.' Through a love-hate relationship with the Alpine Club, the RGS organised and co-ordinated the Everest expeditions from 1921 until 1953. Certainly the role of the RGS was not always that constructive, but as a conduit of knowledge – between mountaineers, polar explorers and their suppliers- it was unrivalled as witnessed in the massive equipment collection in the Everest Files. They contain correspondence between successive equipment officers and suppliers and sometimes this is just pure exchange of information. But at times – as in the correspondence between mountaineer Frank Smythe and the inter war

Manchester designer Robert Burns – it was a lively and thoughtful interaction contributing in tangible ways to the development of better clothing and equipment . This chapter will track the way knowledge developed and was reinforced during the quest for Everest. It also assesses the impact of new understanding and technology which emerged during the Second World War as a result of the requirements of mountain warfare.

Everest as the Third Pole: The Building of Knowledge Before 1918

In the nineteenth century Europeans did little more than measure and map the world's highest mountain. Named after George Everest, the Surveyor General of India and superintendent of the Great Trigonometrical Survey from 1830 to 1843, Everest was formally placed on a map in 1856 following many years of surveying.[4] But at this time it was impossible to approach it since the borders of both Nepal and Tibet were closed to foreigners. The achievement of a height measurement from 200 miles away, that is within 10 metres of the modern figure, was truly remarkable. In any event in the mid nineteenth century mountain climbing in the Alps, let alone at high altitude, was in its infancy. But the driving force behind nineteenth century Himalayan exploration, and indeed mapping, was nothing much to do with sport and a lot to do with politics and imperial power. For the East India Company, the substantial expenditure of time and resources devoted to the mapping of India was partly symbolic. The building of a uniform and systematic map was a reflection of British political and imperial control as well as being of scientific interest. It was also strategic since the 'Great Game' for the domination of Asia, between Britain and Russia, also gave momentum to early British exploration of the high passes of the Himalayas. Although geographers thought the idea of an invasion of India via the Himalayas ridiculous, the Crimean War (1854-5) made the army take it very seriously indeed.[5]

Francis Younghusband was the father of British Himalayan exploration and the promoter of the 1920s Everest expeditions. Born in India, his early journeys into the Karakoram gave him a passion for mountaineering. He saw climbing mountains as useless in practical terms, but as a basic human urge. His three journeys between 1887 and 1890 began with a crossing of the Karakoram by the Muztagh pass (c 5500m) to the Baltoro Glacier and to Baltistan and Kashmir. He had no technical mountaineering knowledge and was without tents and any specialist equipment. In 1889 he investigated recent Hunza raids on the Karakoram Pass and he had a small escort of men from the 5th Gurkha Rifles including Charles Bruce. Destined to lead both the 1922 and 1924 Everest expeditions, Bruce was then a young subaltern who was already training his riflemen to be mountaineers. A third Younghusband journey followed in 1890 to the Pamirs, but this was less significant for the history of mountaineering.[6]

These journeys whetted Younghusband's appetite for mountaineering but they were essentially defence initiatives. The pacification of the borders of the Karakoram made it possible for Martin Conway to organise a major expedition from England, before which he consulted with Younghusband. This trip in 1892 was the first Himalayan expedition to be funded by the Royal Geographical Society. It was especially significant for the way it helped to build knowledge of the organisation and equipping of high altitude expeditions. Later President of the Alpine Club and a leading light in the RGS, Martin Conway was already an experienced mountaineer and traveller, having climbed extensively in the Alps. Although he took mountain guide Mattias Zurbriggen, he recognised the need for a different type of planning from that needed for an Alpine tour. As a result he explicitly modelled his ideas and equipment on Whymper's Andes Expedition of 1879-80. This list included:

'Tent, alpine sleeping bags, snow spectacles, felt covered water bottles, self cooking soup tins, chocolate, warm coverings for hands and feet, strongly nailed boots, cloth gaiters, soap –cerate plaster, Lloyd's cold cream for sun blistering ....'[7]

He used Mummery and Whymper tents and carefully analysed the effects of altitude and diet, pulse rates and wear and tear on equipment.[8] Oscar Eckenstein, who pioneered the 10 point crampon in 1910 was for a short time a member of the party, before he and Conway fell out and Eckenstein pulled out – something for which he believed Conway never forgave him. But his early presence may explain why crampons were used on this trip. Their use by the British was very unusual at this time probably as a result of their close relationship with their Swiss Guides, for whom step cutting was viewed as craft not a slog. However, Freshfield does confirm in his 'Hints on Mountain Travel,' published the following year, that crampons did allow wearers 'to reach a point which would be unattainable by step cutting'. Even more surprisingly – since most crampons were manufactured in the Alps, they were available from the Albion Iron and Wireworks Company in east London, with webbing straps from Buckingham's the rope makers. Almost certainly these were the English made crampons described by A.W. Andrews in 1907.[9] Conway's expedition did not achieve very much in mountaineering terms and his alleged height records were doubtful. But, based on Whymper's logistical mountaineering principle, it was the precursor of large scale Himalayan expeditions. It acted as a model for the Duke of Abruzzi for his K2 expedition in 1909, though he also brought polar experience derived in Greenland and Alaska in the 1890s to the Himalayas.[10] Since Abruzzi had climbed in the Alps with Alpine Club members, Collie and Mummery in 1894, it is inconceivable that information on logistics, equipment and planning was not exchanged. Conway's inclusion of Bruce – the future leader of the 1922 and 1924 Everest expeditions- was also important for building a knowledge base for Himalayan mountaineering. This especially brought an appreciation of the natural mountaineering and portering abilities of local people. For fifteen years following the expedition Bruce remained in the Himalayas gaining unrivalled experience both of the mountains and its people.[11] This understanding was an invaluable foundation for Himalayan exploration generally and Everest in particular.

Other British expeditions in the 1890s included Fred Mummery's fated trip to Nanga Parbat, which could not have been more different from the large scale organisations of both Conway and Abruzzi. However Tom Longstaff, another lightweight enthusiast first visited the Himalayas in 1905 and became an 'oracle to whom no subsequent traveller has ever turned for advice in vain.'[12] In 1907 Longstaff was joined by Bruce and A.L. Mumm and guides Alexis and Brocherel and explored the area around Kamet reaching 6150m. This was the first time that there was any suggestion that oxygen might help climbers at high altitude and Mumm took some small pneumatogen oxygen cartridges prepared by Siebe Gorman and Co, though he was not taken very seriously by his colleagues.[13] Longstaff's earlier trips to the Caucasus had demonstrated an interest in developing the lightest possible equipment for he was an enthusiast for silken ropes and oiled silk tents. But in the Himalayas his medical skills were vital to begin understanding the effects of altitude on the body and on physical performance. However, on the 1922 expedition, on which he was both medical officer and naturalist, he remained sceptical about the benefits of oxygen.[14]

Kamet (7756m), became an important focus for pre First World War British Himalayan activity and between 1907 and 1914 there were 7 more expeditions involving C.F. Meade (1910, 1912 and 1913) A.M. Kellas (1911 and 1914) and A.M Slingsby (1911, 1913). Of these C.F. Meade, guided by Alpine guide Pierre Blanc, reached a high point of 7160m.[15] His perceptions on equipment and most particularly on the adapted Whymper tent ,which came to bear his name are frus- tratingly absent from his own writings. However, as the future equipment officer for the 1920s Everest expeditions, his pre-war knowledge was clearly valued. Much of the development of knowledge of Himalayan travel in the late nineteenth century was inevitably concentrated among Alpine Club members before 1914 and embedded in their travel books and articles in the *Alpine Journal*.

Political tensions and problems of access meant there were no Everest expeditions before the First World War, although in 1913 Captain Noel travelled illegally to within 40 miles of the foot of the mountain.[16] That nothing more substantial was achieved was also partly because the Royal Geographical Society – whose support became crucial –was preoccupied with Antarctica until 1912, while some of its members were sceptical about the scientific merit of climbing mountains.

It was not until after the Great War that the quest for the Third Pole really began to take shape. The inspiration came from a lecture by Captain Noel in March 1919 about his illicit trip and the possibilities for further reconnaissance. He touched a chord with Percy Farrar, the President of the Alpine Club and also with Younghusband, his opposite number in the RGS and the Mount Everest Committee was formed.[17] The collaboration of a mountaineering club with a scientific society was not always a marriage made in heaven ; objectives could vary and by no means all Alpine Club members were happy to see Everest expeditions run by a committee. What this uneasy collaboration did create was a mechanism for sharing experience from pre-war Polar and Himalayan exploration. Some of the experience was already shared as some mountaineers had climbed in the Arctic. But increasingly through the 1920s and especially into the 1930s the strengths and weaknesses of Arctic and Antarctic clothing and equipment for high altitude climbing was explicitly appreciated by climbers.

The Fight For Everest 1921-24

The formal announcement of the Everest Reconnaissance Expedition came on 10 January 1921 and was predictably sensationalised by the press. With more than a whiff of the imperialist and heroic age of polar exploration the headlines ran: 'WHERE NO WHITE MAN HAS TROD'. They were indeed about to walk off the map, into the previously closed regions bordering on Tibet. The 1921 Reconnaissance Expedition was not a *tour de force* in any respect. There were all kinds of blunders in the composition of the team (not least the omission of George Finch), in terms of leadership, age mix and the sheer chemistry of the party, although it did succeed in finding the route in.

Undoubtedly 1921 lacked the depth and care of preparation of clothing and equipment found on the later expeditions. But part of the purpose of any reconnaissance expedition is to assess what is right and what is wrong and use the knowledge to improve kit and technique for subsequent assaults. That was precisely what was happening – they were using the best of what was available and what had been tried and tested before the war, to see how it performed. The organisation of equipment was in the hands of Farrar and Meade, who undoubtedly were competent to advise –especially given Meade's pre-war Himalayan experience. But Harold Raeburn – one of the most distinguished mountaineers of his generation – was to be in charge of the climbers and the mountaineering equipment. He was not an ideal choice, more because of his personality than for his knowledge. On the face of it he was well qualified – he had climbed in the Himalayas before 1914 and in 1920 had published *Mountaineering Art*, which demonstrated a comprehensive knowledge of all aspects of clothing and equipment, though admittedly for the Alps. But at 56 he was arguably too old for the expedition and was a difficult and obstinate man ,whose ill health on the trip made him understandably cantankerous, and quite unsuitable as a climbing leader. George Mallory found Raeburn inept on mountaineering equipment giving insufficient thought to the need for special provision for cold and altitude, though this was partly compensated for by Farrar and Meade.

If some mistakes were made, the expedition was anything but under-resourced. Climbers were left to arrange their own clothing and footwear and given a sum of £50, which could be raised to £100 if necessary. This was not a sign of neglect, for most climbers – as witnessed in the pages of the *Alpine Journal* – understood clothing and equipment well and were used to discussing their requirements with specialist suppliers who often worked to specialist patterns. The mountaineering suppliers like Hills and Co, Silver and Co and Benjamin Edgington in London and numerous hardware manufacturers in the Alps were used to working closely with knowledgeable mountaineers. In any event the £50 earmarked for each mountaineer's personal equipment was hardly a derisory sum – especially since all climbers would have already have had much of the standard kit already. The expedition was to supply all communal equipment , such as tents and heavy carrying equipment. It can be assumed that this sum was to supplement and upgrade clothing and other kit. At 1921 prices this sum was worth almost £1400 in modern terms – just imagine the kind of gear you could buy for that sum. Recommendations on personal clothing and equipment included:

Boots, 2 pairs	*New but broken in*	*Shirts, 4*	*Wool or silk*
Ice Axe, 2		*Stockings, 6 pairs*	*Wool medium thick*
Crampons		*Socks, 6 pairs*	*Wool or silk*
Rope, 60 or 80 feet	*Standard AC*	*Sleeping socks,*	*Shetland*
Woollies, 2	*Shetland*	*2 pairs*	
Helmet , 2	*Shetland*	*Waterproof*	*Thin and light*
Hats, 2	*Felt Broad Brimmed*	*Sleeping bag*	*Down with cover*
Gloves, 2 pairs	*Wool*	*Puttees*	*Thin and smooth*
Clothes	*2 suits climbing and some spare material*	*Rucksacks, 2*	*One Light*
		Head or hip cushions	*Down or air*
Underclothes 3-4 suits	*Wool or silk*	*Lantern*	*Excelsior folding* [18]

The 'best available' tents were those that had been tried, tested and improved – first in the Alps and in the Himalayas – the Whymper and the Mummery – and were supplied by Benjamin Edgington.[19]

Equipment was not just taken on trust and, before being dropped from the expedition, George Finch produced a report on tests on the performance of the

Primus at altitude carried out by Mr Dreyer at Oxford. The silent Primus was undoubtedly found to be more reliable than the roarer but both were unreliable above 6000m.[20] The resulting modifications were not entirely successful as Mallory complained of malfunctioning Primuses at altitude. However it is a sign that potential problems with equipment were being taken seriously and investigated. But another consequence of these tests was that they introduced George Finch to the idea that oxygen enhanced performance at high altitudes – in both people and in stoves. His experience in a decompression chamber was enough to convince Farrar and the Everest Committee to take the controversial step of including oxygen on the 1922 expedition.[21]

The 1921 expedition was undoubtedly poorly led and was, at times, an ill-conceived expedition with grossly inadequate food and fuel and, above all, under-equipped porters. This was a rather nasty reflection of the pejorative way 'coolies' were viewed by the organisers, if not the climbers. Mallory was justifiably critical of the equipment complaining that:

> *'Mummery tents may be well enough in fair weather , though even then the low roof suggests a recumbent attitude ; it makes a poor dining room even for two men and is a cold shelter from snow. '[22]*

But replacement with a heavier Whymper tent remedied the problem. Bullock's diary records having only a wet coat or two pullovers at 6000m. Even so the impression of the tweed Norfolk jacket and knickerbockers, which so amused Bernard Shaw, may be misleading . These were certainly used and photographed on the march in and at base camp, but the climbing suit on the kit list was not necessarily of tweed. There is no evidence of windproof sledging overalls, such as those which Shackleton took to Antarctica in 1921, but tailored Burberry windproof climbing suits had been advertised in the *Alpine Journal* since 1901. Being lightweight, tough and breathable they were ideal for mountaineering and whilst there is no conclusive evidence that they were taken, Raeburn certainly endorsed the idea of using light, rather than heavyweight clothing, and silk and woollen layers (dismissing cotton as cold and clammy). He also pointed to the regular use of gabardine, not least for its power to repel snow.[23] Surprisingly canvas, rather than Burberry, was used for the tents, even though the windproof gabardine had been used for tents by both Scott and Amundsen in the Antarctic.[24]

If bad leadership left elements of the 1921 expedition a shambles, there was a constant learning process through both the 1920s and 1930s, with systematic attempts to improve and build on experience. Howard-Bury recorded that all members of the expedition had been consulted as to their feelings about provisioning and equipment of the reconnaissance. This exercise had highlighted the shortcomings of diet, tents and the poor equipment of porters as

Alpine Club Collection

1922 Expedition at 23,000 showing 16 lb. Meade Tents.

being the prime difficulties. This experience was used to ensure mistakes were not repeated the following year – especially the unforgivable neglect of the Sherpas, who were to be provided with the same clothing issued to troops in Northern Russia during the First World War. The few going to high altitude were equipped in the same way as European climbers.[25] That the mistakes of 1921 were digested was borne out by Bruce, the leader in 1922. He appreciated the work which Farrar and Meade put into improving kit on the basis of what had been observed by Mallory and others in 1921. Accordingly:

'The tents were improved in accordance with the experience gained. Most particular attention was paid to the boots. Clothing and bedding light in weight but warm to wear were specifically designed. Ice axes, crampons, ropes, lanterns cooking stoves and also warm clothing for the porter and much else besides...'[26]

The improvement to tents was the adaptation of the Whymper tent to make what was to be christened the Meade. Basically at 19lbs, compared with 35lbs for a Whymper, the Meade was a lighter Whymper with a fly sheet, and was clearly developed in response to Mallory's 1921 plea for a more comfortable small tent than the Mummery. Mallory was much happier with the tents in 1922 than the previous year, though he still preferred Whympers to either smaller tent, simply because he found them more comfortable and also warmer. Like his companions he had not a good word to say about the 'ingenious circular opening' – imported from Polar designs which were used on some of the Meade and Mummery tents. In common with his generation he was obsessed by the lack of ventilation in both Mummery and Meade tents. Why the constant cries for more air when the door fastening must have brought in a healthy draught not to mention spindrift? One reason may be that he and his contemporaries had grown up in draughty houses, where sleeping with open windows, whatever the weather, was the norm. This stemmed from the widely held belief at this time that diseases were airborne. But headaches are a fact of life at altitude and it is possible that the 1920s climbers blamed the tents, when the real culprit was altitude. In summing up his assessment of tentage he concluded that the exchange of a little weight for greater comfort was worthwhile.[27] With further improvements following in 1924, the Meade was to become an enduring feature of Everest expeditions not least because it was easy to put up in high winds. In 1953 lighter, more modern tents – some Swiss and some American – were available but 'undoubtedly the best was the two man Meade'.[28]

George Finch in eiderdown suit on skis on Everest 1922, the first known use of a down jacket.

National Library of Scotland Courtesy of Mrs J.N.I. Russell

Farrar and Meade gained considerable, if sometimes unpopular, technical advice from the unconventional George Finch. Australian born and educated in Switzerland, Finch was something of a misfit among the public school dominated Alpine Club. But he was a strong climber, with a formidable pre-war reputation for guideless climbing in the Alps. He was also an innovator whose impact on successive Everest expeditions was applauded by John Hunt in 1953.[29] Although best known for championing the then unpopular cause of oxygen for high altitude climbing, he was also the first man to take down clothing to the Himalayas and was unusual for taking his skis. This intensely practical man was to be the expedition handy man and was deeply frustrated on the march in to be separated from tools and Primus stoves as this meant that he could not make alterations and improvements to boots etc en route.

Nevertheless he devised an ingenious method of waterproofing his maps using a duroprene coating, after first mounting them on Willesden canvas.[30]

Down had been used for bedding for centuries and in down petticoats in the 1860s, but eiderdown sleeping bags and camping quilts had been around for 30 years, favoured for their excellent insulation qualities. Quite what inspired Finch to design a down suit is not clear, other than the careful and considered thought he gave to equipment and clothing generally. He has been credited with being the first man to replace a jacket with a light hooded anorak in the Alps in 1909, so he was no stranger to innovative clothing.[31] His suit was made up by S.W. Silver and Co to his own design and consisted of 'eiderdown lined coat,

trousers and gauntlets' and was covered in balloon fabric [32] His companions
thought it a huge joke – one of his eccentricities – but it was a great success and
ridicule soon turned to envy when he was warmer than they were. On 12 April
1922 during the march in he wrote:

*'The wind was poisonous from the beginning. I wore flying boots... we also wore all
manner of warm head gear. Everyone felt the cold except myself – my eiderdown coat,
trousers, flying boots and flying helmet kept me as warm as toast all through... [while
six days later he confirmed] everybody now envying me my eiderdown coat and it is
no longer laughed at. May it do its job well on Everest...'* [33]

Up to a point it did, though conditions when he camped with Geoffrey Bruce
at 7770m were as bad as they could be and even with his down clothing he was
cold. His diary says it all for at that altitude and without protection from the
savage wind their tent threatened to blow away:

*'Room for our Meade tent was found on the very background of the ridge leading
up from the North Col to the North East shoulder of Everest, height 25,500 feet
(7770m) about.... The cold was bitter. We got no sleep, we dared not for ever so
frequently we all had to do our best to hold the tent down. At about 2.00am I
clothed myself up in all my warmest clothes (good old eiderdown suit) and going
outside, firmly belayed down the tent by passing all the alpine rope over the ridge
and poles and fastening both ends firmly to boulders. But the effort was all I could
manage and I returned to the tent chilled to the bone and utterly exhausted.'* [34]

While there is much evidence of a cumulative learning process on some
elements of kit, he remained the lone Everest down enthusiast until the 1930s.
It is possible that the suit was insufficiently robust for heavy and sustained use,
but it does seem to have been ahead of its time. Even Finch himself, while
arguing emphatically for totally windproof garments and even suggesting a
rubber coating, which would of course have caused condensation, ceased to
champion down in his writings of 1923 and 1930. In 1924 although Norton
noted the attractions of Finch's eiderdown suit the experiment was not
repeated. The idea was, however, revived again when Ruttledge began
preparing for 1932 and consulted the reports of earlier expeditions. He was so
impressed that he wrote to Finch:

*'In going through the equipment reports of the previous Everest Expeditions I
have been very struck by the unanimous opinion that the balloon cloth eiderdown
quilted clothing worn by you proved very warm and windproof. I am great
believer of eiderdown myself, and it seems to me that your idea is worth going into
very carefully for the expedition being planned for next year.'* [35]

What happened is not quite clear because down was not used on a British
expedition again until 1936.

Without the insulation of down, windproofing and protection against frostbite, was an even more crucial issue than it might have been. Mallory seemed reasonably content with the clothing that he used in 1922, describing it as 'generally sufficient'[36] Sledging suits were certainly used by some as Morshead put one on above the North Col around 7600m.[37] But several 1922 climbers suffered from frostbite, suggesting that there were problems. Finch – apparently having abandoned faith in his beloved eiderdown suit – was concerned to see further improvements in windproofs, gloves and footwear for future expeditions. He indicated that different altitudes brought varying insulation needs, giving a lie to the notion that in the 1920s climbers believed they should simply dress as for the Alps. For him the crucial divide over keeping warm came between 6400m and 7000m or above the North Col. At that altitude, the combined effects of oxygen deficiency and the loss of any shelter from the relentless wind made staying warm far more difficult. In describing conditions above 7000m, in a 1923 *Alpine Journal* article, he drew the analogy with conditions at the poles but with one key difference – the impact of altitude. It was this which made the case for oxygen so compelling for him, because it improved climbing performance, made it easier to keep warm and reduced appetite loss.[38] His clothing recommendations below this altitude were broadly Alpine, while for the upper zone providing the mountaineer had oxygen, combined light layers, with windproofs and gave particular attention to hands and feet. He included six or more layers of silk, wool, with an outer windproof, preferably lined with flannel and covered with a layer of light duropreened canvas and final layer of transparent oiled silk. He also recommended a hooded jacket with a fur collar to prevent air penetrating and a fur band around the body. To prevent frostbite to fingers he suggested thin woollen gloves under a lambskin pair and topped by a durorpreen over glove.

'The RNAS (Royal Naval Air Service) pattern helmet is the most suitable form of headgear, with a chin piece covering the whole of the face up to the nose. Crookes' glasses, let into a mask lined with soft fur and large enough to cover the remaining exposed portion of the face complete the headgear....'

The proposed outfit was not perfect, since it is hard to believe that a rubber coating would not have led to condensation, but Finch remained convinced that 'against the storm winds of Everest …nothing short of an absolutely non-porous material, such as oiled silk, rubber or gold beater's skin is wind proof enough'.[39] He was by no means infallible and like others at this time, he believed smoking was beneficial at altitude and recommended cigarettes. These were not just as a distraction from discomfort, but as a stimulant –which of course nicotine is. But this was before any scientific understanding of the carcinogenic and respiratory damage caused by cigarettes and based on observation of his and Geoffrey Bruce's experience. Yet elements of his advice

– especially on footwear – were spot on and almost certainly contributed to future developments. For instance he realised that leather conducted heat too well for it to be a good source of warmth. He proposed a light felt upper, covered and protected by duropreened canvas and a thin leather sole over 3-ply wood and a thin layer of felt and that the sole should be lightly nailed.[40] His ideas were adapted for subsequent expeditions and elements – particularly the outer protective layer- look remarkably like a predecessor to the SATRA boot used on the 1953 British Everest Expedition.

Most people associate Finch with oxygen and the controversy which this caused in 1922 and beyond. The mirth which accompanied his down suit partly stemmed from the suspicion which his championing of 'English air' aroused in some circles. Climbers such as Mallory and Longstaff saw it as unnatural or unnecessary. Opinionated Arthur Hinks, the parsimonious Treasurer of the Everest Committee, had never been on a mountain in his life, but disliked and distrusted everything about Finch and was only too happy to pour scorn on his enthusiasm for oxygen. But there was another reason for his opposition – the sum of £400 or the equivalent of over £15,000 at current price and income levels must have appalled him. For a man who begrudged every penny spent over budget – especially if it was to go on frivolous climbing, rather than the serious business of science and mapping – the expenditure was little short of outrageous. A deeply frustrated Farrar pointed to the contradictions in the climbing community which led oxygen to be condemned for high altitude climbing after all he said , echoing Finch:

'One may use extraordinary clothes to counteract the cold, any kind of food or drink, yet when an essential to full efficiency requires to be administered by a tube from a receiver, instead of being drunk out of a bottle, it is liable to condemnation as sinning against the canons of 'legitimate mountaineering'.[41]

Certainly the oxygen sets which were used in 1922 caused problems by being too heavy –at 32 lbs. per set – and very unreliable. But Finch and Geoffrey Bruce reached 8320m using oxygen – a new Everest high point and 150m above Mallory's high point without oxygen and did so about a third faster. To some at least the case for oxygen seemed proven, even if the technology required much improvement and simplification and some climbers still retained a suspicion of it.[42] Certainly Mallory was convinced, but Longstaff still retained a healthy scepticism about oxygen. He feared that it could encourage an unfit man to climb beyond his limits while the weight of the sets displaced vital food and fuel. He did acknowledge that its use could reduce the dangers of frostbite but blamed the deterioration of the weather for the problems of the 1922 party.[43] However, in summing up the failure of Everest 1922 he was quite clear that it was a learning experience:

'Mount Everest, the Goddess Mother of the Snows, with all her formidable array of natural defences, had conquered. But the value of reasoned determination, unwavering confidence, really warm and windproof clothing and, last but not least, the proven worth of oxygen – weapons to break down the innermost defences of even the highest mountain in the world – are now, perhaps, better understood.'[44]

Everest 1922 was not a blueprint for an expedition but, as in 1921, the experience was not lost and, quite apart from those like Finch and Longstaff who published at length about their experiences, all participants fed back comments into the growing bank of information. Compared with the sometimes cursory discussion of kit in the modern expedition reports housed at the RGS, the Alpine Club and the British Mountaineering Council (BMC), these could be very revealing and none more so than George Mallory's. In 1922 Mallory's equipment notes were detailed , intelligent and informative and quite at odds with his image as impractical. He may have been forgetful, but like so many of his generation he was used to discussing kit and its improvement with suppliers. This made him perceptive and observant and he took his obligation to feed back comments seriously, making numerous practical suggestions for improvements. He had after all already seen the benefits of his 1921 observations on tents in the Meade improvements. He remained sceptical about Primus stoves and was appalled by the rucksacks which he believed 'were pitiful – artless square bags made of unsuitable material and having straps improperly attached; they were much too small'. He seems to have been complaining about the high altitude sacks rather than those used by the porters for load carrying. For a supposed impractical dreamer he was much concerned with the inadequacy of the tool kit . He also complained that the crampons provided for porters were too long and suggested that 'it might be worth while to devise a stand fitted with 4 small spirit lamps to heat the wings of crampons and a special instrument for bending them.' It may have required innovators like Finch to improvise and improve kit on a trip and beyond, but Mallory was clearly alert to demands placed on equipment and how to improve it.

Had Finch been included on the 1924 expedition he would almost certainly have been in charge of clothing and equipment. But he was left out, deemed unsuitable by the Everest Committee and especially by Hinks. This was partly for his continental lecture tours and use of his photographs, deemed to be breaking the Committee's control of all lecture tours and agreements made prior to the expedition. But it was not the whole story of his unpopularity of course, and he believed firmly that a prime reason why he was suspect with the climbing establishment initially lay with his championing of oxygen and that it was a prejudice that stuck. His practical skills were doubtless sadly missed on the 1924 expedition. However, Sandy Irvine was an inveterate tinkerer, who took over much of the day to day care

Andrew Irvine in Shackleton suit on Greenland trip, 1923

and improvement of the temperamental oxygen and cooking equipment and indeed anything that needed mending.

Some mountaineering photographs seem to sum up an age and the 1924 base camp photograph of Irvine, Mallory, Norton, Odell and John Macdonald is one of them. The climbers do not seem to be dressed very differently from three years previously. In many ways this photograph epitomises the myth of the Norfolk jacket and knickerbockers and it has come to symbolise the tragedy of Mallory and Irvine. But it was a posed photo, taken at base camp rather than a true reflection of clothing for high altitude climbing. Anyway the kit notes make it clear that 'an old tweed coat and knickers are useful for the march, base camp etc.' implying that thereafter something more robust was needed.[45] A photograph of Sandy Irvine, probably taken on his trip to Spitzbergen the previous year, paints a very different picture, showing a young man who, apart from his flying helmet and pipe, looks remarkably modern and well equipped. He was dressed in an adaptation of the Shackleton windproof sledging suit and in well insulated footwear. Unlike the ubiquitous Everest base camp photograph, this image of 1920s cold weather clothing seems never to have been reproduced, other than in Norton's official history of the 1924 Expedition. It is not what we have come to expect of 1920s mountaineers and that is the secret of the perpetuation of the myth. We think they were poorly equipped because they did not have the benefit of modern clothing and because photographs confirm our prejudices. But what they wore was far less primitive than it might seem and had been improved on the basis of experience, both on the previous two expeditions but also from polar exploration.

Norton's much quoted description of his outfit has also been interpreted to mean that there had been little progress in the personal outfit of high altitude mountaineers:

Nielson's lightening fastener. Sandy Irvine ordered several lengths of Auster's lightening zipper directly from the Birmingham works. His pockets had zips but some of the lengths (4 feet and 6 feet) suggest he may have been experimenting with zips for tent fastenings).

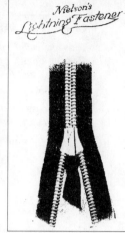

A Lightning Fastener for Tent Doors, etc.

Several Members have written in for particulars of Messrs. Nielson's invention, and we, therefore, reproduce this illustration for their information.

The fastener certainly is a most ingenious device, but it is a little difficult to describe. Imagine a row of metal paper fasteners on either edge of the tent door with a cord running through them, and a clip which, when pulled downwards rapidly and smoothly closes the opening and interlocks these paper fasteners and *vice versa*—and you have it. Possibly light-weight fabric will need to be reinforced, but this, probably, will need the test of experiment to determine. Anyhow, it's a fascinating and novel invention, and completely took us by surprise.

'Personally I wore a thick woollen vest and drawers, a thick flannel shirt and two sweaters under a lightish knickerbocker suit of windproof gabardine, the knickers of which were lined with light flannel, a pair of soft elastic Kashmir puttees and a pair of boots felt bound and soled with leather and lightly nailed with the usual Alpine nails. Over this I wore a very light pyjama suit of Messrs Burberry 'Shackleton' windproof gabardine; on my hands I wore a pair of long fingerless woollen mitts inside a similar pair made of gabardine; though when step cutting necessitated a sensitive hold on the axe haft, I sometimes substituted a pair of silk mitts for the inner woollen pair. On my head I wore a fur-lined leather motor cycling helmet and my eyes and nose were protected by a pair of goggles of Crookes glass, which were sewn into a leather mask that came well over the nose and covered any part of my face which was not naturally protected by my beard. A huge woollen muffler completed my costume.'[46]

But far from being stuck in a time warp this was very much in line with many of Finch's suggestions – including double windproofs and special high altitude footwear. And, compared with 1921 the kit notes are detailed and explicit in the need to use the most modern and effective clothing. The Shackleton smock, overalls, (together weighing 2lbs) RAF helmet and mitts were all deemed essential and while the tailored Burberry windproof climbing suit was optional, it was strongly recommended. [47] To appreciate the quality of what was worn requires an understanding of both the variety and capabilities of fabrics in a country renowned for the variety of its textiles. Developed in Lancashire and tested by the Manchester Chamber of Commerce, Burberry windproof gabardine was extremely versatile and had the added advantage that snow did not stick to it. It was also superior as a wind repellent to many modern windproofs. The inclusion of two rather than one windproof layers, as well as layers of wool and silk, is significant while the flannel lining was also most

Firms Supplying the 1924 mount Everest Expedition.

Army & Navy Stores Ltd	*Groceries and other foodstuffs*
Benjamin Edgington Ltd *1 Duke Street London*	*Tents and camp equipment* *Sleeping Bags for Europeans and Coolies* *Mattresses and Rucksacks*
Och Freres, St Moritz	*Skiing Socks*
Bergans Meis Og Rygnaak *Christiania*	*Packing case carriers and straps* *Sick Man carriers*
A.C. Cosser Ltd *Aberdeen Works, Highbury London*	*Thermos Flasks and food containers*
Fritsch and Co Zurich	*Aluminium Camp Equipment,* *Crampons, Nails for boots*
McGruer Hollow Spar Co Ltd., *Commercial Rd London*	*Duralumin Ladder and bridge*
Fortnum and Mason Ltd *Piccadilly London*	*Canteen boxes and contents* *Skiing Gloves*
Condrup and Co Ltd *Fore Street London*	*Primus stoves and spares*
Meta S.A. Basle	*Cooking stoves for high altitude* *Meta solidified spirit*
Hudson Bay Company	*Blankets*
Frost Brothers *Commercial Road, London*	*Alpine Rope*
Dowie and Marshall Ltd *Strand, London*	*High Altitude boots for porters*
Burberry Ltd, Haymarket, London	*Shackleton sledging outfits for Europeans*
Fagg Bros., 101 Jermyn Street London	*High Altitude boots for Europeans*
W.T Avery Ltd	*Spring balances*
R. Melhuish Ltd, Fetter lane	*Tool Outfit*
W.H. Smith and Son	*Stationery*
Negretti and Zambra Ltd	*Max and Min Thermometers*
C.F. Casella and Co and *Cary-Porter and Co Ltd*	*Air Temperature Thermometers*
Aitchison and Co Strand, London	*Compasses*
Siebe, Gorman and Co	*Carrying frames etc for oxygen apparatus*
Armstrong, Whitworth and Co Ltd	*Cylinders for oxygen apparatus*

Source: List of firms supplying Mount Everest Expedition 1924:RGS Archives: 402/EE/38/2

normally made of wool. Modern climbers are used to being able to buy their clothing off the peg from outdoor shops, but their predecessors built up close relationships with specialist manufacturers. In addition sporting outfitters made up suits of a standardised design to the personal measurements of the climber, and this careful fitting was one of the keys to their performance. Climbers were instructed, when they went to Messrs Burberry in Haymarket, to ask for Mr Pink who would doubtless measure them carefully. This was all part of the growth of understanding between the climbing community and their suppliers. There were also notable innovations since Sandy Irvine used custom made zip fasteners.[48] Their clothing was clearly state of the art. Breathable cotton windproofs had been found very effective and versatile at the Poles and especially during high exertion activities. Indeed the most uncomfortable part of the 1920s Everest trips will have been the walk in through tropical rain, since no really effective waterproofs had been developed.

Footwear too had evolved as Norton's outline had shown, but the kit notes reveal even more of the evolutionary process and were clearly influenced by Finch:

> *'For climbers one pair of special felt boots. Mr Fagg has the specification, though the boots are so far in the 'experimental stage'. Members would be well advised to get a pair made in time to test them and make any minor adjustments before sailing. These boots are the result of last year's experience and the essential feature is that that the leather sole should be nailed (with the points of the nails turned down) before being attached to felt soles ... these should be supplemented by one pair of good Alpine climbing boots in case they fail; Mr Carter supplied two members of last year's party with particularly good boots of Lampar pattern to take stockings and two pairs of socks; the soles should be treated similarly to the above to avoid conductivity of nails and with a felt sole between the welt and the nailed sole if possible...'[49]*

There was no explicit mention of the distinctive V shaped nails which, according to Mallory in 1922, had 'stayed in better than any others'[50] but these were used and can be seen on the boots recovered from Mallory's body in 1999.

The development and improvement of clothing and equipment required a good dialogue between suppliers and the expedition leaders. The preceding table shows the firms involved and with many of them there developed a valuable interchange revealed in the ongoing correspondence in the Everest files in the RGS.

Although the surviving correspondence for the 1920s is limited, there are tantalising insights into innovations that occurred and some quite surprising ideas investigated. For instance the Norwegian company Bergan supplied the carrying frames and some of the rucksacks for the 1920s expeditions and as always concerns were expressed over weight according to the equipment notes:

> *'The Bergan Meis weighs 3lbs. Is it considered desirable to reduce this weight? The frames can be made lighter by being made of pure aluminium and the sacs can possibly be made of lighter material.'[51]*

This pre-dated the commercial development of modern aluminium pack frames by a generation.Sometimes the initiative for changes and modifications came from climbers or those who were carrying out testing on behalf of the expedition and company responses varied. Some companies-like Bergans- saw this was an opportunity to improve their product while others, including somewhat surprisingly the manufacturers of Primus, sat on requests and did very little. Cooking at altitude had been a problem in both 1921 and 1922, for much the same reason that climbers struggled – the lack of oxygen. George Finch had worked hard to improve the performance of Primus stoves and make them more versatile and his design proposals both for stoves and for oxygen were continued by P.J.H. Unna before and after the 1924 expedition. He found Messrs Hjörth and Co of Stockholm, the makers of the Primus, slow and unresponsive, especially compared with their competitors the Swiss Meta company. Unna pulled no punches in a letter to Hinks in March 1924 commenting on his forthcoming article on the expedition. He was frankly frustrated with the Primus' manufacturers for lack of response throughout. Perhaps the success of their stoves for polar work and general camping had made Hjörth a little complacent in a highly specialised niche. Meta, in trying to build their market share, were far more responsive.[52]

Even so Unna believed that the Swiss would need some incentive – such as the promise of future expedition contracts – to make the modified cookers commercially available.[53] In fairness pressure stoves remained unreliable above 6500 metres and it was not until gas stoves were added to the repertoire after the Second World War, that a solution to the 'stove problem' was found.

The Illusive Summit: Everest in the 1930s

There were no more Everest expeditions in the 1920s mainly because access from Tibet again became a problem. But, when planning began again in 1932, there was still a significant knowledge base on which to build, because while Everest may have been temporarily abandoned other parts of the Himalayas and the Poles were not. When denied access from Tibet climbers turned their attention back to the Karakoram and in 1930 a four nation party of Swiss, Austrians, Germans and British, led by the Swiss Dyhrenfurth, attempted Kangchenjunga (8586m) while the next year a party led by Frank Smythe climbed Kamet.

Frank Smythe was a very different personality from George Finch and had none of his unconventionality. But he was considered 'difficult' by many of his contemporaries and treated with some suspicion within the Alpine Club, for being almost a 'professional' mountaineer who lived off his writing. But he did emerge as knowledgeable about kit, not so much as an innovator but as a careful adaptor, whose understanding was valued by fellow climbers in the 1930s and by the War Office during the Second World War. Regular visits to the Himalayas in the 1930s brought him an understanding of the special demands of that extreme environment as well as an appreciation of others' experience. He was quite clear that a bedrock of understanding had developed, and anyone reading his introduction to *Kangchenjunga Adventure* is left in no doubt that there was expertise embedded in the history of Himalayan climbing and polar exploration, which the aspiring Himalayan climber ignored at his peril. Echoing George Finch, he distinguished between climbing up to 7000m when normal Alpine kit was perfectly adequate and above that height which requires:

> *'...more specialist equipment, for owing to the effects of altitude and subsequent lowering of vitality and bodily wastage, the winds that mercilessly sweep the upper ridges, and intense cold, it is essential to prevent frostbite.*
>
> *There is only one way of efficiently clothing an expedition, and that is to study the lessons of the past, and to take heed of the lessons learnt, often at considerable cost, on expeditions such as Sir Martin Conway's in the Karakorams and the three Mount Everest expeditions. These lessons and the recommendations derived from them are all laid down and should be studied with the utmost care. Nor should the late Sir Ernest Shackleton and the clothing which he provided for his expeditions into Antarctica be neglected, for he was one of the first to make a scientific study of light wind and cold resisting clothing.'*[54]

Accordingly he poured scorn on Dyhrenfurth for ignoring the conventional wisdom and insisting on heavy rather than light equipment for Kangchenjunga. Certainly the equipment does sound on the heavy side. Indeed at 20 lbs. for clothing and a further 6.5 lbs. for boots, 4lbs for crampons and 2.5 lbs. for an ice axe it is surprising anyone got out of base camp. The sheer effort of lifting his feet at 7000m in the expedition boots, was not something that Smythe forgot in a hurry and he was quick to point out the fallacy that one warm thick layer is better than several light ones. Of course he may have been suspicious of the Continental liking for loden – probably the material used for the coat. However the other kit does seem pretty excessive and may reflect limited Swiss experience outside Europe, while pursuing differing climbing games from the British. Continental companies dominated technical climbing equipment in this period and were inseparable from the development of climbing in both the Western and Eastern Alps. Smythe certainly has nothing but praise for the camping equipment supplied by Messrs Schuster of Munich which 'stood up well to wind and rain'. But:

> *'The best thing of all among the camping equipment was the synthetic rubber ground sheets. These were about one third of an inch thick. Not only do they keep one dry, but they insulate one from the cold ground or snow, and are soft enough to eliminate the 'inevitable stone'.*[55]

This pre-war forerunner of the Karrimat proved immensely popular whenever added to the kit. But for Smythe his sleeping bag was the most crucial bit of kit and in getting this just right he began a most fruitful partnership with gear-maker, Robert Burns of Manchester.

The dialogue between the two men began before Kangchenjunga ,when as Smythe admitted he began fussing about his bag a bit like a cricketer worried about the brand of bat. Earlier sleeping bags for Everest had been too narrow, often required a contortionist to get in them, and above 7600m the sheer effort of doing that was exhausting. Quite simply he wanted his bag to be 'invisible' and set about eliminating all causes of irritation, adding only those features which improved comfort and insulation. Side lacing was abandoned as was the notion that the tightest bag was the warmest. He preferred eiderdown and designed a double sleeping bag and approached Robert Burns to make it up.

> 'It was seven feet long, 32 inches wide at the head end, tapering to seventeen inches at the feet end, and weighing eight pounds fourteen ounces. It consisted of two quilted eiderdown bags, one inside the other. The inner one was lined with Jaeger fleece, and the two bags were enclosed in an outer covering of jaconet (light muslin). Both bags and the outer covering were fitted at the head end with a string bag arrangement. The length was so ample that I was able to snuggle up right inside it with only my nose and mouth projecting through the drawn opening.' [56]

It was very versatile because of the range of possible combinations that the two bags allowed and was used throughout the trip from the tropical forest right up to the climbing high point. Interestingly he had also found a solution to the problem of condensation which was prevented by the air space between the two bags. This was a crucial step forward since damp sharply reduces the insulation qualities of down and he slept well and comfortably throughout the six week expedition. A bit like Finch and his eiderdown suit it was with a certain smugness, that he listened to the grunts and groans of his companions, as they struggled to get comfortable in their inferior sacks issued by the expedition leaders.

This was the basis of the design which went to Everest in 1933, and which had a pedigree built on Alpine experience. Burns showed that the ideas behind Smythe's sleeping bag came directly from bivouacing on the Brenva face of Mont Blanc which made him think a lot about how to adapt and improve existing designs. He had

> '...a Zdarsky tent which was merely a large bag made from a sort of rubberised cambric, he tried this out on one occasion. The method of using it is to pull it over the head and sit inside supporting it with the body. One would no doubt coil the rope or line and sit on that, and endeavour to hold the tent off the body with the ice axe. However, it is impossible to keep it from touching all round and where ever it does touch the cold strikes through. Another disadvantage is that, being air proof it is necessary to lift it at frequent intervals to get air to breathe. Finding its utility in its original form so very small he converted it into a cover for an ordinary down sleeping bag, and with this outfit he bivouaced under the Red

Sentinel, when he made his wonderful ascent of the Brenva face of Mont Blanc. He spent a fairly comfortable night, although the bag was too tight and condensation formed inside the outer cover.'[57]

It was this experience that brought him to the double bag, while the wider dimensions allowed him to keep his boots on, which stopped them freezing during the cold of the night.

Smythe's Kangchenjunga sleeping bag marked the beginnings of a highly fruitful dialogue with Robert Burns – a genuine relationship of innovation- which continued right through the 1930s and made Burns a challenger to established suppliers like Benjamin Edgington. Burns began as the designer for E. Buck and Co – the Bukta brand beloved of the Scout movement – but was already semi-independent in the late 1920s. His challenge was not confined to sleeping bags, but included other elements of the market which Edgington's had

Everest and the Himalayas became crucial marketing platforms for manufacturers like Robert Burns. From the *Oxford Mountaineering Journal 1935-7.*

dominated for so long – tents and rucksacks. He also experimented more generally with down and by 1935 R. Burns Ltd of Hanover Mills, Buxton Street advertised as supplying Tents, Sleeping Bags, Rucksacks, Padded Clothing and Mountain Stretchers for a number of major Himalayan expeditions, including Kamet, Kangchenjunga, Nanda Devi and Everest.[58]

Burns' initial reputation came from the hiking and camping craze. He was a bit like Mike Parsons and Pete Hutchinson who, thirty years later built Karrimor and Mountain Equipment and benefitted from Annapurna 1970. A keen climber himself, he could not believe his luck when the expeditions of the 1930s catapulted him into the world of high profile mountaineering. Even in the 1930s these trips brought national media exposure and ample advertising opportunities. However, again like his successors Parsons and Hutchinson in the 1960s and 1970s, his enthusiasm for making good functional kit leaps out of his letters, while the two way benefits of his dialogue with Smythe led to steady improvements in his designs. The wider commercial benefits of providing specialist kit for mountaineers and explorers were perfectly clear to him as was the importance of years of experience and experimentation. After all:

'Great expeditions, record breaking and even stunts, almost always influence the design and construction of equipment or machines used afterwards in everyday affairs and the Everest Expedition of 1933 [shows this]. Many of the gadgets have been devised specially for the Expedition, but the majority have been adopted because they have proved useful on previous Himalayan expeditions, in the Alps or in the Arctic.'[59]

The man who made 'it safe to sleep out for democracy' was delighted to get a letter from Frank Smythe in September 1932 about the lessons from Kamet and inviting improvements for Everest 1933. Smythe suggested a reduction in the weight of the sleeping bag, a hood and a tapering at the foot end (really a move to what we now think of the classic mummy design) otherwise he thought the sleeping bags were excellent. But he was keen to use a really lightweight climbing pack and asked him to think about whether he could make one like that used in the Alps by Kirkpatrick and Hope before the First World War. This was made of a Macintosh fabric and weighed 6 oz. Two or three loofahs were substituted for the metal frame and provided the same level of ventilation for a fraction of the weight.[60] Burns obliged with a sack weighing just 4 oz – although Hugh Ruttledge, the expedition leader rejected this as too flimsy, choosing another weighing 11 oz.[61]

Smythe was also keen to improve the design of high altitude tents and find one which combined lightness, warmth and strength. He initially favoured a Norwegian pattern which tapered at the feet – a classic lightweight shape. He returned to the idea of a tunnel entrance in preference to the overlapping flaps more normally used on the Meade tent because:

'Not only could wind driven snow penetrate, but the tapes when tied frequently froze up and could not be untied with gloved hands which might easily lead to frostbite on Everest'.[62]

He favoured the entrance design used on the Watkins' Arctic expedition. Despite Smythes' faith in Burns' custom made products, the Everest Committee were a conservative bunch and initially preferred to play safe and rely on tried and tested Benjamin Edgington, rather than an obscure Manchester designer. Disappointed but irrepressible, Burns persuasively talked of taking a prototype tent:

'to Wales if there is likelihood of gales, pitch it on top of Carnedd Llewellyn and spend the night in it. I shall then be able to test the new kind of door I have embodied in it. If anyone can come along and accompany me I shall be glad.'[63]

The trip took place –vividly recalled in his obituary – and his enthusiasm paid off.[64] Although Benjamin Edgington remained significant suppliers of tents, sleeping bags and rucksacks Burns cornered the market for some of the more specialist items. Three of his adapted Meades with a triangular door were used, along with sleeping bags and lightweight rucksacks –some of which he supplied to the expedition *gratis*.[65] He was nonetheless very doubtful about another tent taken by Jack Longland for emergencies. It incorporated the old Victorian weight-saving idea of substituting ice axes for poles and had an Arctic tunnel entrance. According to Burns it was awkward to erect and of course we know how the 1920s Everesters had hated tunnel entrances, but it was only meant as a last resort.[66]

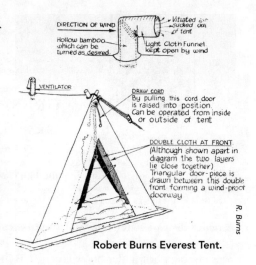

Robert Burns Everest Tent.

Burns was, however, very impressed by a tent design from the rival company Camtors, which was a genuine departure from the standard mountaineering shape and had been used by Gino Watkins in Greenland by the British Arctic Air Route Expedition. The 'pyramid' tent was shaped like an igloo and was made of Jacqua, one of several windproof materials.[67] High up at Camp V it was invaluable, enabling parties to 'continue up the mountain in full strength instead of being half frozen, battered and weary from loss of sleep on that wind lashed platform at 25,700 feet.(7830m)'.[68]

The success of his 1933 products established Burns' reputation as an expedition supplier and this continued through to the Second World War. Maybe inspired by George Finch's 1922 prototype, about which he will have heard or by experiments that were taking place on the Continent, Burns began to develop down clothing that was first used on the 1936 expedition. But he dealt more with Shipton than Smythe and communication was not perfect and the chemistry between the two men, so vital in any exchange of ideas, does not seem to have been right, so that it took a while for a rapport to build up. First in a curt note on 12 November 1935 Shipton dropped Burns' sleeping bag designs. Burns, having begun work, was justifiably irritated since they were specialist items unsuitable for commercial sale, though happily the order was restored. Secondly some of Burns' ideas were fairly whacky and definitely experimental. This was particularly true of his 'Cubi-cell' down clothing, which consisted of eiderdown waistcoats and shorts (eventually replaced with down breeches) designed to be a substitute for woollen layers. They were unfortunately very fragile and when Shipton put the shorts on they immediately split down the front. Burns was worried that Shipton had misunderstood the precise purpose of garments which

The sketch shows the design of the GRENFELL Cloth climbing suits used by the Everest Expedition, 1936. Grenfell Cloth is absolutely Wind-proof, so care had to be taken to keep the suit openings draught-proof.

It's only on rare occasions that one wears a garment like this.......but one often has need for a :: ::

GRENFELL

RAINCOAT

3 Gns.

JOHN KENT & Co. Ltd.

Exchange Street East,

LIVERPOOL.

Grenfell climbing suits. From 1937 *Wayfarer's Journal.*

were to be worn under other layers.[69] By return Shipton told Burns that the problem was nothing to do with putting the garment on and that what was needed was some strengthening of the waistband. If the exchanges lacked some of the natural meeting of minds which Burns had built up with Smythe, Burns got the order for eight eiderdown suits and Shipton was soon feeding valuable design ideas to improve them. But the fact that they were to be used instead of woollen layers does not seem to have registered, for Shipton talked of using layers of woollens under them.[70] Described as 'good for sitting around in, but hardly worthwhile elsewhere than at extreme heights they were very warm, light and at 10 guineas a suit expensive, but delicate and soon fell to pieces'.[71]

Burns also supplied his newly designed high altitude tent – the Yak which had evolved from his 1933 experiments and been tested on Shipton's 1935-6 Reconnaissance Expedition. These small relatively lightweight (11lbs) tent were made of Grenfell cloth and two could be joined together by a sleeve entrance with one sleeve tucked into another to form a wind and snow proof joint. Climbers could then communicate with each other –a major psychological advantage which was later echoed in the Karrimor Instructor Survival Unit.[72]

What is interesting though is that whereas in 1933 Burns had been on the fringes as a supplier, by 1936 he had completely ousted Benjamin Edgington for sleeping bags and tents – to say nothing of supplying the new-fangled down clothing. Whether because they were becoming complacent or were too expensive, Edgington's were entirely dropped from Everest 1936. [73] The company were clearly stunned and offered to supply tents free of charge, but received in return a dismissive and rather irritable letter from the Mount Everest Committee in January 1936:

Alpine Club Collection

Everest 1933, Harris and Wager descending from Camp VI wearing Grenfell Suits.

'...as I told you in our recent interview we have got all the tents that we require for the coming expedition and I greatly regret that it will be impossible for us to take any more. I would like, however, to thank you for your most generous offer to present us with a number of tents, but the difficulties of transporting a large bulk of surplus goods prevents us from accepting this kind offer...'[74]

It was clearly a case of don't ring us we'll ring you ! Given that in 1934 they had been passed over for Andrew Croft's Oxford University Arctic Expedition, in favour of Thomas Black and Co, this was doubtless a chastening experience.[75]

Robert Burns was not the only supplier to make his debut in the expeditions of the 1930s, challenging the position of long established firms. Two others were from the North West of England – Robert Lawrie, the Burnley boot-maker and Eric Taylor of Baxter, Taylor and Woodhouse the Manchester firm which, through the 1930s, marketed Haythornthwaites' Grenfell cloth. This was an interesting story of how a new community of knowledge developed. In the first place all three men were keen outdoor people and climbers and came to know each other both professionally and through sport. Burns had used Grenfell for both rucksacks and tents while working for Bukta and advised Eric Taylor to contact the Mount Everest Committee in 1932.[76] Similarly Lawrie like Burns had a reputation among hikers and along with Haythornthwaites was a Burnley firm – he was also a great fan of Grenfell cloth. Whatever the initial catalyst, during the 1930s Robert Lawrie came to replace James Carter and Co – who had been advertising in the *Alpine Journal* since 1867 – as the leading mountaineering bootmaker. Similarly Grenfell cloth rather than Burberry became the favoured windproof from 1933 until the Second World War, despite Burberry's long pedigree.[77]

Invented for the Arctic missionary Sir Wilfred Grenfell in 1923, Grenfell cloth was a tightly woven, high quality, cotton fabric that was used for flying suits, high quality leisure wear and, in the 1930s , for mountaineering for both tents and clothing. The origins of the fabric and Haythornthwaite's have been described in an earlier chapter and by 1930 the fabric had been perfected. It was an extremely specialist and technical fabric, which needed skilled weavers to produce it without a flaw and was exceptionally difficult to finish. It is a measure of the high relative skill of Lancashire textile workers that, when the Americans, with their more standardised textile traditions, tried to copy it to make 'Byrd' cloth, they could not produce it in any volume.[78] Tested by the Manchester Chamber of Commerce against Cupra – another windproof considered by the Mount Everest Committee- Grenfell was both lighter (at less than 6 oz per square yard) and stronger.

As well as being chosen by the Labrador Missionary, Grenfell began to be used for other high performance purposes. It went to the South Pole with Byrd in 1931 and a Grenfell suit was used in the flight over Everest in 1933. During the 1930s Haythornthwaites marketed the cloth through the Manchester company of Baxter, Taylor and Woodhouse and it was within this association that the key to its popularity for mountaineering lies. The secret of the success of Grenfell in this period lay in the combination of a light windproof fabric with Eric Taylor's specially designed climbing suit, which became a classic for a decade. It was far more sophisticated than the Shackleton overalls and more modern than the Burberry climbing suits. A climber himself, Taylor recognised that however good a cloth was, it was useless if the design of the suit was inappropriate. He developed a 'standardised' climbing suit, with variations for winter and summer, including a detachable hood, a jacket with zipped front and windproof wrists which could then be made up by a tailor. But like all good outdoor designers he wanted to improve it and invited readers to contact him. [79] The response he got from climber Marco Pallis, published in the next edition of the *Mountaineering Journal*, could not have been more helpful. It incorporated suggestions from Howard Flint, who Pallis believed was the only man in the country who really knew how to make a climbing suit. It is the first article to address one of the most crucial issues faced by any expedition climber – the subject of passing water – though interestingly he stopped short of discussing defecation. Flint's main suggestion was for the front fastening:

'This is a Zip with an inner lining of cloth to prevent the metal searing the flesh. It may be due to reasons of false modesty, but the question of passing water is generally ignored in discussions of this type, and more damage has been caused to climbers through this than any single thing. There are scores of young men today suffering from internal troubles caused by inattention to this important problem. In the past, suits designed for low temperature wear have not had front fastenings. Obviously the fly front would not do as it admitted the wind and the snow. The practice was,

therefore, to have a completely enclosed front, and when relief was desired partially to remove the garment. Now as the diet of most expeditions consists largely of hot liquid food, the necessity of relief is comparatively more frequent than in normal life, and this meant that often during the day, there was an exposure of the body to the cold. But worse than this followed. After the function had occurred, the climber found it quite impossible in the open to tuck in his shirt etc., into their positions, leaving that part of the body semi- unprotected. The result is now apparent in the frequency of stomach trouble amongst members of recent expeditions.

The Zip fastener on the trousers designed by Mr Flint obviates this as far as the male is concerned.[80]

Taylor's Everest suit was an adaptation of the general purpose suit and appears to have taken on board many of Flint's suggestions, while adding some of his own. The crucial innovations included an integrated quilted hood with a windproof gusset, a draw string and fur linings, wind traps on the cuff and zip fasteners on both pockets and flies. It was also made double thickness to increase wind resistance. He recognised that high altitude clothing needed to be comfortable, windproof and sun-proof as well as being easy to manipulate. Crucially he grasped that kit should be 'invisible' saying:

'I had to take into consideration the men working at such high altitudes could be subject to nervous tension so that the slightest irritation in the lie of their kit would become an intolerable burden.[81]

Grenfell cloth was used for clothing and for some tents for Everest right the way through the 1930s and, like Burns, Taylor was always trying to improve what he made. One piece windproof climbing suits did not appear on the scene until Pete Hutchinson and Don Whillans developed them in the 1960s. The one piece Sidcot flying suit had first appeared shortly after the First World War[82], but there were obvious limitations for prolonged use in extreme climates because of toilet needs. There is evidence that the overalls used by Sherpas in 1922 had been one piece, but without zips they were doomed to failure. Based on his own designs for flying suits, Eric Taylor was talking about the possibility in 1935 in a letter to High Ruttledge, pointing out that the advantage would be the removal of anything tight around the waist, making bending down in the tent more comfortable. [83] He sent a sample for Frank Smythe to try but, in the event the suits that were ordered were two piece. He also continued to experiment with zip fasteners believing they were wonderful devices 'so long as they are used with knowledge of their limitations' and not used indiscriminately. But most intriguingly he experimented with synthetic resin zips which would not cause frost burn in the way that metal does, again probably with the one piece suit in mind. These were being made by ICI and did not become brittle in sub-zero temperatures and Ruttledge was keen to try them. However, for unspecified reasons, neither innovation was taken to Everest. That they were discussed at all

One of the many types of boots always in stock.

Mark VIII. Weight : unnailed. Size 8, 3·lb. 15·ozs.

A copy of our fully illustrated catalogue and self measurement form will be sent to you post free on request.

SPECIAL HIGH ALTITUDE MODEL

Recent expeditions to which we were the official suppliers include :

1933 Mount Everest Expedition.
1933 Marco Pallis Gongatri Expedition.
1934 Wordie's Arctic Expedition.
1934-37 British Grahamland Expedition.
1935-36 Kaulback and Tracy Tibetan Expedition.
1935 International High Altitude Expedition.
1935-37 Oxford Arctic Expedition.

ESTABLISHED NEARLY HALF A CENTURY AGO—THE KEY-NOTE OF OUR BUSINESS IS QUALITY AND SERVICE.

ROBERT LAWRIE, LTD.
38 BRYANSTON STREET, MARBLE ARCH, W.1

TELEPHONE : PADdington 4993   *Inland Telegrams :* Alpinist, Wesdo, London.   *Cablegrams :* Alpinist, London.

Robert Lawrie moved to London in 1935 and built on his Himalayan reputation.

is an interesting reflection on the process of clothing development.[84] Taylor maintained great respect for Flint as a tailor and was convinced that the performance of any garment was related to the quality of the fit.[85]

The third new north west supplier was Robert Lawrie, who was interestingly the only one to supply Everest 1953 as well as those in the 1930s. Mention of Robert Lawrie now brings affectionate memories of a man whose unchanging London shop became an institution in his lifetime. It is hard to think of this link with the past –his boots remain collectors' pieces- as an innovator. But, as well as crafting bespoke nailed boots he also developed high altitude boots for the Everest expeditions of the 1930s and made his name as a result. Like Robert Burns, his background at the heart of the interwar hiking boom has been traced in an earlier chapter. Climbers had a choice of boots which could be bought from either James Carter or Lawrie. Lawrie's new high altitude design contained several novel elements, including interior felting and a lambskin inner sole. He also used asbestos webbing as an important source of insulation – a practice found in the Alps before the First World War. The boots were not universally popular and in 1936 there was a note that Carter's boots were generally better.[86] That said, Lawrie was able to build a reputation on these expeditions and removed from Burnley to London on the strength of his new found status as an Alpine Equipment Specialist. It was an interesting move which reflects that, despite the growing popularity of provincial companies as suppliers of outdoor clothing and equipment, the action remained based in London and the Alpine Club. Lawrie's roots may have lain in the north but, as a craftsmen making bespoke climbing boots, the future still seemed to lie with the elite.

The 1933 and 1936 Everest expeditions achieved relatively little in climbing terms and there were few if any fundamental changes in approach to the mountain. Disputes over leadership, organisation and appalling weather made 1936 an embarrassing and expensive failure to the tune of £10,000. At a time when much of industrial Britain remained in the grasp of the Great Depression, it was more of an outrage than an embarrassment, for many people and had parallels with Ken Wilson's condemnation of the 1970s Bonington expeditions.[87] It helped to create a reaction against extravagant, large scale expeditions in favour of Shipton and Tilman's 'back of the envelope' lightweight trips, which were both philosophically and, at around a quarter the cost, economically much more attractive. But, if 1933 and 1936 had achieved little in mountaineering terms, Tilman was quick to acknowledge their contribution in terms of kit to his attempt in 1938:

'The sole innovation in the matter of equipment was that we took only essentials and not too many of those. Three very good types of tents have now been evolved from bitter experience so that many of the discomforts suffered by earlier parties are things of the past. It cannot be pointed out too often that each party draws on the experience and profits by the example of its predecessors – we of course benefited most. The types of sleeping bags, warm clothing and windproof suits, as now used will not easily be improved upon, but the search for ideal boots and gloves for climbing still goes on.'[88]

This remarkably perceptive comment sums up the very significant incremental progress that had been made on clothing and equipment through the inter war period. The solution to the high altitude boot lay with the SATRA in 1953. But in the 1930s the interchanges and understanding had built up between climbers and their gear makers – who were themselves committed outdoor people. For the first time, the elite of the Alpine Club had come into contact with that group of provincial based designers and manufacturers, who were also climbers and whose knowledge and experience of sport lay in the Peak District and the Pennines. It has already been shown that on these gritstone crags a climbing tradition had emerged that was quite different from the Alpine Club and of which their members were largely ignorant. From the perspective of kit development, it marked a break with the past, where firms like Benjamin Edgington had built a strong reputation for military and ceremonial tents and also interpreted the designs of mountaineers. As climbers themselves, Burns, Lawrie and Taylor were better able to appreciate their customers needs and this was reflected in the advances in clothing and equipment.

The impact of polar knowledge also became particularly noticeable in this period as well. This of course began earlier, for the experiment with the unpopular tunnel entrances used on some of the Meade and Mummery tents and the introduction of windproof sledging suits from 1922, suggest the direct influence of polar experience on the improvement of kit. Certainly in preparing for 1922, the Mount Everest Committee had used equipment notes from Scott's 1910 preparations looking especially at the footwear and crampons used.[89] Nor was the impact confined to clothing and footwear, for in 1921 two Nansen cookers, surplus from a pre-war polar expedition, were taken. The 1923

Spitzbergen expedition which, as well as Irvine included both Odell and Tom Longstaff, will also have brought experience to Mount Everest. But in the 1930s the links and the interchange of knowledge became much more noticeable. One reason for this was that J.M Scott, who had been with Wager to Greenland, became Secretary of the Mount Everest Committee. There developed a cross-fertilisation of ideas as so many of the suppliers and designers, like Eric Taylor and Robert Lawrie, also provided clothing and footwear for the Arctic.

The British may have had Everest to themselves in the 1930s, but not of course the entire Himalayas. Mention has already been made of the ill-fated four nations trip, but there were others including those organised by the German Paul Bauer and by the Frenchman, Pierre Allain. International differences in 'climbing games' were reflected in technical equipment as has been shown in an earlier chapter. But there were also differences in less specialist kit at this time, which transferred themselves from Europe to the Himalayas. Smythe's bivouac equipment was a case in point for, although he was an enthusiast for lightweight expeditions, the British summit game – until after 1936 – was based on large scale expeditions. By contrast, both the Germans with Bauer and the French with Allain were committed to a much more streamlined approach to the Himalayas. Both Allain and Bauer talk of a pragmatic and philosophical shift in the approach to climbing in the Alps after the First World War. Climbing without guides, the Germans and the Austrians had pioneered big wall climbing in the Eastern Alps from around 1910. After the First World War Germany was a bankrupt nation and so a simple approach to climbing became an imperative. This philosophy was not confined to Germany and also emerged in France after 1928, when again growing economic stringency led French Alpinists to reconsider the extensive use of guides. In both cases this had an impact on the equipment they used and in some instances –especially with Allain- contributed to some of the most significant clothing and equipment innovations of the twentieth century. They transferred their ideas to the Himalayas at the very time, when the British, under the influence of Shipton and Tilman, were also reconsidering the viability of large scale expeditions.

Lightweight Munich climber Paul Bauer told of how they transferred their new ideas from the Alps to the Himalayas in the 1930s and, like all mountaineers, built on past experience:

'We restricted our baggage, and our necessary comforts, to the minimum we relied rather on companionship, self sacrifice and good organisation, than upon the quantity of supplies and elaborate outfit...We paid continual visits to Schuster, the sports outfitters. We invented new devices, made models of them, discarded them and built them up again in better forms, until at last everything was shipshape.

There was only one really possible way of getting such an outfit together, and a thoroughly good outfit it was too – the English in India spoke of our 'splendid equipment' and our Tenchedar who wielded the cook's spoon with the Everest expedition was continually astonished at its simplicity and comprehensiveness. That was because we had taken care to go into every possible detail for years beforehand. We also had at our disposal the experiences gained in our journey to the Caucasus in 1928 and those of the German and Austrian Alpenverein's expedition to the highlands of Pamir and South America. Finally we could compare these experiences with those of the English expedition and fill any gaps first hand'. [90]

Bauer was an outstanding mountaineer and, like Pierre Allain, he was also an equipment innovator. His ideas included a very short wide ski, the forerunner of the Salewa 'firmgleiter'. He also learnt the techniques of igloo construction and snow holing and applied them at altitude. His other innovations included a small dynamo torch and an integrated sleeping bag and air mattress – a forerunner of the Gore system launched in 2002. The approach of Bauer and Munich climbers differed from British lightweighters, in that their mountain assaults were Alpine style but their planning was logistical rather than being 'on the back of an envelope'.

As chapter 6 has demonstrated Pierre Allain's experience was very similar and his ideas for creating a better weight to insulation ratio were revolutionary, he combined down clothing with a light rubberised silk garment – the cagoule. [91]

Whereas Smythe was ingeniously adapting existing designs, Allain's ideas represented fundamental platform breakthroughs which, in time, were to transform mountain bivouacing. The combination of the down jacket and the pied d'elephant saved weight and improved insulation. The rubberised waterproof cagoule, which kept the down clothing and sleeping bags dry, was the forerunner of its coated nylon namesake which became a synonym for a waterproof from the 1960s.

It is interesting just how much work was being done, world wide, relating to down in the early 1930s. While Allain and Burns were experimenting in Europe an earlier chapter showed that Eddie Bauer had patented the down parka called the Skyliner. [92]

The Impact of War

The Second World War inevitably ended all attempts on Everest, but it brought improvements to fabrics, materials, clothing design and equipment which were to benefit post war expeditions. It also disrupted existing patterns of knowledge and created new ones, especially through mountain warfare and through the development of specialist cold weather kit for the airforce and the navy, as well as mountain troops. These communities inevitably involved mountaineers, some of whom like Frank Smythe, also advised the War Office on cold weather clothing and in Mountain Training. But they were also international, including those countries like the United States and Canada that took mountain warfare infinitely more seriously than the British.

Outdoor companies ceased to manufacture for leisure needs and often shifted almost seamlessly into the war effort. For tent makers like Benjamin Edgington and John Edgington, the transition was relatively easy as pre-war both companies had been significant suppliers of ceremonial and military tents. So we find John Edgington producing mountain warfare tents, their designs being tested by the Ministry of Supply at Farnborough using the slipstream of an aircraft for a wind test.[93]

Robert Lawrie got out of London almost as soon as war was declared and decamped to 53 Stodman Street, Newark-on-Trent, Nottinghamshire on 30th September 1939. He stayed there for the duration of the war specialising in making military boots and equipment. He promised to continue making mountaineering boots, though for how long he managed is unclear.[94]

During the first 18 months Haythornthwaites, the manufacturers of Grenfell cloth, produced 5 million yards for the three services and then faced a bombshell. The grave cotton shortage, brought on by the need to conserve scarce shipping space for food and armaments, led to an acceleration of the policy of concentration of production in far fewer mills, so that around half of spindleage and loomage across Lancashire was made compulsorily idle. Only those mills concentrating on Government orders or for export were to remain open. Walter Haythornthwaite was incandescent when he found that although 84% of their machinery ran on government orders, they were to be closed down. He complained to his MP that:

'If a closing down order by the Cotton Control is their interpretation of JUSTICE and RIGHT we can only presume that they have been educated upon different lines to ourselves or is there a faint suspicion of 'Fifth Column Activity' impeding the War Effort'[95]

He had a point, for Grenfell Cloth was a highly specialist cloth, ideally suited for military purposes. But family rumour has it that the problem lay, not with the cloth or the efficiency of the factory, but with relations between the Ministry of Supply and Haythornthwaite himself. He could be short tempered, but impatience with the bureaucracy of the Ministry of Supply often had one result – shifting contracts- and he certainly was not the only manufacturer to be deprived of a contract by sometimes vindictive officials.[96] Whatever the cause Grenfell cloth went out of production in 1941 and did not reappear until 1945.

But crucial wartime fabric and clothing development was to have a lasting impact on what was available for peacetime mountaineering and exploration. Fine cotton nylon fabrics were developed for parachutes while Ventile – very similar to Grenfell – was developed by the Shirley Institute because of the high casualty level of airmen on convoy duty ditching into the icy waters of the Atlantic. This became a problem because home based RAF fighter escort was impossible – they just did not have the range and so Churchill had promoted the idea of catapulting Hurricane aircraft from the decks of merchant ships to provide local cover. Of course they then had nowhere to land and the pilot could either ditch or bail out. Although they were relatively easy to find as they had lights, within only minutes most died of exposure – until the development of a new 'miracle'. In 1941 The British Cotton Industry Research Association (the Shirley Institute) perfected a fabric using long stapled cotton which kept out water when the yarns swelled. Garments in this fabric dramatically improved airmen's survival chances from a few minutes to 20 minutes which made rescue a real possibility. As a result 80% of anti-submarine pilots who fell into the sea survived, as compared with a mere handful previously.[97]

As a potential peacetime outdoor fabric it was not impermeable – like rubber or plastic coated cloths – and so was also breathable, making it ideal for a wide range of active pursuits. Whilst there were some doubts about the durability of the lighter versions , the tests on British ventile clothing in the Arctic in late 1940s 'proved superior to any other type of arctic clothing similarly tested'.[98] And almost as soon as the war ended its benefits were trumpeted in the press by a cotton industry anxious to recover:

'Lancashire has found a new world beating use for cotton. It has produced a cotton cloth which is rainproof, storm proof windproof and warm.'[99]

Tests in 1985 showed it compared very favourably with modern fabrics like Gore-Tex and for Polar work it still remains the preferred option for some explorers.[100]

Shortage of supplies of hemp and the specialist requirements of the Admiralty, the Air Ministry and the Ministry of Supply for reliable cordage was the catalyst for the development of nylon rope. Experiments with nylon fibre began quite early in the war at the Leith factory of British Ropes Ltd and by the end of the war they were producing nylon cordage for glider tow ropes, marine purposes, parachute cords and climbing ropes.[101] Although hemp ropes did reappear after the war, the advent of nylon rope proved to be one of the single most important innovations in the history of climbing In Himalayan climbing they were used for the first time on Shipton's 1952 expedition to Cho Oyu.

The war also acted as a catalyst for a fundamental change in mountaineering footwear, the shift from the nailed boot to the rubber Vibram. The pattern on these soles mimicked the nail design on traditional boots but offered far better insulation.

Changes in fabrics, materials and the design of clothing and equipment was not of course confined to Britain and some of the most important and far reaching changes, from the point of view of post war mountaineering came from the United States. Interestingly the Americans could not compete with the British on cotton textile development and in 1943, in trying to develop a better water resistant fabric, were forced, somewhat shamefacedly, to send a technician to the Shirley Institute to get details of the construction of Ventile. This is not that surprising, since historically American cotton cloth was both coarser and more standardised than in Lancashire and so the development of skill and technical knowledge was more limited. However, the United States soon took the lead in the perfection of synthetic fibres and polymers, which were to transform outdoor kit post war.[102]

With potentially different theatres of war the Americans, and indeed the Canadians and Europe's mountain nations, devoted far more attention to mountain warfare and the development of specialist clothing and equipment than was the case in Britain. Indeed in Britain, although the mountain warfare school was established at Braemar with first Frank Smythe and then John Hunt, the future leader of Everest 1953 as chief instructor, the military establishment only really took such training seriously post war.

In addition, and crucially for post war clothing and equipment, it created new communities of knowledge. Wartime demand and the 10th Mountain Division gave a massive stimulus to what became the modern American outdoor trade . For instance members of the 10th Division, like Gerry Cunningham founder of Gerry Mountaineering Equipment Co ,Ward, Colorado were to make a real and genuine contribution to the development of mountaineering equipment. Cunningham became a supplier of Everest 1953 and was author of *Lightweight Camping Equipment and How to Make it.*[103] Similarly Eddie Bauer turned to military contracts, making 25,000 flight suits and a million sleeping bags to meet military demand. Such was the quality of the clothing and bags he produced that he was the only supplier able to display his label on his products. This undoubtedly raised product awareness and helped make his post war mountaineering market. [104]

The impact of the war on American specialist clothing and equipment for mountaineering was particularly noticeable if the 1938 American attempt on K2 is compared with later expeditions in 1953 and in the 1960s. Before the Second World War they bought virtually all their specialist clothing –from woollen underwear, through lightweight sleeping bags, high altitude tents and boots in Europe.[105] In 1953 the military influence was clear with the newest type of Army underwear, socks boots and insoles. Gerry Cunningham was also a prominent supplier, providing nylon windproof parka and pants as well as a lightweight tent, while a down jacket was specially designed by Eddie Bauer of Seattle. Likewise on the 1962 Everest trip, suppliers were all American with Gerry Mountain

Sports and Eddie Bauer remaining prominent.[106] Interestingly boots were still a problem and they tried a variety including a Lawrie high altitude boot. But they concluded that 'the ideal boot should be insulated along the lines of the Korean boot, and should not freeze'.[107] In addition relatively open lines of communications developed between the British and American and Canadian military for testing cold weather clothing. From the late 1940s through the 1950s there were regular mountain warfare trials where British, Canadian and American clothing was tested and compared and improved where necessary.[108]

The Ascent of Everest 1953

John Hunt's 1953 Everest expedition was the best equipped team ever to go to the Himalayas. John Hunt had had a distinguished army career which stretched back before the War. He had served in India in the inter war period and had climbed in the Karakoram in the 1930s, taking part in three expeditions. He had initially been selected for the 1936 Everest expedition but was dropped when a minor heart murmur had been detected. During the war, he worked for a time with Frank Smythe at the Braemar Mountain Warfare School. Compared with Eric Shipton, who was dropped as leader in 1953 in favour of Hunt, his climbing career was quite modest.[109] But Hunt was chosen more for his proven logistical and organisational skills than his respectable climbing record. His expedition style and philosophy was the antithesis of Shipton, that master of the lightweight. Hunt, by contrast, applied military logistics and planning, which were second nature to him, to what was effectively a siege of the mountain. The two preparatory chapters in his book are immensely thorough while the planning documents included in the appendix – covering the ascent, preparatory period and expedition timetable, were designed to 'lead [the climbers] methodically towards achieving [their] aim'. They certainly would not have fitted on the back of either Shipton's or Tilman's envelope. The published planning document included an organisational chart and full logistical analysis and quite apart from extensive notes on diet, fluid intake, and equipment, including oxygen, filled 43 pages of the book. [110]

Hunt used all of his international and army contacts – a massive and influential network- to source the best possible products from around the world. Fabrics, for the most part came from Britain where the combination of Government research organisations and Lancashire producers manufactured new cotton nylon fabrics.[111] There were some pre-war fixtures – not least Howard Flint the climbing clothing tailor who also had a range of army contracts. Benjamin Edgington reappeared, doubtless on the strength of a strong wartime performance in tents. But one of the earliest casualties was Grenfell cloth, by then established back in production and used by Shipton on the 1951 reconnaissance expedition and on Cho Oyu in 1952. Anguished letters from Haythornthwaite and Sons Ltd began to wing their way to the RGS in Kensington Gore, as soon as rumours that alternatives were being considered reached Burnley. At first there came a reassuring letter from climber W.H. Murray, a veteran of 1951 and Cho Oyu saying:

> '*I do not think you need worry at Hunt's testing out other clothing than Grenfell. It is only his duty to try out new stuff and I know that he is very conscientious... I imagine that Hunt's question is: 'Is there a cloth of similar weight and quality as Grenfell but which is even more windproof?' It is his duty to experiment. I do not believe that a satisfactory test can be made in the Alps, which are relatively windless mountains. It is thus possible that he may be forced to take the experimental garments to the Himalayas to test there. In any event I cannot believe that Grenfell will not be taken too....*'[112]

But Murray was wrong and just 3 days later the news came back that a cotton nylon cloth was to be used for both windproofs and tents. It may or may not be significant that the Mount Everest Committee had been assisted by Haythornethwaite's wartime bête noire, the Ministry of Supply, who did the testing:[113] This is not to suggest that a conspiracy went back over a decade to 1941 when Haythornthwaites were closed during the war, but that the gap in production meant they were superseded by new fabrics.

Hunt's myriad of military contacts proved an invaluable basis for sourcing the best possible kit , but in no sense did he throw aside the experience of past expeditions. Preparations included reviewing the interwar trips , but most crucially the experience of especially the 1952 Cho Oyu trip and the failed Swiss attempt on Everest. This build up of knowledge had major implications in 1953 for use and design of oxygen equipment, high altitude boots, tents and stoves as well as diet and rehydration. Perhaps the most outstanding innovation of Everest 1953 was the SATRA boot. Working in collaboration with the British Boot, Shoe and Allied Trades Research Association the problem of frost bite was solved by a combination of inner vapour barrier, mesh insoles and an integrated rubber outer gaiter. The waterproof vapour barrier's inner layer stopped boots becoming sweat soaked and then freezing, the mesh insole allowed sweat to disperse from the socks, (equalling or perhaps improving for the first time on the age old use of arctic sedge grass by the Lapps), while the outer gaiter prevented snow melt soaking in. In addition, there were 5 layers of kapok, a natural hollow fibre and forerunner of the synthetic versions produced today[114] and the boot lasting technique was very special to prevent compression of this vital insulation material. The Italian Vitalio Bramani had developed a revolutionary new moulded rubber sole in the 1930s, making metal nails practically redundant. However this sole was still quite heavy. The outer sole developed for Everest 1953 was not the new Italian Vibram sole, but was made by Dunlop and used micro cellular rubber to further improve insulation and decrease weight, although the loss of durability was accepted, this was a summit boot. This was a breakthrough and no-one on Everest 1953 had cold feet let alone frostbite.[115] This boot was expensive and whilst used on Kanchenjunga first ascent by George Band and Joe Brown, never went into commercial production at all. In terms of insulation and weight it was not bettered until the development of plastic Koflach boots in the 1978.

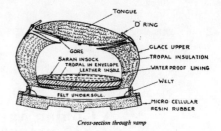

Cross-section through vamp

The greatest breakthrough product of all time which was never commercially exploited; vapour barrier inner, mesh insoles, micro cellular rubber soles, stretch rubber outer gaiter, kapok insulation with special lasting to avoid compression. See center color section for a picture of Hillary and Tensing.

The direct impact of Everest 1953 on the British outdoor trade at first sight was minimal, because it was too early, the austerity of the immediate post war period was too close. But chapter 8 shows it was indirectly one of the triggers for the emergence of a number of internationally competitive companies.

CHAPTER 8
A Golden Age of Innovation
1960-1995

Harry Griffin mused that in the 1920s:

'You didn't see climbers in the fells, there was no television to picture their antics, no climbing magazines, no climbing equipment shops, no lectures, films or slide shows and 'no outdoor pursuits'. The whole business of climbing was a complete mystery to most people – if they ever thought about it. What was the rope for? Did they throw it up to catch on a rock and then swarm up it? Nobody seemed to know. To most people, climbing must have seemed a strange game played out on dangerous cliffs, probably by crazy people from the universities. None of us leaving school, and certainly not before then, had ever seen a climber or anybody with a rope. Although we lived on the edge of the Lake District and were adventurous youngsters it was right out of our world.'[1]

This perfectly sums up how mountaineers were viewed before the Second World War: they were 'crazy people' who sometimes got themselves killed in a largely hidden sport. But the world changed dramatically after 1953 and mountaineers and mountaineering became more visible and accessible. Some had gained a taste for climbing at the Mountain Warfare Schools or through Outward Bound Training. This was the brain child of German-Jewish refugee Kurt Hahn. Laurence Holt, of the Holt Shipping Line, had alerted Hahn to the need to improve the survival rate of the young sailors, forced to abandon ship after being sunk by German U-boats . After the war, mountaineering stopped being just for the wealthy and mountaineers became folk heroes rather than mad people. The War itself had created a need for a national mountaineering organisation to liase with government over equipment and training. This organisation – the British Mountaineering Council (BMC) founded in 1947 – became a basis of training, of standards and had broad membership along the lines the Continentals had embraced in the late nineteenth century. The real catalyst of change, however, was Everest 1953 – which succeeded without a fatality – and made mountaineering seem safe as one letter from a 12 year old girl to John Hunt highlights:

Dear Sir John,

'...Last year we went with Mummy and Daddy to Wales and climbed Snowdon. Next year we are going to Scotland to climb Ben Nevis. Will you please send us details about climbing Mount Everest so we may climb it the year after.'[2]

On the strength of this mountaineers became influential and it was this which helped to institutionalise outdoor education, which had a massive impact on a whole generation. After the doldrum years of the interwar period British mountaineers bounced back, in the 1950s and 1960s. They played catch up effectively with an amazing energy and dynamism. Chapter 6 has shown how this working class generation brought practical skills to climbing and to the equipment they used and designed. Men like this became working class climbing heroes.[3]

All of this was a prelude to what now looks like a 'Golden Age' of innovation for the British outdoor trade. For outdoor companies it was reminiscent of the Victorian 'Golden Age' of Alpine climbing, when British climbers and their guides collected the 4000 metre peaks and it was almost as unexpected. It was a period recalled by Cameron McNeish when firms like Karrimor, Mountain Equipment, Troll and Berghaus became world beaters. [4] But like the Victorian 'Golden Age' it did not look in anyway inevitable in 1953 and the companies which became so innovative were not Everest suppliers.

They were new companies, whose owners were keen and active outdoor sportsmen and who understood the needs of climbers, skiers or backpackers. This chapter explains how they emerged and why they were so successful. They were not the only innovative companies in this period and to track every company, every innovator, every innovation in this extraordinary era would be a book in itself. But they help to give the flavour and essence of what drove the trade. The appearance of these new companies was linked to the post war upsurge of mountaineering, skiing and outdoor sports world-wide and to the resurgence of British climbing at the leading edge – as compared with its moribund pre war performance. But it was a more complicated story than this. It was linked to the war, the first ascent of Everest, to the leaps forward in ice climbing and technical equipment, to changes in leisure and to new sports, to changing attitudes to clothing. That it did not always feel like a Golden Age, for those involved, is easy to forget with the comfort of hindsight. But it spanned one of the most troubled periods for the British economy and for labour relations. Mike Parsons, then Karrimor's owner, has described the 1970s as one of the most difficult periods of his life and the 1980s as a battle for survival. But, in terms of innovations across the outdoor trade, the 1960s to the 1990s were extraordinarily creative.

War inevitably has had an impact on the design of specialist clothing and equipment. This can be traced through from the Napoleonic Wars – with the introduction of the two strap rucksack, the Crimean War and the balaclava. But other effects of war on outdoor activity included the development of ski training for Continental Mountain troops in the First World War and Outward Bound of course. There was also the appearance of what became known as the Via Ferrata in the Dolomites, which enabled battles to be carried out in the most severe terrain. 70 years later these became the focus of a new sport. The immediate impact of the Second World War has already been tracked for the improvements used for Everest 1953 – including nylon rope, cotton nylon fabrics and Ventile. The Second World War is an important backdrop to the post 1945 world and even to the Golden Age. The British outdoor trade underwent a period of renaissance and restructuring between 1950 and 1969 and it was then that the vital seeds of change were sown. But it was little more than that until the late 1960s. Certainly new companies and new products appeared at this time, but the industry was really just a cottage industry and could have gone either way. The vital spark or ignition came in the 1970s with the take off of Scottish ice climbing and a range of other winter activities. This was at precisely the same time as media attention made mountaineering a spectator sport and Chris Bonington's Annapurna South Face expedition flung firms like Karrimor, Mountain Equipment and Troll into the public view. These changes drove a second phase of development, which lasted until 1980. From 1980 onwards there was a boom in clothing and footwear innovation linked to a combination of technology, outdoor changes and new attitudes to dress.

Renaissance and Restructuring: The Everest Effect
The 1950s were a period of post war recovery throughout the world and one where differing wartime experiences had striking and surprising implications for the development of mountaineering and outdoor sport. Far from ceasing, climbing, mountaineering and skiing all developed during the war. In German-occupied France, for instance, the Vichy government instituted a programme of youth training called 'Jeunesse et Montagne – youth and mountain, using the Saussois limestone cliffs, outside Paris, as a training ground. Mountains were the focus of the 1940 film by Frison Roche, adopted Chamonix guide, journalist and film-maker – to 'give our youth some hope and a little inspiration'. In any event the resistance was heavily mountain based and climbers like Terray, Rebuffat and Lachenal – who were to have such an impact post war – continued to climb.[5] One of the results of France's youth and mountain programmes was the formation of École Nationale de Ski et Alpinisme (ENSA) in 1947. It was to gain world-wide status for training and

accrediting professional mountain guides and ski instructors. The French were in a position to put together an expedition to climb Annapurna in 1950 –the first ascent of an 8,000 metre peak. Of course the Swiss too as a neutral nation did not interrupt their climbing during the war. They mounted an expedition to Everest in 1952 which narrowly failed through inadequate footwear and frostbite, rather than from poor climbing experience. German climbing took longer to recover in the post war period and relied on US ex-army surplus equipment and yet, in the 1950s and 1960s, German speaking climbers took the largest share of the 14 Himalayan 8,000 metre peaks as well as the coveted first winter ascent of the north face of the Eiger in 1961.[6]

In England the picture was rather different and, at first sight, it is extraordinary that by the 1960s Britain had returned to the leading edge of climbing and become the home of a number of innovative companies. But the two trends were not unconnected. Unlike their Continental contemporaries, service men, who were trained in mountain warfare by John Hunt and Frank Smythe never saw active service in the mountains. But their training introduced them to ropes, and even pitons, and for the first time karabiners were made specially by the War Office. The war time advisory role of a number of leading climbers highlighted the need for a national organisation and the British Mountaineering Council (BMC) was the result.[7] There followed an explosion of affiliated club formations and, for the first time, Britain had the kind of club structure that had been normal on the Continent. With the formation of the BMC, Britain at last had an institute open to all not restricted by class, education or climbing standards. Mountain training began to flourish and the Mountaineering Association, formed in 1947, trained 15,000 people in the next 20 years and the BMC mountain guide scheme followed. The process was simple, based upon knowledge of a specific region and involved letters of recommendation from two clients. Interestingly Peter Lockey, co-founder of Berghaus, was granted a BMC Guide Certificate in 1958.[8] Climbing club membership ceased to be socially elitist and became open to all. With employment levels high, working class climbing enthusiasts – many of whom, like Joe Brown and Don Whillans had honed their skills on Peak gritstone – climbed extensively in Britain and, for the first time, on the Continent.

There was massive post war enthusiasm for the outdoors and for mountaineering in the UK and people returned to the hills in droves. Perhaps partly created by wartime mountain training and simply by a post war return to normality, there was a pent-up demand for the outdoors and John Barford's 1946 *Climbing in Britain* sold 50,000 copies on the first edition. It was a level of sales most current mountain writers only dream of. The outdoors also became more accessible for the British in the 1950s and 1960s. The creation of National Parks, under the 1949 National Parks and Access to Countryside Act, was the culmination of a campaign stretching back before the First World War to broaden access to wild places. The first was the Peak District in 1951 with seven others following through the 1950s. The opening of the Pennine Way from Edale to Kirk Yetholm in 1965, championed for many years by Tom Stephenson, marked Britain's first official long distance path. By the1980s ten such paths, covering some 1,550 miles, had been created by the Countryside Commission, with more to follow.[9] Despite the large number of participants, there was no large market for outdoor clothing and equipment from specialist companies in the immediate post war period. In the late 1940s and the 1950s, if you went into the mountains you used ex-army surplus, and fairly awful stuff much of it was.

> *'Everything was in short supply and there had been a lot of making do. Almost to make matters worse the Government off-loaded enormous stocks of cheap surplus mountaineering equipment which was little short of useless, if not dangerous. There were boots which heeled over to one side after a week or so's wear, paper thin cotton anoraks, ice axes with sharp steel edged heads that wore through gloves in a few hours or so and karabiners that opened under low stress...'[10]*

It was the successful first ascent of Everest in May 1953 that really provided impetus for a new generation of innovative companies, even if the impact was neither immediate or obvious. Anyone able to read 'climbing form' in the period would not have given British climbers a chance of being the first to climb the world's highest mountain. Experience we had yes, but we had fallen behind the leading standards of climbing over the previous thirty-five to forty years. The news of the first ascent of Everest was announced over the loudspeaker system to the crowds along the route of the Coronation procession in London on June 3rd 1953. Many people still remember exactly where they were on this occasion, just as they did at the time of the announcement of the assassination of Kennedy and other significant events. Ten year-old Mike Parsons heard the news whilst camping in the Lake District. Even at that age he was already rather conscious that Britain had been in continuous decline for at least 50 years – growing up in Lancashire this would have been hard to miss. He remembered:

> *'I felt the thrill of the occasion like nothing before or since, wondering if indeed this could the beginning of a second Elizabethan age, of exploration and of leadership. In most ways it was sadly not. In other ways, this story being one of them, it certainly was!'*

Everest became a symbol of national status and mountaineers the new adventurers:

> *'a subject of sermons and for the Goodies[a cult comedy show], an incentive for export drives, a target for charitable appeals, a trade name for Italian wine and*

for double glazing against the rigours of the British climate. The names of some members of the expedition have been given to schools and school houses, to streets, to youth clubs, Scout troops, exploration groups and even to three tigers in Edinburgh Zoo.'[11]

Everest then struck a vital chord and changed attitudes to mountaineers and mountaineering.

As the last chapter showed, Everest 1953 needed a change of heart and ethic to succeed. Tom Bourdillon, summed up the need for change when he wrote to the Himalayan Committee in 1952:

'*Everest attempts have become an international competition in which, as against almost all other mountaineering, the pleasure of the climbing takes second place to national prestige.*

Knowledge of this has caused dismay in this party at the way in which this and last year's British expeditions have been run... To put it bluntly, the expeditions have been based on the spare time efforts of people in London [and] they are not an adequate basis for an expedition of this type... It is not suggested that any person is to blame for this situation, but rather the whole method of organisation, which is the natural outcome of the British attitude to mountaineering... On Everest a different approach appears necessary, and the key to the solution is clearly money.'[12]

This strong plea for professionalism changed the whole mood, we suspect. Gone was the 'by fair means', the bringing back of geological specimens and dying as Scott did, or thoughts of brilliant survival as with Shackleton. Gone were both the authoritarian style of the pre war generals or the 'look round the next corner, back of the envelope style' of Shipton and Tilman. Success meant pulling in John Hunt, a man who had served under Monty, the master of warfare logistics. . The decision caused a furore, Shipton being a well liked public figure, and he sadly turned down the offer to be climbing leader.

As noted previously John Hunt sourced clothing and equipment far and wide. Looking at the list of British suppliers, which included Benjamin Edgington, Robert Lawrie and Blacks, it is initially puzzling why this outstandingly successful expedition was not a platform for the outdoor brands which supplied it. But the expedition provided the springboard for a virtual tidal wave of new materials as was shown in chapter 7. At first the direct impact on commercial outdoor products was very slow but, as it spread from the late 1960s, this necessitated new manufacturing processes and machinery and therein lies the problem. Many of the new specialist products were custom made and the few British outdoor companies who did supply Everest 1953 could not survive as the new polymers spread and they had gone or were ailing by the late sixties – or as with Blacks-had largely lost their reputation in the mountaineering market. On the surface, then, it looked as though Everest had had little or no impact in encouraging the development of outdoor brands and mountaineering activity. It was, in any event, too early for a sizeable product market to emerge even though the enthusiasm was there. But the successful expedition proved an ignition for a new type of outdoor education which was ultimately to provide a bulk market for firms like Karrimor. It was also a great stimulus to setting up new climbing clubs, most of which succeeded in setting up their own club huts in the mountain regions of the UK. The Mount Everest Foundation (MEF) was established and provided £800,000 over the next 50 years to support exploratory expedition to all parts of the globe. Mountaineering began to flourish.

Most important of all, mountaineers became respected people and occupied positions of influence throughout society, the education system and even in politics. Through these positions they were able to keep mountaineering and outdoor activity in the public and political arena. Yes this was the ignition point, the takeoff, for it provided the bedrock of demand for products which had been lacking in Britain in previous decades. In the first 10 years of the Duke of Edinburgh award scheme, which was headed by Hunt at the personal request of HRH Prince Philip, there were 150,000 awards and by 1978 over a million young people had taken part.[13] Outward Bound – a scheme like the Scouts (with its Boer War origins) was partly spawned by war – also flourished in schools scattered through wild places in Britain. Today it is embedded in the local culture of 35 different countries under a licensing system. In 1955 Hunt became the first Chairman of the national centre for outdoor pursuits at Plas-y-Brenin in Snowdonia and was President of the BMC from 1965-68, when he played a fundamental role in developing Mountain Leadership Training culminating in the controversial Hunt Report of 1975.[14]

Another earlier Everester, Jack Longland – a veteran of both the 1933 and 1938 Everest attempts- also promoted the rising level of participation in outdoor activities. He became Director of Education for Derbyshire in 1949 and masterminded the opening of the first Local Education Authority (LEA) outdoor centre, at Whitehall near Buxton, in 1950. The 1944 Education Acts had 'made it the duty of every education authority to provide facilities for recreation, social and physical training in primary, secondary and further education and enabled them to establish and manage, amongst other facilities, camps and holiday classes... and organise expeditions.' Longland's success led the majority of LEA's to open outdoor pursuits centres over the next 30 years, especially in the 1960s and by 1980 there were some 350 centres. This was the market volume which provided the initial platform for companies like Karrimor in the 1960s – the crucial bulk market. It also introduced a generation to the outdoors.

Some older established organisations, like the Boy Scouts, provided a route to outdoor activity for some of the toughest and most unconventional post war working class climbers. In the 1940s the Scouts allowed Don Whillans, who as an adult hated all organised activity and despised authority, to escape from the back streets of Salford. He described a week's camp in Ennerdale as 'a dream come true'. [15] Another working class climber who initially caught the outdoor bug from the Boy Scouts was the seemingly anarchic climber, Mo Anthoine, the founder of Snowdon Mouldings, business partner of Joe Brown and manufacturer of helmets, axes and clothing. He remembered:

KARRIMOR

WEATHERTITE

CYCLING EQUIPMENT

QUEEN'S WORKS, RAWTENSTALL, ROSSENDALE
TELEPHONE. ROSSENDALE 1013   LANCS.

Karrimor Weathertite Products advertisement. Cycle bags were Karrimor's first products in 1946.

'I joined the Boy Scouts [Scout Association since 1966] and they took me camping That was a real breakthrough: it meant that I could get away from home and also enjoy myself. For a few bob I bought myself an ex-US Army bivouac tent and I used to go away every weekend.'[16]

As a trainee manager with a carpet firm he went on an Outward Bound course and became completely hooked. Other Outward Bound graduates include Ken Wilson, the editor of the highly influential international magazine *Mountain,* John Brailsford, the originator of the first manufactured nut and Bill O'Connor the Mountain Guide, photographer and writer.

Karrimor was one of the first of the new generation of companies and had its origins in an interwar cycle shop in Rossendale. The Karrimor Bag Company was originally set up in 1946 by Charlie and Mary Parsons, to make cycle bags for their Rawtenstall cycle shop. Post war shortages left the Parsons without supplies for the shop and they decided to start making their own cycle bags. Everything was short and food was still rationed and Charlie remembered the frustration of trying to cut through the yards of red tape and start making anything:

'Early in 1946 I applied for a licence to manufacture saddle bags in the name of Karrimor and after a lengthy exchange of correspondence between my accountants and the Offices of the Board of Trade the necessary document was obtained. This licence, however, was but another stage in the struggle to get the Karrimor Bag Company, as we called it, off the ground. Although it gave us the right to manufacture, it did not give us the right to procure the materials to

manufacture with, only 10 square yards of cotton canvas every three months, which of course was nothing but a token supply.[17]

That getting even this involved a shady incident with a chocolate cake, baked with all the neighbours' egg ration and delivered to the man from the Ministry about sums the period up. But Karrimor was born.[18] Manufacturing began on a home sewing machine in an attic above the shop in 1946 and, six years later, Karrimor Weathertite Products was registered as a private limited company, manufacturing cycle bags and goods to meet a range of specialist contracts. [19] The move into rucksacks came in 1958 when the bottom fell out of the cycling market. But manufacturing continued to be attached to the retail store, though in a purpose built workshop until 1965. Apart from government surplus, the choice of rucksacks was strictly limited in the late 1950s. Norwegian Bergans –promoted under the slogan the 'Best rucksack in the World' – and Brown Best occupied the top of the British rucksack market. [20] The key to the success of these two companies was their long standing reputation and deep skill base in stitching and leather working. Brown Best was a nineteenth century luggage manufacturer, which supplied the 1953 Everest expedition with rucksacks. [21] Founded in 1909 Bergans' reputation for quality became legendary, first with Amundsen, the polar explorer, and later with Everest Expeditions in the interwar period.. Other leading specialist brands in the late 1950s and early 1960s included the French firm Millet whilst, apart from retailers' own models, Bukta occupied the general walking and hiking slot .[22]

This was the world in which the first Karrimor rucksack was made for climber Dave Thomas in 1958 – a rucksack he still had 25 years later when he described it for the 1983 Karrimor Technical Guide:

'My work with the Geological Survey took me all over Lancashire and I presently found myself outside Charles and Mary Parsons' cycle equipment shop. We discussed rucsacs in general and the Bergan types they had on sale...They seemed a little doubtful when I sketched out my ideal sac. It had to be made of canvas with webbing straps for cheapness: to carry the load vertically rather than across the back; to have a waterproof sleeve inside that could be pulled out in a bivouac and the sac pulled up over a pied d'éléphant to provide protection and warmth, and big enough for me to get into and have the straps to hold an ice axe and a steel ring so the sac could be hauled. 'They won't sell' they said but they made, I think half a dozen, and I had the first. Modesty prevented me from calling it the 'Thomas Sac' but we settled for Sac de Grimpeur', Later the Outward Bound adopted it with the addition of side pockets and Don Whillans, looking for a Himalayan Sac, was shown the Grimpeur and said 'Just like that but twice as big'.[23]

The naming of the sac was significant in commercial terms for, if the Bergan was the 'best pack in the world' for the walker, the Millet sac was preferred choice of the mountaineer. The key to success lay in the functionality of the product but a good product name could also be important. When Charlie Parsons asked his son Mike to come up with a French name in 1958, he hoped it would be linked in customers' minds to quality.[24] The 'Joe Brown' followed and was first advertised in 1960 – the year Mike Parsons joined the family business at 18. Brown had been introduced to Parsons by outdoor retailer Frank Davies and actually had little directly to do with the pack's development – it merely bore his name. However, this pack marked the beginning of a process which, by 1970 was to make Karrimor Britain's leading rucksack manufacturer with products positioned at the top of a number of crucial markets.

Karrimor's initial success was based in part on price competitiveness for Karrimor climbing packs were, on average, a third cheaper than equivalents from Brown Best.

Prices of Frameless Mountaineering Packs 1962

Company Name	*Pack name*	*Price*
Karrimor	*Pinnacle*	*£2 11s 8d*
	Chamonix	*£2 19s 3d*
	Joe Brown	*£4 7s 0d*
Brown Best	*Snow Cap*	*£5 0s 11d*
	Cairn	*£4 18s 0d*
Lafuma	*Super Altitude*	*£3 19s 6d*

Source: Pindisports Mountaineering Catalogue 1962

Similarly Bergans, previously Blacks' favoured brand, were undercut by Karrimor. As Alan Day manager of Jackson and Warr of Sheffield, by then part of the Black's group, commented in 1963:

> *'I regret to say that we cannot report more favourably regarding Bergans and I have been disappointed in sales. The reason for the drop in sales is perhaps such people as Karrimor are now marketing a high-loading rucksack at a very much lower price and this is quite an attraction since Karrimor have a good name for quality and price.'[25]*

Two years later the picture was even bleaker for a complacent Bergans, still living off its past success. As a frustrated Day observed:

> *'It is rather difficult for me to comment on Bergans because we cannot sell sufficient to warrant comment. We have in fact tried hard to sell these but it is like trying to revive a 'dying duck'. ...this is because Bergans are still living on their reputation... I strongly disagree with the view put forward at our last Port Glasgow meeting that Bergans have 'not deteriorated' but in fact other makes have greatly improved. Also quite frankly, I do not believe advertising will 'revive' them.'[26]*

But if Bergans stopped innovating, other Continental firms like Millet did not and Parsons' designs were undoubtedly innovative. Peter Gildersleve, who produced Karrimor's catalogues from the 1960s, vividly remembered Manchester retailer Bob Brigham telling him in the mid 1960s:

> *"'there's a chap up in Rossendale I'd like you to meet who wants a catalogue doing". So I went to meet this chap and of course he meant Mike Parsons and ...he'd just moved into the Mill in Haslingden and he was, I think, probably the first man who was making the type of rucksack that... was not an 'A' frame. If you go back to those days and see what was available you'll find that the leader was probably Bergans with the old 'A' frame and Mike was creating something new.'[27]*

Inevitably, initial selling was quite low key and visits to Continental trade shows needed a whole new set of skills. But as Peter Gildersleve remembered, as his margins grew Parsons became very good at marketing the product. He never skimped on promotional print and the Karrimor technical guide always had priority in the budget.[28]

Given the prominence Karrimor was to achieve later, it would be easy to assume that Mike Parsons was initially fulfilling a dream. He was an outdoor enthusiast after all – a keen cyclist, fell runner and climber and so many outdoor companies almost began as hobbies. But this was not the case for Karrimor and Parsons – he may have wanted to go into the business and certainly from the start cared passionately about making good gear. But, until the mid 1960s, he felt trapped in dead end Lancashire, disliked the workshop and was deeply frustrated with the prospects. He felt that people despised his manual work and recalled:

> *'To be precise when I arrived in the business I was the seventh employee. Manufacturing was around 2/3 of the turnover of the retail store and comprised 2 rooms on the middle floor, which were curtained off from the retailing. Visitors who went through to the top floor to see the tent display could smell the pungent smell of leather. I was really the poor relation. I hated it and I knew I was going to do better or get out.'[29]*

However, the work could be extremely varied and brought him a deep understanding of the process of manufacturing and a wide range of contacts within the Lancashire textile industry. This gave Parsons two of his key sources of competitive advantage, but it did not seem like that at the time. Karrimor's main business had always been cycle bags and while still at school Parsons plotted the downward trend of that market to almost zero. This was because, if outdoor activity generally was popular, the bicycle was not. This was the age of the motor car and cycling ceased to be the everyday activity it had previously been and national cycle sales fell by more than half during the 1950s.[30] Whilst rucksacks proved to be the making of Karrimor this was not obvious in 1960.

The most rapidly growing outdoor market in the 1960s was family camping and this stemmed from increasing levels of paid holiday, the developing motorway system and the emerging love affair with the motor car. It was also the era of motorway building and the spread of modern gadgetary, which made weekends away and holidays much more accessible. For instance the opening of the M6 and its extension to Carlisle in 1970 made the Lake District accessible to many in the conurbations of the North West and the Midlands.[31] Rising economic prosperity meant people had more to spend on labour saving devices which in turn also meant more leisure. For instance Mary Parsons, who with her husband Charlie, founded Karrimor, bought her first fully automatic Bendix washing machine in the 1950s, expressly so she and her family could go cycling on a Sunday, rather than catching up with the household chores.[32] The family camping craze began in France and is captured in the pages of the catalogues of the leading French company Aux Vieux Campeur. The firm had its origins in the 1930s and what became Aux Vieux Campeur was set up in 1941. Almost all the products used in the UK, including tents, stoves, furniture were produced and imported from France and the large companies and retailers, such as Blacks and Pindisports, focused on this obvious and very clear boom area. Car based camping, trailer tents and of course caravanning, both in England and on the Continent, became the family holiday craze in the 1960s and early 1970s. It altered the whole character of the Camping Club, soon to become the Camping and Caravanning Club of Great Britain and Ireland, from its original image of self propulsion.[33] The British outdoor trade of the 1960s then was camping based. The outdoor trade association therefore was named COLA, Camping and Outdoor Leisure Association, (originally the Camping Trades Association, now the Outdoor Industries Association) because camping activity and sales of products absolutely dwarfed all others. Blacks, with its growing number of stores, and widely distributed catalogue dominated that trade. However the style of family camping could not have been more different from the pre – war Baden-Powell style of scout camping. A model of comfort emerged, with suspended inner tents and zipped entrances which were entirely insect proof. The growing use of normal height tables and chairs and clean, easy to operate, liquid gas stoves were an important inducement for women. Many of these developments were then transferred to lightweight tents and to backpacking in the 1970s. Though it should be remembered that, even today, only a tiny proportion of lightweight tents and equipment sold are actually used for backpacking – they continue to be car based. Family camping also provided an introduction to the outdoors for many children in the 1960s – low cost accommodation for the whole family and a base from which to go walking.

The expansion of climbing in the Alps and Britain's return to the leading edge provided a market for Karrimor's frameless climbing packs, of which the orange Whillans Alpiniste, was the most distinctive. But the specialist mountaineering market was still comparatively small and whilst gaining a slot

KARRIMOR CLIMBING SACS

Developed by well-known alpinists and expedition members, the Karrimor climbing sacs are highly recommended for climbers everywhere. The two shown below are already used by hundreds of climbers, both at home and abroad for ordinary weekend excursions or expeditions of months' duration all over the world. All British in design, materials, and workmanship, Karrimor Rucsacs represent excellent value at a moderate cost.

'ALPINIST' SAC

DON WHILLANS 'ALPINIST' CLIMBING SAC (*right*)

Special features are:

1. The wedge shape and large removable flap give maximum protection when carrying equipment to the base of climb. When climbing the flap can be removed and the sac drawn up to a small size.
2. Canvas is bright orange with a black leather base.
3. 'D' ring attached to each shoulder harness has two uses:
   (*a*) for attaching the 'armslength' cord of the piton hammer;
   (*b*) for holding pitons via a karabiner or piton holder.
4. A strong hauling ring has been incorporated.
5. There is a small loop on the right to hold a piton hammer.
6. Crampons are fastened to flap by cord and eyelets.
7. The detachable flap has a map pocket.
8. Flap can be used as a cover for crampons when inside sac.

Size 21 in. deep, wide bottom, 14½ in. wide top. Weight 3 lb. 2 oz.

£6 10s. 1d.

Bivi sheet 3½ oz.   *extra* **19s. 9d.**

CONTINENTAL SAC

JOE BROWN 'CONTINENTAL' CLIMBING SAC (*right*)

As illustrated. Is made of high quality canvas with leather base. Supplied complete with strap attachments for crampons and ice axe. A waist strap is also incorporated. Shoulder harness of leather is felt padded for comfort. Design of the rucsac features the sides, widening towards the top to ensure that the load is properly balanced and carried high.

Size 21 in. x 15 in. wide with 5 in. base gusset widening to 6½ in. at top. Weight 2 lb. 14 oz.   **£5 14s. 4d.**

Don Whillans and Joe Brown captured the imagination of the nation, their packs dominated the UK market place for more than a decade. Illustrated in Black's catalogue 1967.

in the widely circulated Blacks catalogue in 1964 helped, it would not have sustained the business. In the 1960s Karrimor's real bulk came from the early blossoming of outdoor education. During the 1950s Brown Best had developed a traditional steel-framed cotton duck pack- 'The Senior' – specifically for the Scouts and Youth Organisations. Through the use of new designs and materials, most particularly nylon and aluminium, Karrimor was able to replace Brown Best in both the scouting and the growing outdoor pursuits market by 1970. Parsons is quite clear in his mind that the Keswick outdoor retailer, George Fisher, was instrumental in this breakthrough:

> '*George Fisher brought us the Outward Bound Pack. You know he came from OBS and they had a need for a pack that was BOYPROOF . At the time it used to be said that when boys got tired it was not unknown for them to kick the rucksack down the hill. So there were very specific performance requirements! We got the early samples made, developed the business and then rather later developed a critically important dialogue with Outward Bound Schools and training centres using Ken Ledward*'.[34]

By supplying the growing number of outdoor pursuits centres and participants on the Duke of Edinburgh award scheme Karrimor gained a crucial bulk market, though of course it was extremely seasonal with all orders coming in April.[35] But if Fisher introduced Karrimor to the Outward Bound Schools,

Ken Ledward played a vital role in reinforcing the company's links with outdoor education. He was senior instructor at OB Eskdale from 1959-1962, had a two year spell as Chief instructor at Loitokitok in Kenya before returning to Eskdale to work on the Mountain Leader Training and Assessment Courses.[36] He had been introduced to Karrimor and Parsons through another Lake District retailer, Frank Davies of Ambleside, who had brought a selection of rucksacks to Eskdale OB – including the Karrimor OB pack.[37] Ledward, a passionate lightweighter built up a rapport with Mike Parsons and Karrimor, eventually worked for them as a tester and product developer in the 1970s, playing a key role in developing the lightweight Marathon tent and later the lightweight boot the KS-B.

The combination of the specialist mountaineering market and the outdoor education market was the basis of Karrimor's 1960's growth. Parsons had identified a number of gaps or potential opportunities in the market and produced distinctive products –often in new materials – to fill them. It was a strategy that lay at the heart of Parsons' manufacturing philosophy and was the basis of the development of the Karrimor range – one the keys of the firm's dominance of the rucksack market in the 1970s and 1980s. Business began to grow in the mid 1960s and the first factory opened in Haslingden in 1965. Between 1960 and 1970 the real value of Karrimor's turnover had grown 8 fold to reach £1.5m.[38]

Another company to have its origins in this period of renaissance was Mountain Equipment, which became renowned for its quality down clothing and sleeping bags. As British climbing began to catch up with standards on the Continent, climbers may not have cared much about style, but they did care about staying warm and dry. As leading climbers began to travel to the Alps and further afield, they became increasingly aware of what their Continental contemporaries were using to stay warm on precarious bivouacs. Down jackets combined with pied d'éléphants were widely used in preference to the Zdarsky bivouac bag. After the War Blacks were manufacturing sleeping bags and the Icelandic bag had a good reputation with mountain campers –especially after the early introduction of wall quilting. They were also among the first to move into synthetics,but the combination of synthetic cover and filling was very bulky and quite unsuitable for mountaineering – it was intended for family camping. But all good quality down clothing was imported, mainly from the Continent. Pete Hutchinson, the founder of what became Mountain Equipment, remembered being unable to get any decent supplies other than from France for the tiny shop in Manchester, which he had started with fellow climber Pete Crew in 1961. Very much like Mike Parsons, Pete Hutchinson saw a niche for high quality products. He began making his own and, after the shop folded, he decided to concentrate on making down gear – first sleeping bags and then jackets. Pete Hutchinson's Mountain Equipment began in a shack on a farm near Glossop where he lived and worked. Peter Gildersleve remembers visiting Pete in the 1960s, with the outdoor retailer Bob Brigham:

'I got the shock of my life – I went into a chicken shed and it was full of down and Pete was stuffing duvet jackets... he was a prime mover at the time.'

It was hardly a glamorous existence – he would clean out the cattle sheds to pay his rent and then go back to his tiny shack and make a jacket.[39] But his down jackets and soon sleeping bags, produced initially on a bespoke basis, developed an enviable and justifiable reputation. Hutchinson was a good mountaineer and his hallmark was a craftsmanship which reflected a deep understanding of the demands placed on climbers at high altitudes and an empathy with his gear. He is one of very few designers to whom climbers have consistently paid tribute for over 40 years. The exceptionally good relationships he built with climbers brought commercial benefits too, for he got the earliest expeditions photographs, which he always used immediately in advertisements or catalogues. But, in the 1960s, before the expansion of winter climbing, winter walking and backpacking and skiing, there was not a bulk market for his down clothing and sleeping bags in a way that there was for rucksacks. Whilst he certainly would not agree that he was not pleased that Mountain Equipment grew, in some ways, Hutchinson was most comfortable with this position. He loved design work but disliked the rising tide of administration as the firm grew. He returned to his original specialist niche in the 1990s after Mountain Equipment went into receivership. He founded PHD – Pete Hutchinson Designs – and won a Millennium Design Council Award for his lightweight sleeping bag.[40]

Innovative designers do not work in isolation and rely on advice and feedback from suppliers, retailers and users to evolve and improve their ideas. This is especially the case in the outdoor trade, where functionality is vital and can, in some circumstances, be a matter of life and death. Product development was based on a number of frank dialogues between informed outdoor people who spoke the same language. These often took place between outdoor manufacturers and a number of influential and knowledgeable retailers, including Alan Day of Jackson and Warr and later Blacks, Tony Lack of Pindisports, George Fisher at Keswick, Frank Davies in Ambleside, Bob Brigham in Manchester, Tanky Stokes in Sheffield and Graham Tiso in Edinburgh. Developing a good and open relationship with these men was crucial in the 1960s. They not only understood the outdoors, but they knew their way round numerous Continental workshops and trade shows, at a time when barely anything of quality was made in the UK. Everything from rucksacks, through duvet jackets to technical hardware was imported; there were Millet rucksacks and Pierre Allain's rock boot from France,

Erve down clothing and sleeping bags from Switzerland, Fairy Down sleeping bags from New Zealand, Austrian Dachstein mitts, and Norwegian knitwear. To get round some of the shortages retailers sometimes co-operated by making joint imports as Tony Lack remembered:

'At Pindisports we had a very successful arrangement to do this in conjunction with Graham Tiso [for Fairy Down sleeping bags which were posted from New Zealand] and we eventually extended it to bringing in Chouinard hardware, Camp Trails pack frames and various brands of footwear – mainly Italian. This continued until a viable supply of equal or better products became readily available from suppliers in the UK.'[41]

Because retailers were so close to the market place and knew all the products available in Europe, they provided an invaluable basis of knowledge for manufacturers. They also used this knowledge to have their own products made when they saw gaps in the market. A few, like the Brighams and Tanky Stokes initially did some manufacturing and designing themselves. They knew about both the changing needs of their sport, specific shortages and often applied the kinds of craft skills, so much talked about in the technical climbing chapter. Bryan (Tanky) Stokes was a committed climber, who was taught to mend boots by a skilled leather craftsman while still working for the Milk Marketing Board. Based in Sheffield, the very Mecca of Peak, gritstone climbing, he began repairing and making boots and climbing shoes for himself and friends in the 1960s. Soon he expanded into rucksacks and began doing repairs across the UK. He developed the first climbing harness in the early 1960s, after he witnessed a friend being asphyxiated by a rope in an accident in the Dolomites. It was made of harness leather and, according to Tanky, would have 'held a bloody elephant' He could have gone down the manufacturing route in the mid 1960s, but an enforced change of premises and early moves by Tony Howard and Troll into harnesses led him to shift into full time retailing.[42]

Another highly influential retailer, in the 1960s and 1970s with origins in manufacturing, was Ellis Brigham. The pre war story of Brigham and his back street Manchester shop has already been told. In the 1940s specialist nails like Tricounis were often hard to come by – so F.E. Brigham invented his own – the Brigham plate to be followed by the 'Brigham-Peacock plate (when he collaborated with an engineer) which was similar but had replaceable screw-in nails. He also sold a special fine oil for boots –called Feb (his initials).[43] After their father's death the Brigham brothers Ellis and Bob, themselves keen skiers and mountaineers, took over the business and quickly moved the shop to a city centre location. The firm expanded in the 1960s to include shops in Liverpool and Capel Curig and, in 1966 with Peter Gentil (who soon left to open The Alpine Centre at Blackpool), Bob Brigham set up an associated company for manufacturing technical gear. MOAC (Mountaineering Activities) was partly to fill the gap left by the defunct Mountaineering Association, which had put much effort into developing equipment and manufactured John Brailsford's nut as described in chapter 6.[44] Brigham, like his father, was an innovator as well as a retailer and by 1970 his developments included:

> 'the MOAC bandoleer climbing harness, the MOAC alloy chockstone, the Gollies rock boots, his trail boots which sold well in the United States, and the nylon Annapurna tent'.[45]

These specialist retailers were closely integrated into the emerging outdoor education and climbing world and were quite different from Blacks and Robert Lawrie- the London based retailer from a past generation. Already in 1963 D.C. Black felt that the family camping image conflicted with Blacks' sales to serious mountaineers:

> 'Our chief competition in climbing is Brigham in Manchester whom climbers claim carries a wider variety and in some cases sells cheaper. Mr Day says Brigham puts out a mountaineering leaflet so climbers think he specialises in climbing goods, whereas they think, because of our catalogue, that we are in general camping equipment. It would help Mr Day to compete with Brigham if we were to print a climbing leaflet and he said that if we did so it should include the Icelandic sleeping bag, because he had discovered that Sheffield climbers consider this a must.'[46]

On the other hand Robert Lawrie, who had been so influential in the 1930s, became a legend from a bygone age. Climber, Bill Ruthven bought a pair of Lawrie boots in 1976 and his story exactly mirrors Bob Lawford's leisurely experience in the 1930s described in a previous chapter:

> 'I had been told not to look for a shop, but it was only on my third 'pass' along Seymour Street that I noticed the two doorbells on the door of number 54 with their discreet brass plates 'Robert Lawrie – Business' and 'Robert Lawrie – Private'. I rang the 'business' bell, and an elderly lady opened the door. 'Yes?' she enquired. 'Er, I need some new climbing boots', I said, slightly taken aback. She ushered me down the hall and into a room on the left, which seemed to be a cross between a private sitting room and a small showroom for climbing equipment. Here was another elderly lady and a man of similar age, who introduced himself as Robert Lawrie. I said again 'I need some new climbing boots'. 'Why have you come here?', he asked. More surprised than ever, I said, 'Well, I have several friends who use your boots, and they have recommended that I come to see you.' 'Who?' came the reply. I said the first name that came into my head: 'Bob Pettigrew'. 'Ah, Bob Pettigrew', he said, shuffled over to the mantelpiece and returned with a postcard sent by Bob when he had been in India several years earlier. We discussed our mutual connections: this looked like being a long session!'

It certainly was and, having been told he did not sell boots but fitted them, Bill was personally measured by Lawrie, after which there was much walking around in a trial pair of boots. During the hour and a half that this took and, on a number of subsequent visits, Bill never saw another customer.[47] The contrast with the bustling, if sometimes cramped, outdoor shops that were appearing in the provinces could not have been greater. Not surprisingly it was to the new breed of retailers that manufacturers turned.

Some were easier to deal with than others and part of the success of any relationship was personal chemistry, but many found George Fisher increasingly difficult. George Fisher set up his Keswick shop in 1957, after spending three years as an Outward Bound Instructor at Ullswater and from the 1940s he had been the leader of the Keswick mountain rescue team. His second premises, at the junction with Lakes Road in Keswick was at the Abraham Brothers', the mountain photographers', old premises and contained some of the old equipment. Fellow retailer Alan Day summed up the key to his success when he said:

'the great thing about Fishers is because George was active he knew what people wanted and they got it for people at a sensible, honest price'[48].

But even in those early days Fisher could be reclusive and manufacturers, like Mike Parsons, found him quite difficult to deal with. He would give inspired advice or contacts, but he could be extremely moody. One trade rep. used to arrive at Fishers and say 'are you all right then, are you in a good mood or shall I bugger off and go and talk to your brother?'[49]

Called by Parsons the gentleman of the trade, Tony Lack of Pindisports in Holborn was another important influence. Later an outdoor consultant, Lack developed an encyclopaedic knowledge of specialist clothing and equipment and was responsible for importing equipment for the 1970 Annapurna expedition. Parsons saw him as one of the three corners of his retailing 'advice triangle' with Tiso in Scotland, either Frank Davies or Bob Brigham in the north and Tony Lack in the south. These men were thus far more than mere customers, they would react to designs and advise on changing customer tastes. A climber himself, like so many in the outdoor trade, Lack was in close contact with user needs but the design of the Holborn shop also helped because as mountaineering buyer he did not separate himself from the shop. Instead his office directly overlooked the trading area giving him a unique view of customers.[50]

Described by Alan Day as 'arrogant but most honourable' Graham Tiso, had one of the most respected reputations in the trade. His career began as a sales rep. with Cadburys in southern Scotland. He was also a very keen climber and the prospect of moving away from the mountains as his career progressed encouraged him and his wife Maud to open their shop in Edinburgh in 1962. His earliest suppliers were Blacks' and Peter Storm but, from the start, he travelled the Continental shows looking for new gear and suppliers and bluntly advising new UK suppliers about what they got right and wrong. He could be intimidating to the faint hearted or inexperienced and did not suffer fools gladly so that:

> 'A meeting with Graham Tiso was much more comfortable in his office, where he could talk frankly, than on the shop floor or at a trade show, where he liked to project a certain image to his staff and scare the pants off company representatives at the same time !'[51]

Like so many in the trade at this time Mike Parsons relied heavily on Tiso. Comparing him with Fisher he commented:

> '...whereas if something was wrong with a Fisher product he would not take the trouble to lift the phone. He would send you a long letter but he wouldn't lift the phone or he wouldn't come down or he wouldn't even meet you half way, whatever, he was not serious on that dialogue. So for me what Graham Tiso was was about a serious dialogue, very often fierce, but it achieved results'[52]

He had strong views about what was suitable for his specific customers and in those early days choice was distinctly limited. Mike Parsons undoubtedly gained from this since 95% of Tiso's rucksack sales were of the GT sac, made by Karrimor and designed especially for Scottish needs with long walks in to climbs. This was the beginning of a long relationship between Parsons and Tisowhich included the development of one of Karrimor's most distinctive and memorable products – the Karrimat. Mike Parsons recalled one day in the mid 1960s:

> 'Graham Tiso said that when he was next down at the Karrimor factory he wanted to discuss a new idea and sounded a little bit excited. When he arrived he indicated that it was something to do with the closed cell foam that we were using for harness. Graham explained that he had an idea and could he see one of the pieces of foam? I said yes was he thinking of using it as a sleeping mat, because I had had the same idea but hadn't had time to try it? We took out a piece and immediately laid down on the floor. Here, take a piece and try I said. At this time Tiso was acting as a part-time instructor at Glenmore Lodge and they were beginning to teach snow holing techniques. [53]

In 1969 Tiso enthused about the closed cell mat in an article in the *Alpine Club Journal*, following a trip to Greenland: it proved 100% waterproof and an almost perfect insulator. At just 9.5 ounces it was also remarkably light and, because it was perfectly waterproof, it did not matter if it got wet in carriage, all you had to do was wipe it dry.[54] The Karrimat became the euphemism for the sleeping mat and the distinctive yellow mats appeared on postage stamps celebrating the Duke of Edinburgh award during the 1970s. But Tiso could be impatient and uncompromising when he thought he was right (which he usually did) and he had especially strong opinions about boots. This finally led to the parting of the ways when Parsons introduced the lightweight fabric K-SB, of which Tiso strongly and vociferously disapproved.

Upsurge in Activity 1970-80
New sports, new companies and new boundaries

Ask any of the leading outdoor retailers or the owners of the tiny manufacturing companies for the defining moment which, more than anything else, transformed their companies and changed the outdoor trade and they would say, without hesitation: Annapurna South Face 1970. From the standpoint of the history of mountaineering when Dougal Haston and Don Whillans climbed the South Face of Annapurna on 27th May 1970, their success marked a turning point in a process which began outside Britain. It was based on developments in technical gear and big wall climbing on the Continent in the interwar period and in post war America. These techniques had been learnt and improved by a post war generation of leading British climbers. They drew on the skill of a quite different breed of climber from either Everest 1953 or the interwar attempts on the Third Pole. The film and the book *Annapurna South Face* and the London lectures, sponsored by Pindisports, were like a breath of fresh air, compared with what had gone before. Chris Bonington summed up Annapurna South Face as pure 'siegemanship', but it was a marvellous example of grasping the opportunity, of leadership and also of marketing. Funding of expeditions took a whole new leap forward with City expertise and involvement. Annapurna 1970 was also landmark in terms of gear innovation too, and although some of the developments were quite short-lived the innovating companies, like their climbing users, became household names. As well as being discussed in a book and getting wide media coverage, equipping of the expedition was reported at length in Ken Wilson's prestigious and international journal *Mountain*.[55]

In a retrospective interview with Tony Lack (who was responsible for obtaining much of the imported equipment for Annapurna 1970) in 1992, one of the Troll founders Tony Howard saw Annapurna South Face as the key turning point for his company's development. He and his partners had designed the Whillan's sit harness, which was accorded a 'high profile on photographs, on TV and in the lectures' and raised both their national and crucially their international standing.[56] But this was not just publicity hype, as the sit harness was a break through which started a whole new level of safety and performance in climbing. Bonington described it as, 'an outstanding success, for it enabled one to rest back in the seat while jumaring up snow slopes.'[57]

Annapurna 1970 had a similar impact on Karrimor for rucksacks, the Whillans box – the special aluminium framed high altitude tent designed to Whillans' specification and made by Karrimor using pack frame technology– and the Karrimat. The Whillans box and its successor the MacInnes box, used on Bonington's 1975 Everest expedition, were fairly short-lived, as they were

The Annapurna Expedition will have some rather nice climbing equipment

We supplied it!

Above we show the ultimate reality can opener. This and all the other sophisticated gear can be admired at any of our branches

Join the expedition yourself — come to Pindisports

PINDISPORTS

14-18 HOLBORN, E.C.1   373-375 UXBRIDGE ROAD, ACTON, W.3.   1086 WHITGIFT CENTRE, CROYDON.

Pindisports advertisement following Annapurna. *Climber and Rambler, 1970.*

synonymous with the 1970s siege expeditions and quickly disappeared with them. But other innovations had a lasting impact and quite simply changed the experience of the outdoors. The Karrimat was used as the floor covering for the high altitude tents and replaced other forms of camping insulation for two decades. Karrimor also made neoprene over-boots – which again used closed cell foam but of the kind used for diving suits not the Karrimat. It was 1978 before plastic boots were available for British climbers and these were worn together with the leather Galibier-Hivernale boots. These gave the necessary insulation to prevent frostbite at altitude.[58] For Karrimor the visibility and prominence of the expedition caused some difficulties, according to Mike Parsons, because his company found it hard to keep up with the demand encouraged by the publicity. However, the most important impact for Karrimor was on the company's international standing – such was the profile of the expedition that when the company exhibited on the Continent they were seen as being in a new league of manufacturers.[59]

Pete Hutchinson's down clothing earned its justified reputation partly from this expedition and according to Bonington:

'The Hutchinson down jackets were so successful that we found we needed only the single jacket either for climbing in or for wearing inside the sleeping bag at night. They had the advantage of being quite close fitting and did not make one feel like the Michelin tyre man.'[60]

Annapurna 1970 was the first of Bonington's high profile Himalayan expeditions and was followed by others to Everest in 1972 and 1975. But Bonington was not a gear specialist himself and where specialist equipment needed designing Bonington turned to people like Don Whillans in 1970 or Hamish Macinnes in 1975 and they collaborated with the manufacturers. Don Whillans was blunt, outspoken and as he used to say to amused lecture audiences 'they call me working class but I haven't worked in years'. A plumber by trade and later a forester he was intensely practical and at the height of his climbing career he designed some really classic gear, ranging from the Whillans Box, through the sit harness to clothing. Some of his ideas were inspired and this included the Whillans box, one of the symbols of the 1970s siege expeditions which began as a rough wooden framed prototype in Patagonia in the 1960s. Whillans lived in Rossendale and was already collaborating with Karrimor on the design of his pack. A second stage product design of the box using angle iron and orange rucksack canvas (and almost identical to those he used as a forester) had been made for his second Patagonia expedition, on a casual request along the lines of 'Mike do you think you could make me a cover of rucksack canvas for an angle iron frame.' 'No problem Don, you realise it will be heavy?' This meant that the obvious company to approach to develop the tent further for Annapurna was Karrimor and Mike Parsons. Building on expertise developed making pack frames, Parsons used aluminium tubing for the frame and was confident the tent would cope with extreme conditions.. Whillans was also convinced, but one of the other members disagreed and proved his point by hurling himself on top of the prototype flat topped tent – which promptly collapsed. Parsons wryly recalled that:

'Personally I was a bit surprised but the look of disgust on Don's face was something to be remembered and not long afterwards when the clothing was being discussed by a super slick salesman called Arnold Angel, Don seemed to have mysteriously disappeared. A quick check of my watch indicated that it was just before Sunday closing time, but no one else seemed to have spotted the coincidence.[61]

The second version did not fare much better as Parsons recalls as it blew away during testing on Ben Macdui in the Cairngorms:

'About seven days later, Don came into the shop, because the shop was always the front entrance to the manufacturing at the time, and said, 'I've been given this, this pile of bones.' I said, 'Oh my God, where d'you get this from Don?' 'A friend of mine found them ten miles over from the top of Ben MacDui'. The friend had recognised what it was, and put it into Don's hands and Don brought it back to me!'[62]

But it was this kind of testing which enabled Parsons to improve the box. Whillans did not see any need for further innovation once a product had served its purpose. This was deeply frustrating for Parsons who not only had the future of his company to think about, but who positively thrives on change and innovation. When asked in the early 1970s for ideas for improving the classic orange Whillans Alpiniste rucsac – first launched in 1964 – Whillans just was not interested; he was no longer climbing in the Alps and had lost touch with what was suitable, as the requirements were so different from the Himalayas. Parsons has contrasted his frustration with Whillans with the development of a new Alpine sac with Dougal Haston. Haston helped him develop the Haston Aiguille – described by Tony Lack as one of the key innovations of the 1970s . It was designed precisely to accommodate the specific demands of 1970s

Alpine climbing.[63]

Pete Hutchinson of Mountain Equipment also worked closely with Whillans. He found he was one of those designers who had 'an analytical approach to gear' and this is a view with which Mike Parsons agrees. Together they developed the first one piece down suit and wind suits. He has vivid memories of dealing with Don on designs for Annapurna 1970 and other expeditions. He had strong and highly practical views on clothing for high altitude climbing putting functionality above all else. He believed that:

'once you get into the higher reaches of a peak, you don't want to bother about your gear really, you just want to be warm and protected and get on with it You don't want to think about changing things and all the rest of it.'[64]

This was exactly the kind of approach Pete understood and, as they both knew what they were talking about, the design process was a genuine interaction until the garments were right . Hutchinson went for one piece down suits for the Annapurna expedition based on ideas evolved with Don Whillans in the 1960s. They were a novel idea for climbing at that time, though of course there were one piece work overalls and flying suits. The main problem was nothing to do with textiles or the quality of down, but all to do with arranging the zips to make 'going to the toilet' easy. It was crucial not just because of the potential for messy accidents, but because:

'just ordinary practical things like this are so important when you are up there because all you want to do is plod on and get up this thing and they say the best gear is invisible. ...we chose the one piece wind suits, which once they put them on, sort of round Camp Four or something, they just keep them on all the way, and as long as you can go to the toilet in them and so on there is no reason why you should take them off. [They were so successful] that we went the next step [for later expeditions] following that into down suits. Again the same idea really, once you got into it you sleep in it, you just live in it, and then you don't have to think about putting gear on and off, and all the rest of it.'[65]

What Hutchinson really appreciated was the feedback gained from climbers:

'I like to hear that the gear is good but the useful information for me is when the climbers come back and say, 'It would work a lot better if ...'.[66]

Relationships with climbers on high altitude expeditions was one of the keys to innovation in both Karrimor and Mountain Equipment. But leading edge climbing was a tiny market although it brought considerable advertising opportunities. The high profile face climbs of the 1970s were only part of a rapidly changing world which brought new techniques, new sports, and new companies. The late 1960s, until 1980, saw the take off of Scottish ice climbing, backpacking, of mountain marathons, the beginning of trekking companies and of skiing in the British Isles, all of which created new markets and encouraged innovation in the trade.

There began an extraordinary period in Scottish climbing which was to have a major impact on the profile of both UK outdoor sports and the outdoor trade. The combined impact of the Salewa twelve point adjustable crampon and the use of two curved axes on the development of ice climbing, has been shown in chapter 6. This in turn had far wider implication for the outdoor trade. Outdoor activity, had previously been heavily summer based which of course had created major problems of seasonality for any supplier or retailer. Tony Lack recalled that at Pindisports in the early 1960s they combined family camping with skiing gear and their mountaineering equipment was a small part of total sales. So great was the degree of seasonality that Pindisports did no advertising in August and September. But the family camping boom was coming to an end in the early 1970s to be replaced by a range of self-propelled activities. The upsurge of winter mountaineering, winter camping and hill walking from the late 1960s began to change the pattern of seasonality for ever and helped to create a demand for a growing range of specialist gear.[67] This was certainly reflected in the climbing and walking press where, from 1968 there were a growing number of articles on winter walking, climbing and equipment. Previously people had certainly gone into the hills in the winter – indeed for cyclists walking had normally been the preferred winter activity, but there has been little thought of wearing anything specialist.

This period also coincided with the early development of skiing in Scotland . Interestingly Graham Tiso, with his passions firmly allied to ice climbing, was vehemently anti ski. For other companies, like Nevisports, the development of Scottish skiing was inseparable from retailing. The founders of Nevisports were Ian Sykes, Ian Sutherland and Alex Gillespie. Ian Sykes originally worked for the British Antarctic Survey and is an enthusiastic skier and set up the Aonach Mhor ski development. The increase in winter activity eased the problem of seasonality for both retailer and manufacturer and created opportunities for new products, whilst a higher profile encouraged, and was encouraged, by new and distinctive methods of marketing. Modern discursive and visually pleasing catalogues appeared from Pindisports and Tiso along with the Karrimor Technical Guides. Similarly advertising space in Ken Wilson's *Mountain* – the first truly international, prestigious mountaineering periodical, with a circulation of 11,000 was highly sought after.

It was not just retailers who faced seasonal fluctuation and in 1973 the editor of *Practical Camper*, Peter Lumley, faced the difficult task of making the magazine viable in the barren winter months. Backpacking – an American enthusiasm- proved the solution though many doubted that the word would ever catch on here. But Peter's chirpy enthusiasm and some sponsorship from the magazine's publishers created the 'Backpacker's Club'. During the winters of the 1970s, *Practical Camper* became filled with Peter Lumley's articles on lightweight camping. Rather like Thomas Holding, 70 or 80 years before, he positively relished finding ways of making camping and independent travelling comfortable and pleasant. Like Holding he relished writing about it and in 1974 published the first edition of *Teach Yourself Backpacking.* Talk to Peter today and the enthusiasm for outdoor living is as keen as it was thirty years ago – it positively spills out. Just like Holding and his passion for cycle camping, for Lumley backpacking was and is a way of life, a source of freedom which also happens to be cheap.[68] Very quickly most companies had a product with the word backpacker or backpacking attached to it. This coincided with another international development which began slowly at first to gather momentum in the 1970s – the birth of Himalayan trekking. With the reopening of Nepal in 1969, Jimmy Roberts, an officer in the Gurkha regiment advised the Nepalese king to allow mountain tourists into the kingdom. The commercial end of these early treks was run by Thomas Cook, the originators of Alpine excursions in the 1860s, and were led by Himalayan veterans Eric Shipton and Bill Murray.[69] Whereas Cook's nineteenth century excursions were a product of the railways, this new brand of mountain tourism was inevitably closely linked to air travel. But the gentle beginning was transformed by the success of Bonington's Annapurna expedition in 1970 and the 1975 Everest expedition and the base camps of these major expeditions became regular objectives for trekking companies from the mid 1970s onwards.

The late 1960s and early 1970s then were a period of change in the UK outdoor trade and not surprisingly this created opportunities for both innovation and new companies. But the 1970s was also an intensely difficult time economically, with a combination of spiralling inflation and intensely difficult labour relations. This caused particular difficulties for Karrimor, which as the dominant producer employed over 300 people in two factories by 1974. It was also a period when Karrimor faced growing levels of competition. In the walking market Karrimor secured a strong position by supplying packs with aluminium frames. The aluminium pack frame was an American innovation based on welding technology developed in the aircraft industry. In the 1960s the leading U.S. firm making packs and pack frames was Camp Trails of Phoenix, Arizona. Their combination of high quality engineering and the impressive productivity levels that have distinguished U.S. from British manufacturing from the industrial revolution, terrified Parsons. With scale economies from a large domestic market, Camp Trails could afford to automate to a far greater degree than the small Lancashire company. Parsons vividly recalls the sense of impending doom he felt when he realised what the high tech, low cost American products, when moved to an Eire manufacturing location, could do to his market:

'I looked at the product for three years, and when I got my industrial engineer to actually check it and check the number of minutes in it I nearly died, I mean I nearly died. I couldn't believe how few minutes there were in it [and] I got my work study guy to check it. I think there were six minutes of stitching and assembly work only to put the cross band pieces on the frame and mount the belt that stitched it automatically. And we had about 20 to 24 minutes in ours.'

In addition Camp Trails had already moved part of their activities offshore into Mexico, shipping their high-tech fabric across the border. Combined with semi-automated pack frame production they could produce an enormous volume, at low unit cost . This looked a dire threat to Karrimor should they really begin to penetrate the U.K. market [70] and, when Camp Trails set up a factory in Ireland in 1971, Parsons believed that the game was up. If he had simply tried to match US productivity and low Irish labour costs, the market would have been lost before he was even half way there. This is not to say he did not **want** to raise productivity levels in the longer term but, for a small company, it was a matter of finding a route to short term survival.

Karrimor's initial response capitalised on a quirk of the British purchase tax system, (the predecessor to the current VAT) and of differing consumer and retailing tastes from their American rival . Parsons first of all simplified his product to make it easier to manufacture and for the customer to use. However, the crucial difference was that, whereas Camp Trails sold a range 3 packs and pack frames, Karrimor sold packs and frames separately. Since pack frames were not subject to the 25% Purchase Tax charged on rucksacks this immediately brought a price advantage. Additionally selling packs and frames separately was popular with both retailers and consumers. Karrimor's ten-pack sacs and three adjustable packframes brought thirty possible combinations, and consumers were encouraged to 'tailor their own pack frame and sac' to meet particular needs.[71] But crucially the retailers loved it too because if they had a single frame and pack left they could still make a sale when new stocks arrive. Parson's longer term response drew on his understanding of processes and aimed to dramatically improve productivity and hence reduce costs. This involved major new investment in the most modern German sewing machine technology which automated the positioning of fabrics, trimming and cornering. In the early 1970s, at over £1750 these machines were ten times the price of a conventional sewing machine. Karrimor initially bought sixty or more than £100,000 worth. But over an 18 month period combined with further redesign and work study they reduced production times by 40%.[72]

Mike Parsons, Karrimor demonstrating new Pfaff (German) sewing machines (Part of the £100,000 investment) to Japanese visitors.

In the 1960s Parsons had used pack frames to develop a pack to compete against the Bergan, the Whillans Alpiniste became an alternative to Millet climbing sacs and he had penetrated the outdoor education market with the OB sac. Karrimor also of course continued manufacturing distinctive cycle bags as well as the popular child carrier, the papoose. With Eddie Creig, Parsons formed the product development group which worked closely with retailers, climbers and outdoor education and was crucial in stimulating the company's rapid reaction.[73] The strategy of segmenting the pack market by positioning a product at the top of each segment and then developing a flexible range around it was a powerful one. It depended to a large part on Parsons own deep knowledge of design and factory processes – gained in the early days in the workshop and first factory. But it also relied on an eye for the development of a niche. In the 1970s one new sport which Karrimor almost made their own, through a combination of sponsorship and product development, was the mountain marathon. Mike Parson's decision to sponsor the event from 1971 proved a significant one for the company, the event and the company quickly became synonymous. The Mountain Marathon combines fell running, orienteering and survival techniques and is run over two days, the elite class covers 50 odd miles with 10,000 to 15,000 feet of ascent. Economy of weight became crucial for performance. Coming originally from a cycling tradition, Parsons was at home with the need to save weight and, initially at Chris Brasher's request produced a nylon rucksack weighing just three ounces. However, it was

Ken Ledward, employed as a full time tester and product developer at Karrimor from 1972-78, who contributed most to the development of truly featherweight gear in the 1970s. In 1972, working for a week with a sewing machine technician he produced two full sets of gear for himself and Mike for the next marathon. Tents, sleeping bags, jackets, overtrousers breeches and packs – Mike's weighed just 6.5 lbs and working on the principle that he was pint sized and older and so needed

COME AND SEE OUR NEW SHOP

LD Mountain Centre 1971 the retail origins of Berghaus.

P. Lockey and G. Davison Collection

lighter gear, Ken's was just 5.5 lbs.[74] This was the beginning of Karrimor's move into lightweight gear and the origin of the Marathon I and II tents launched in 1972 – again very much Ken's project. The wedge shaped tent weighed just 2lbs including poles, pegs, sewn in ground sheet and frost liner.[75] At the same time Ledward developed an up dated version of the Zsardsky Sac – Karrimor Instructor Survival Unit (the KISU). It provided immediate shelter for up to 6 people and gave the psychological advantage of face to face contact in emergencies. It is today widely copied and in stock with every outdoor centre and mountain rescue team.[76] Ledward's testing and improvement of the lightweight design continued into 1973 in often awful weather, as on January 6th when he recorded in his testing log:

> *'Fast run to the Lakes, Mike's van broke down again. Late evening climb to the Saddle between Scales and Souterfell; good windy site. Water some distance, so I chose to erect the tents. After 40 minutes no sign of water carrier, started to search and saw a hunched figure moving over Southerfell towards Mungrisdale and away from the tent. Quite a funny sight, Mike had an old canvas water bucket, and with beard and hair out horizontal appeared as Noah looking for his Ark.'[77]*

Competition came from new companies, including Newcastle-based Berghaus. Like Karrimor, Berghaus began with a shop – LD Mountain Centre in Newcastle which friends Peter Lockey and Gordon Davison started in 1966 and was initially one of Karrimor's top retail customers. The shop still exists and as late as 1989, Berghaus owner, Peter Lockey concluded:

> *'We will always keep the shop. It may have reduced in importance as Berghaus has grown but it is still quite central- firstly because it's profitable and secondly because it helps us to analyse the market and do market surveys of certain items.'[78]*

One of the key differences between Parsons' experience with Karrimor, where until the early 1970s he was both designer and salesman and Berghaus, lay in the

MACH 1 AND 2 FRAMES
An anodised coated alloy frame of 2 vertical and 3 horizontal tubes combines lightness with rigidity. Designed so that the sac can be attached at two different levels and fitted with tubular padded harness. The MACH 1 has a webbing waist strap and is 5ins. shorter than the MACH 2, which extends below waist level. A shaped and padded hip harness fitted with adjustable straps is standard with the MACH 2 frame. The straps of the hip harness are designed so that a proportion of the weight may be carried on the hips, so easing the load on the shoulders. This weight transference may be effected without taking off the frame.
HEIGHT 31 Inches
WIDTH 15 Inches
WEIGHT 2 lbs. 11ozs.
PRICE: MACH 1 £6.96
PRICE: MACH 2 £8.90

BERGSAC 272
Manufactured from Topspan or 9oz. proofed nylon in colour red. The sac is designed to attach to most frames, but specifically designed for the Berg Mach 1 and 2 frames. The flap has a large zipped external pocket 14" x 8" x 3". Inside the flap is another zipped pocket. The sac may be reduced in size by internal lacing for use on shorter expeditions. It is complete with padded tubular shoulder straps, waist strap and ice axe loop. Attachment to all frames is by means of the top loops.
HEIGHT 24 Inches
WIDTH 15 Inches
DEPTH 9 Inches
PRICE: £8.50

QUALITY EQUIPMENT
BERGHAUS
OF NEWCASTLE

ASK YOUR LOCAL STOCKIST FOR DETAILS OR WRITE DIRECTLY TO:
Berghaus Limited,
34 Dean Street,
Newcastle upon Tyne, 1.
Telephone: 22139

The first advertisement for Berghaus Rucksacks, 1972.

partnership between Gordon Davison and Peter Lockey. The pair brought complementary skills and personalities and of course the accompanying networks. Peter Lockey had worked in marketing and selling with Rowntrees and Gordon Davison had been a mechanical engineering lecturer at Newcastle Polytechnic. Like Parsons, they were keen sportsmen concentrating on skiing and climbing, enthusiasms upon which they built the LD Mountain Centre from 1966. Indeed initially they ran a ski school part-time in conjunction with the shop as Lockey recalled:

'... we used to take people out skiing at weekends and teach them and all that... and it gave us a wonderful entree into selling skis. So that undoubtedly gave the business quite a push, quite an impetus at the beginning. I mean, all this frenzied activity Friday, Saturday and bringing skis back Monday caused a constant traffic through the shop'.[79]

If skiing helped them build their shop, their interest in climbing indirectly created one of their most significant network opportunities. Prevented from climbing by storms and mudslides in the Italian Dolomites in 1967, Davison, accompanied Bill Wilkins (who became the LD Mountain Centre shop manager) and who was eventually to go on to found Ultimate Equipment, went in search of suppliers of good quality Italian boots for the shop. They came away with the agency for Scarpa, which was the start of the wholesale side of the business and the beginning of Berghaus. In 1972 Berghaus, encouraged by retailer Frank Davies of Ambleside, shifted into manufacturing, having tried and failed to become distributors for Karrimor.[80] They began manufacturing rucksacks and waterproof clothing with twelve employees in a small workshop in Washington, Tyne and Wear.[81] Interestingly one of the earliest employees was Bill Wilkins. Quirky, talkative, original American Bill, like so many of the innovators in the outdoor trade at this time was a fanatical climber but had no previous knowledge of making gear. He learned to make garments by a process of trial and error, first in a room with a couple of sewing machines at LD working half time in the shop and half time on making waterproofs. This arrangement did not last, and relations cooled as LD did not want to build up their manufacturing. He moved to Northumberland and set up Ultimate Equipment where eventually he made tents, clothing and sleeping bags. [82]

Like Mike Parsons at Karrimor, Peter Lockey and Gordon Davison had the greatest respect for Graham Tiso, even if Lockey's first professional meeting with him did not bode too well:

'The first time I met Graham in the trade, rather than as a friend was when I was selling our line of Scarpa boots to the Brigham brothers in Manchester. I was well into my presentation and doing rather well, when in walked Graham, picked up one of my sample boots, bent it in half and said 'Crap'. Steam was coming out of my ears, but the Brigham brothers knew Graham well enough and we got a good order.'[83]

Like Parsons, Lockey and his designer partner Gordon Davison saw Tiso as one of the major forces in the trade and a major influence on design in Berghaus:

'...clothing design, colours and features were directly influenced. They [Tiso's] had an in-house buying team who were very proactive and we would have meetings with them where Gordon and his key design team were present, the idea being to get as close to the end customers' (the buying public) views as possible. In those days, Tiso's were probably the most vociferous people in the trade as to what they wanted to see, and some manufacturers got short shrift if they couldn't react. However, we had to be careful as we could not produce solely for Tiso's tastes, as that would not necessarily be what the rest of the UK (quite apart from export markets) would want. Most other retailers might have some input into the design process but in a much more general way'.[84]

As Parsons has said of the competition with Berghaus, 'You think competition is healthy until it happens to you and then it becomes uncomfortable'.[85] The rivalry between the two companies was legendary and personal and from the start Mike Parsons recognised the potential threat that Berghaus represented to his dominant position in the rucksack market. They were initially tiny and designs experimental, but Lockey's background in selling gave Berghaus an advantage over Karrimor, as Parsons is the first to admit. He knew that once they hit on a good design they would be able to sell it. It was an advantage which Berghaus keenly pursued in an effort to dislodge Karrimor.

Lockey explained:

'...they were the first movers and to dislodge them would require quite a big marketing campaign and we decided as well we had to reorganise selling [under

Tony Sharp who had joined the organisation in 1969 from a sales management position in Nestle]. We spent quite a lot of money in those days establishing this marketing and it was very successful.[86]

Nevertheless, despite sustained Berghaus competition, Karrimor remained the dominant rucksack manufacturer right through to the purchase of the company by 21 Invest in 1996.[87] Mike Parsons' first response was to concentrate on his relationship with retailers, by getting delivery right. To do this he had to improve factory organisation and responsiveness and much of his ability to do so came from his sister Jen Longbottom, who joined him in manufacturing in 1972. According to Peter Gildersleve it was Jen who was like a spider at the centre of the web making production run smoothly and her brother agreed. 'Her brilliant administration' said Parsons 'ensured we always delivered exactly to promise, a critical weapon against the Berghaus onslaught'.[88] Jen Longbottom introduced new systems which ensured 'they delivered on time every time. If it was six weeks we delivered in six weeks... when a production batch was ready we knew all of the customers, so we hit it right.'[89]

The combination of niche development and regular process change helped Karrimor to remain the UK's dominant rucksack manufacturer for 30 years, despite the very real Berghaus threat. But it was combined with other responses when Berghaus threatened specific segments. In the mid 1970s Parsons became aware of the danger of Berghaus moving into the Outdoor Education market. In addition Berghaus hired, Jon Gale an outdoor centre principal as shop manager for LD:

'This scared me because they were going to be able to use both the manufacturing margin and the retail margin to compete against me'

commented Parsons. He chose to respond by collaborating with Graham Tiso, who was himself building up his outdoor education business and who had some concerns himself over the potential threat from the mail order company Field and Trek. The result was Adventure Equipment set up in 1975. The arrangement was that Karrimor sacs were supplied to outdoor centres with very special price structures and was initially highly controversial.[90] The deal brought other benefits to Karrimor, because with it came 50/50 distribution rights for Salewa. This along with those for Trangia stoves, which became so popular in the camping market (an entirely separate arrangement) added to Karrimor's position in the market place. It also brought some seasonal balance to both Karrimor and Salewa. Adventure Equipment served its purpose until the late 1970s, by which time the outdoor centre trade was falling off. Where Berghaus really scored was in the military market during and after the Falklands War for both rucksacks and for their newly developed Yeti gaiter. In

September 1979, at the Spoga exhibition in Cologne something new appeared:

'unlike ordinary gaiters, which hook onto the boot laces and are laced beneath the boots, Yeti gaiters fit right over the boots. Around the base of each gaiter is a rand and instep strap cut from a single piece of strong rubber and this is sewn to the gaiter canvas. Then, instead of putting the gaiters on after you put on the boots you put the gaiters on the boots.'[91]

The origins of the Yeti were on the notoriously wet Cheviot where Berghaus owners Gordon Davison and Peter Lockey had their testing days- they even originally called it the Cheviot. Fed up with constantly wet feet Davison wanted to put a seal on gaiters and the prototypes actually used old tractor inner tubes whipped from the local scrap yard. Putting them on was quite a struggle and they were not suitable for all boots. However what really made them was the Falklands War of 1982 when Berghaus got a contract with the MOD . Peter Lockey remembered:

'The Marines... were marching over this very inhospitable terrain which was very, very boggy... with Yeti gaiters on they could keep dry all the time and they were absolutely fantastic for doing that....'.92

The intense competition between Karrimor and Berghaus, for the rucksack market undoubtedly stimulated innovation and led to improved products not least in the soft pack market. The development of the Karrimor Jaguar and the Berghaus Cyclops and the introduction of the differing adjustable back systems were major steps forward. One of the big challenges, when rucksacks began to be made of nylon was proofing. All early users of nylon for packs had problems with coating. As Mike Parsons recalled:

'There were two problems with coating at this period and they were that it was extremely difficult to get a physical and/or chemical bond between the coating on the nylon. Even when a very basic bond was achieved the tear strength of the fabric dropped very dramatically to as low as 50% of the original tear strength. Kelty solved the problem from the early 50's by not coating the fabric and then hot wire cutting single plies to avoid seams bursting Millet of France was one of the first companies using nylon fabrics. As I had a comfortable dialogue with most of my competitors I asked Raymond Millet how long his proofing lasted and his reply was immediate and emphatic, "three big alpine routes" so I knew at that point that I was not alone in having this problem.'[93]

Parsons initially turned to textile BM Coatings based in Middleton. After an unpromising and quite slow start, a dialogue developed which provided a growing mutual understanding of what was needed. This included new compounds which were used for Ken Ledward's lightweight tent for the Karrimor International Mountain Marathon, which for the first time ever improved the tear strength of the fabric after coating. This deep and lasting relationship with BM Coatings proved important in the rucksack war with

Berghaus, for it resulted in the development of KS-100e in 1979, described as 'a completely new rucksack fabric with a new elastomer coating. The first fabric purpose designed for rucksacks'. It marked 'the culmination of two decades of technical research and development in fabrics as well as development of quality assurance'.[94] The product was launched with a very special leaflet with a piece of fabric attached and was immensely successful. Very quickly no one wanted a pack that was not KS-100-e. Confidence in the quality and performance of this fabric was such that Karrimor was able to launch lifetime guarantees on rucksacks made of the fabric. It was a radical move and a 'first' for the industry and crucial for Karrimor's competitive advantage. It was also controversial with some retailers who viewed it merely as a marketing ploy.[95]

Yet, by the 1980s there was some sense of a drive for ever more technical packs which, whilst an integral part of the competition process, may have left both consumers and retailers slightly baffled. As Alan Day commented:

> '...there's all these packs, all these packs bamboozled me, bamboozled the public but they were too technical... from the retailer's point of view most rucksack users do not go on expeditions like the professional expeditions, they don't go on them. So the packs were far too technical and costing far too much. We still don't want all these bells and whistles. Er, when they were bringing these out, backpacking as such was more popular than it is today. So both these companies were producing these very technical sacks for backpackers and things but ...people didn't understand how to use them. So although highly technical they were not getting the best out of them.'[96]

That packs did become too technical for the average fell walker may well have been the case. However, at the heart of the success of both Karrimor and Berghaus and indeed all the outdoor companies in this period was a commitment to and knowledge of the outdoors. Both companies took testing 'on the hill' as the crucial way of ensuring functionality. Parsons, Lockey and Davison and their staffs were involved in the regular practical testing of gear and of course Karrimor employed Ken Ledward as their tester during the 1970s. The Berghaus testing days became legendary and originated as a way of Gordon and Peter escaping from the interruptions of the office to talk over developments. Lockey and Davison at Berghaus had Wednesday test days on the Cheviots when they tried out new designs and pursued their own personal networking. As Davison said in a 1983 newspaper interview: 'We make all our major decisions on the hills without the interruptions of phones and people knocking at the door.'[97] They did, however, sometimes also invite outdoor journalists to join them, as in September 1982, when Roger Smith of *The Great Outdoors* described a visit to Berghaus when a trip round the factory to see the 1983 designs was followed by a product testing trip.

'The party consisted of a number of journalists and writers, three Berghaus
people and their bank manager – getting to know his clients on the hill instead of
on the golf course! We were kitted out with Bionic boots and Yeti gaiters,
Stormbeta waterproofs and AB rucksacks which Peter and Gordon had
generously filled with a 30lb load.'[98]

Without such outdoor credentials none of the dynamic companies of this
period could have achieved such a depth of knowledge and understanding.

The 1980s: A Clothing Revolution

The 1960s and 1970s saw remarkable equipment developments. But the
functional changes in down, waterproofs and the use of pile for clothing were
not accompanied by any shift towards more stylish, specialist clothing in the
UK. The lack of specialist clothing for the outdoors was very much a British
phenomenon. In both the United States and Continental Europe – partly from a
more extreme climate and partly from the seriousness with which mountain
warfare was treated, there was a longer manufacturing tradition for high quality
cold weather clothing. In the United States it has already been shown that Eddie
Bauer had been able to capitalise on his war time reputation and manufactured
down clothing in volume. In addition on the Continent outdoor activity
developed very much on a multi-sport basis, with climbers naturally shifting into
skiing in the winter. This meant that Continental outdoor clothing companies
had both a summer and a winter market for their products. Historically, skiing
has been associated with stylish, if functional outdoor dress and this was
translated across to walking and climbing wear in Austria and Switzerland
where typically, over half the population ski. There were no such traditions in
Britain where, until the 1970s and 1980s, only a tiny social elite skied and even
today it remains a minority sport. For UK mountaineering and outdoor activity
there were until the Second World War, two clothing traditions. There was one
derived from field sports and used to convey respectability in official
photographs, but for the majority discarded work-wear was the norm for outdoor
activity. The idea that you needed specialist clothing was anathema to the
majority of British outdoor enthusiasts. You walked or climbed in your cast off
work gear and not just because there was precious little else available. This was
the time when everyday clothing was very functional – the era before universal
central heating and when most people went to work on foot, by bicycle or on the
bus and so needed to dress warmly. Alfred Wainwright's son recalls he and his
father never bought anything new for walking in the 1940s and 1950s:

'We had no special walking clothes at all...Dad always walked in his shoes and
his suit... he had four suits all tweed. His best one was for council meetings. His
second best was for work. Third best for walking. Fourth best was for gardening.

RAIN-WEAR

PLASTIC CAPES

CYLING CAPE: This highly protective plastic cape with re-inforced thumb grips can be rolled small enough to pack into tool-bag or pocket when not in use. In Yellow or Black. 10/6d. (inc. P..T 5d.)

NYKAPE: A featherweight plastic rambling cape which gives full protection. Length 47 ins., skirt circumference 12 ft. Press-stud fastening at neck with 7 in. slide fastener opening. Smoky Grey shade. Weight 12 ozs. 18/11d. (inc. P.T. 9d.)

SOU'WESTERS: to match above capes, small, medium, large. 2/9d. (inc. P.T. 3d.)

MEN'S LIGHTWEIGHT RAINCOAT

A superior well-fitting plastic raincoat of extremely smart appearance. Absolutely waterproof. Colours, Grey, and Smoky Black. Length 46 ins., 48 ins., and 50 ins. with appropriate chest and sleeve measurements. Weight 12½ ozs.
18/6d. (inc. P.T. 9d.) d

FULL LENGTH OVERTROUSERS

Smart overtrousers to match raincoats. Plastic waist and two re-inforced let-through pockets. In 28 ins., 30 ins., and 32 ins. inside leg size.
9/6d. (inc. P.T. 4d.) d
The above garments and the plastic capes below fold up to pocket size when not in use.

P.V.C. RAMBLING CAPE

A cape which being of P.V.C. coated cambric and having generous length affords as near complete protection as possible. Buttoned at front, two slash armholes, gusset at back to cover ruc-sac. Colours, Black and Grey. Weight 3 lbs.

Two Sizes
Size 1 — 48 in. front, 50 in. back
Size 2 — 46 in. front, 53 in. back
£3 12s. 0d. (inc. P.T. 3/2d.) e

SOU'WESTERS TO MATCH: Lined. Small, medium, large. 11/- (inc. P.T. 10d.) d
Also available: Capes, size and style as above, in Fawn Indiana rubber. Weight 4 ozs.
Size 1 — £2 10s. 0d. (inc. P.T. 2/-) d
Size 2 — £2 12s. 6d. (inc. P.T. 2/3d.) d

Rambling Cape, 1958.

We had no anoraks either. We tried an oilskin cape once, but you got blown away in that if there was a wind. Then we tried those cheap plastic macs, but they immediately got torn to shreds... [99]

The ubiquitous Pacamac was not confined to English hills, however, and Joe Brown and Don Whillans used it to keep dry on the West Face of the Dru, above Chamonix, in 1954. They must have looked like nothing on earth and there was doubtless a Whillan's 'one liner' when he first put one on. [100]

Some changes did begin in the 1960s, when the orange nylon cagoule became the uniform, first of the outdoor centres in the UK and rapidly of all self-respecting outdoor enthusiasts. The French origins of the cagoule, which literally translates as cowl, have already been discussed. It was a long rubberised silk garment designed to be used on bivouacs with a combination of a down jacket and pied d'éléphant. The pioneer of the cagoule in the UK was Noel Bibby, who owned Peter Storm. Until the early 1960s Peter Storm anoraks and ski jackets were double texture poplin – closely woven cotton fabric which, like both Ventile and Grenfell, swelled with water making the weave even tighter and blocking out water. But in 1962 Bibby pioneered Bri–nylon sailing smocks which marked the beginning of their 100 lightweight PU coated nylon range. It was the forerunner of the 101 overjacket or cagoule which appeared very shortly afterwards. Pointing to its growing popularity by 1965 one set of guidance notes for hill-walkers concluded:

'A completely waterproof garment which is finding increasing favour is the cagoule – a voluminous lightweight nylon smock reaching to the knees and fitted with a hood. It is usually large enough to be worn over a rucksack, and its roominess allows enough air circulation to avoid the condensation normally caused by nylon waterproofs. One brand of cagoule embodies several valuable

features including an air vent in the back as an added safeguard against condensation, elasticated cuffs inside the sleeves, draw string at the hem, and a vivid orange colour to make the wearer easily visible in an emergency'.[101]

The Lake District wet is legendary and Eric Shipton told staff at OB Eskdale to 'dress for Lakeland hills as if you are going sailing'. And they did, using Henri Lloyd and Helly Hansen sailing gear.[102] Anyone who ventured onto the UK hills in the late 1960s and 1970s will remember that they positively teamed with 'day glo' ants. This was less so in the Alps where, without the concentration of outdoor centres, individuals made their own choices. Even with features designed to limit condensation, being wet most of the time in these garments was normal,as one Scottish walker warned:

'I also have an expensive nylon anorak and trousers and quite frankly I never expect them not to become wet inside if I am walking any faster than two miles per hour. The condensation element has to be taken into account.'[103]

The acceptance of an element of discomfort was an integral part of walking and climbing in the UK in this period. In addition climbers and walkers just did not care how they looked and scruffiness was almost a badge of honour. But by the early 1980s this began to change, through the coincidence of sporting and technological changes with a change in attitudes to outdoor sporting clothing. One key influence was the growing popularity and accessibility of skiing. Although though even today, only about 1% of the British population are active skiers, participation grew dramatically in the late 1970s and early 1980s. This came from cheaper air travel and the rapid expansion of winter sports holidays, while the popular television programme Ski Sunday brought skiing into people's homes. The Continental trade shows had become a mecca for product development during the 1970s. They were networking centres par excellence for an eclectic mix of people who were at one the same time both mountaineers, skiers, and business people. Gradually, as more and more professional guides/skiers and the newly emerging class of professional mountaineers became involved with business, the date became an important part of this mix. The dates of trade shows in that period conveniently coincided with the end of the alpine season so that the trade show to some extent also became an end of season reunion. In these often fleeting stand-up discussions in the exhibition corridors, the conversation always began with activity and almost invariably flowed into the product that was used. Vital confirmations of new product suitability were quickly passed from mouth to mouth, but most importantly between two people who trusted each other's opinion. Innovations therefore were quickly validated or otherwise and those manufacturers with a close ear to this could benefit significantly. In the 1980s this began to apply to clothing as well as equipment and design trends began to move between sports as Peter Lockey of Berghaus remembered:

'It was probably our move into the ski clothing market that was influential in the changes to the mountaineering garments. At that time we were also the UK distributors for Atomic skis, Marker ski bindings and Nordica ski boots, so we were always very active at the major international ski exhibitions, getting us closer to what was happening in the ski clothing markets also. So yes, the mountaineering clothing was influenced by the ski clothing, and of course we also manufactured a range of pure ski clothing as distinct from more crossover clothing.'[104]

In addition close relationships with ski schools were also important as Lockey confirmed:

'We made a determined drive to increase visibility through doing special deals with ski schools, both in Scotland and in the Alps. We also encouraged our agents/distributors to get our clothing worn by ski school instructors in Italy, France and to a lesser extent in Germany. Our drive was with specialist ski clothing rather than fancy fashion clothing. It was successful, both in terms of the effect on the foreign markets, but also on UK skiers who would arrive in a resort and find their French/Italian instructors using Berghaus jackets. Our clothing was often more acceptable to those instructors especially with a bias to ski mountaineering and 'extreme' skiing. I wouldn't say that there was an especially strong relationship with holiday and tour operators. They were happy to have special deals and BH had the right 'cred'!'[105]

The interplay between skiing and mountaineering clothing was part of the story which created a shift, but climber's own attitudes began to change. Alex McIntyre was one of a new breed of 'super alpinists' who, in the early 1980s, were taking alpine-style climbing to the Himalayan 8000 metre peaks. He was also notoriously scruffy, earning the nickname 'dirty Alex'. But in 1982 he commented to Mike Parsons, for whom he was a technical advisor, 'scruffy gear and clothing is no longer good enough for what we need to achieve and in some cases it is downright dangerous.'[106] It was a comment which also coincided with a range of technological changes to fibres, fabrics and garment design, which were to transform what was possible and practical in outdoor clothing and footwear. As Tony Lack was to conclude in 1989:

'There seem to be two systems of outdoor clothing in general use. The traditionalists still think in terms of string vest, loose fitting woolly shirts, baggy tweed breeches (or jeans) hairy wool socks and clumpy boots. The moderns are using close fitting underwear, fleece or fibre-pile for warmth, light wind shirts and jackets, trousers or stretch breeches and lightweight trainer style boots or moulded (plastic) footwear'.[107]

Increasingly the 'moderns' outnumbered the 'traditionalists' as special clothing became the symbol of participation as well as being purely functional. It is often said that outdoor clothing has become 'fashionable' and certainly in the

1980s there was a dramatic change in the language of clothing. However as central heating became ever more pervasive in the home, school and the workplace, the need for the high street fashion brands to provide warm clothing became less and less. Eventually almost the only warm and weatherproof clothing available was provided by the outdoor industry. But until the mid 1980s clothing still retained the look and feel of work-wear. From then on it began to look good as well as functional and more important conveyed a particular image.

Change began in waterproofs during the 1970s following the almost 200 year search for the 'holy grail' of the breathable waterproof for mountaineering and outdoor activity. The Victorian Macintosh, with its rubberised coating had been universally disliked by climbers because of both its smell and build up of condensation. There were also paraffin wax impregnated fabrics, developed towards the end of the nineteenth century by Norwegian Helly Hansen and the English company Barbour for fishermen and sports people. These were totally waterproof but did not breathe, though they did not smell unpleasant like Macintosh. One solution to breathability lay with Burberry gabardine, patented in 1879 and also originally developed for field sports. It used tightly woven yarn dyed and proofed cotton threads to keep out the rain. For 40 years, from the 1880s until the 1920s, it was unrivalled for mountaineering and for exploration. This was less because it was waterproof than because it repelled snow and wind and did not cause condensation during exertion. As such it was the first breathable fabric. The appearance of the lighter Grenfell in the 1920s and the wartime Ventile undermined Burberry for mountaineering. All these cotton fabrics were certainly breathable but they suffered eventually from water penetration and also froze solid in cold conditions. In the 1930s PA's silk rubberised cagoule certainly solved the problem of protection of down clothing on a bivouac but, like Macintosh, it still condensed.and when coated nylons were used for cagoules in the 1960s – the 'battle for the breathable' continued.The 1973 Cagjac by G. and H. Products of Batley in Yorkshire- soon to become Craghoppers-was one solution. It was three-quarter length and it used zip fasteners to allow for ventilation. It needed to be well ventilated though because it was really a glorified Macintosh, for a rubber coating was used at a time when PUs would not stick to nylon.[108] Noel Bibby at Peter Storm also experimented with breathable coatings to produce 'No Sweat'.[109]

In recalling the 1980s, Ken Ledward remembered that 'Berghaus had this beautiful glowing thing above Gordon and Peter'.[110] The 1980s became the Berghaus decade, when they emerged as the UK's leading mountain clothing company. Part of the 'golden glow' stemmed from their relationship with W.L. Gore, the American patentees of Gore-Tex which affected their position as outdoor clothing manufacturers. The timing was genius or pure luck. This is because extremely expensive Gore-Tex clothing could not have been commercially successful unless there was a need for technical clothing, that also made a statement about the status of the wearer. The jury is still out as to whether Gore-Tex waterproofs really are the most effective breathable garments, but it certainly changed the market and contributed to the evolving world of outdoor clothing. Certainly the massive advertising budget which the company threw at Gore-Tex and its licensed garment manufacturers gave the concept incredible visibility. Conversely had the advertising budgets on Sympatex –which for a period outsold Gore-Tex in the European market- matched those of Gore, the picture could have been very different.[111]

Wilbert L. Gore was a research supervisor at Du Pont in the 1950s. After trying and failing to persuade the company of the wide commercial potential of Teflon, he left to set up his own company W.L. Gore. Working with his son he used the PTFE coating for cable insulation before moving on to develop a porous film based on Teflon. One of the principle breakthroughs involved regenerating tissues destroyed by disease or traumatic injuries and this provided the basis for an extension into outdoor clothing.[112] The patent for Gore-Tex, which was ultimately to transform the market for outdoor clothing was filed in 1973 and issued in 1976.[113]

Gore saw their laminate as only part of the story however and, a bit like the manufacturers of Grenfell, believed that its success depended upon the development of high performance goods and clothing. This could only be done through the formation of a number of strategic alliances with outdoor manufacturers. Two pioneers included Peter Hutchinson at Mountain Equipment and Banton's of Nottingham which showed a Gore-Tex sleeping bag cover at Harrogate as early as 1975.[114] However, if in 1976 Berghaus was not the first company to experiment with Gore-Tex, they made an enormous contribution to the evolution of Gore-Tex clothing where they were perceived as 'first movers'. The alliance with Gore established Berghaus as the UK's premier outdoor clothing manufacturer. Heralded as the 'miracle fabric' which, with its millions of tiny holes, would mark the end of discomfort and chilling caused by condensation, 'first generation' Gore-Tex was problematic. Ken Ledward tested a Berghaus Mistral jacket made of Gore-Tex in 1978 and, although he found the fabric was good, he highlighted problems with the seams and found the heat conservation properties were poor, compared with conventional neoprene – because of its high breathability.[115] However, soon other difficulties with first generation Gore-Tex became apparent with prolonged wear . The two main problems were contamination from sweat and leaking seams. This led to returned garments, endless complaints in the outdoor press and Peter Lumley went so far as to say that using such a garment in the

Cairngorms had led to potentially life threatening hypothermia. [116]. The imperfections of first generation Gore-Tex virtually lost Gore the German market but also encouraged improvements . The addition of a hydrophylic membrane helped to remove the contamination problem . But the real problem was that the seams were stitched and so leaked like sieves. The next step was high frequency welding but, as Neville Whitley, Berghaus' production manager remembered,that was pretty hit and miss too because, 'if you got a slight mismatch [in the welding] you got a leak.'[117] The answer lay in taped seams – first used for waterproofs by Macintosh in the 1880s. This involved using technology which had already been developed for polyurethane in 1971. Gore finally sourced a taping machine for use by Berghaus and their designer Marion Barnes recalled:

> *'When I went into design...Gore developed a taping machine and I can remember coming in over Christmas and Gore came to train me on being able to use the taping machine.'[118]*

But it was improvements in taping which really transformed Gore-Tex garments. Berghaus's development work was critically important to the success of these breathables in wet and windy climates in Northern Europe. Of course Berghaus's own reputation was also on the line and it was crucial that outdoor enthusiasts quickly forgot the weaknesses of the first generation garments. In a letter in *Great Outdoors* in 1982 David Ulberg of Berghaus commented:

> *'The garment used by Mr. Rhodes is one of the models using 'first generation' Gore-Tex material. During the past few years W.L. Gore have (like all forward thinking companies) followed a policy of continually improving and upgrading their product.'[119]*

But if Berghaus were primarily responsible for salvaging the reputation of Gore-Tex, there was a mutual commitment. The advertising budget which came with the alliance had a far wider commercial significance for the company's external profile. For the first time outdoor products were advertised outside the mountaineering press and Berghaus' Gore-Tex products even appeared in the *Sunday Times* supplement. This was far beyond the means of small outdoor companies and only the resources of a major US textile company made it possible.[120]

Gore-Tex and Berghaus products were promoted simultaneously and generally raised both companies' profiles. Peter Lockey was in no doubt that it was the relationship with Gore which put them on the map regarding clothing:

> *'Once we were working with Gore, we knew that we had a strong potential performer, supported by W.L.Gore's own marketing and advertising budget. We therefore tried to dominate the market for Gore-Tex clothing with 'first mover' advantage, and it did put us on the map for specialist clothing. Again, we used our sponsored climbers to project this image.'[121]*

Whilst controversy still remains whether any synthetic fabric can be rendered truly breathable and whether Gore-Tex is superior to its competitors, its appearance broke the mould and clearly had fundamental implications for Berghaus, seen as the first to develop its use for clothing in Europe. As Gore imposed ever tighter specifications on its users, Berghaus gained from the relationship. Combined with Gordon Davison's stylish and adventurous designs for high performance clothing, Gore money helped to make the 1980s 'the Berghaus decade'. It also increased their competitive threat to Karrimor, for which the 1980s seemed more like an uphill struggle to survive.[122]

Gore-Tex created a demand for breathable clothing, but it was very expensive and it prompted an explosion of activity in the manufacture of waterproofs and in proofing. Some established companies, like Henri Lloyd chose to go with Gore while Peter Storm remained staunchly independent. In 1982, the year that 2nd generation Gore-Tex burst on the scene, Noel Bibby opened his own proofing factory – Stormproofing – in Manchester. He launched his relatively cheap, breathable version of the light nylon waterproof, using a hydrophylic coating at the Harrogate Trade Show in 1984 but it had little impact – drowned out by the roar of Gore-Tex advertising.

Through its links with Gore, and with the leading edge climbers who used their products, Berghaus undoubtedly helped to change attitudes to clothing for the outdoors in Britain. Their own image had changed a great deal from the 1970s, boosted by their memorable Italian designed trademark. Berghaus clothing became 'collectable' and a status symbol far beyond the mountaineering community, aided in part by national advertising. Other technical developments – including the development of fleece, as an alternative to pile and of Pertex as a down proof wind proof layer also had significant implications for both the appearance and the performance of clothing for outdoor sports. At the same time changing sporting demands – especially in climbing contributed to new approaches and new designs as well as more new companies.

However, sustained, intense competition in the production of waterproof jackets eventually became counterproductive, because there are ultimately only so many features and gismos you can add to a jacket which actually enhance its performance. A new outdoor player began to have an impact in 1991. Risol – to be renamed Regatta in 1996 – was a sales led company which set out to capture the general as opposed to the specialised outdoor market.[123] The firm had a long history in the Lancashire rainwear industry (spawned initially by Macintosh) and their owners saw an enormous potential market for cheap, breathable waterproofs for the general walker and they began experimenting in the late 1980s. And they were right as there was an estimated 10 million occasional walkers in the U.K. in 1995.[124] Good breathable waterproofs in the 1990s were expensive and arguably the vast majority of walkers did not even venture onto the hills and were over-equipped. Of course some jackets like the Berghaus Trango were bought as much as fashion and status symbols as for the hills. The Blacks, who owned Risol, had been rainwear manufacturers from the 1930s and used their knowledge of coatings and garments to build a mass market brand. Keith Black, the current MD of Regatta, drew a clear line between his family's textile clothing background and the sports and mountaineering enthusiasm of many in the outdoor trade. It was this background and the use of offshore manufacturing which he believed allowed Regatta to break the mould by producing the first mass market, affordable, breathable clothing using their own brand of coating.

Regatta were not trying to emulate companies at the specialist end of the market, but rather create a brand in its own distinctive mould. [125]

Another development to transform clothing for outdoor sports was fleece. The military pioneered use of a natural pile – using alpaca or wool during the Second World War and aircrews were being issued with Acrilan pile underwear in 1963.[126] Two years earlier the Norwegian company, Helly Hansen, pioneered the use of pile in outdoor sports, though it really took off in the 1970s. Pile was highly functional but looked tatty from 'pilling' or bobbling very quickly. Fleece, by contrast, was a velour which combined the warming qualities of pile with an attractive appearance and a comforting feeling. It came from Malden Mills in Lawrence, Massachusetts owned by Aaron Feuerstein. Development began in the late 1970s of a lightweight, quick drying fabric that did not absorb water and stemmed from the company's work on seating fabrics for public transport.[127] This new fabric revolutionised outdoor gear, because most things that had been used previously for mountaineering looked scruffy. It was invaluable as part of layering systems and ultimately graced every high street fashion store as well as outdoor gear world-wide. Yvon Chouinard's clothing company, Patagonia, pioneered the use of fleece in the early 1980s under their own brand name Synchilla. Such was the impact of their launch that, when Malden introduced their own product 18 months later the whole outdoor trade was beating a path to their door. Again the market and attitudes to clothing were changed, for here was a product that was not only functional but looked too good for outdoor sport.

In the 1970s and early 1980s Pete Hutchinson's Mountain Equipment had dominated the market for high performance down clothing and sleeping bags but as ME grew and shifted into an ever broader range of leisurewear, a niche had emerged at the very top of the down market that was eventually to be filled by Rab Carrington.

Rab Carrington began climbing in 1965 in Scotland, just before he went to university. Seven years later, not long after he moved to Sheffield, he teamed up with Al Rouse. At the centre of the Peak gritstone edges Sheffield was, by the early 1970s, a vibrant climbing centre and a magnet for many leading climbers, so it was an obvious and fruitful move. During the 1970s Carrington emerged as a leading edge climber with a reputation for hard, lightweight routes in the Alps, South America and the Himalayas. In 1973 he organised a trip to Patagonia with 5 friends including Al Rouse, and a dock strike in Liverpool delayed the arrival of the climbing gear. This gave him the chance to learn how to work with down from an Argentinian who put them up. After the trip Rab stayed on until Christmas, learning how to make sleeping bags, though he did not make use of that knowledge until 1980.

When Rab Carrington first went into business, he concentrated on sleeping bags, though he displayed his first down jacket at Harrogate in 1982. His philosophy was simple – as a top climber he knew what other climbers wanted and, like Hutchinson's, his gear has always had an integrity based on its high quality and performance. But of course in 1980 he was 'a well known commodity' himself and by calling his company Rab, he was able to build on something that was already public knowledge and which inevitably appealed to retailers.[128]

From the start Carrington's main competitor was Pete Hutchinson but, throughout, both men retained a deep respect and liking for each other. There was none of the personal antagonism that characterised say, the rivalry between Karrimor and Berghaus. At the start, Carrington was making gear at home and thought of himself as the small guy rather than as a competitive threat to a firm like Mountain Equipment. He is quite clear that the shift in his position just crept up on him and that he did not consciously seek it out.[129] By the 1990s Rab had become synonymous with high quality down gear, with an integrity which continues to reflect the values he originally brought into the trade.

One fabric which helped to transform both the performance and appearance of Rab Carrington's gear was Pertex – which he had heard about from Hamish Hamilton – the originator of the Vango Force 10 tent. Through his clothing company, Buffalo, Hamilton really began to break new ground using combinations of new fabrics in layering systems. He explored using pile in combination with another material, the idea being that the two worked in tandem – the pile kept you warm and helped to keep moisture away from your body and his search for another complementary fabric to disperse moisture led him to Perseverance Mills, Steve Laycock and to Pertex – an 'almost' micro fibre fabric. Perseverance Mill in Padiham was founded in 1901 and, from the first, was one of Lancashire's more specialist mills producing balloon fabric, then moving into typewriter ribbons and then computer ribbons. Perseverance is now part of the multinational textile group Scapa and Steve Laycock began applying typewriter ribbon technology to the outdoor trade and Pertex- patented in 1980, was the result. Its legendary 'wicking' ability stemmed directly from the typewriter ribbon function of moving ink back to the area just hit by the key.

Pertex's ability to move moisture out of the fabric made it ideal for Hamish Hamilton's needs and he was their first outdoor customer.[130]:

Hamilton's Buffalo was on the same Sheffield industrial estate as Rab Carrington and Hamish put him in contact with Laycock and Perseverance. This was the beginning of a highly successful and innovative relationship which parallels the ties companies like Karrimor have with their suppliers. Laycock really listened and a genuine dialogue developed which benefited both companies and crucially genuinely improved products. Superficial changes to fabrics that created cosmetic changes to products had no attraction for Rab. He became the first commercial down sleeping bag company to use Pertex and Carrington and Steve Laycock of Perseverance developed highly functional, versatile fabrics to meet specific needs in the outdoor trade, including sleeping bags, down jackets and windproof shells.

Footwear changed as much as clothing during the 1980s with the emergence of lightweight boots, a development in which Ken Leeward and Mike Parsons at Karrimor were key players. The story began in 1974 when the pair were competing together in the KIMM. Parsons recalled:

> *'We had made ourselves an ultra lightweight outfit (tent, packs, jackets etc) but I was going very slowly and Ken was impatient. When he saw the state of my heels which had been torn apart by the leather running shoes he was more sympathetic, but only slightly. Not long afterwards I purchased a pair of the first running shoes made in fabric, the Adidas SL 72 (first produced for the Olympics of the same year in Munich). Together with two friends Don and Guy we took three days to go from Langdale to Eskdale and back, our packs weighed only 12lb each plus a rope and three runners. The idea was to do easy rock climbing in running shoes, and carrying all gear The descent from Napes ridge was the real test when we had to run a rather vicious scree but my shoes were still holding up at the end of the day and after three days were still very comfortable. Every time other people on the hills saw that we weren't wearing boots you could see them drawing in breath and oozing and aching and obviously considering us rather foolish people to be going on the hills without boots.'[131]*

At this time Ken Ledward had been trying to produce a lightweight canvas boot. His faith in lightweight footwear goes back to the 1960s when he used a hockey boot to break the running record on Kilimanjaro. Having personally proved that light footwear could function on steep ground he became more and more conscious on returning to England that people were using heavier boots than they needed. He recalled:

> *'everywhere in the UK was over-booting, everybody was buying a pair of boots that would have lasted them a life time and they were spending horrendous time trying to break them in. And I tried to persuade somebody that what we needed was something that would be closer to a fell running shoe, which I knew well as a studded shoe but had some rigidity and I couldn't get anybody interested.'[132]*

Later Ledward's research showed that the traditional Vibram sole was a major source of erosion on British mud. He developed a sole which combined traction on steep ground with edging for traversing and was well suited to British conditions.[133] The next step was to find someone who could marry the sole to a lightweight boot and he approached Parsons who, whilst interested, was unable to find a manufacturer prepared to produce a run of under 10,000. Eventually, having set up his own independent testing service, Ken Ledward Equipment Testing Service, (K.L.E.T.S) Ledward found his first partner, a cricket boot firm called Winit run by John Little and the first boots became available by 1980. However, as Ledward ruefully observed:

'it went pear shaped, it really went pear shaped because the first firm he got to manufacture and sell it was a caving company and they were selling them as ideal for caving.'

In the meantime Parsons remained keen on the idea of a lightweight boot and had been pursuing his own path in collaboration with the Italian firm ASOLO for whom Karrimor were acting as UK distributors. ASOLO had already developed a fabric boot which they said had been selling extremely well in Italy, despite being a very basic design, with a poor sole. Parsons was baffled and found that the secret lay in the price – they looked like a boot but were the same price as the Adidas TRX running shoe and so people used them for the Tour de Mont Blanc. Neither the ASOLO nor the product that Ken Ledward developed with Little were remotely near what Parsons had in mind. He told ASOLO that their design was unsatisfactory and obtained Ledward's permission to work with Little. One of the keys to what became known as the KS-B was combining a new shock absorbing material – Sorbothane – with the K.L.E.T.S. sole and a fabric upper. The boot, the first with a sole which did not ape nailing patterns, was launched by Parsons at Harrogate in 1980. Shortly afterwards ASOLO came up with a good upper design which, if combined with the K.L.E.T.S. sole, would make a good product. But time was immensely tight if orders from the Harrogate Show were to be met. Parsons remembers the whole deal being on a knife edge with a hint of cloak and dagger:

'The principal of ASOLO, Giancarlo Tanzi called me and said that if he was going to deliver something before the factory closed in the first week of August we would now have to work exceptionally fast. Within seven days I was on the plane to Milan, with instructions to go to a village called Vigevano, just north of Milan and wait in a bar at 3 pm. No name of a person or a company, just wait there at 3 pm that day. A friend, Peter Cooper had spotted that the moulds must come from this certain factory, and lo and behold when the person arrived he had the original KLETS drawings. This was critical in order to meet our time-scales but we made a new design with some improve- ments from Kens suggestions. At the meeting were also the ASOLO factory manager and a sole moulder. With this group of people around the table we could get exact

*delivery promises for each of the three phases; manufacture of the moulds, moulding
the soles, making the footwear. Incredibly it worked exactly to time and ASOLO
shipped a full container load of KS-B's before the factory closed for holiday the first
week in August.*[134]

The KS-B, as the pioneering lightweight fabric boot, was by no means problem free as would be expected with any new design. Anyway fabric boots in a climate like Britain would always cause difficulties. But, as with early Gore-Tex garments, the big problem with them was that they leaked, especially at the seams while breathable laminates like Gore-Tex or Sympatex were simply not yet available for footwear. But whilst leaking remained a problem, there were improvements during the second year of development. These included the moulded mid sole. Until this point footwear had been constructed with a mid sole of uniform thickness. This meant that experienced retailers did not stock some manufacturers' models over say size 10 and other manufacturers' models were not stocked below say size 5. With the KS-B mid sole the thickness not only differed with each individual size, but also along its length. Every size of the boot therefore had the correct strength of flex. The nature of the material also meant that the natural spring and flex of the boot was maintained more or less for the life of the boot.

Outdoor writer Chris Townsend, whilst acknowledging the shortcomings of the new boots, concluded that:

*'Despite problems, I am reluctant to go back to conventional leather boots. After
KS-Bs, they feel clumsy and heavy. Wearing them is rather like putting on
conventional rainwear after wearing Gore-Tex. It is no longer satisfactory and the
disadvantages are suddenly very noticeable when you know there is an
alternative. The KS-Bs are really a breakthrough so I hope the problems that have
arisen can be quickly solved.'*[135]

In the third year of the KS-B's life a leather version, which kept the lightweight construction, was introduced. In theory, it should have meant that the problem of waterproofing was solved. Unfortunately it coincided with the appointment of a new designer by ASOLO. He not only made some significant and misguided modifications to the K.L.E.T.S.sole of the leather version, but also introduced a fabric tongue which entirely negated any waterproofing benefits and it would not sell. The timing could not have been worse for Karrimor faced growing competition from the Berghaus Bionic SF and the Meindl Gore-Tex boots, as well as light leather boots such as the Brasher Boot. The leather Brasher boot quickly emerged, again with a K.L.E.T.S. sole, and became the most popular and best selling lightweight boot, transforming perceptions and expectations of leather mountain footwear and maintaining a strong position today. Certainly the teething troubles of the KS-B contributed to the major commercial crisis at Karrimor in the mid 1980s – though a combination of an overvalued currency, continued inflation and the bankruptcy of their French distributor in 1984, turned a blip into a near catastrophe. The relationship with ASOLO inevitably deteriorated and Karrimor pulled out of KS-Bs.[136]

By pioneering lightweight footwear, Mike Parsons, Ken Ledward and Karrimor changed the trade. Derryck Draper (who handled Karrimor's PR from 1977-1989) commented wryly that the KS-B was a genuine path-breaker, but 'If he (Parsons) could just have held back and been second he and Karrimor would have been better off'.[137] Eventually though Karrimor became 'second' movers when they re-launched the KS-B in 1990 following advice and help from Alan Day – by then retired from Blacks. The relented KS-B used Gore-Tex and within 2 years Karrimor were Gore's largest UK footwear customer.[138]

The extraordinary period from 1960 until the 1990s was in many ways a golden age for British outdoor companies. It was a period when British climbing returned to the forefront internationally, when first outdoor education and then mountain tourism flourished and it was a period when new sports gained popularity. But it was not an easy period economically. Karrimor, Berghaus and Mountain Equipment succeeded because of their determined commitment to the performance quality of their products. They were not the only innovative outdoor companies but they were often the most prominent, each having a niche with which they were easily identified.

What Does the Future Hold for the Outdoor Industry?

Projecting the future is always hazardous but, since part of our message has been that history matters, it follows that past trends will have some bearing on the future. Most people through time have come to understand their clothing less and less. Modern living has rendered the once instinctive skills of staying warm and dry obsolete. Unlike animals, for whom grooming and preening are a crucial element of survival, humans now see it as personal adornment – in much the same way most of them now view their clothes. Central heating and the motor car have removed the need for primarily functional everyday clothing. Attitudes to physical exercise have changed too and a new generation of young people will reach maturity when only a few have had the opportunity to walk or play on an unprepared surface. The cult of the gym – those 'factories' of exercise for the hard pressed young executive- has already influenced sportswear and also has physiological effects. For outdoor exercise there are several ways clothing and footwear can go and the following look to be the most important. One way may be to ape the development path of homes and cars with temperature and ventilation controlled by the ubiquitous micro chip, which would open and close fastenings at will. The other route is to study the myriad of different ways that all kinds of wild life keep warm and dry.

Most visual projections show sleek aerodynamic clothing. What is clear, however, is that design will go on changing and evolving as it has done in the past. As in the past it will depend heavily upon the versatility of the textile industry – that much maligned but most innovative of sectors.

Acknowledgements for Illustration Reproductions

We should like to thank the following for permission to reproduce images: Scott Polar Research Institute of Cambridge, Alpine Club, the British Library, the Royal Geographical Society, the Fell and Rock Library of the Lake District, the Royal Geographical Society , Westminster City Libraries, Jaeger, Hazel Constance ,the Thomas Cook Archive, the Camping and Caravanning Club of Great Britain and Ireland, the Deutschen Alpenverein, the National Library of Scotland, Mrs J.N. I Russell, *Mountain Equipment*, Blacks Leisure Group, Patagonia, Vibram, Bill O'Connor, Hermann Huber, Stéphane Pennequin and the John Noel Photographic Collection . All credits are also included with images in the text. Others are from our personal collections.

NOTES AND REFERENCES

Chapter 2

1   The Hot Arctic, John Dyson, 1979.
2   James P. Delgado, *Across the Top of the World : The Quest for the North West Passage* (London : British Museum Press, 1999) pp.8-15.
3   David Mountfield *Polar Exploration* (London : Hamlyn Group 1974) pp. 24-56.
4   Cameron, *To the Farthest Ends of the Earth* p. 27.
5   Fergus Fleming *Barrow's Boys* (London,1998) p.1-12.
6   Fleming, *Barrow's Boys* p. 64; Delgado, *Across the Top of the World,* p. 167.
7   Barbara F. Schweger, *Documentation and Analysis of the Clothing worn by Non Native Men in the Canadian Arctic prior to 1920, with an Emphasis on Footwear* (MSc Dissertation, University of Alberta, 1983) p. 182
8   J.Ross *Narrative of the Second Voyage in Search of the North-West Passage in the years 1829, 30, 31, 32 and 33)* reprinted from 1835 edition. First Greenwood Printing) pp 721-22.
9   Schweger, *Documentation and Analysis of the Clothing* ,p. 86
10 Ibid p.181.
11 Ibid p.106
12 Ibid p. 82 and 95
13 quoted ibid p. 98
14 Ken McGoogan, *Fatal Passage : The Untold Story of John Rae, the Arctic Adventurer who discovered the fate of Franklin* (Toronto, Canada: Harper Flaminge, 2001) p. 130
15 Ibid pp. 67-9.
16 Mountfield, *Polar Exploration* p. 86
17 F.L. McClintock, 'Antarctic Sledge-travelling' in (ed.) G.Murray, *The Antarctic Manual* p. 301.
18 Ibid p. 298.
19 Ibid 298.
20 Mountfield, *Polar Exploration* p. 97. Fleming, *Barrow's Boys* p. 424; C.R. Markham, *Life of Admiral Sir Leopold McClintock* (London, 1909)
21 Roland Huntford, *Nansen,* (London1997). p151
22 ibid
23 Ibid. p65
24 Life and Times of Fridtjof Nansen J .Arthur Bain
25 J.S.Garrow et al *Human Nutrition and Dietetics* (2000); Roland Huntford, *Nansen* (London, 2000) p.460; The Past, Present and Future of Vitamins An Essay by Jack Challem Copyright © 1997 by Jack Challem, The Nutrition Reporter™.
26 (introduced in English language 1792.Websters)
27 PRIMUS catalogue (fuel comparisons)

Energy value	heat kcal/kg	BPI=boiling power index *(an adjustment for specific gravity of fuel)*
Methylated spirit	6,300	53
Kerosene/paraffin	10,100	85

Paraffin gives an effective BP Index increase over meths of 60% and this can be translated directly into distance covered on an expedition.)

[29] J Arthur Bain *Life and explorations of Fridtjof Nansen.*, p 162.

[30] Roald Amundsen *The South Pole;*, p77

[31] A folding tent is still there unused at Cape Evans in Scott's hut according to Roger Mear.

[32] Michael Pearson Sledges and sledging in polar regions Polar Record 31(176):3-24 (1995)

[33] First source Michael Pearson Sledges and sledging in polar regions Polar Record 31(176):3-24

[34] This and other ski wax info from email correspondence with Harald Bjerke and Leif Torgersen Axell (lab manager)of Swix company. Aug 2001.

[35] US Forces 10th Division museum web site.

[36] 'Nice Goin' My Life on Skis by Friedl Pfeifer with Morten Lund 1993.

[37] 'Notes on aluminium running surfaces (not successful) and new "Sohm" skins' *British Ski Year Book,* 1920; 'Test of Sohm's ski skins – favourable' *British Ski Year Book,* 1921.

[38] Michael Pearson Sledges and sledging in polar regions Polar Record 31(176):3-24 (1995)

[39] Mirsky 1970 Jeannette Mirsky (d. 1987)Visiting Fellow, Department of East Asian Studies, Princeton University, 1970–74. Co-author of The World of Eli Whitney. 'To The Arctic! the story of northern exploration from the earliest times to present'

[40] Roger Mear interview.20/11/2002

Chapter 3

[1] An excellent and detailed over-view of the early development of mountaineering is provided by W. Unsworth *Holding the Heights* (London, Hodder and Stoughton, 1993) pp. 20-52)

[2] R.H. Greg , *Travel Journal1816-7,* manuscript quoted Mary B. Rose , *The Gregs of Quarry Bank Mill: The Rise and Decline of a Family Firm, 1750-1914* (Cambridge: Cambridge University Press, 1986) p. 49.

[3] Walt Unsworth *Holding the Heights* p. 37; T. Graham Brown, "Early Mountaineering" pp34-38 "Lonsdale Library, Mountaineering, "

[4] Jim Ring, *How the English Made the Alps* (London: John Murray, 2000) pp. 49-51

[5] Quoted Piers Brendon: *Thomas Cook: 150 Years of Popular Tourism* (London Secker and Warburg 1991) pp. 55-6

[6] Douglas W. Freshfield, 'Preliminary Hints', *Hints to Travellers* (London, Royal Geographical Society, 1893) p. 1.

[7] T. Graham Brown, "Early Mountaineering" pp34-38 "Lonsdale Library, Mountaineering, "

[8] Fergus Fleming, *Killing Dragons: The Conquest of the Alps* (London: Granta Books, 2000) p. 155-6.

[9] Robert E. Schofield, 'The Industrial Orientation of Science in the Lunar Society of Birmingham' in (ed.) A.E. Musson, *Science, Technology and Economic Growth in the Eighteenth Century* (London 1972).

[10] Ronald Clark , *The Victorian Mountaineers* (London: B.T. Batsford 1953) p. 152

[11] Alison Adburgham, *Shops and Shopping, 1800-1914* (London: George Allen and Unwin,1964)p. 80.

[12] Quoted Cunningham, Phillis and Mansfield, Alan (1969) *English Costume for Sports and Outdoor Recreation* (London) p.320

[13] We are grateful to the staff of the Castle Museum, York for drawing our attention to examples of these in their collections.

[14] W.E.Durham (1916) *Summer Holidays in the Alps, 1898-1914* (London: T. Fisher,1916), p. 46

[15] Girdlestone, *The High Alps* p. 170

[16] Charles Boner, *Guide for Travellers: In the Plain and on the Mountain* (London: Hardwicke

and Bogue, 1873) p.37

[17] Clinton Dent, *Mountaineering* (London, Longman, Green and Co, 1892) p. 48.

[18] Adburgham, *Shops and Shopping,* p.87.

[19] Girdlestone, *The High Alps* p. 166

[20] Dent, *Mountaineering* pp.48-9

[21] Quoted , Julie Summers: *Fearless on Everest: The Quest for Sandy Irvine* (London ; Weidenfeld and Nicolson, 2000) p. 4

[22] R. Ascott Hope, (1888) *Romance of the Mountains* (London) pp. 55-6.

[23] J. Tyndall, *Hours of Exercise in the Alps* (London, 1871) p. 168-9

[24] Davidson, *Hints to Lady Travellers* p. 155-6

[25] G. Scriven, 'The prevention of sun burning and blistering' *Alpine Journal* 1886-8

[26] Quoted Unsworth, *Holding the Heights* pp. 50-1

[27] A.G. Girdlestone, *The High Alps without Guides* (London: 1870) pp. 13-14.

[28] Girdlestone, *The High Alps,* pp. 90-1.

[29] Edward Whymper, 'Camping Out' *Alpine Journal* Vol II, p. 2

[30] Whymper, 'Camping Out' pp 4-6

[31] *Alpine Journal* Vol III, 1867; Benjamin Edgington Catalogue 1967

[32] A. Adams-Reilly, 'Some New Ascents and passes in the chain of Mont Blanc' *Alpine Journal* Vol 2 1865-6, p. 105.

[33] Whymper, 'Camping Out' pp.7-11; *Report of the Special Committee on Equipment for Mountaineers* (London: Alpine Club, 1892) p. 17.

[34] R.W Clark, *Six Great Mountaineers* (London: Hamish Hamilton, 1956)pp. 67-75; Unsworth, *Holding the Heights* p. 125-6

[35] A.F. Mummery, *My Climbs in the Alps and the Caucasus* (London: 1895) p.150-1

[36] Walt Unsworth, *Tiger in the Snow: The Life and Adventures of A.F. Mummery* (London 1967) p. 22

[37] Mummery, *My Climbs in the Alps* p.295-6

[38] *Report of the Special Committee....*1892, p. 25

[39] Ellis Carr, 'Two days on an Ice Slope' *Alpine Journal* Vol XVI p. 429-30

[40] Tom Longstaff *This my Voyage* (London: John Murray, 1951) p.43

[41] John Norman Collie(1902) Climbing in the Himalaya and other Mountain Ranges (Edinburgh) p.175-6 and p. 182

[42] Mummery, *My Climbs in the Alps* pp. 159-60

[43] 'An Easy day for a Lady': the unpublished letters written by Lily Bristow to her family while climbing with A.F. Mummery in 1893, printed in the *Alpine Journal* Vol 53, p. 371.

[44] 'Easy Day for a Lady' p. 371

[45] Quoted Ronald Clark , *The Victorian Mountaineers* (London: B.T. Batsford 1953) p. 99.

[46] Whymper, 'Camping out' pp. 3-4.

[47] F.F. Tuckett, 'A Night on the Summit of Monte Viso' *Alpine Journal* Vol 1 p. 27.

[48] Tuckett, 'Night on the Summit' p. 32

[49] 'Alpine Art and Appliances at the Winter Exhibition' *Alpine Journal* 1886-8 Vol XIII p. 464.

[50] Jaeger archive, Westminster City Record Office; 'Report of the Special Committee on Equipment for Mountaineers' *Alpine Journal* 1892 XV p. 18; 'Alpine Club Equipment Exhibition' *Alpine Journal* 1900-01, Vol XX.p.40

[51] Heals archive: Archive of Art and Design – Victoria and Albert Museum

[52] *Report of the Special Committee....*1892 pp. 26-7.

[53] W.M. Conway, *The First Crossing of Spitzbergen* (London 1897) p. 344.

[54] L.W. Rolleston 'Climbing in Suanetia' *Alpine Journal* 1904-5. Vol XXII pp. 102-3

55 August Lorria 'An Ascent of the Hohberghorn' *Alpine Journal* 1886-8 , Vol XIII, pp. 527-8.

56 *Alpine Journal* Vol XIII 1886-8 p. 465.

57 *Report of the Special Committee....*1892, p. 9

58 C.T. Dent, *Mountaineering* (London: Longman Green and Co 1892), p. 66

59 Girdlestone, *The High Alps* p. 97.

60 Mrs E.P. Jackson, 'A Winter Quartette' *Alpine Journal* 1888-9 Vol XIV pp. 207-9

61 F.F. Tuckett 'Ascent of the Aletschorn' *Peaks, Passes and Glaciers* Vol 2 ,(2nd series London 1862) p. 46 and p. 70.

62 G. Hastings 'Over Mont Blanc, by the Brenva Route, without Guides' *Alpine Journal* 1894-5 p. 346.

63 *Catalogue of Equipment for Mountaineers Exhibited at the Alpine Club,* December 1899, p. 7; 'The Alpine Club Exhibition' *Alpine Journal* Vol XX pp. 37-8

64 Girdlestone, *The High Alps* p. 171

65 Tuckett, 'Ascent' p. 64

66 Jennifer Davies *The Victorian Kitchen* (London: BBC Enterprises Ltd 1989) p. 103-114

67 Tuckett 'Ascent of the Aletschorn' *Peaks, Passes and Glaciers* Vol 2 ,(2nd series London 1862) p. 46

68 *Report of the Special Committee....*1892, p. 11-13

69 Charles Boner, *Guide for Travellers: In the Plain and on the Mountain* (London 1873: Hardwicke and Bogue) pp. 35-7

70 Tom Price, *Travail so Gladly Spent* (Ernest Press, 2000)

71 *Refined Camping:* Catalogue for Thomas Holding, Maddox Street c 1906 – kindly lent to us by Mr Alan Day; Holding, *Camper's Handbook* p. 321

72 Tom Longstaff, 'Eccentric Holiday' *Alpine Journal* 1902-3 Vol XXI p. 377.

73 W.T. Kirkpatrick and R.Philip Hope *Alpine Days and Nights* (London: George Allen and Unwin

74 Thomas Hiram Holding, *The Campers' Handbook* (London 1898), p. 307.

75 Dedication to Macgregor in *Cycle and Camp.*

76 Holding *The Camper's Handbook* 1898 p. 3

77 We are very grateful to Hazel Constance for supplying obituaries and biographical material relating to Thomas Holding, part of her forthcoming book on the History of the Camping Club of Great Britain.; Arthur Ransome, (ed.), *Voyage alone in the yawl 'Rob Roy. John Macgregor* (London: Grafton 1987, originally published London 1867);

78 Transcription of Royal Canoe Club Newsletter 1887, in the possession of Hazel Constance.

79 W.J. Pearce, *Fixed and Cycle Camping* (London , 1909) p. 44

80 Pearce, *Fixed and Cycle Camping* (London, 1909) p. 44; W. Hamish Fraser: *The Coming of the Mass Market, 1850-1914* (Basingstoke: Macmillan, 1981) p. 39.

Chapter 4

1 Mary Mummery in A.F. Mummery, *My Climbs in the Alps and the Caucasus* (London: 1895), p. 68

2 McCrone, Kathleen E. *Sport and the Physical Emancipation of women, 1870-1914* (London Routledge, 1988) p. 217

3 Jennifer A Hargreaves, 'The Victorian Cult of Family and the early years of female sport' in Eric G. Dunning et al *The Sports Process: A Comparative and Developmental Approach* (*Champaign: Human Kinetics, 1993)* p. 73.

4 Kathleen E. McCrone, *Sport and the Physical Emancipation of English Women* (London:

Routledge, 1988); Jennifer Hargreaves (1994) *Sporting females: critical issues in the history and sociology of women's sports* (London Routledge) pp. 90-106

[5] Hargreaves, *Sporting Females, p. 92.*

[6] *Ladies' Alpine Journal* 1925, 'List of Members', pp. 44-8

[7] Quoted Jennifer A. Hargreaves, 'The Victorian Cult of Family and the early years of female sport' in Eric G. Dunning, et al *The Sports Process: A Comparative and Developmental Approach* (*Champaign:Human Kinetics*, 1993), p. 73

[8] L.C. Davidson, *Hints to Lady Travellers* (London 1889) p. 152

[9] Burberry Advertisement, *Fell and Rock Club of the Lake District Journal* 1907-8; *Burberry for Ladies* Gallery of Costume, Platt Hall Manchester. We are grateful to Barbara Burman for drawing our attention to this collection.

[10] Williams, *Women on the Rope* p. 28

[11] Quoted Ronald Clark *The Victorian Mountaineers* (London, 1953, p. 176)

[12] *Catalogue of Rational Dress Exhibition* 1883, Exhibit 33 Mrs Blair of Manchester: Mountain Climbing Costume as worn by her.

[13] C.T. Dent, *Mountaineering* (London, Longman, Green and Co, 1892), p.51.

[14] Joanne Entwistle, *The Fashioned Body: Fashion Dress and Modern Social Theory* (Oxford: Polity, 2000), p. 168.

[15] Derek Hudson *Munby: Man of Two Worlds: The Life and Diaries of Arthur J. Munby, 1828-1910* (London: John Murray, 1972) p. 255-6

[16] Hudson, *Munby* p. 168 and 271

[17] Cecily Williams *Women on the Rope* (London, George Allen and Unwin 1973) pp 62-5

[18] Mrs Aubrey Le Blond *Day in Day Out* (London 1928) p. 90

[19] Rubinstein, *Before the Suffragettes, p.* 218

[20] 26 August 1871, *Punch* Vol 61, p. 86.

[21] W.Unsworth *Holding the Heights* (London, Hodder and Stoughton, 1993) p. 119 and 142

[22] Obituary of Lucy Walker, *Alpine Journal* 1917, Vol XXXI p. 98-101

[23] Williams, *Women on the Rope* pp. 47-8 ; Nea Morin *A Woman's reach* (Eyre and Spottiswoode, 1968) pp.. 257-278

[24] Nea Morin *A Woman's reach* (Eyre and Spottiswoode, 1968) pp.. 257-278

[25] Williams, *Women on The Rope* p. 65-70

[26] Quoted in *Ladies Alpine Journal* 1935, editorial on the death of Mrs Aubrey Le Blond, p. 4

[27] Morin *A Woman's Reach* pp 257-78

[28] A.F. Mummery *MyClimbs in the Alps and the Caucasus* (London 1895)

[29] Morin *A Woman's Reach* pp 257-78

[30] Quoted Williams, *Women on the Rope* p. 78; Obituary of Gertrude Bell *Alpine Journal* 1926 Vol 38 p. 299

[31] Freda du Faur *The Conquest of Mount Cook and the climbs ; an account of 4 seasons mountaineering on the Southern alps of NZ (*London: Allen and Unwin, 1915)

[32] Quoted Jennifer Hargreaves *Sporting females: critical issues in the history and sociology of women's sports* (London Routledge, 1994) p 90

[33] John Lowerson *Sport and the English Middle Classes, 1870-1914* (Manchester, Manchester University Press, 1993) p. 211

[34] Mrs le Blond, 'Then and Now' *Alpine Journal* p. 4

[35] Quoted by W.P. Haskett Smith, 'Memories of Some Women Mountaineers' *Journal of the Pinnacle Club*, 1929-31, p. 15.

[36] Cunningham and Mansfield, *English Costume* p. 339

[37] 'How we slept at the Châlet des Chèvres' *Cornhill Magazine* 1863 p. 326

[38] Quoted Lord Schuster *Postscript to Adventure* (London: Eyre and Spottiswood, 1950) p.163.

[39] Williams, *Women on the Rope* pp. 58-9

[40] Madeliene Eno 'Girl Power' *Appalachian Mountain Club* October 1999, p. 2

[41] Quoted Clark, *Victorian Mountaineers* p. 177

[42] Julian Grande, 'Lady Alpinists from a Man's Point of View' *Daily Mail* May 6 1910.

[43] Information provided by Marian Parsons who has climbed extensively world wide.

[44] Och Brothers, Sporting Outfitters, Montreux, Switzerland, 1909; W. Bocher of Munich Catalogue, 1912.

[45] Sarah Levitt, 'Clothing' in (ed.) Mary B. Rose *The Lancashire Cotton Industry: A History since 1700* (Preston: Lancashire County Books, 1996), p.166

[46] Annemor Sundbo *Everyday Knitting* (Kristiansand, 2000) p. 56

[47] *Fell and Rock Club of the Lake District Journal* Volume 12, 1938-40, p. 232.

[48] Dent, *Mountaineering* p. 51.

[49] E.M. Symonds, 'Mountaineering for Girls' *The Girl's Realm* 1899, p. 1258.

[50] Mrs Le Blond, 'Then and Now' *Alpine Journal* 1932, p. 6.

[51] Ibid p. 6

[52] Quoted Dorothy Middleton, *Victorian Lady Travellers* (London: Routledge and Keegan Paul, 1965) p. 8.

[53] Mrs Le Blond, *Day in Day Out* pp. 101-2.

[54] Greater Manchester Record Office, B/CHA/16/11 CHA archive *Useful Hints to lady ramblers c 1900*

[55] Emily Hornby, *Mountaineering Records* (Liverpool, 1907) p. 158.

[56] David Rubinstein, *Before the Suffragettes*, p. 218

[57] Julian Grande, 'Lady Alpinists from a Man's point of view' *Daily Mail* May 6th 1910.

[58] Harold Spender, 'Should Women climb snow mountains' *Woman at Home* August 1908, p. 931

[59] David Rubinstein, *Before the Suffragettes* (Brighton: Harvester Press, 1977) p. 14

[60] Le Blond, 'Then and Now' *Ladies' Alpine Yearbook*, 1932, pp. 5-6

[61] Rubinstein, *Before the Suffragettes* p. 191.

[62] Lady Bell, *The Letters of Gertrude Bell* (London 1928)

[63] Unsworth, *Holding the Heights* P. 269

[64] Rubinstein, *Before the Suffragettes*, p. 218

[65] *The Tatler* 1908

[66] Fanny Bullock Workman, 'Some Hints on Preparing for Mountaineering: What to wear and How to Diet' *For and About Women* July 1905

[67] Annie S. Peck 'Practical Mountain Climbing' *Outing* September 1901, pp. 688-9.

[68] Constance A. Barnicoat 'Through the Copland Pass': Where no woman ever went before' *World Wide Magazine, 1904*. pp. 567-8.

[69] *Ladies' Alpine Journal* 1925, 'List of Members', pp. 44-8

[70] *Morning Post* 2 May 1910.

[71] Mrs Le Blond, *Mountaineering in the Land of the Midnight Sun* (London: Fisher Unwin, 1908)

[72] E.H. Daniell, 'Reminiscences' *Pinnacle Club Journal,* No 4 1929-31, p.26

[73] C.E. Benson, *British Mountaineering* (London, Routledge and Sons, 1909), p. 185

[74] Thomas H. Holding *Ladies' Cutting* (T.H. Holding: London, 1885), p. 3 and p.36.

[75] Lady's climbing bloomers, viewed at the Museum Store, Castle Museum York, dated c1900-1914. We are grateful to Mary Brooks of the Textile Conservation Centre for drawing our attention to these.

[76] Jane Inglis Clark, *Pictures and Memories* (Edinburgh: The Moray Press) p. 28

77 Constance Barnicoat, 'Women and Mountains' *The Ladies'Realm*, 1911, p. 362

78 W. Bocher, Catalogue, Munchen, 1912

79 Jane Inglis Clark, *Pictures and Memories* p. 28

80 See advertisements for Burberry in *Public schools Alpine Sports Club Yearbook 1909-1930*

81 A.W. Gamage Ltd *Winter Sports Hints,* 1926-7, p. 13.

82 Dame Katherine Furse *The Great Game* (London 1926) pp. 11-12

83 Katina Bill, 'Attitudes towards women's trousers in Britain in the 1930s' *Journal of Design History* Vol 6, 1993 pp. 43-54

84 Greater Manchester Record Office B/CHA/HIST/5 'Memories of the CHA in the 1920s

85 Quoted Ann Holt, 'Walking Women: Defying Convention' *TGO* February 1996

Chapter 5

1 Richard S. Tedlow , *New and Improved: The Story of Mass Marketing in America* (Cambridge Mass., Harvard University Press, 1996) p.259-328

2 'A Century of Business', *Puget Sound Business Journal* September 17th 1999; L.L.Bean Website.

3 H. Taylor *A Claim on the Countryside: A History of the British Outdoor Movement* (Keele: Keele University Press, 1997)p. 154

4 Roger-Lloyd Jones and M.J. Lewis, *Raleigh and the British Bicycle Industry: An Economic and Business History, 1870-1960* (Aldershot: Ashgate 2000) pp. 9-10

5 Again we are grateful to Hazel Constance for this biographical information on Thomas Holding; *Cycle and Camp* , dedication to John Macgregor.

6 Lloyd Jones and Lewis *Raleigh* p. 35; Zoe Lawson, '*Wheels within Wheels – the Lancashire Cycling Clubs of the 1880s and 1890s*' in (ed.) Alan Crosby, *Lancashire Local Studies in honour of Diana Winterbotham* (Preston: Carnegie Publishing 1993)

7 *Camping: The Official Organ of the Amateur Camping Club* Vol 6 No 3 March 1911

8 Pearce, *Fixed and Cycle Camping* p. 44.

9 *Refined Camping* p. 2

10 *Refined Camping* p. 10

11 Holding, *Camper's Handbook* p. 310

12 Holding *Watery Wanderings,* 16-7, and 20.

13 Thomas Hiram Holding, *Watery Wanderings: Mid Western Lochs* (London 1886)

14 *Refined Camping,* Introduction

15 *Refined Camping* p. 10

16 Victor George de Freyne Bridges *Camping Out for boy scouts and others* (London: C.A. Pearson, 1910) p. 83.

17 *Camping* , July 1909 , p. 1

18 *Camping*, September 1909, p. 1

19 Taylor, *Claim on the Countryside* pp. 54-80.

20 Tom Stephenson, *Forbidden Land: The Struggle for Access to Mountain and Moorland* (Manchester: Manchester University Press 1989) p. 114

21 Taylor, *Claims on the Countryside* p. 165

22 Greater Manchester Record Office, Archives of Co-operative Holidays Association, *Comradeship* Vol 5 No 5 p. 80; Stephenson, *Forbidden Land* p. 70; S.G. Jones *Workers at Play: A social History of Leisure, 1918-1939* (London, Routledge and Keegan Paul 1986), p. 11

23 John Springhall, *Youth, Empire and Society* (London: Croom Helm 1977) pp.53-70 and pp. 134-8.

[24] Advertisements in the *Rucksack Journal* 1907-8 and *Journal of the Fell and Rock Climbing Club of the Lake Disitrict* 1913-5.

[25] W. Shakespeare, *Macbeth* Act I

[26] Quoted Eric Byne and Geoffrey Sutton, *High Peak: The Story of Walking and Climbing in the Peak District* (London: Seker and Warburg 1966) p. 70.

[27] Byne and Sutton, *High Peak* p. 90.

[28] Quoted Taylor *Claim on the Countryside* p. 185.

[29] C. S.Davies *North Country Bred: A Working Class Family Chronicle* (London, Routledge and Kegan Paul, 1963) p. 136 and 178

[30] J.B. Priestley, *English Journey* (London, First published 1934, Penguin Edition) p. 166

[31] Taylor, *Claim on the Countryside* p. 228

[32] Quoted, Taylor, *Claim on the Countryside* p. 227

[33] Jones, *Workers at Play* (London 1986) pp. 11-15

[34] Jones, *Workers at Play* pp. 11-15; Taylor, *Claim on the Countryside* p. 236

[35] Stephenson, *Forbidden Land* p. 153-64

[36] Katrina Honeyman, *Well Suited* (Oxford University Press, 2000) ; Fraser, *Mass Market* pp.118-9.

[37] Advertisement in *Wayfarers' Journal* 1928

[38] Official History of Blacks; Roger Smith, 'Company Profile: Blacks of Greenock' *The Great Outdoors* December 1978 p. 34.

[39] We are very grateful to Hazel Constance for giving us access to her research on Thomas Holding and Club formation which, along with the early history of Camtors is a part of her forthcoming book on the History of the Camping Club of Great Britain.

[40] Camping Club of Great Britain, *Handbook of Lightweight Camping* (London, Camping Club of Great Britain, 1920) p. 36; W.T. Palmer, *The Complete Hill Walker, Rock Climber and Cave Explorer* (London: Isaac Pitman, 1934) p. 90.

[41] Advertisement, Sport and Camp Co-operators *Rucksack Club Journal* 1935.

[42] We are extremely grateful to Alan Day for allowing us to use his collection of Black's catalogues and for sharing with us his deep knowledge of the development of Blacks as a company.

[43] 1932 Thomas Black and Sons (Greenock) Limited *Good Companions Catalogue*, p. 4.

[44] 1932 Thomas Black and Sons (Greenock) Limited *Good Companions Catalogue*, p. 6

[45] Advertisement for Camp and Sports Co-operators, Royal Geographical Society *Hints for Travellers* 1935.

[46] Advertisement, Camp and Sports Co-operators *Rucksack Club Journal* 1935; 1935 Thomas Blacks and Sons (Greenock) Limited *Good Companions Catalogue*, p. 47

[47] I.D.S. Thomson, *May the Fire Always be Lit: A Biography of Jock Nimlin* (The Ernest Press 1995) p. 32.

[48] 1933 Thomas Black and Sons (Greenock) Limited *Good Companions Catalogue*, p. 29

[49] Advertisement, Camp and Sports Co-operators Ltd 'The Eleven Pound Kit' *Out-O'-Doors* April 1933.

[50] RGS Everest Files Box 45.

[51] W.T. Palmer, *The Complete Hill Walker, Rock Climber and Cave Explorer* (London: Isaac Pitman, 1934) p. 14

[52] Advertisement for James Carter, Alpine Bootmaker and Outfitter in *Alpine Journal* III, 1867.

[53] Report on a lecture by Frank Smythe at the Mechanics' Institute in Burnley, published in *Among the Deep Sea Fisheries* Vol 7 1934 p. 73. These boots are discussed in more detail in Chapter 6.

[54] A. Harry Griffin, *The Coniston Tigers: Seventy Years of Mountain Adventure* (Sigma Press, 2000) p. 73

[55] Obituary of Robert Lawrie by Charles Warren, *Alpine Journal*, 1983 Vol. 88 pp.260-261.

[56] Interview with Bob Lawford by Mary Rose 18 August 2000.

[57] Obituary of Robert Lawrie by Charles Warren, *Alpine Journal*, 1983 Vol. 88 pp.260-261.

[58] 'The Gear –makers: Ellis Brigham' *Climber and Rambler, 1970* p. 298.

[59] Bob Brigham, 'Underfoot information: the story of the climber's boot' *The Alpine Journal* 1976, p. 134.

[60] 'The Gear –makers: Ellis Brigham' *Climber and Rambler, 1970* p. 298

[61] See below chapter 8 for more discussion of Ellis Brigham.

[62] Obituary of Robert Burns, *Rucksack Journal,* 1972 p. 57.

[63] Advertisement, R. Burns Wanderlust Rucksack, *Wayfayers' Journal 1928*

[64] *Out-O'-Doors* July 1931 p. 145.

[65] Advertisment, Robert Burns *Out-O'-Doors* 1927.

[66] Discussed in Chapter 6.

[67] Advertisement R. Burns, *Oxford Mountaineering*, 1935-7.

[68] Haythornthwaite archive: typesript: 'The beginning of Grenfell Cloth.'

[69] 6 August 1923 Dr Wilfred Grenfell to Walter Haythornthwaite.

[70] The development of the Grenfell climbing suits will be discussed in chapter 6.

[71] Interview with Bob Lawford by Mary Rose 18 August 2000.

[72] Mary Rose's father in law.

[73] Byne and Sutton, *High Peak* p. 116-7 and 127

[74] Griffin *Coniston Tigers* p. 3.

[75] A. Harry Griffin *Coniston Tigers: Seventy Years of Mountain Adventure* (Wilmslow: Sigma Press, 2000) p. 73 ; Advertisement Robert Lawrie Ltd *Rucksack Club Journal* 1933.

[76] 8 October 1934, W.Russell Flint *The Times*

Chapter 6

[1] Herman Huber was born 20th September 1930 in Munich, just as alpine mountaineering swung into its most dangerous and most notorious phase. He grew up during the war period and an early experience was digging out the precious historical remains from the DAV in Munich after the Allied bombing raids. He began his lifelong mountaineering passion accompanying his father on mountain trips. In due course he passed on these passions and experiences to his two sons. Since 1947 he has climbed more than 500 alpine routes, more than 150 of them at UIAA grade 6. He knows many of the big routes of the eastern alps (and it must be mentioned seven routes on Lalidererwand) plus the ice walls of the Western Alps. He can count 1400 alpine summits between Monte Viso and Rax, and has climbed on four continents plus Greenland and New Guinea. He was an expedition leader in 1955, 68 and 74 and has plenty of new routes to his credit.

[2] Friedrich Ludwig JAHN, 1778 – 1852 who became known as TURNVATER JAHN, (Gymnastics father JAHN)

[3] (Union Internationale des Associations d'Alpinisme) the scale can be found at http://www.uiaa.ch/

[4] Interview with Herman Huber August 2002 and e-mail from Herman Huber to Mike Parsons 16 November 2002.

[5] *Alpine Journal* , 1912, Advertisement 'Tricouni nails & their advantages'.

[6] Email correspondence with Herman Huber Sept 2002

[7] Discussion with Bill O'Connor an ex-lecturer in Physical Education at Loughborough University, and Hermann Huber who helped me make these links.

[8] Frison Roche, 'A history of Mountaineering' (Paris, 1996) p. 302.

[9] Interview Gill Aldersley FRCC Nov 2001.

[10] Le Diable des Dolomites, Tita Piaz.

11 Welsh rock, Trevor Jones and Geoff Milburn, 1986

12 Grivel archives and website www.grivel.com and discussion with Gioachino Gobbi, Feb and Sept 2002.

13 Arthur Westlake Andrews (1868-1959) wrote the highly persuasive article on crampons He climbed with Eckenstein and with him and others undertook early exploration of Lliwedd – with J.M.A Thomson he wrote The Climbs on Lliwedd in 1909.

14 A.W. Andrews, 'The Use of crampons in mountaineering' *Climbers' Club Journal,* IX, pp.131-42.

15 C.F. Meade, *Approach to the Hills* (1940)

16 Grivel archives and website www.grivel.com and discussion with Gioachino Gobbi, Feb and Sept 2002.

17 Eric Roberts, *Welzenbach's Climbs* (London 1980).

18 list of his first ascents p199 Handbuch Alpin Geschicte im Museum. Kempten

19 interview Aug 2002.

20 In 1978, Slatkine published a reprint of "Alpinisme et Compétition" in which Yves Ballu wrote an excellent preface with some information on climbing equipment made by Pierre Allain. In this preface, Yves Ballu quote.

21 Pierre Allain, *Alpinisme et Compétition* (1949) chapter entitled L'Arête Sud du Fou

22 Maurice Herzog *Annapurna,* ,(Paris, 1953, French edition) p. 191

23 Stephane Pennequin; email correspondence with Mike Parsons July 2002.

24 Stephane Pennequin ; email correspondence with Mike Parsons July 2002

25 'Pierre Allain, Pure Lumiere de Rocher' Gilles Modica.

26 Stephane Pennequin ; email correspondence with Mike Parsons July 2002

27 Lindsay Griffin, *High Mountain* e-mail to Mike Parsons Nov 27th 2002.

28 Frances Ashcroft *Life at the extremes, the science of survival,*

29 Hampshire County Record Office ITS RUBBER LTD – 58 YEARS ON' (Issued c 1977 as retrospective on company history)

30 AJ 1970 Polar Notes SPRI visit.doc and origin is La Montagne 1967 p 76

31 R. Cassin, *Five Years of Alpinism* (Diadem / The mountaineers 1981) page 88

32 Herman Huber interviews Feb 2001 and Aug 2002

33 correspondence from Huber 28/10/02

34 Beal web site, www.beal.com and conversation with Michel Beal Feb 2002.

35 Interview with Tony Howard by Mike Parsons, September 2001.

36 A. Alvarez, *Feeding the Rat* (2001 2nd Edition) p.79.

37 Big Wall Climbing, Doug Scott 1974.

38 Interview with Mark Vallance, FRCC dinner November 2002; e-mail from Mark Vallance to Mike Parsons, 6 November 2002 .and Ray Jardines web site www.rayjardine.com

39 email correspondence Nov 2001

40 Jeff Connor, *Creagh Dhu Climber: The Life and Times of John Cunningham* (Ernest Press, 1999) p.185.

41 Climbing Ice; Yvon Chouinard.

42 UIAA web site November 2002.

Chapter 7

1 Conrad Anker and David Roberts *The Lost Explorer: Finding Mallory on Mount Everest*

(Robinson, London 1999) p. 166

2   Roger Frison-Roche and Sylvain Jouty *A History of Mountain Climbing* (New York: Flammarion, 1996) p. 85

3   Ian Cameron, *To the Farthest Ends of the Earth: The History of the Royal Geographical Society* (London: Royal Geographical Society) p. 155

4   Cameron, *To the Farthest Ends of the Earth* p. 160-1

5   Cameron *To the Farthest Ends of the Earth* pp. 159-61; Gordon T. Stewart, 'Tenzing's two wrist watches: the Conquest of Everest and Late Imperial Culture in Britian 1921-53' *Past and Present* 1995, No 148 pp. 172-4.

6   John Mason, *Abode of Snow* (London, Diadem Books, photo-reprint, 1987) pp. 99-102

7   Douglas W. Freshfield, 'Mountain Travel' in RGS *Hints for Travellers* 1993 p37

8   Mason, *Abode of Snow* p. 104.

9   Freshfield, 'Mountain travel' p. 37; A. W. Andrews, 'The Use of Crampons in Mountaineering' *Climbers' Club Journal,* Volume 9, June 1907 pp. 131-42.

10 Frison-Roche and Sylvain Jouty *A History of Mountain Climbing* p.186.

11 Mason, *Abode of Snow* p. 105

12 Mason, *Abode of Snow* p. 114

13 Scottish National Library, Acc 8338 George Finch Diary 21 March 1922 p. 9.

14 Mason, *Abode of Snow*, p. 117.

15 Frank Smythe, *Kamet Conquered* (London: Victor Gollanz, 1932) p. 27.

16 Peter and Leni Gillman, *The Wildest Dream: Mallory: His Life and Conflicting Passions* (London, Headline 2000) p. 173

17 Cameron, *To the Farthest Ends of the Earth* p. 167

18 RGS Everest Files Meade's Personal Equipment List, 1921

19 RGS Everest Files

20 RGS Everest Files, 28 March 1921 Report by George Finch on Primus stoves.

21 Walt Unsworth, *Everest:A Mountaineering History* (London: Baton Wicks, 2000)pp 76-77

22 Walt Unsworth, *Everest: A Mountaineering History* (London: Baton Wicks, 2000) p. 56

23 Harold Raeburn, *Mountaineering Art* (London, 1920) p. 28

24 Burberry *Gabardine in Peace and War* (1911) p. 22.

25 C.K. Howard-Bury *Mount Everest: The Reconnaissance, 1921* (London: Edward Arnold 1922) p. 315.

26 C.G. Bruce *The Assault on Mount Everest 1922* (London: Edward Arnold , 1923) pp. 8-9

27 RGS Everest Files Box 38.2 G.L. Mallory, 'Notes on Equipment' 1922 Expedition.

28 L.G.C.E. Pugh, 'Scientific problems on Mount Everest 1953' *Himalayan Journal,* 18, 1954 p. 49

29 John Hunt *The Ascent of Everest* (London: Hodder and Stoughton, 1953) p. 226

30 Scottish National Library Acc 8338 George Finch Diary 21 March 1922 p. 22

31 Aldo Bonacossa, 'Reminiscences' *Alpine Journal* 1965, p. 218.

32 RGS Everest Files Box 38/1 13 February 1922 Letter from S.W. Silver and Co to RGS.

33 Scottish National Library Acc 8338 George Finch Diary 12 and 18th April 1922 p.65 and 74.

34 Scottish National Library Acc George Finch Diaries, 1922 Expedition, 25 May 1922.

35 RGS Everest Files 20 September 1932 Ruttledge to Finch

36 RGS Everest Files Box 38/2 'Notes on Equipment' by George Mallory

37 Walt Unsworth, *Everest: A Mountaineering History* (London: Baton Wicks, 2000) p. 86.

38 G. Ingle Finch, 'Equipment for High Altitude Mountaineering, with special reference to Climbing Mount Everest' *Alpine Journal* Vol. XXXV p. 69.

39 George Finch , *Climbing Mount Everest* (London, George Philip and Son, 1930) p. 2

40   Finch, 'Equipment for High Altitude Mountaineering'… p. 73-4
41   P.J. Farrar, 'The Everest Expeditions: Conclusions' *Alpine Journal* Vol XXXIV, 1921-2 p. 455
42   Walt Unsworth, *Everest: A Mountaineering History* (London: Baton Wicks, 2000) p. 95.
43   T.G. Longstaff, 'Some Aspects of the Everest Problem' *Alpine Journal* Vol XXXV 1923 pp. 57-68.
44   George Ingle Finch , *The Making of a Mountaineer* (London: Arrowsmith 1924) pp. 333-4.
45   RGS 1924 Mount Everest Equipment
46   Norton, *The Fight for Mount Everest* pp. 103-4
47   RGS 1924 Mount Everest Equipment
48   Clothing list for Irving, 1924. We are grateful to Julie Summers, Sandy Irvine's great niece and biographer for supplying a copy of this list.
49   RGS 1924 Mount Everest Equipment
50   RGS Mallory Equipment notes 1922
51   RGS Everest Files Notes on Everest 1924 Equipment.
52   RGS Everest File Box 40/2 Letter from P.J.B Unna to Hinks 20 March 1924
53   RGS Everest File Box 40/2 Letter from P.J.B Unna to Hinks 10 December 1924
54   Frank Smythe, *The Kanchenjunga Adventure* (London, Vicotor Gollanz, 1930) p.61.
55   Smythe, *The Kanchenjunga Adventure* p. 65
56   Smythe, *The Kanchenjunga Adventure* pp. 65-6
57   R. Burns, 'Everest Equipment' *Rucksack Journal* 1933, pp.261-2
58   Advertisement in *Oxford Mountaineering* 1935-8.
59   Burns, 'Everest Equipment' *Rucksack Journal* 1933, p. 259.
60   Smyth, *Kamet Conquered* pp. 403-4
61   RGS Everest Files 21 December 1932 Letter from Robert Burns to Frank Smythe
62   RGS Everest Files 15 September 1932 Letter from Frank Smythe to Robert Burns
63   RGS Everest Files 18 October 1932 Letter from Robert Burns to Frank Smythe
64   Obituary of Robert Burns, *Rucksack Club Journal* 1972, p. 57.
65   RGS Everest Files 21 December 1932 Letter from Robert Burns to Frank Smythe
66   Burns, 'Everest Equipment' *Rucksack Journal* 1933 pp. 260-1; H. Ruttledge, *Everest 1933* (London: Hodder and Stoughton, 1934) p. 30
67   Burns, 'Everest Equipment' p. 259
68   Ruttledge, *Everest 1933* p. 160; *Manchester Guardian* 10 February 1934.
69   RGS Everest Files 10 December 1935 Robert Burns to Eric Shipton.
70   RGS Everest Files, 11 December 1935 Eric Shipton to Robert Burns
71   RGS *Hints to Travellers* 11th Edition, Volume 11 1938.
72   'New equipment' *Mountaineering Journal* 1937, p. 142.
73   RGS Everest Files Equipment List, Everest 1936.
74   RGS Everest Files 9 January 1936 Mount Everest Committee to Benjamin Edgington.
75   Scott Polar Research Institute MS 399 Benjamin Edgington bid for Oxford University Arctic Expedition 5 October 1934
76   RGS Everest Files, 12 September 1933 Letter from Eric Taylor to Hugh Ruttledge
77   RGS Everest Files, 16 September 1933 Letter from Burberrys Ltd to Hugh Ruttledge
78   Erna Risch, and Thomas Pitkin *Clothing the Soldier of World War II* (QMC Historical Studies, 1946) p. 92
79   Eric H.Taylor, 'Climbing Suits' *Mountaineering Journal* 1932-3 p. 168-71
80   Carl K. Brunning, 'Further remarks on Climbing Suits' *Mountaineering Journal* Volume 1 1932-3 p. 251

[81] Interview with Eric Taylor in *Daily Mail* 20th January 1933

[82] Information supplied by Tony Lack from his essay 'Development of Outdoor Clothing in the Twentieth Century'.

[83] RGS Everest Files 19 June 1935 Letter from Eric Taylor to Hugh Ruttledge

[84] RGS Everest Files Correspondence between Eric Taylor and Hugh Ruttledge 8 July 1935, 12 and 18 November 1935.

[85] RGS Everest Files 8 July 1935

[86] RGS Everest Files 24 October 1932 Equipment advice;

[87] Walt Unsworth, *Everest: A Mountaineering History* (London: Baton Wicks, 2000) p. 210

[88] H.W. Tilman, *Mount Everest 1938* (Cambridge University Press 1948) p. 17.

[89] Scott Polar Research Institute British Antarctic Expedition, 1910-12 , manuscript note attached to description of Finneskoe Crampons that it had been lent to the Mount Everest Committee, 24 January 1922.

[90] Paul Bauer,(translated by Sumner Austin) *Himalayan Campaign* (Oxford: Basil Blackwell, 1937) pp. 4-5.

[91] Translated by Nea E. Morin *Himalayan Assault: The French Himalayan Expedition 1936* (London Methuen 1938) p. 190

[92] www Historylink.org: biography of Eddie Bauer 1899-1896.

[93] *From Old Kent Road to Alamein*

[94] *Fell and Rock Climbing Club Journal* 1938-40, Robert Lawrie advertisement.

[95] Haythornthwaite Archive, in possession of David Haythornthwaite, Statement to Wilfrid Andrew Burke MP by Walter Haythornthwaite.

[96] Interview with David Haythornthwaite by Mary Rose, July 2000.

[97] Public Record Office (PRO) WO/32/13587 'The Development and Use of 'Ventile' Cloths' Directorate of Equipment and Stores, Ministry of Supply 1949; Ventile Cloth Website: www.ventile.co.uk

[98] PRO WO 32/12960 Arctic Mountain Warfare trials, 1947-9

[99] *Daily Express* January 1946.

[100] 'Trading Post' *Great Outdoors* July 1985.

[101] British Ropes Ltd *Ropes Made from Nylon: Report on the Evaluation of Properties and Characteristics of Cordage Made from Nylon* (British Ropes Ltd, 1949) pp. 5-6

[102] Risch, Pitkin *Clothing the Soldier of World War II* (QMC Historical Studies, 1946) p. 92; Mary B. Rose, *Firms, Networks and Business Values: The British and American Cotton Industries since 1750* (Cambridge: Cambridge University Press, 2000) pp. 1-249.

[103] Gerry Cunningham and Meg Hansson, *Lightweight camping equipment and How to Make it* (Ward Colorado: Highlander Publishing Co., 1959)

[104] www Historylink.org: biography of Eddie Bauer 1899-1896.

[105] Robert H. Bates *et al Five Miles High* (London:Robert Hale Ltd 1940) pp. 41-42.

[106] James Ramsey Ullman, *Americans on Everest* (London: Michael Joseph 1963) pp.330-4

[107] Charles Houston and Robert H Bates *K2: The Savage Mountain* (New York: Mcgraw Hill Book Company) pp. 280-3

[108] PRO WO 32/12960 Arctic Mountain Warfare trials, 1947-9

[109] John Hunt, *Life is Meeting* (Newton Abbot: Readers Union 1978) p. 1-70.

[110] John Hunt, *The Ascent of Everest* (London: Hodder and Stoughton) pp. 21-53 and 239-250

[111] RGS Everest Files, Box 70 Press Release, Everest 1953

[112] Haythornthwaite archive, in possession of David Haythornthwaite 10 December 1952 Letter from W.H. Murray to W. Haythornthwaite.

[113] Haythornthwaite archive, 13 December 1952 Letter from C.G. Wylie to The Managing

Director of Haythornthwaite and Sons Ltd.

[114] seed-hair fibre obtained from the fruit of the kapok tree or the kapok tree itself. The kapok is a gigantic tree of the tropical forest canopy and emergent layer. Common throughout the tropics, the kapok is native to the New World and to Africa and was transported to Asia, where it is cultivated for its fibre, or floss. The floss has been used in life preservers and other water-safety equipment, supporting as much as 30 times its own weight in water. Buoyancy is lost slowly, with one test showing only 10 percent loss after 30 days of water immersion.

[115] RGS Everest Files, July 1953, SATRA bulletin on Everest boots with photos & diagram.

Chapter 8

[1] Harry A. Griffin, *The Coniston Tigers: Seventy Years of Mountain Adventure* (Wilmslow, Sigma Leisure, 2000) p. 26.

[2] John Hunt, *Life is Meeting* (Newton Abbot: Readers' Union 1978) p. 137.

[3] Roger Frison-Roche and Sylvain Jouty: *A History of Mountain Climbing* (Paris 1996) p. 128.

[4] Cameron McNeish 'Go Outdoors: A Plea to Gear Manufacturers' *TGO* January 2001

[5] Lionel Terray (translated by Graham Sutton) *Conquistadors of the Useless* (London, 1963).

[6] Roger Frison-Roche and Sylvain Jouty: *A History of Mountain Climbing* (Paris 1996) p. 320.

[7] British Mountaineering Council, *The First Fifty Years of the British Mountaineering Council* (London 1997, pp.1-22.

[8] BMC Lake District Sub-Committee minute book

[9] T.G. Millar, *Long Distance Paths of England and Wales* (Newton Abbot: David and Charles, 1984) pp.7-16

[10] BMC, *The First Fifty Years: A Political History* (Manchester:BMC,1997) p. 17.

[11] John Hunt, *Life is Meeting* (Newton Abbot: Readers' Union 1978) p. 123

[12] Everest Files, Letter from Tom Bourdillon to the Himalayan Committee 1952 and endorsed by Eric Shipton.

[13] John Hunt, *Life is Meeting* (Newton Abbot: Readers' Union 1978) p. 140

[14] John Hunt, *Life is Meeting* (Newton Abbot: Readers' Union 1978) p. 141.

[15] Don Whillans and Alick Ormerod *Don Whillans: Portrait of a Mountaineer* (London: Heinemann) p. 10.

[16] A. Alvarez, *Feeding the Rat* (Adreniline Classics: 2001) pp. 6-7.

[17] Excerpt of a fragmentary memoir by Charlie Parsons in the possession of Mike Parsons.

[18] E-mail from Mike Parsons to Mary Rose, 8 May 2000.

[19] Companies' House: First Incorporated 9 April 1952. Registration No: 00506817

[20] Black's catalogue 1954 and 1958

[21] Pindisport catalogue 1956

[22] Bergans Catalogue 1958; *Camping and Outdoor Trade Reference Book* 1964 p. 28

[23] 'Then (1958) *Karrimor Technical Guide 1983* p. 10.

[24] E-mail from Mike Parsons to Mary Rose 2 October 2002

[25] 14 November 1963, Alan Day to Mr Black.

[26] 27 July 1965, Alan Day, Sheffield to Robin Duthie, Black's, Port Glasgow

[27] Interview with Peter Gildersleve, by Mary Rose, 17 January 2002.

[28] Interview with Peter Gildersleve, by Mary Rose, 17 January 2002

[29] Telephone conversation by Mary Rose with Mike Parsons 29 September 2002.

[30] CC Digest of Leisure Statistics 1979.

[31] Countryside Commission, *Digest of Countryside Recreation Statistics* 1974 and 1979 (London: Countryside Commission); Caroline Harrison, *Countryside Recreation in a Changing Society* (TMS Partnership Ltd:1991) p.131-9

[32] Information supplied by Mike Parsons

[33] Hazel Constance, *First in the Field: A Century of the Camping and Caravanning Club*

(Coventry, Camping and Caravanning Club, 2001), pp188-9, 194-215.
34 Interview with Alan Day and Mike Parsons 13 October 2000
35 Pindisport Mountaineering Catalogue 1968, Black's catalogue 1969 Tom Waghorn, 'Pack up your troubles in nylon' *Climber and Rambler*, February 1969; Company accounts 1960 and 1970.
36 E-mail from Ken Ledward to Mary Rose 7 February 2002.
37 E-mail Ken Ledward to Mary Rose 7 February 2002
38 Karrimor Annual Reports 1960-1970.
39 Interview with Peter Gildersleve by Mary Rose 17/01/02; Profile of Pete Hutchinson by Andy Kirkpatrick, PHD Website.
40 Interview by Mary Rose with Pete Hutchinson 3 August 2002.
41 Letter from Tony Lack to Mary Rose, 16 February 2002.
42 *Great Outdoors* 'Meet the Retailer: Tanky's shop in Sheffield' by Roger Smith p. 76; Interview with Tony Howard by Mike Parsons, 24 September 2001.
43 'The Gear –makers: Ellis Brigham' *Climber and Rambler, 1970* p. 298.
44 Alan Reid, 'Meet the Retailer: The Alpine Centre, Blackpool' *Great Outdoors,* March 1980, p. 51.
45 'The Gear –makers: Ellis Brigham' *Climber and Rambler, 1970* p. 299.
46 20 May 1963 Report on Sheffield Branch by Mr D.C. Black
47 E-mail from Bill Ruthven to Mary Rose 22.01.02
48 29 September 2000 Interview with Alan Day and Mike Parsons by Mary Rose.
49 29 September 2000 Interview with Alan Day and Mike Parsons by Mary Rose
50 Interview with Tony Lack 14 March 2001
51 E-mail from Paul Bibby to Mary Rose 29 January 2002
52 Interview with Alan Day and Mike Parsons 13 October 2000
53 E-mail from Mike Parsons to Mary Rose 3 October 2002.
54 'New Waterproof Sleeping Pad' by Graham Tiso *Alpine Journal* 1969 pp. 324-5.
55 'Annapurna briefing" – report on preparations and equipment for Annapurna south face' *Mountain* 1969.
56 *Mountain Ear* January 1992, 'Troll Safety Equipment' Report by Tony Lack.
57 Chris Bonington, *Annapurna South Face* (London: Cassel and Co, 1971) p. 246.
58 E- mail from Mike Parsons to Mary Rose 3 October 2002.
59 Chris Bonington, *Annapurna South Face* (London: Cassel and Co, 1971) p. 244.
60 E-mail from Mike Parsons to Mary Rose 3 October 2002.
61 Interview with Mike Parsons by Mary Rose 7 June 2000
62 Interview with Tony Lack by Mary Rose, 14 March 2002; Conversation between Mike Parsons and Mary Rose, 21 June 2002.
63 Interview with Pete Hutchinson by Mary Rose 3 August 2000
64 Interview with Pete Hutchinson by Mary Rose 3 August 2000
65 Interview with Pete Hutchinson by Mary Rose 3 August 2000
66 Telephone interview with Tony Lack, by Mary Rose, 9 September 2002.
67 Interview with Peter Lumley 19 June 2001.
68 Advertisement for Cook's Himalayan Treks, *Alpine Climbing,* 1971, p. 94.
69 Interview with Mike Parsons by Mary Rose 8 November 2001.
70 Karrimor advertisement 'Tailor your own pack frame and sac' *Great Outdoors* April 1979
71 E-mail from Mike Parsons to Mary Rose, 4 October 2002.
72 E-mail from Ken Ledward to Mary Rose 31 October 2002
73 Mike Parsons, 'Brief History of the KIMM'
74 Tom Waghorn, 'Equipment '73' *Climber and Rambler* April 1973, p. 164
75 E-mail from Ken Ledward to Mary Rose 31 October 2002.
76 Extracts from Ken Ledward's Equipment Log 1972-3 reprinted In Karrimor Outdoor Pursuits Equipment Guide
77 *Mountain Ear,* November 1989.

78 Interview with Peter Lockey and Gordon Davison 10 August 2000.
79 Interview Gordon Davison and Peter Lockey 10 August 2000; e-mail Mike Parsons to Mary rose 11 August 2000.
80 Berghaus Catalogue 1983, Company Profile
81 Interview of Bill Wilkins by Mike Parsons, August 2001; Interview with Peter Lockey and Gordon Davison by Mary Rose 10 August 2000.
82 E-mail Peter Lockey to Mary Rose 30 October 2000
83 E-Mail Peter Lockey to Mary Rose 30 October 2000
84 Interview with Mike Parsons 30 April 2001.
85 Interview Peter Lockey and Gordon Davison 10 August 2000.
86 28 October 1996 *Financial Times*
87 Interview with Peter Gilderseive by Mary Rose 17 January 2001; E-mail from Mike Parsons to Mary Rose 13 February 2002.
88 Interview with Mike Parsons by Mary Rose 8 November 2000.
89 22 January 1975 Letter from Ken Ledward to Mike Parsons; E-mail from Mike Parsons to Mary Rose 23 January 2002; E-mail from Ken Ledward to Mary Rose 28 January 2002.; Email from Mike Parsons to Mary Rose 3 October 2003.
90 John Lloyd, 'Tried and Tested: Berghaus Yeti Gaiter' *Practical Camper* April 1980.
91 Interview with Peter Lockey and Gordon Davison by Mary Rose 10 August 2000.
92 E-mail from Mike Parsons to Mary Rose, 4 October 2002.
93 Tom Waghorn 'Harrogate' *Climber and Rambler,* January 1982; Karrimor advertising material for KS100e *Climber and Rambler* 1980
94 Interview with Alan Day 29 September 2000
95 Interview with Alan Day 29 September 2000
96 *Sunday Times* 25 September 1983
97 Roger Smith 'Testing with Berghaus' *The Great Outdoors* December 1982
98 Hunter Davies *Wainwright: The Biography* (London: Michael Joseph, 1995) p. 123
99 Chris Bonington *The Climbers* (1995) p. 166
100 J. Rivers-Smith, 'Clothing' *The Climber* August 1965 p. 14
101 E-mail from Ken Ledward to Mary Rose 31 October 2002.
102 Letter from A. Macdonald, Edinburgh to Editor, *Climber and Rambler* January 1968.
103 E-mail from Peter Lockey to Mary Rose 31 October 2000.
104 E-mail from Peter Lockey to Mary Rose, 21 October 2002.
105 E-mail from Mike Parsons to Mary Rose 4 October 2002.
106 Expedition Advisory Centre: *Expedition Equipment Manual* 13th edition, edited and revised by Tony Lack February 1989.
107 Tom Waghorn ' Equipment '73' *Climber and Rambler* August 1973 pp. 347-8.
108 E-Mail from Paul Bibby to Mary Rose 29 January 2002; *Great Outdoors* September 1982 Roger Smith questioning Paul Bibby: 'Kit Check: What is waterproof' p. 40
109 Interview with Ken Ledward and Mike Parsons 8 September 2000.
110 E-mail from Derryck Draper to Mary Rose 21 November 2002.
111 Hounshell and Smith, *Science and Corporate Strategy* pp. 484-5; W.L. Gore website; e-mailfrom Derryck Draper to Mary Rose, 21 November 2002.
112 E-mail Heidi H. Cofran to Mary Rose 30 July 2002.
113 24 March 1977, Letter from Alan Daley (Director of Banton and Co) to Peter Lumley.
114 Tom Waghorn: 'Gore-Tex: does it work?' *Climber and Rambler*, June 1978, p. 42; Chris Townsend 'Keeping out the Elements' *Great Outdoors,* October 1983
115 Interview with Peter Lumley 19 June 2001
116 Interview with Neville Whitley by Mary Rose and Mike Parsons 25 September 2001.
117 Interview with Marion Barnes, Berghaus, 2 August 2000
118 D.C. Ulberg, Berghaus ' Gore-Tex Berghaus Reply' *Great Outdoors* June 1982, p. 67

119 Berghaus Catalogue, Company Profile 1983;
120 E-Mail from Peter Lockey to Mary Rose 28 February 2001
121 Interview with Mike Parsons by Mary Rose 30 April 2001.
122 John Traynor, 'Risol: Stock Service and Profit' *Mountain Ear* February 1993 p. 6.
123 Mintel Outdoors 1996 pp. 1-2
124 Interview with Keith Black and Tony Wood by Mary Rose 24 April 2000.
125 15 July 1963 Report of Trial SCS 3/63 Cold Weather Flying Clothing Trial; David Brook interview 20 September 2000
126 E-mail from Derryck Draper to Mary Rose 21 November 2002.
127 Interview with Rab Carrington by Mary Rose 11 May 2001.
128 Interview with Rab Carrington by Mary Rose 11 May 2001
129 Interview with Dave Brook by Mary Rose 20 September 2001
130 E-mail from Mike Parsons to Mary Rose 4 October 2002
131 Interview with Ken Ledward and Mike Parsons 8 September 2000
132 Chris Conroy, 'Kit Check: The Lightweight Revolution' *Great Outdoors,* July 1983,Chris Townsend on sole patterns and performance pp. 53-4.
133 E-mail from Mike Parsons to Mary Rose 4 October 2002
134 Chirs Townsend, 'Test Report: Karrimor Asolo K-SB III Boots, *Great Outdoors* January 1982
135 E-mail from Mike Parsons to Mary Rose 4 October 2002; Chris Conroy 'Kit Check: The lightweight revolution' *Great Outdoors* 1983.
136 Interview with Derryck Draper, 24 April 2001
137 Interview with Alan Day by Mary Rose 13 October 2000

Index

Dent, Clinton · 51, 54, 73, 89, 95, 97, 101.

Derbyshire (Peak District) · 3, 115-6, 118, 120, 130, 132, 166, 179, 207, 220, 222.

Dibona, Angelo · 139, 148, 153.

diet · eskimo & polar 18, 20, 26, 29-32; Victorian 53, 76-9, 141, 184; Everest 8, 189, 194-5 199, 210, 220-1; scurvy 21, 29.

DMM · *see Moorhouse, Denny.*

dog (& sledge hauling) · 2, 14-8, 20, 22-5, 36-7, 41, 43, 80, 92

down gear · *see clothing, down, also sleeping bags.*

Draper, Derryck · 262.

Dress Reform Society & movement · 86, 88, 117.

Dulfer, Hans (& Dulfersitz)· 138, 146, 148, 151, 153.

Dunlop, John Boyd · 10, 215, *see also bicycles.*

Du Pont · 254.

E

Eckenstein, Oscar · 72, 149-51.

Ecole Nationale de Ski et Alpisme (ENSA) · 151, 174, 218.

Edgington, Benjamin & John · 61, 64, 70, 104, 111, 121-2, 179, 184, 194, 199-200, 217, 210, 213, 221.

Edinburgh, Duke of (Prince Philip) & award scheme · 1, 222, 228, 234.

education & training · 39, 45, 93, 116-7, 135-6, 164, 166, 168, 180, 209, 212, 216-8, 222, 228, 232, 242, 246, 262 *see also Outward Bound & British Mountaineering Council.*

eiderdown · *see clothing : down*

Elbsandstein · 83-4.

Ellis Brigham · *see Brigham*

Erve (Swiss) · 141.

Eskimo · 16-9, 21-4, 28, 30-2, 36-7.

etrier (stirrup) · 85, 91-2, 101.

Europe, Continental · 9, 11, 38, 48, 52, 144, 165, 174, 178, 249.

Everest · 1920s British expeditions & earlier 180-196; British 1930s expeditions 196-209; 1953 1st ascent 213-5; SW Face 1, 6-7, 236; impact of WW2 209-13; Mount Everest Committee 182, 202-4, 207-8, 214; Mount Everest Foundation 222.

F

fabric · 2, ,9, 24, 26, 36, 68, 70, 80, 88, 96, 104, 112, 126, 131-2, 178, 188,

193, 200, 204, 209-13, 218, 234, 241, 247-8, 250, 253-4, 257-8, 261.

Fairy Down · 231

Farrar, Percy · 183-7, 190.

feedback · *see knowledge.*

Fell and Rock Climbing Club of the Lake District · 104, 147.

Fiechtl, Hans · 138-9, 147-8, 153, 170.

Finch, George · 59, 144, 154, 183-5, 187-91, 193, 196-8, 201.

finnesko · 30.

fire & fire lighting · 9, 23, 57-8, 60, 62, 65, 74.

Fischer, Walther · 137.

Fischli, Hans · 40.

Fisher, George · 228, 230, 233-4.

flannel · 53, 69, 87-8, 98, 189, 193.

fleece · 69, 178, 198, 252; 256-7.

Flint, Howard · 204-6, 238.

flying suit · 204-5, 238.

food, processed & preserved · 20, 77-8 *see also diet.*

footwear · *see boots and footwear.*

Fram · 24-7, 107.

France ·19, 39, 45-7, 90, 98, 102, 128, 130, 141, 146, 148, 151, 154-6, 160, 162-3, 167, 171-5, 208, 218, 224-5, 227, 229-30, 247, 250, 252, 262.

Franklin, Sir John - expedition to North West Passage · 16, 20-3, 25, 29, 37, 47-8.

Freeman, Hardy & Willis · 121.

Freshfield, Douglas · 47-8, 51, 181.

frostbite · 6, 9, 13, 20, 54,, 72, 158, 178, 189, 197, 200, 215, 219, 236.

fuel · 30, 32-4, 42, 58, 73, 185, 190.

Fuhrer, Ulrich · 93, 101.

Fuller, Buckminster · 35-6.

fur · 9, 22-5, 54, 71, 178, 189, 293, 205.

G

G & H Products · 253.

Gamages · 107, 114, 121.

Genecand, Felix · 142

Gentil, Peter · 167, 231.

Germany · 8, 12, 34, 37-9, 52-4, 58, 69, 77, 95, 110, 134-41, 144-55, 158, 160-5, 168, 175, 196, 208-9, 216, 218, 241, 252, 255.

Gerry Mountaineering Equipment Co · *see Cunningham, Gerry.*

OTHER BOOKS OF INTEREST
From Northern Liberties Press and Old City Publishing

INVISIBLE ON EVEREST: INNOVATION AND THE GEAR MAKERS
By Mike Parsons and Mary B. Rose
320 pp + 4 pp of color illustrations + 90 b&w illustrations
ISBN 0-9704143-5-8 • Price: UK £24.99 • USA $36.00

LUCKY TO BE ALIVE By Angela Benham
186 pages • 18 color illustrations • ISBN 0-9704143-6-6 • Paper • $14.95 • £9.50

A PRICE GUIDE TO BOOKS CONCERNING BRITISH MOUNTAINEERS AND
MOUNTAINEERING IN THE BRITISH ISLES 1781-1999 By DEK PALMER
122 pages + i-viii • ISBN 0-9704143-0-7 • £9.95 • $14.95

A PRICE GUIDE TO BOOKS CONCERNING MOUNTAINEERING IN THE HIMALAYAS
By DEK PALMER • 152 pp + i-viii • ISBN 0-9704143-2-3 • £9.95 • $14.95

ORDER FORM

AUTHOR/TITLE	ISBN	QUANTITY	PRICE

☐ CHECK (payable to Old City Publishing)
☐ CREDIT CARD   ☐ CASH   ☐ BILL

CREDIT CARD INFORMATION:
☐ MASTERCARD   ☐ VISA   ☐ DISCOVER

ACCOUNT NUMBER_____

EXPIRATION DATE ☐☐ / ☐☐

TOTAL _____

NAME _____
ADDRESS _____
_____
CITY _____ STATE _____ ZIP _____
COUNTRY _____
TELEPHONE _____
E-MAIL _____

SIGNATURE _____

Old City Publishing
628 NORTH 2ND STREET,
PHILADELPHIA, PA 19123
USA
TEL: +1 215 925 4390
FAX: +1 215 925 4371
e-mail: info@oldcitypublishing.com
web: www.oldcitypublishing.com

OLD CITY PUBLISHING
NORTHERN LIBERTIES PRESS
Fax orders to: +1 215 925 4371